THE RED COUNTESS

Hermynia Zur Mühlen in the garden of the estate at Eigstfer, Estonia, c. 1910. Courtesy of Dr. Patrik von zur Mühlen.

The Red Countess

Select Autobiographical and
Fictional Writing of
Hermynia Zur Mühlen (1883-1951)

*Translated, Annotated and with
an Essay by Lionel Gossman*

https://www.openbookpublishers.com

© 2018 Lionel Gossman

The text of this work is licensed under a Creative Commons Attribution 4.0 International license (CC BY 4.0). This license allows you to share, copy, distribute and transmit the text; to adapt the text and to make commercial use of the text providing attribution is made to the author(s), but not in any way that suggests that they endorse you or your use of the work. Attribution should include the following information:

Lionel Gossman, *The Red Countess: Select Autobiographical and Fictional Writing of Hermynia Zur Mühlen (1883-1951)*. Cambridge, UK: Open Book Publishers, 2018. https://doi.org/10.11647/OBP.0140

Copyright and permissions for the reuse of many of the images included in this publication differ from the above. Copyright and permissions information for images is provided separately in the List of Illustrations.

Every effort has been made to identify and contact copyright holders and any omission or error will be corrected if notification is made to the publisher.

In order to access detailed and updated information on the license, please visit https://www.openbookpublishers.com/product/834#copyright

Further details about CC BY licenses are available at http://creativecommons.org/licenses/by/4.0/

All external links were active at the time of publication unless otherwise stated and have been archived via the Internet Archive Wayback Machine at https://archive.org/web

Digital material and resources associated with this volume are available at https://www.openbookpublishers.com/product/834#resources

ISBN Paperback: 9781783745548
ISBN Hardback: 9781783745555
ISBN Digital (PDF): 9781783745562
ISBN Digital ebook (epub): 9781783745579
ISBN Digital ebook (mobi): 9781783745586
DOI: 10.11647/OBP.0140

Cover image: Hermynia Zur Mühlen (drawing of late 1920s) drawn by Emil Stumpp. Reproduced with the friendly permission of the Emil Stumpp Archive, Gelnhausen, Germany.

All paper used by Open Book Publishers is SFI (Sustainable Forestry Initiative) and PEFC (Programme for the Endorsement of Forest Certification Schemes) Certified.

Printed in the United Kingdom, United States, and Australia
by Lightning Source for Open Book Publishers (Cambridge, UK)

Contents

Translator's Introductory Note	1
Acknowledgements	5
1. *The End and the Beginning: The Book of My Life* Hermynia Zur Mühlen	7
2. Supplement to *The End and the Beginning* Hermynia Zur Mühlen	163
3. Notes on Persons and Events Mentioned in the Memoir Lionel Gossman	175
4. *Feuilletons* and Fairy Tales: A Sampling Hermynia Zur Mühlen	279
Editor's Note	279
The Red Redeemer	282
Confession	287
High Treason	291
Death of a Shade	294
A Secondary Happiness	300
The Señora	304
Miss Brington	308
We Have to Tell Them	313
Painted on Ivory	318
The Sparrow	325
The Spectacles	340

5. *Our Daughters the Nazi Girls*. A Synopsis in English 347
   Lionel Gossman
6. Remembering Hermynia Zur Mühlen: A Tribute 407
   Lionel Gossman
7. Works by Hermynia Zur Mühlen in English Translation 435
8. Image Portfolio 437

List of Illustrations 441

Additional online resources available at
https://www.openbookpublishers.com/product/834#resources

Translator's Introductory Note

In the first two chapters of this volume we present Hermynia Zur Mühlen's 1929 autobiographical memoir, *The End and the Beginning* (*Ende und Anfang. Ein Lebensbild*), in a revised and extensively corrected version of Frank Barnes' translation of 1930 (New York: Jonathan Cape and Harrison Smith), which, though readable enough, contains many errors. A surprisingly large number of words and phrases in the 1930 translation were simply misunderstood (e.g. *ochrana* [*okhrana* in the usual English transcription] – the Russian secret police – translated as "the Ukraine"), and on more than one occasion Zur Mühlen was made to say quite the opposite in English of what she wrote in German. In addition, the original title has been restored in the present edition, as has the original lay-out of the text. The title of the 1930 translation, "The Runaway Countess," was doubtless designed to attract a particular class of readers, probably readers of the popular romances of the time. As the present edition is directed rather toward readers interested in the social and cultural history of the period covered by the narrative and, in particular, in women's writing and women's history, it seemed appropriate to restore Zur Mühlen's own title, which has a political rather than romantic resonance. The original German title was intended to evoke the end of one social and political order and, with the Russian Revolution of 1917, the beginning of another, in the author's eyes far better one, and at the same time, in her own personal life, the end of dependency and the beginning of a new existence as a free woman, capable of determining her own identity and her own destiny instead of having to submit to those imposed on her by history and tradition. Zur Mühlen also gave titles to the 77 sections of varying length into which she divided her narrative. These were dropped from the 1930 translation, which was divided instead into 24 untitled sections. There seemed to be no reason to prefer that arrangement of the text to the author's own. The latter has therefore been reinstated.

A supplementary chapter, written by Zur Mühlen in 1950 for a post-World War II re-publication of the 1929 German text in the Socialist magazine *Die Frau*, has been translated and placed, as Chapter 2 of the present book, at the end of Zur Mühlen's original text, immediately after the final section, "Zdravstvui Revolyutsia."

It was not always possible to reproduce certain characteristic features of Zur Mühlen's literary style in English translation – notably the effect of impressionistic immediacy achieved by means of punctuation and the elision of co-ordinates like "and" – and it was virtually impossible to convey the Viennese flavour of her language. Translation is inevitably subject in considerable measure to conditions imposed by the target language. Every effort was made, however, to stay as close to the original as possible.

The attraction of Zur Mühlen's memoir lies not only in the charming freshness with which it narrates a young woman's struggle to be a full, free, and independent human being, in defiance of the conventions and expectations of her time and social class, but in its sharply observed and often humorous portrayal of a bygone world from the unusual angle of the headstrong, rebellious daughter of an Austrian aristocrat and minor diplomat. The numerous individuals and events referred to in the memoir, some quite prominent and well known, many obscure or now forgotten, serve as a reminder that the world that disappeared in the fires of the First World War was full of colourful characters whose often surprising careers can be unexpectedly revealing. In addition, the memoir touches lightly and naively on major issues of the time, such as the interconnected Balkan and Moroccan crises and the climate of revolution in czarist Russia. In the hope of restoring some sense of the author's world, a fair number of the individuals and events mentioned in the narrative have been identified and described, most often quite briefly, sometimes at considerable length in Chapter 3. In a few especially interesting cases, these notices take the form of little essays. As much information as could be accommodated in the book without expanding it unduly has been provided, in particular, about Zur Mühlen's family members and about figures little known in the

English-speaking world, such as the poets Freiligrath and Anastasius Grün. Where information about those figures was hard to come by, the editor has listed some of his sources for the convenience of the reader. Thumbnail images accompany some of the descriptive endnotes.

This revised edition of the Open Book Publishers 2010 publication contains material not included in the earlier volume. Chapter 4 contains a sampling of the hundreds of short narratives that Zur Mühlen wrote for newspapers and magazines. These were selected and translated for this edition because of the light they shed on Zur Mühlen's principles and practice as a politically committed writer, who also earned her living by writing and translating. In addition, translations of two of her socialist fairy tales for children have been included in order to give the reader an idea of the work for which she won an international reputation in left-wing circles in the 1920s and 1930s. Chapter 5 consists of a substantial synopsis in English of a vigorously anti-Nazi novel written by Zur Mühlen in 1934, suppressed in Germany and Austria, and never translated into English. This is followed in Chapters 6 and 7 by the translator's essay on Zur Mühlen's life and literary career and by a list of her works in English translation. To close, Chapter 8 offers a sampling of illustrations by the artists George Grosz and Heinrich Vogeler of two of Zur Mühlen's fairy tale collections and one of her numerous translations. This new edition of Zur Mühlen's memoir is supplemented by an online appendix available at https://www.openbookpublishers.com/product/834#resources. It contains a short extract from the *Memoirs* of Sándor Márai, in which the celebrated Hungarian novelist gives a vivid, highly personal, and amusing account of his association with Zur Mühlen and her partner Stefan Klein in Frankfurt in 1919–20; a study of Zur Mühlen's relation to the aristocracy and to her own past by the historian Patrik von zur Mühlen; and two short essays by the editor – one on Zur Mühlen as the translator of Upton Sinclair into German, the other on the background of Zur Mühlen's widely read "socialist" fairy tales.

The English translations of three of Zur Mühlen's novels, which are no longer covered by copyright – *We Poor Shadows*, *Came the Stranger*, and *Guests in the House* – have been posted on a women's literature website and may be read at http://digital.library.upenn.edu/women/_generate/authors-Z.html

Lionel Gossman, May 2018

Acknowledgements

The translator and editor wishes to acknowledge his indebtedness for help, counsel, and encouragement to Professor Ritchie Robertson, Dr. Deborah Viëtor-Engländer, Dr. Ailsa Wallace and, not least, Dr. Patrik von zur Mühlen of the Friedrich-Ebert Stiftung in Bonn, to whose liberal and generous spirit Hermynia Zur Mühlen would undoubtedly have responded as warmly as she responded, a century ago, to that of his great-grandfather, "Uncle Max." He also wishes to thank Dr. Alessandra Tosi, his editor at Open Book Publishers, for much valuable advice and infinite patience.

Neuerscheinung!

Soeben gelangte zur Ausgabe

Ende und Anfang

Ein Lebensbuch

von

Hermynia Zur Mühlen

Geheftet 4 RM, in Ganzleinen 6 RM

Diese Erinnerungen einer altösterreichischen Aristokratin haben bei ihrer Vorveröffentlichung in einer großen Tageszeitung ungewöhnliches Aufsehen erregt. Aus allen Volkskreisen ohne Unterschied der Partei sind der Verfasserin Äußerungen zugegangen, die sich leidenschaftlich zu dem Werk, seinem Gehalt und seiner Form bekennen.

Mit geistreicher Anmut und klugem, natürlichen Urteil erzählt Hermynia Zur Mühlen, was sie im alten Österreich, später in ganz Europa und Nordafrika erlebte und beobachtete, während sie ihren Vater, einen hohen österreichischen Diplomaten, auf seinen Reisen begleitete. Für die Farbigkeit und den künstlerischen Zauber der Lebenserscheinungen hat sie überall ein offenes und williges Auge; aber früh entwickelt sich in ihr auch ein nachdenklicher, starker und redlicher Sinn der Kritik. Torheit und Unrecht in den überlieferten Lebensformen sind ihr überall von Anbeginn unerträglich; bis zur Unwiderstehlichkeit regt sich ihr kämpferischer Freiheitsdrang, als sie als Gattin eines baltischen Adeligen in eine Hölle der sozialen Stumpfheit und Roheit verbannt ist. Die Nachfahrin einer Kaiserlichen Palast-Dame (K. P. D.) wird schließlich zur Anhängerin der Kommunistischen Partei Deutschlands (K. P. D.). Wir begleiten die Verfasserin auf ihrem kühnen, klaren Entwicklungsgang durch ein anschaulich offenes Werk von hohem zeitgeschichtlichen Wert.

S. Fischer Verlag / Berlin

Advertisement by Samuel Fischer Verlag, Berlin, for the newly published *Ende und Anfang*.

1. *The End and the Beginning: The Book of My Life**

by Hermynia Zur Mühlen

In the well tempered glass-house

When I was a small child there was a cuckoo clock in the hallway across from my bedroom. I was very fond of it and never tired of hearing it. One night, however, the beloved clock played me a nasty trick. I was awakened from a deep sleep by a dull sound and started with fright as I heard in the stillness of the night eleven terrifying cries. Screech owls, I thought, and screech owl cries mean death. I was very frightened and began to scream and call for help, but no one heard me. A horrible feeling of despair surged over me: everyone in the house, in the little town, in the whole world was dead, and I had been left all alone in a world of the dead. Thinking back now on those childhood days, I am often reminded of that eerie night when my friend the cuckoo prophesied the death of a world. The world in which I grew up is dead. Even if many of its former denizens are still alive, the old refined, high-spirited levity is gone, as is the contempt for money and the natural, unmediated high-handedness with which middle-class people were treated, even when they were millionaires.

---

* The note numbers refer to 'Notes on Persons and Events Mentioned in the Memoir' immediately following the text (Chapter 3).

Translation © Lionel Gossman, CC BY 4.0

The "aristocratic" diplomatic service, which in those days — such, at least, was the conviction of the diplomats themselves — was distinguished by a kind of aura, was among the glories, now lost, of that bygone world. We in our family belonged to the "career," and the "career" meant one thing and one thing only: the diplomatic service. For us nothing else was conceivable. This reverence for the "career," it should be added, did not in any way prevent Austrian diplomats from making merry at the expense of their chiefs. The Austrian ambassador in London, for example, was known only as "the Superlative" — "dumb, dumber, Dehm."[1] In general the diplomats took nothing in the world seriously, including themselves. One of my uncles,[2] for instance, who was himself in the service, taught me to give to the question "What is your father?" the following fine reply: "My father is a poor devil who wears a green monkey suit, writes stupid reports and costs the state a lot of money." And my father[3] never lost an occasion to explain that "Austria has only one real interest: the continued piety of the Muslims. As long as these people continue to wear the fez everything will be all right for us." Most fezzes were manufactured at that time in Bohemia.

Yet we ought not to have looked upon other callings with so much scorn, for my paternal grandfather[4] had risen in the military to the rank of general, been appointed First Adjutant-General of Emperor Franz Joseph and been made a Knight of the Golden Fleece. And a great-uncle[5] had been a cavalry general and governor of Mainz. His wife[6] was a typical representative of her caste, a lovable, pretty, exceptionally pious old lady who followed the teachings of the Gospel by giving away half of her not too large income to the poor — a fact which, nevertheless, did not prevent her from saying to me one day: "The bourgeois, you know, are perfectly fine, and I know that before God we are all alike, but I just can't see them as people like ourselves." And she used to tell of charity balls where a ribbon was stretched across the middle of the ballroom — the bourgeois danced on one side, the aristocrats on the other. She was certainly a most consistent old lady; when her niece, Sophie Chotek,[7] married the crown-prince, Franz Ferdinand, she said: "That person shall never cross my threshold again. She is a wicked young woman and has done the Kaiser a grievous wrong in depriving him of a rightful heir."

I found remarks of this kind extremely amusing because I had already, at a quite tender age, been "corrupted" by reading the *Neue Freie Presse*[8] and other liberal newspapers. Only the *Fremdenblatt*[9] was supposed to be read in our circles in those days, but my grandmother[10] was an Englishwoman with the liberal views of the English at that time, and so it happened that, at the age of eight or nine, I considered the editorials of Herr Benedikt[11] a Revelation and a new Gospel, and an unshakable conviction crystallized in my mind: the government is always wrong. One of my great-uncles[12] was Minister of Agriculture and belonged to the clerical party. He pushed a law through which is called after him the *Lex Falkenhayn,* and the *Freie Presse* attacked him vigorously. Once, when we were paying our obligatory call on his wife in Vienna, this uncle also came into the room, and I, a little brat of eight, was astonished that such an "infamous scoundrel" could seem so innocent and friendly.

My republican feelings were also awakened early, though I cannot claim that they were the product of logical thinking. They sprang from a purely personal thirst for revenge. About thirty minutes from the little health-resort of G.[13] in the Salzkammergut, a veritable eyesore of a chateau towered over the beautiful landscape, disfiguring it horribly; it belonged to the Duke of Württemberg. The old duke had a particular aversion to dogs, and any dog that had somehow or other crept into his park was shot. I considered this proceeding most reprehensible and condemned it, as one condemns a wrong which does not directly concern one, coolly and without special anger — until one evening my little fox-terrier Grip did not return from one of his customary explorations of the countryside. Nor did he come back the following day, and when a week had passed we had to conclude that poor Grip had met his death in the Duke's park. My condemnation, purely on principle, now flared into raging indignation. The old Duke embodied for me all the tyrants of history, all the murderers and criminals. Day after day, on our walks, I would drag my poor governess to the red-coloured castle, collecting on the way all the little stones I could find. I then threw them amid a torrent of curses into the park. From that moment on I was through with monarchs, princes, and dukes. And when many years later, during the German Revolution, the throne was taken from the house of Württemberg too, I thought of poor Grip and felt a quiet personal satisfaction, because my little murdered dog had been avenged.

Quite slowly and gradually the "New Age" penetrated into our little lake-side town. The first female clerk to run a branch of the Post Office created a sensation. Most people had the feeling that letters deposited in this office would never arrive, and important insured letters were generally not entrusted to the fat, friendly *Fräulein*. I think that some of the old ladies who lived in villas and wore gloves all day long to protect their hands thought it improper that a woman should sit behind a window, and considered the respectable female postal clerk a lost creature.

But "society" had scarcely recovered from this first sensation when it was shocked by a far worse one. On the smooth, beautiful streets brazen creatures suddenly appeared: bicyclists, women who dared display their limbs half-way up to the knee. In our home, we did not see the matter in such a tragic light, since grandmother believed women had a right to do anything they were capable of doing well, and even my mother rode a bicycle. But the other women were less indulgent; old Countess Szapáry[14] had her gardener collect flint stones and lay them on the garden table. Then she sat behind the hedge of her garden and watched for women cyclists. If one of the immodest creatures passed her way, she was showered with a rain of stones, and the old Countess would shout with all her might after the bicycle: "Hussy! Hussy!"

Yet it must be said to our credit that there was actually a woman in our circle with bobbed hair. In those days this was called a "Titus head." The possessor of this Titus head was a romantic apparition in my eyes for another reason too: she had been an actress before her marriage to Count Prokesch-Osten and, under the name of Friederike Grossmann,[15] had enjoyed great success. Herr Wiesinger, the stationer, was even then still selling a picture of her in her most celebrated role as "The Cricket." I still remember the lively figure and large eyes of the "Cricket," who cannot but have been extremely bored in the rather ceremonious atmosphere of our local society. Once during the Dreyfus affair, she allowed her feelings to get the better of her and, in her capacity as head of the Red Cross in G., sent a telegram to Madame Dreyfus in which she expressed the sympathy of the Red Cross. Wild excitement seized the little town; some were anti-Dreyfusards, but the others also shook their heads, for after all, Dreyfus, though innocent, was still a Jew, and therefore one ought not to act so impulsively, especially when one had been a member of the bourgeoisie before one's marriage. I, naturally, was an ardent Dreyfus supporter, and had constantly to be reminded by grandmother, who moreover was also one, that a child must be polite even to those adults who hold different views. When Zola published his *J'Accuse*, a new world was opened up for me, and Zola took the place of all my other heroes.

***

But the "Cricket" was not our only celebrity. Right next to the large garden of our villa there was another garden, which belonged to Pauline Lucca.[16] The famous singer had just retired at that time; she was married to a Baron Walhoven and gave singing-lessons. I can no longer recall her face; I only know that she had beautiful, merry blue eyes and spoke with a frightful Viennese accent. Every year, towards the end of the season, she gave plays in the little theatre installed in her villa, and at one of these performances a young creature made her appearance — the freshest, most attractive, most enchanting being that one can imagine. Even the old ladies were charmed by her and her voice. "What is the name of the little one?" they asked after the performance. And the answer was: "Fritzi Massary."[17]

A little old white-haired man lived on the promenade and I knew that he was the composer Goldmark,[18] a most remarkable personality. You could also find Peter Altenberg[19] on the promenade, as well as the painter Angeli,[20] whose celebrity in England was due to his being the best waltzer in London — so, at least, his friends maintained.

But we also had local celebrities. There was a young instructor who was attacked by all the priests because he told the children about Darwin's theory of evolution. The prefect of our district, Baron A., a wise and sensible man, took his side and informed us, often in great anger, of their persecution of Herr Lebida. Naturally, I immediately saw the young man with the pale face and dark hair as a hero and martyr. Since I did not know him I began to run after his two elderly sisters, on foot and on my bicycle — for grandmother had at last yielded to my pleas and given me a bicycle. The moment I saw the Lebida sisters in the distance (they always went out together) I would race after them, give them a look full of admiration, and hope that they would condescend at some point to speak to me. But they never did, and it may be that this circumstance increased my respect for their family. For notwithstanding all one's liberal feelings, one was accustomed, after all, as the "little Countess," to having the bourgeois feel honoured when one spoke to them.

Naturally one was courteous towards everyone — but not on account of the individuals themselves. It was a matter of self-respect. "Don't forget that you are a little lady." How often have I heard that in my childhood. But in those days "lady" did not mean a well-dressed, idle, rich woman, but a person who was tactful and sensitive to the feelings of others, obliging and polite in every life situation, careful to hide her own feelings, and, however bad she might be feeling herself, capable of not letting others notice it. It was not solely their fault that the aristocrats considered themselves the *umbilicus mundi*; the bourgeoisie's abject veneration of them also played a part. I remember quite clearly a doctor, otherwise a wise and very nice man, who had been called in to see me, saying on the occasion of the big fire at the charity bazaar in Paris: "It's terrible to think how many aristocrats were burned to death there!" And I recall, too, my grandmother's quietly asking "Do you think, doctor, that it was less horrible for the others?"

Nor have I ever forgotten the explanation of my catechist, when, to the astonishment of the entire class, at the age of about ten, I declared: "I don't believe our dear Lord is just; if he were, he wouldn't permit there to be rich and poor." The worthy gentleman stared at me grimly for a moment — he was horrified, I think, every time I opened my mouth — then he quickly found an answer. "There are rich and poor in order that the rich may get to heaven by giving alms to the poor."

It was likewise an unwritten law with us, moreover, that one had to be gracious in one's dealings with the bourgeois and even more gracious — in a far more natural way, as though one had to do with one's equals — in one's dealings with the "poor," the common people. A little incident seems to me to illustrate this well. In our little town the river Traun frequently overflowed its banks, threatening to bring down the old wooden bridge that spanned it. One day what we feared happened. With a horrible crack the bridge broke in two. Three working men fell into the river and were drowned. The prefect of the district (not Baron

A.) who was in charge of the rescue work turned to his servant and said: "Go home, Johann, and tell the Countess that only working men were drowned." I believe that even the working people were not as outraged by these words as the aristocrats. Count S. would most certainly have been boycotted from society had not some one found an excuse for him. "What do you expect? His wife's mother is a bourgeoise."

Contempt for the bourgeoisie was so ingrained, even among the most unprejudiced members of our class, that it was impossible to dislodge it. My father was far too wise to harbour any belief in aristocratic superiority; he required of people only that they be intelligent and have their wits about them, and he sought these attributes mostly in vain among the members of his own class. Yet even he took care to use the inevitable prefix "poor" when speaking of his acquaintances in industry. A number of years ago, when I was translating a book in which the enormous wealth of a Rhineland industrialist was described in great detail, I had to burst out laughing in the midst of my tiresome task when I suddenly remembered how my father always spoke of the founder of this gigantic fortune — he was a good friend of his and could have bought us up, lock, stock, and barrel, a hundred times over — as "poor H., really quite a nice fellow all the same."

In those days, in our circles, money really counted for very little, even if, as a child, I long believed — perhaps not altogether mistakenly — that the "S. M. Rothschild" on the seal of the Rothschild business letters meant "Seine Majestät Rothschild."

***

Likewise, relatively little importance was attached to clothing. "One" wore tailor-made things from Jungmann in Vienna and the inevitable diamond buttons. It was not proper to be too elegantly dressed. That was left to the wives of the wealthy bourgeois. The old ladies sometimes ran around so shabbily dressed — like the women we in Austria used to call "church wives" — that an outsider unfamiliar with our ways could easily have felt like handing them ten *kreuzers*. "Church wives" were poor women whose greatest pleasure consisted in sitting for hours on end in church telling their beads. They attended nearly all the services on Sunday. I had little love for them, because, when the pews were full I had to give up my seat to them and stand. I had to do this for the elegant bourgeois women only when they were quite old. I also had to get up for working men and women because they had toiled hard all week.

It was grandmother who taught me this respect for working people. In our garden we had a day-worker, an old woman we called Höllerin, and grandmother told me the story of her life. She was sixty years old, and she had three grandchildren at home whom she had to raise. She worked from morning till night, yet she was always friendly and always ready to chat with me. She had a pig at home, for which she would collect horsechestnuts, and when I had been good I was allowed, as a special privilege, to gather horsechestnuts in the garden for Höllerin. I was also allowed to give her toys for her grandchildren, and grandmother explained to me that one should never give ugly, broken toys to the poor. That would be an insult. One should give them the finest one had. Somewhere inside me there was a feeling for self-castigation, perhaps inherited from a distant ancestor, Saint Ignatius Loyola, who was the cousin of a remote ancestress, and so I followed grandmother's injunction to the letter. But my asceticism seems to have been not quite genuine, for I remember that I once gave away my beloved black doll — her name was Bella and she said "Mama" and "Papa" when you pulled on two strings attached to her middle — but regretted it bitterly afterwards and for a long time could not get over my loss.

***

We inhabitants of this old world were actually living as if in a beautiful well-tempered glass-house, filled with the scent of flowers. Outside, all sorts of horrible things were happening, but we saw only confusedly through the windows, which were overgrown with greenery, and did not let these things disturb us. To be sure, the glass-house also allowed many good attributes to sprout: genuine love of beauty, real culture, self-control (inseparable from good manners); but it also estranged us from the real world and created a helplessness in practical matters that was passed off as disdain for "business." In our own personal green-house, however, the wise hand of my grandmother had cleaned off one of the panes. Through it I could look out on reality and there, even as a child, I caught sight of the problem of problems — riches and poverty — or what in those days was called the problem of "the poor."

Discoveries

There were not many "poor" in our little watering-place. Still enough, however, to set an intellectually curious child, hungry for justice, thinking. This was all the more inevitable as in my earliest youth I took the Gospel literally — and would announce to horrified grown-ups: "You are not Christians. If you were, you would not have two coats, for whoever has two should give one of them to someone who has none."

Why were "the poor" poor?

Children and primitive people are always inclined to displace blame on to individuals or political classes. And so it was with me. If there were people who did not have enough to eat, this had to be due to the malevolence of individuals — in effect, of those individuals who held power. But who were these individuals? Not the bourgeois, for they also belonged in some measure to "the poor." In those days I looked upon anyone as poor who did not have a house of his own as well as a carriage and at least four servants. And as we did not mix with the wealthy bourgeois, manufacturers and financiers existed for me only as a very vague concept. A banker was someone who took care of one's fortune, and reported on his activity every month in a fine sealed letter, and a manufacturer was a sort of glorified tradesman. My sociological investigations were advanced by a work by Hans Blum[21] on the revolution of '48. Later I discovered that Robert Blum's son had actually written a reactionary book. Yet at eleven — I was that age when I read the book — it appeared to me extremely revolutionary: bourgeois heroes fell in the struggle against monarchs and aristocrats and died in order to give the people a parliamentary constitution and freedom of the press. I discovered three important things: the bourgeoisie, magnanimous, virtuous, and industrious, in contrast to our idle, frivolous, and profligate class; the parliament, which expressed the will of the people (I was then eleven years old); and the press, which is called on to contribute to the victory of truth and justice. I had aspired at one time to be a circus rider or the female leader of a noble robber band, but from now on I recognized only two really superior callings: that of member of the House of Delegates or that of journalist. My uncle Anton[22] gave me a statistical map of the House, on which the different parties were represented by different colours. On the reverse side were the number and names of the members. I learned them until I could reel them off by heart. The particular platforms of the various parties did not interest me. I was moved only by a burning hatred of the clerical party, because most aristocrats were in it. For I was by then already fully convinced of one thing: the aristocrats were to blame for all the misery in the world. To this conviction my uncle Anton had certainly contributed his share. He who was known at the Ministry of Foreign Affairs as the "Red Count," and whose career had been considerably harmed by his liberal opinions, would call me into the drawing-room with special pleasure when there were guests and ask: "Where do the aristocrats belong?"[23] To which I was to respond with unshakable conviction: "Strung up on the lamp-post." Uncle Anton was altogether the highest authority for me in intellectual matters. When he came to visit us, I never left his side, and he often declared that he knew of nothing more exhausting than the hours he spent with me, for no one could answer all the questions I asked. But he did me the greatest kindness one can do to a child: he took me seriously, tried to explain everything to me, and if I often understood his explanations differently than he intended, that was not his fault. Grandmother also took me seriously, and I recall long debates with her on passive and active voting rights for women. She was in favour of women's having the vote in principle; however, she thought that women were not yet ready for it, and that in Austria they would vote almost without exception for the clerical party. I naturally had a better opinion of the good sense of my sex; today, I have to admit that in many of her views grandmother was right.

The "Anchor Society"

After intense study, from my eleventh to twelfth year, of the "social question," which for me was exclusively a question of politics and had nothing whatsoever to do with economics, I reached the conclusion that since the year '48, when the brave and generous bourgeoisie had taken to the barricades, nothing had been done for the improvement of the world. But now I had come along and would take matters in hand. Down with the aristocrats!

And so one rainy Sunday morning I founded a Society for the Improvement of the World — the "Anchor Society." It was all quite simple. I wrote to two cousins in Vienna, to a friend in Lisbon, and to three bourgeois acquaintances in our little town, telling them that I had founded a society for the improvement of the world and had appointed them members. I despotically drew up the rules myself. The first proclaimed the abolition of the nobility; the others, as I recall, were of a more practical nature and concerned membership dues: twenty-five kreuzers a month for regular members and one gulden for honorary members. With these funds the misery of the world was to be assuaged. All members were to wear an anchor badge so that later, when the number of members had swollen to millions, they would recognize one another in the wide world beyond and be able to work together. (The badge, which had a hook on the back, always tore our clothes and thus caused us all kinds of unpleasantness — but all that was part of our martyrdom for the Cause.) Of course, I was the head of the society, and my youngest cousin in Vienna was treasurer.

The society issued a monthly bulletin composed by me and consisting of six copies written out in my own hand. It "appeared" on four lined folio pages, and was made up of one leading political editorial, in faithful imitation of the editorials of Herr Benedikt of the Vienna "Free Press"; an endless novel about an unbelievably noble anarchist, who lived with his sister in a hut on the heath, manufactured bombs, and held forth in speeches from morning to night, so that he never got around to throwing the bombs; news of the society, of which there was very little; and poems by Lenau,[24] Freiligrath,[25] and my special favourite, Anastasius Grün.[26] Grandmother, who was our first honorary member — later, Uncle Anton also joined — and who with touching patience had me read the entire paper to her each month, presented me with a seal stamped with an anchor. Since, for some reason or other I had at the time a deep respect for the Freemasons, I would draw a triangle next to the seal on the back of the envelope, hoping that this secret sign would be noticed by the police and that one fine day I should be arrested.

***

As a first step towards abolishing the nobility — aside from the wild editorials of the Anchor Journal — I omitted titles on all addresses and wrote only the names. One of my aunts whose mother had been a commoner felt insulted and wrote to grandmother, who explained to me that one should be considerate of the weaknesses of others; but her gentle, faint smile betrayed to me that she was really on my side, and I defended my conviction with glowing words. Finally we agreed that the half-bourgeois aunt should be allowed "Countess" on her address, but that I could limit myself to the name only in the case of her children, who were more "truly" aristocrats. My admiration for the bourgeoisie received something of a jolt from this incident, but I assumed that my aunt had been corrupted by her marriage to an aristocrat.

The cousins raised no objection to being deprived of their nobility. (I think I was an extremely unpleasant, domineering brat, who simply terrorized them.) But the three bourgeois girls, whom I invited every Sunday and tried to work on "politically," were less malleable and harder to influence. They both wanted and did not want to acknowledge that the old aristocracy was the cause of all the evil in the world. At first I worked, despite my young years, with purely feminine means, played one off against the other, favoured the one who allowed that I was right and turned against the one who refused to see what an evil the aristocracy was, turning up my nose and haughtily playing the "Countess" to the hilt. If that did not succeed either, I resorted to plain rudeness and cuffs on the ear. But the bourgeoisie proved itself the stronger; I did not succeed in bringing a single one of the three girls round to my view.

As we had still not been honoured by the vigilance of the police, I decided, as a last resort, to write a play which would naturally be accepted by every theatre company and banned by the censor. It was a fine drama with many corpses and a tirade, in hexameters, against the aristocrats. Children were freezing and starving, and the wicked Count, who in the midst of a snow storm had refused to let them into his palace, just laughed demoniacally, "Ha-ha," until he was silenced by his mother's many pages-long curse on him. Quite exceptionally, I showed my masterpiece, out of authorial vanity, to my parents. Mother was irritated and responded with her customary: "You are an idiot." But father laughed and laughed and finally said: "A second Goethe" — which filled me with satisfaction for several days until I realized that he had been making fun of me, and in discouragement burned my play.

***

Meantime, the editorials of my paper had been getting better, for I had been diligently reading the speeches of the Social Democratic delegate Daschynski,[27] who was a brilliant and powerful orator, and I had now abandoned Herr Benedikt in order to devote myself to Herr Daschynski. At that time I read the newspaper regularly. I had had to promise not to read the court proceedings, but the promise was not hard to keep, since in the court-room the government was not attacked, and nothing else was of interest to me. Grandmother, who was also interested in politics, catered to my passion, read articles to me, and called my attention to this and that; Uncle Anton, too, helped to strengthen my interest in politics. Father laughed at me, but he too would sometimes condescend to discuss politics when he could ride his favourite hobbyhorse, the Balkan question. While I insisted firmly that everything bad comes from the aristocracy, father maintained just as firmly that everything bad comes from that cursed storm-centre, the Balkans. For that reason, for a long time, the Balkans represented for me the entire field of foreign policy.

The Anchor Society had been in existence for a year now, and yet the nobility had not been overthrown in Austria. I began to feel slightly discouraged. The finest editorials, the most powerful speeches of my noble anarchist seemed to be of no avail. The number of members was not growing. I had a vague presentiment that only a mass popular party, with me at the head, would be able to accomplish anything, but where were these masses to come from? Then, too, something was not quite right with the treasury; there was always less money in the cashbox than there should have been. In choosing a treasurer I had not taken into consideration my little cousin's extreme fondness for bonbons. One day when I categorically demanded all the money in the cashbox to aid the victims of a flood, it was found to be empty. My little cousin humbly and woefully confessed that she had "eaten up" the money. In shame and disgrace she was removed from her post and one of the bourgeois girls living in G., whom I could keep an eye on, was appointed treasurer in her place. But this incident had shown me clearly that one could not depend on help from the aristocrats to overthrow the nobility. I still struggled to keep the Anchor Society alive for a while, by loudly crying out to any members I encountered as I bicycled through the little town: "Down with the government! Down with the nobility!" But even that did not produce a sympathetic policeman willing to arrest me and so bring the whole society to the attention of the public.

The last number of the paper appeared; a swansong with the wildest of all wild editorials. It happened that just at that time Uncle Anton was visiting us, and I read my work aloud to him. The last words of it were: "And so we proclaim that this criminal government belongs where all governments belong — on the gallows!"

When I ended my uncle was silent, and I thought joyfully that he was so moved he could not speak. But he looked at me for a long time with his big dark eyes, and then he turned, shaking his head, to grandmother: "The child will end up on the gallows herself one day."

Despite this prophecy I have not yet come to that point; I have only been tried for high treason[28] before the supreme court in Leipzig, because I published a little story of some thirty pages in which I allegedly "undermined" the morale of the police. In fact, that story was a small pacifist tract in comparison with the editorials I wrote for the defunct Anchor Journal.

Servants

The entire little town by the lake was actually a collection of islands. Each one of its villas, set in a beautiful garden of its own, was the retreat of someone who wanted to lead a separate life. Most of these people were extreme individualists, even if many of them — in true Austrian style — would have adamantly refused to be so described. "Stop using those horrible foreign words," many would have said, and they would be the very same people who would say to you reproachfully, if you used the simple German past tense in conversation, instead of the usual compound past: "Get along with you, don't talk so affectedly!"

The calm and peace that reigned in those beautiful houses seems incredible today, unreal. Was life truly so harmonious, or did good manners simply create the illusion of harmony? The feeling of being a community, expressed in immediate use of the familiar second person by everyone who was part of "society" when addressing other members of "society," extended in some measure to the servants. They "belonged" almost as much as family members and they often ruled over the children even more tyrannically than the family. I stood in real awe of our old valet Albert. He would on no account permit me to slide down the banisters — I think he considered it improper — and when at table I made a spot on the cloth and hastily pushed a plate over it, a relentless index finger came down and marked the spot and a deep voice announced: "The Countess has already made yet another spot!" 'Mr. Albert' — for I was not allowed to call him simply by his first name — owned a squirrel which he kept in a big cage in the servants' room. If he was in a good mood, he would take out the little animal, and I was permitted to stroke it; if he was in a bad mood, he would say: "I haven't time!" And woe unto me if I so much as touched the cage without his permission. One fine day, the squirrel escaped, but that did not diminish my interest in Herr Albert. There was a mystery attached to him, which I would have given my life to unravel: did he wear a wig or not? It was impossible to tell for sure. Uncle Anton spurred on my curiosity; whenever he came to see us, he would ask: "Have you discovered yet whether he wears a wig or not?" I would willingly have asked Herr Albert himself, but grandmother forbade me to ask such a tactless question, and so, to this day, I do not know whether he wore a wig or not.

The second-tier servants never stayed very long with us, and I can remember only one. His name was Alois, and he never missed an opportunity of telling you that he was the only son of a widow. Alois sported a black moustache — which was contrary to all the rules of propriety — for in those days no servant was permitted to wear a moustache. But he was apparently a vain young man, and besought grandmother with tears in his eyes and allusions to his widowed mother, whose only son he was, to permit him to keep his moustache — and he was allowed to do so.

I remember likewise the gardener. He was a small, silent man with two burning passions: elaborate flowerbeds and veterans' reunions. He would have liked to lay out the entire garden in flower-beds, and grandmother had to fight strenuously against each one. At veterans' reunions and funerals he wore a uniform and thus clad marched proudly in the procession. He called them both "celebrations," because both made him equally happy. He was afflicted with a thin, constantly scolding wife whom I, as a small child, took for a witch. How often, terrified yet full of anticipation, I would creep to the gardener's house on dark autumn evenings, hoping to see his wife ride through the air on a broomstick. Grandmother did not need to tell me to be polite to her.

When I saw her I greeted her respectfully from afar, for fear of being bewitched.

Fräulein Marie, the chambermaid, was also thin, and constantly felt offended. She had a brother who was a court councillor in Bavaria, and to whom she referred as often as Alois referred to his widowed mother. I received many a scolding because of her. Her presence disturbed me in my religious exercises more than anything else. It sometimes happened that she was there when I was saying my evening prayers and on every one of those occasions, I refused, for reasons no one could understand, to say the Ave Maria. I was firmly and stubbornly convinced that *Fräulein* Marie would assume I was referring to her when I said: "Hail, Mary, full of grace, the Lord is with thee." And as I could not endure her, I would not have had her think for a moment that I was praying to her.

For the cooks also I had a keen antipathy; they were always the one discordant note in our harmonious existence. Besides, my first act of social justice went so badly awry with one of them that my young soul was beset by evil doubts. We had a most lovable little kitchen maid, pretty and very young. She sometimes played with me and I was very fond of her. One day, as I was walking in the garden, I approached the kitchen window and heard the cook giving the girl, who was weeping bitterly, a terrible scolding. I became very angry. Then I noticed that directly under the window a large bowl of stewed fruit had been set out for our lunch. Here was my chance to punish the wicked cook. I quickly determined to scoop up some sand from the path and throw it into the bowl. When at lunch the sand was discovered, I was delighted, but not for long. The cook immediately announced that she suspected me, whereupon I admitted haughtily that I had wanted to "punish" her. I was severely reprimanded and told to beg the cook's pardon. But I refused because of my confused feeling that she had tormented a weaker creature than herself. Grandmother, who was a good pedagogue, tried to explain to me, that the eternal heat of the oven and smell of the food made cooks nervous and irritable, and that a silly little girl like me had no right to punish a hard-working person. I did finally give in and apologize. But my dislike for cooks has remained with me to this day.

The beautiful circus rider

Sometimes a circus came to our little town, and that was glorious. About ten minutes from our villa there was an empty plot of ground; and it was there that the tents were set up. How splendid it was to see the circus enter the town — the horses, the dogs, the clowns. And then the show! The most beautiful girls, who performed the most daring tricks; the elegant lady who demonstrated all the equestrian arts; the ring-master with his cracking whip. And it all smelled so strangely, of sand and horses and wild animals. It was a marvellous world, inhabited by fortunate people who rode horseback, walked the tightrope, and were allowed to wear brilliant clothing covered with spangles. My admiration for the tight-rope dancers cost me many black and blue marks, so many, that I gave up thinking of tight-rope dancing and transferred my desires and longings to riding a horse over a wooden plank. On one occasion an exceptionally beautiful equestrienne arrived with the circus. She had pink cheeks, golden hair, and a sweet smile such as one normally sees only on dolls. I admired her infinitely and would have given almost anything to make her acquaintance. My wish was to be fulfilled. One day someone told us that "stupid August" had been thrown from his horse and could not appear in public. Grandmother sent me with a bottle of French red wine to the injured man — perhaps in order to dampen somewhat my circus ardour. I went into a miserable little tent; on a plank bed lay a melancholy, oldish man, the last person in the world one would have thought capable of dashing exploits and clever repartee. Near him, darning stockings, sat a thin, weary woman, pale, fretful, her hair already turned grey — it was the beautiful equestrienne. My governess, who had accompanied me, thought it was out of compassion for the two poor devils that I almost began to weep. However, it was not pity that brought tears to my eyes, but disappointment, perhaps also the horror by which one is overcome when, for the first time in one's life, one sees behind the scenes.

Shopping

It was an exciting adventure to go shopping in our little town. In a tiny street near the church lived the shoe-maker who had an enormous goiter, which even his long black beard could not cover. He would have one place one's foot on a sheet of paper, and would draw an outline of it with a pencil — a procedure that tickled terribly. In the little workroom there were two extremely interesting works of art: one was a youthful portrait of Kaiser Franz Joseph, not in the form of a drawing, but in that of a piece of writing that told the story of the emperor's life. Whenever you went to the shoe-maker's, he would fetch this portrait and tell you that it had been made by a school teacher who had spent a whole year at the task. The second treasure was a little wooden flask on which was carved the martyrdom of Christ — the scourge, the crown of thorns, the vinegar sop, the cross, and the spear. This marvel had come from a convict. The shoe-maker was always glad to talk at length about these two precious objects, and I was always delighted when I got to hold them in my own hands.

Not far from the cobbler's was the glove-maker's workshop. The glove-maker was a friendly old man who always spoke with great pride of the distinguished ladies for whom he had made gloves. The gloves were tried on like clothes. They had to fit without a wrinkle, as though they had been poured on.

The shopkeepers were part of the place and seemed to have grown with it. It was as though they had always been there. It did happen once that a young stationer opened a new shop, but as he was the son of the old stationer, it was not an act of disloyalty to buy from him. But then a brand-new shop opened, an elegant shop that sold blouses and underclothing, hats and lace collars. The owners were foreigners — as the inhabitants of G. described everyone who did not hail originally from the town — and they were not only foreigners, they were Jews, and their name was Sonnenschein. This first Jewish shop gave rise to all sorts of discussions. Most of the ladies declared that they would never, in any circumstances, buy from the Sonnenscheins, that one should not take the trade away from the old-established Christian shopkeepers. For a few months they held heroically to their decision, but after half a year the prerogative of the Christian merchants was forgotten, and all "society" bought from the Sonnenscheins. We had gone to them from the beginning, and grandmother had more than once held little, mobile, dark-eyed Frau Sonnenschein up to me as an example of amiability and kindness. I can still see the thin little woman now; she never seemed to be still for an instant; her hands were busy, her big black eyes moved continually, she talked incessantly, and always found the right thing to say. Within six months she knew what all her customers were interested in, asked this one about her roses, that one about her dogs, and chatted about swimming, bicycling, or the latest fashions, while she pulled out different articles in order to show them and sent Herr Sonnenschein, who was slow and deaf, to fetch this and that. Within a year the most Catholic ladies bought only from Frau Sonnenschein, the shop became bigger and bigger, business got better and better, and everyone loved the little Jewess. When she died a few years later and very soon afterwards Herr Sonnenschein married one of his Gentile salesgirls, everyone was in a state of righteous indignation: how upset the poor little woman would have been had she known that her husband would marry a Christian! The new Frau Sonnenschein was regarded with hostility, the customers stayed away, the shop began going down, and the Christian tradespeople got their old clients back again.

Woman in the year 1900

The woman of the year 1900 was a martyr who concealed the tortures she had to suffer behind heroically maintained smiles. In those days the most important thing for a woman was to have "a waist." The ideal waist was one that could be encompassed by two hands of normal size. This was achieved in the following manner: a corset was put on unlaced, one pressed one's arms close to one's sides, and held in one's breath, while the maid pulled with all her might at the corset laces. Then came a pause, one took another breath, and the maid gathered new strength. Then the procedure was repeated, and finally, after that, the dress, plentifully equipped with whale-bones, was put on. At the waist there was a strong band with hooks and eyes. Most of the time the ends of the band did not meet, so another tug had to be given to the corset, until at last the dress could be fastened. It took about two hours to do one's hair. Countless small and large hairpins held together real and false switches and curls. Then the enormous hat was set in place and hatpins were stuck in. Frequently the hat was trimmed with birds and flowers only on one side, so that all the weight pulled at one spot. After ten minutes one had a headache; with the corset it was impossible to breathe; the collar stays bored into one's neck; and the monstrous balloon sleeves hindered all free movement. So, heroically smiling, women went out to promenade holding up their skirts with hands that were soon weary from the weight.

The disposition of purses and handkerchiefs was a chapter in itself. The clothes had a slit in back, a dangerous thing because it came open so easily. Such occurrences were signalled by the phrase: "there's lightning!" A horrified hand would then immediately feel behind. If one wanted to reach into the pocket, one had first to open the slit and then begin to feel around for the pocket. I cannot explain how the pocket managed never to be where one expected to find it — but it did. One constantly saw women on the streets with anxious expressions, searching behind, frantic, desperate. Once the purse was found, they would forget to close the slit, or would be unable to locate the hooks and eyes.

Naturally, it was not admitted that one had legs. A man at that time had to precede a woman when going upstairs so as not to fall under suspicion of wanting to see her legs. From the moment a young girl put on her first long dress — and how proud we were of those dresses, and how often we tripped over them — no one was even to suspect that she was supported on anything more than ankles and even ankles were not supposed to be seen. On the street one wore laced boots; for some reason open shoes were not respectable outside the house. The boots had a long row of buttons, and if one was in a hurry, a button would inevitably come off. The same thing happened with the gloves worn at balls; they came almost all the way up to the shoulder, were always too tight, pinched, and stretched, and were very expensive.

How the women of 1900, with their balloon sleeves, wasp waists, and the flower-beds and aviaries on their heads, still managed to be pretty is an enigma today. But they were. Yes, they even managed to be graceful and to move elegantly. To be sure, one was in training for it from childhood. I still remember with horror the board with two diverging rods, which, held in place under the armpits and stretched across the back, was intended to develop an erect carriage. Another exercise for the same purpose was more entertaining: one placed a bottle full of water on one's head and was then to walk the length of the corridor several times without holding on to the bottle and without spilling a drop. One also learned how to sit down, how to rise, and how to enter a room. Young girls were never supposed to sit in easy chairs. I still recall my father's fury when once, weary from a long horse-ride, I lay down on a chaise longue in his presence.

"Sit up straight! What kind of a position is that?" How often I had to hear that. And how many angry glances were directed at my feet, because the forbidden ankles were showing.

Childhood days

We spent the spring, summer and autumn in the little town, which I long thought was the most beautiful place in the world. I loved our spacious garden with the old chestnut trees. In the spring we had breakfast under their white candles, and the hum of the bees mingled with that of the old silver teapot that had been handed down from my beautiful English great-grandmother. Flecks of light played on the blue Wedgwood china; in the tall pines which shaded the gentle slope, squirrels hopped from branch to branch, and blackbirds sang. In autumn the old chestnut trees glowed yellow and filled the dining-room with a warm gold colour. The big green tile stove roared happily, and I ate as slowly as possible, because after breakfast I had to go to my lessons.

I loved our mountain, too, the pride of the little town, rising up on the opposite shore of the lake. On fine summer evenings the whole mass of stone turned pink, like the finest marble, and then, when it was already dusk all around, the Traunstein (as our mountain was called) shone forth out of the shadows like an undying flame. Gradually, however, it paled and turned cold and dead, and everything lost life and became suddenly old and joyless. At that moment, without knowing why, I felt a deep sadness. A day was dead, a day of childhood was irrevocably gone. I especially enjoyed the hour before breakfast when I would go to grandmother's room and sit by her while she was having her hair done.

She always read aloud to me: Dickens, Thackeray, Trollope, Jerome K. Jerome, Swift, Tennyson. I could not endure children's books and stories for young people (the "Leatherstocking" tales excepted), and grandmother often laughed, half pleased, half worried, when I put away *Trotzkopf*[29] and similar pearls of German literature for the young, because they were "much too absurd." We even read Milton's *Paradise Lost* in those wonderful morning hours, and I loved the rebel angel with all my heart.

If winter came early I was doubly happy. The little snow-covered town looked like a picture on the Christmas cards we received from English cousins and friends. I especially liked the little church that stood on an island in the lake and was linked to the mainland by a long bridge. Entirely surrounded by white, it seemed to be floating in the clouds. I gladly sacrificed the pleasure of sleeping late on a Sunday in order to attend early mass in the island church. One stepped from the soft white dawn into the dark building. On the pews, spiral-shaped, faintly-smelling yellow wax lights burned with slender flickering flames, the reddish vestments of the ministrants glowed dully, the figure of the priest moved indistinctly in the chancel, and the little asthmatic organ gave forth its best. It was Advent, the moment of expectancy; the Messiah will soon be born. We all know this, and we cry to heaven that it might open up and send down the saviour of the world: *rorate coeli*. And afterwards, when we walked back across the bridge, the heavens had truly opened, the sun streamed down, the blue sky made the snow seem even whiter, the air was cold, and we were filled with good resolutions — and terribly hungry.

Rules of etiquette

Sometimes we stayed over Christmas in G. If I was alone with grandmother it was marvellous. I was allowed to prepare a Christmas tree for the poor children, buy things for them, and order vast quantities of chocolate and cakes from the cook. Grandmother maintained that only the best was really good enough for the "poor children," because they had so little happiness. The "poor children" enjoyed themselves royally and plundered the Christmas tree with noisy enthusiasm; but the parents were terrible. They sat anxious and unsure of themselves on the edge of their seats, continually making little bows, would neither eat nor drink chocolate, and kept saying thank you over and over again, which annoyed and embarrassed me. It bothered me because it had been impressed on me that my first duty as a "lady" was to make sure that all my guests felt absolutely at their ease. Another point of the social code required that if a person has once been a guest in a house, the mistress of that house should remember for all time thereafter whether or not the person takes milk in his tea as well as how many lumps of sugar he takes. If she asks the person on the second visit what he takes, that demonstrates a lack of interest in the guest's preferences and constitutes a breach of etiquette. There was also another rule: "When you are grown up and give dinners and parties, you must never wear your best dress, because you might happen to have among your guests poorer and more shabbily clad women who would feel ill at ease in their less pretty clothes." One was also instructed in the matter of letter writing. "When you write a four-page letter, make sure that three and a half pages concern the person you are writing to and his or her interests. Never take up more than half a page at most to tell about your own affairs; more than that would almost certainly be of no interest." Also in conversation one should discover as soon as possible what the other's interests are and talk of these exclusively — never of oneself. It was only much later that I discovered the profound significance of this precept and found out how easy it is to give the impression that one is extremely intelligent. All one needs to do is listen with great interest to one's interlocutor. All the women whom history and literature present as uncommonly gifted were, above all else, good listeners, which, when you think of it, requires no special art, since in the end every human being is interesting when speaking of what is closest to his or her heart, whether that be politics, literature or something absolutely inconsequential. When a gardener speaks of flowers or a tailor of clothes, his whole person is transformed; everything good and beautiful about roses or clothing is transferred, as it were, to him, while he in turn invests material things with the interest that inheres in any living human being. As I have said, however, I did not discover this truth until much later; in youth one feels so rich that one thinks only of giving out, not of taking in.

Relatives in Vienna

As soon as it began to get really cold we would leave G. First, there was the traditional three-week stop in Vienna to visit the dentist and various relatives. Going to the dentist was not entirely awful; for one thing it provided an opportunity for heroic behaviour, something I always enjoyed very much; in addition, that heroic behaviour was always rewarded in one way or another. The relatives were a more difficult matter; here one demonstrated heroism by enduring boredom, and that was a good deal harder.

Aunt Maria[30] was tiny, old, and roly-poly. She wore a faded yellow wig, and I think that, except for her chambermaid, no one ever saw her hands. Day and night they were encased in dirty, white, glacé leather gloves. Her rooms were dark and smelled strangely of a mixture of rose-leaves and medicines. Aunt Maria had only one lung (though, for all that, she lived to be seventy); as a result, she kept out of the fresh air and almost never allowed her windows to be opened. Every afternoon at three, her old landau would drive up, drawn by her old horses and with her old coachman on the box, and Aunt Maria would go for a drive in the Prater[31] with both carriage windows shut tight. She had a box at the Burgtheater and one at the Opera, the latter for tradition's sake, for Aunt Maria was a relative of Beethoven's immortal beloved, Theresa Brunsvick. She talked a great deal about music and inquired regularly about my progress with the piano — a painful topic. She suffered from "nerves" and so one had to speak very softly around her and sit still on a stool, so as not to jangle those nerves. When at last one had dutifully answered all her questions, she would ring and the old butler would come in: "Johann, bring the sweets." And with that I was out of the program. Aunt Maria would talk with grandmother while I ate bonbons. Once old Johann brought in two little plates from which I ate alternately — with none too happy results, for on one of the plates had been placed not bonbons but sugarcoated laxative pills.

When I was fourteen years old Aunt Maria gave me a pearl necklace with the admonition that I dedicate myself, with all my strength, to music. I was delighted with the pearls although I was not yet allowed to wear them. My aunt's wish that I should become a good pianist has never been fulfilled. But this was in no way the fault of my piano teacher. Poor Herr Habert[32] with his tired, sorrowful face went to inconceivable pains with me — but all in vain. I loved to listen to him when he spoke of his favourite composers, and under his guidance, learned to recognize the places in Schumann's works that indicated the approaching madness of their creator, but with all that I never kept time properly and was invariably a bit off. Still, I did learn something else, when still quite young, from my music teacher: the tragedy of the unsuccessful artist. Herr Habert was an extremely gifted man; he had composed oratorios and masses, but he had never managed to establish himself as a composer. Finally — he must have been about fifty-seven at the time, which of course seemed utterly ancient to me — one of his oratorios was accepted for performance. Herr Habert was so happy that the piano lessons even became a pleasure. He played phrases and motifs from the oratorio for me, explained them, and no longer noticed when my timing was off. Then something happened, I don't know what it was, and the oratorio was not performed. Herr Habert came a few more times to give me lessons, then excused himself saying he was very tired, and never came back. When I went to see him, he was lying in bed in his — to me — miserable three-room dwelling, his face completely grey, and his body small and shrunken. He did not complain; he only said that he was tired, very tired. A fat ugly wife and three unattractive grown-up daughters said he had to pull himself together. But he was too weary, and shortly after that he went to sleep forever.

After visiting Aunt Maria we generally went to Aunt Vicky's. If it was necessary to speak softly at Aunt Maria's to spare her nerves, here one had to roar, for Aunt Vicky was stone deaf. She would look at you with a frozen face, as though it had been carved out of wood, in which only her little dark eyes seemed to be alive, and would bend down toward you with her huge ear-trumpet in her ear. Walking into her old-fashioned drawing-room with its stiff black ebony furniture was not without its perils. As soon as the door opened four yellow pugs would spring at you, yapping wildly and snapping at your legs. The pugs were old and peevish. Once the servant had quieted them they would crouch down sullenly on their cushions and glower at everything around them.

Aunt Vicky's deafness and frozen expression weighed like a mountain on the whole room. Here everything was lifeless and weird; one's own voice sounded strange and unfamiliar when it roared into the ear-trumpet. The chairs were unwelcoming, even the flowers on the tables were dead. I was always happy when grandmother indicated that it was time for us to go.

Sometimes we visited Aunt Steffi and that was much more agreeable. She was big and strong and, though no longer young, full of life. At her house one did not have to sit still on a stool; one could wander through the rooms and examine the curious things she had brought back from her distant travels. Aunt Steffi was what in those days was called an emancipated woman; she travelled alone all over the world; and would set off for Japan or China as fearlessly as others would go from Vienna to Salzburg.

The wide world

Children create a strange picture of the world for themselves, finding some small detail or other that comes to characterize cities and countries for them for years to come. Thus Vienna to me was the city of pink tissue paper, for the washerwomen there placed sheets of pink tissue paper between individual garments when they returned them — which looked very pretty and dainty. Whenever I heard the name Vienna soft pink sheets of tissue paper immediately appeared before my eyes. Germany, on the other hand, was closely linked to fine railway stations and thick slices of bread and butter. The fine station was the one at Frankfurt-am-Main. We passed through it once and, while the train was stopped, went for a walk on the platform. Grandmother explained to me that this was the finest railway station in Europe. It made a great impression on me, far greater than Cologne Cathedral, which we saw on the same trip. There it was only the mosaic on the floor that pleased me.

As for the thick slices of bread, they were for many years my only memory of the beautiful landscape around Lake Constance. We were travelling from Lindau to Rorschach and on the steamer ordered bread and butter. It came and so completely astonished me — accustomed as I was to paper-thin English sandwiches — that I was almost angry, for I thought, for some unfathomable reason, that thick slices of bread, especially when thickly spread with butter, were vulgar. Grandmother explained to me that in Germany one always gets thick sandwiches. My view of the German Empire was formed immediately: it was a vulgar country with beautiful railway stations.

One of my first travel remembrances is of Venice. It is not a beautiful memory. I was at that time separated from grandmother and was travelling with my parents. It was winter. The lagoons were grey and gloomy and foul-smelling. On top of it all, in an effort to educate me — I was then seven years old — I was dragged through all the galleries. I saw picture after picture and found them all deadly boring. When I shyly explained that I had had enough of the innumerable saints, I received the inevitable "what an idiot you are," which for a long time afterwards completely spoiled the old masters for me. Even at a time when I had begun to take genuine delight in works by Perugino and Luini, I refused — out of spite — to say so and it was not until I was quite grown up and was spending two years in Florence with my parents that I admitted to getting pleasure from painting.

***

When my father was posted to Lisbon, he had the unhappy idea, for me at least, of taking me along with him. And so I was again obliged to leave "home" and go to be with two people who were really complete strangers to me. Of the trip I remember only that I was horribly seasick in the Bay of Biscay. When the ship cast anchor in Lisbon harbour I had a terrible fright. Out of little bobbing boats dark, bearded creatures emerged and clambered up to our ship. I thought they were monkeys. Later I realized that they were men. In Lisbon I saw for the first time the reverse side of having colonies. Soldiers were coming home from the Portuguese colony of Lourenço Marques — wounded men and men sick with yellow fever. They were received with great ceremony; the court and the entire diplomatic corps showed up. Well-dressed, well-nourished, healthy people, gathered respectfully around the beautiful queen and the fat king, stood about the dock, but from the ship came yellow shadows, emaciated, desiccated from the deadly climate. Many staggered as they disembarked, others had to be carried. There were also simple women there, weeping bitterly because their son was not among those who had been shipped back. I remember my father remarking scornfully on the way home: "The blessings of colonialism."

From Lisbon my mother and I went to Madeira. The ship put out to sea in the late afternoon. When we reached the dreaded bar where the Tagus empties into the ocean, the sun went down. The great waves boiled blood-red about the ship like liquid flames, and in the distance lay the ocean, dark and infinite. On this trip I came into contact with a person whom I have never been able to forget in the many years that have passed since that time, and of whom I shall always think with gratitude. The weather was bad, the trip took five days instead of the usual three, and I was seasick the whole time. My mother stayed up on deck: children do not know how to be seasick gracefully and are not a particularly pleasant sight in this condition. To the misery of seasickness would have been added the misery of loneliness had it not been for a big English sailor with red hair and many freckles. Perhaps he had children at home, perhaps he was simply a good man; at any rate he took care of me, as the saying goes, as a father takes care of his child. In the morning he came into my cabin and dressed me. To this day I remember how gentle and careful his big hands were. Then he carried me out on deck and helped me to combat seasickness. To accomplish this he employed the strangest means. I had to eat sour things, drink salt water and when none of this did any good, he resorted to the remedy he no doubt considered a universal cure and forced me to down a large glass of pure whisky. He was bitterly disappointed when that too failed to help. But throughout the entire day, he found time to come to me every little while, tuck me into my blanket, cheer me up, and promise me good weather and a smooth sea on the following day. In the evening he carried me back to the cabin and undressed me. I have forgotten his name, but not the man himself, with his big, strong, soft hands and the kindly smile on his freckled face.

In Madeira an old Baron W. came to meet us. We climbed into the funny little sledge-like oxcart, and I was very anxious to sit on the rear seat. But the old gentleman assumed a pompous expression and said, pointing to the front seat: "Excuse me, Countess, but I know my Gotha." How strong the class feeling must have been in the old man for the sight of an eight-year-old child who had turned quite yellow from sea-sickness to make him think of the Gotha! For some reason or other my memories of Madeira have faded. I see now only the great camelia bushes, the thickly wooded village of Monte from which you slid down the polished cobblestone path to Funchal in a sort of bob-sled, as though it were a toboggan-run. I also remember a dreadful, seemingly endless dinner which the Austrian consul gave in honour of my mother, and at which twenty-five different vintages of Madeira wine were brought out.

Our next stop was in Tenerife. Here it was very beautiful; the hotel lay right by the sea, and the mighty Pic rose up snow-covered into the blue sky. There were weird cacti that produced yellow, edible pears and eucalyptus trees with their wonderfully strong smell. One of the residents of the hotel was a beautiful Englishwoman who played the guitar and showed the most friendly interest in me. My mother forbade me to speak to her. I racked my brains for a reason for this prohibition. What could such a lovely, charming woman have done? And how did my mother — who was not even acquainted with her — know that she had committed a crime? I worried a great deal about the beautiful woman and often, while I was playing alone on the beach, I would think how I might help her get away in case the police came after her.

After a month we returned to Lisbon where the Feast of Saint Anthony of Padua, who was born in the city, was being celebrated with much festivity. There were lights on all the hills surrounding the city, fireworks crackled all around, and against the night sky you could see the saint preaching his famous sermon to the fishes.

By autumn my period of exile was finally over and I was allowed to return to grandmother.

English encounters

We spent one summer on Lake Thun. At the hotel grandmother made the acquaintance of an English family consisting of two tall, suntanned men, their wives, and the daughters of the elder of the two men — one grown-up and two still quite small. When we were alone again she asked me: "Do you know who these people are?" "No." "The sons of Charles Dickens."

The grandchildren of the great man were extremely disappointing. They were passionate mountain climbers and seemed to have no interest in literature. The oldest daughter did very bad water colours, and I still have an album from that time in which under one of Shakespeare's sonnets she sketched an impossible tree of forget-me-nots. Only eleven-year old Olive composed stories, which she wrote into a copybook. But when we compared our stories at one point, I had to note, in all modesty, that mine were not a whit worse than hers. From that moment on Dickens' descendants had no special aura for me.

Olive and I together once had a strange experience. We went into the woods with her big sister Enid to pick bilberries. All along the way we had fun imagining that we would get lost and never be able to find our way back. We thought up all sorts of frightening situations: endlessly wandering around and searching vainly for the way back, having to go without food or water after all the bilberries had been eaten, and finally when winter came on, with lots of snow and ice, freezing to death. On the way back we two young ones ran on ahead. Whether by pure chance or because we were unconsciously led on by the thought of losing our way, we took the wrong path.

After we had wandered down it for a few minutes we looked around for Enid: she had disappeared. We called her name — no answer. We laughed: "Now we really are lost." And we ran on further. But the path became narrower, the bushes became more dense, the trees seemed to get taller. We continued to call vainly for Enid, and kept running on in the hope that her form would suddenly appear at some turn in the way; but we only got ourselves deeper and deeper into the wood.

We were not laughing any more now. Anxiety had us so tightly by the throat that our shouts sounded muffled, strange, and frightening in themselves. All at once the wood had turned into something evil and menacing. The bushes made fiendish grimaces, and the tall pines had become dark as night and hostile. Weird noises filled the air, sounds of scraping and crackling. I turned away, not daring to look Olive in the face, for I had done so once and seen something horrible in her expression — stark fear. Her contorted child's face was so dreadful, that I lost the last little remnant of my courage. All the visions we had conjured up in fun now became grim reality: we would never, never get out of the forest — we were going to perish here, miserably.

And then the miracle happened that saved us: a bend in the path opened on to the highway, and we saw Enid, red with excitement and anger. How good it was to hear the sound of a human voice, even though it was scolding us roundly, how calming and comforting was the slap in the face that Olive got from her sister. The forest was immediately beautiful and friendly again, for there was a human being there, someone we belonged to, someone who spoke with a human voice and who was not alien and impenetrable like nature.

***

Many years later I again saw fear on a human face. We were crossing the Mediterranean. The weather was bad, waves crashed on to the deck; with every breaker the ship seemed to be pitched up to meet the lowhanging, dark, stormy sky only to sink down again, after shuddering violently for a second, into bottomless depths. The few first-class passengers had gathered in the saloon after dinner. A pretty young American sat in a corner speaking. She talked incessantly as though to deafen herself, flirted with the men, laughed shrilly. But there was fear in her dilated eyes, and her hands were clenched together so tightly that the knuckles shone white. Her face was deathly pale, and her smile a frozen grimace. She talked about her husband and little son in America, and behind each word lurked the fear: I shall never see them again. She talked and talked — with the passengers, with the ship's officers, with the stewards. Every one of her words was an entreaty: "Don't leave me alone. Speak, make a noise so that I don't hear the ghastly sound of the waves. Tell me there is no danger, that a ship has never yet gone down." The moment a passenger left the saloon to go to his cabin she cringed: one fewer to stand between her and solitude, between her and her mortal anguish. It grew late; the young woman continued to talk, convulsively, feverishly — only, for the love of heaven, let me keep one other human being here so that I am not left alone. She seemed very fond of her husband — yet on that night she would undoubtedly have betrayed him with any man there, passenger, officer or sailor, anything so as not to have to remain alone with her fear.

***

I too learned how calming the presence of other human beings can be when, as a child of nine, I got lost for the second time — in London no less. I was with my mother visiting an English aunt and was to pay a call on my Uncle Anton who was then at the embassy there. My mother put me in a hansom cab and gave the driver the address. Apparently the man misunderstood it, for when I got out and the carriage had driven off I found myself in front of a strange house in an unfamiliar street amid the tumult of the huge city. Strangely enough, I — who even today, I am ashamed to confess, am fearful when crossing the street — was not in the least afraid. There were people everywhere, so what could happen to me? I walked happily along several streets, enjoying the adventure and paying no attention to the fact that I was getting further and further from my destination. When at last I became tired, I went up to a policeman who put me in a hansom cab again and this time gave the driver the right address.

I was shyly devoted to my English aunt. Like Aunt Maria, she too suffered from "nerves." But she was a beautiful woman, and from earliest childhood I have always loved everything beautiful. This veneration of beauty was in my blood, perhaps because her beauty was the most important thing in the world to my beautiful mother. I have also Aunt Agnes[33] to thank for my first acquaintance with a genuine authoress. Grandmother and Aunt Agnes once arranged to meet in Milan. Aunt Agnes had brought a travelling companion with her. Grandmother, knowing my penchant for hero-worship, told me that Miss May Cromelin,[34] my aunt's companion, was a writer. From that moment on I never left the unfortunate May Cromelin's side. I was absolutely determined to be there when inspiration came to her and to experience the moment with her. I never experienced it. She was a dried-up old spinster who wrote sentimental, extremely moral love stories. Still, I thought she was wonderful and almost expired from adoration of her. Once when we set out on an excursion to Monza, I was horrified when May Cromelin was seated beside me on the rear seat. A writer, a genius by the grace of God, had by rights to be given the place of honour! All in all, however, May Cromelin, like Dickens' sons, was a bitter disappointment. She called my adored Jerome K. Jerome[35] "vulgar." I was astounded. At that time I had no idea that half of England felt the same way about Jerome K. Jerome. When I turned in consternation to grandmother for an explanation, she smiled and said that literary people were often jealous of each other. It was as though I had received a blow to the head, for I had always believed that these people were especially devoted to each other and eager to lend each other mutual support whenever that was possible. Let it be recalled, by way of excuse, that I was then about ten years old.

Strangely enough, though I obviously worshipped her, May Cromelin seemed to consider me stupid. When I asked her to inscribe something in my album, she wounded me deeply by choosing a line that began: "Be good, sweet maid, and let who will be clever." It is unpleasant to be told to be good when one's ambition is to be a writer and an exceptionally clever person!

Thanks to a "Bohemian nose"

Uncle Anton was responsible for my desire to be clever. The whole family, father, mother, grandmother had all been endowed by nature with beautiful noses, but I had been cursed with a Bohemian nose, a heritage from my other grandmother, my Czech grandmother. Father used to tease me about it and said that it would rain into my nose, it turned so steeply up to the heavens. But Uncle Anton looked at me searchingly one day and said:

"With that nose, child, you absolutely have to become a very cultivated and clever woman."

No injunction to be diligent, no scolding for poor schoolwork ever influenced me as much as that remark of my uncle's. I gave up putting clothes-pins on my nose and strove only to become "a cultivated and clever woman."

Father too was much concerned with my education, although in a somewhat peculiar way. Whenever he came to visit grandmother, lunch was a torment for me, because he used that time to investigate the state of my knowledge. Unfortunately for me, he had the idea that a child should know everything he knew, and he was — not just for an Austrian aristocrat, but by any standard — an exceptionally well-educated man. To this day I detest Charles XII of Sweden, because I got my ears boxed when I was not yet eight years old for not being able to give an accurate account of his military campaigns. It was also at that time that father endeavoured to instill in me his own love of Shakespeare, and became furious when I begged him to explain the "improper" words. Nevertheless it was a joy for me to hear him recite the great soliloquies and especially Anthony's speech over the body of Caesar; despite my age I could still understand the bitterness of the words.

Taking a walk with father was also not an unadulterated pleasure. Every time we passed a tree I had to say what it was called in German, French, English, and later also in Italian. It was especially terrible if we spotted cranberries; I could never remember that they are called *airelles* in French.

Father as a young man

If my answers to his questions had not been too stupid, and he was in good humour, father would tell me of his adventures in America. He had run away to America when he was quite a young man, and there, without a *kreuzer* in his pocket, had earned his own living — first as a waiter, which did not last long because he was so near-sighted, then as a salesman in a dry-goods store. He had made an excellent salesman, he claimed, and I think he was telling the truth, for no one was a greater charmer than my father, when he wanted to be. It is not difficult to believe that he could talk up the worst fabrics until he persuaded the American women that they were the best. He was discharged simply because he could never manage to roll up the bolts of cloth correctly.

(I inherited that too from him; to this day I am incapable of making a decent package.)

Later he went to the western states as an election speaker for the Republican party, if I am not mistaken. One story that he used to tell, about a poker game in Texas, was especially fine and exciting. A man was caught cheating and by a very simple method was rendered immediately incapable of doing further damage. One of the players pulled out a knife and stuck it right through the cheat's hand, thus pinning it to the table.

The last job father found was teaching German at a finishing school for girls. When speaking of this period of his life he made remarks to me that at the time were vague and quite incomprehensible concerning the early maturity and forwardness of American girls.

Afterwards he became reconciled with my grandfather and came back to Europe. He was very proud of the fact that he, the spoiled child of an aristocrat, had made his way so well over there, and many years later when he was at the embassy in Washington, he was much amused when at grand embassy receptions he got to lead in to dinner the very ladies to whom he had once sold dry-goods.

Uncle Anton

Uncle Anton came home from Japan where he had been ambassador, the youngest ambassador in the entire Austrian foreign service. All the places and countries where we had relatives "in the service" seemed near and familiar to us; in that easy way we acquired an international outlook.

It was late autumn when Uncle Anton came. We sat in the little salon before an open fire, and he told us about Japan. He had brought back with him many beautiful things, lacquer, porcelain, and for me his big red Japanese visiting card. When a new ambassador had his first audience with the Mikado, a servant went before him bearing the big red visiting card. One ambassador had a great misfortune befall him on such an occasion. He had not taken the necessary precaution of having someone who knew Japanese review the card beforehand. On the great sheet of paper, fluttering in the wind as it was borne before him were inscribed the words:

"Here, humbly creeping on his stomach, a European son of a dog approaches our most high lord to beg grace for his country."

In the eyes of most Austrians the "Japaners," as they called them, were funny little yellow men who had been created by Providence to produce beautiful knick-knacks and silks, to celebrate cherry-blossom festivals, to delight Europeans with lovely Geishas and to provide themes for operettas.

Uncle Anton depicted for us a quite different people, the "Japanese" — striving, industrious, smart, and ambitious, the Prussians of the East. Many years before the Russo-Japanese War he spoke of the inevitable conflict between the two empires, and he was convinced that Japan would emerge victorious from the conflict. In any case, he hated czarist Russia and often announced: "Much as I hate war, should there be one with Russia, I would fight."

That was how I got my first live idea of Russia. Before then, it had been simply an infinitely vast land, with cities and rivers and lakes whose names one could never remember. Now it had become something dark and bad, ruled by an evil power that tortured men, banished them, and exiled them to wildernesses of ice. Alexander III was a blood-thirsty monster surrounded by criminals and scoundrels, and somewhere in the dim and distant depths a martyred people groaned beneath the scourge. At home we had an edition of the Divine Comedy illustrated by Doré, and whenever I thought of Russia the pictures of hell in that book appeared before my eyes.

Uncle Anton was no longer happy at home in Austria. He had never been comfortable with the Austrians and their carefree way of living in the moment, and now he felt doubly estranged from them. He already had at that time the tendency toward solitude and the horror of people that finally drove him to withdraw to an old castle in the country, where, after years of living all alone, he died.

First encounter with the Orient

Father was tired of always having a chief over him, so he switched to the consular service and was sent to Algiers. Thus it came about that we did not go to Italy or the Riviera that winter, but visited my parents in Algeria.

This was the first piece of the Orient that I got to see. It really began in Marseilles. We stayed there in an enormous hotel, which grandmother dubbed a caravansary. What a magnificent word that was! It made me think of long caravans winding across the golden desert, of endless lines of camels trudging heavily along, and of a tiny donkey going ahead as their leader.

This image of the donkey had been impressed on me by an anecdote, familiar in diplomatic circles, about a young man from the high aristocracy who was sent as attaché to a legation where the ambassador was socially his inferior and, in addition, had the reputation of being unusually stupid. At a dinner one evening the ambassador insisted on giving the young man precedence, but the impudent little attaché waived the honour with the remark: "Excellency, your place is without question at the head of the caravan." As the little episode took place in the Orient, even the ambassador understood the allusion.

All cities have a characteristic smell: Dresden smells of high, layered *Baum*-cakes, Munich of beer, Vienna of leather and bad tea, Lisbon of fish and pepper trees, Berlin of benzine and casually washed people, Frankfurt of bourgeois pride and democracy, but in Marseilles the smells of the West mingle with those of the East. Here one already gets that unique odour of the Orient — a mixture of attar of roses, Morocco leather, camel dung and sun-baked filth. An exciting smell that sets the nerves a-tingle and presages all kinds of strange adventures.

The harbour already held out this promise; it was an adventure in itself with its multitude of large and small ships, strange figures of Arabs in white burnouses, Algerian soldiers, and sailors from all corners of the globe.

I had at that time been made a present of my first camera and took the most remarkable pictures (because I always forgot to insert a new film) — of houses upside down, ships running into each other, humans and animals monstrously melded together. In my head too everything was as on the pictures. For the first time I was unable to absorb the many new impressions crowding in on me; they took me by storm, pulled me hither and thither, so that pleasure was mixed with dizziness and exhaustion.

The first impression of Algiers is of blinding whiteness crowned by the glittering gold of the great church on a high hill: Notre Dame d'Afrique. I was enraptured. The overpowering spell of the Orient had seized hold of me. It has never let me go. The North, for me, remains to this day an ersatz of life, sad and colourless, with its ersatz sky, its ersatz sun, and its ersatz flowers.

My enthusiasm cooled somewhat when my parents told me that on the next day I would start attending the Sacré Coeur. I had secretly been hoping for a holiday. However, father softened the blow for me by presenting me with a little donkey, Bichette, on which I made the daily trip to the convent. Ali, the Arab groom, trotted alongside me on foot.

The convent was situated in a big, old garden, quite shut off from the world. Here, in the midst of the sun-drenched Orient, the old traditions of the Sacré Coeur were maintained. The cool austerity of the convent filled the high-ceilinged rooms, and even on the hottest days, the nuns in their heavy black garments and veils never seemed to be warm.

It was a little difficult for me at first, being suddenly obliged to study all my subjects in French, though I soon got used to that. I loved the evenings most of all. My parents were of the opinion that parents should see as little of their children as possible; besides, they had a very active social life and had no time for me. So after I ate my solitary dinner, I was sent to father's study and left to myself. Here, however, there were quantities of books, and I plunged in and indiscriminately read everything that fell into my hands. I recall especially an almost endless four-volume novel about the Thirty Years' War; I read it sitting in an easychair by the window, before which stood a great orange tree. The oranges were just ripe then, and the air was heavy with their perfume; long afterwards whenever I read something about the Thirty Years' War the scent of oranges would return to me.

Sometimes father came in and said: "Reading something? That's right." And he would remove yellow-backed paper-bound French novels. Often he would say: "Read something worth while," and would hand me works by Kürenberger,[36] who was one of his favourite authors, or by Lamartine and Chateaubriand, on account of their good French style. I devoured with equal avidity *Le Génie du Christianisme, Le Dernier des Abencérages, René, Atala, Voyages en Orient*, the novels of Walter Scott — and the Thousand and One Nights tales.

Sundays I spent with Sybil, an English friend. She was fifteen, a year older than myself, and it was she who introduced me to the sentimental side of life, of which, until then, I knew absolutely nothing. When I had come to know her better, she suddenly said, out of the blue:

"I'd like to talk to you about something. But I don't know whether you might not find it shocking. Can't you guess what it is? It begins with L."

As I couldn't guess, Sybil explained, blushing all over: "Love."

Sybil's big sister was engaged to be married, and Sybil herself had nothing in her head but love, love, and more love — sweet, pure, gentle love, such as one encounters in the old triple-decker English novels. She wanted to "play at love," and I was to take the part of the man. At that time I was very much occupied with social issues, and I countered Sybil's theme of "love" with my theme of "socialism." But she would have none of it. Socialism bored her to tears. Finally we compromised. I was ready to pay court to her if I could be a socialist agitator, trying to convert a wealthy maiden to socialism. In this way I got my money's worth out of the deal, for I was able to insert a long speech about socialism between two declarations of love, which I kept as short as possible.

Many years later — I was already married — I received a letter from Sybil, whom I had long since lost sight of and who had chanced upon my address. At the very beginning of the letter she said: "I too am a socialist now." I wonder if, back in that garden sloping steeply down to the blue sea, I did succeed in converting her after all?

Homecoming

In the spring grandmother and I went back to G. Perhaps that journey home after all the travelling was the most beautiful part of it all. As the train passed between two steep banks on which anemones peeked out like white stars through the dead leaves of autumn and liverwort gleamed blue, my heart began to thump with joy and impatience. Then followed the ride from the station past the odd, green-covered hillocks, shrouded in mystery because, it was said, they were mass graves from the Peasant War, over the well-known streets of the little town, past familiar faces, the bath-house, and the riding school, up the steep hill, and through the big garden gate. And there stood the beloved house; the garden was smiling in the spring; and I was once more alone with grandmother. Life was beautiful.

Boarding school

In the fall I went to Dresden to boarding school. The first months were unbearable; I suffered one humiliation after another. I was used to being called an "idiot" by my parents, but I considered it an expression of personal hostility and did not take it to heart or give it another thought. Here, however, people of my own age would say the same thing to me, even if the words were different. Here for the first time I heard the fine expression "gojischer Kopf."[37] The words were unknown to me, but the intonation and the scornful laughter left no doubt about their significance.

The boarding school was divided into two cliques. One was composed of typical well brought up middle-class girls. It sickened and bored me. The other was made up of "intellectuals." It consisted of only three girls, a Berliner, a Finn and a Jewish girl from Bohemia. Naturally I wanted to belong to this clique. The Finn, who was well disposed toward me on account of my socialist views, and the Bohemian, who was a good sort, would have been glad to include me, but it all came to nothing because of the Berliner's resistance. For some reason or other this Käthe Bernhard could not stand me. She was about two years older than me, and most strangely formed, with a short fat body, on which was placed a beautiful head with wonderful eyes and a high intelligent forehead. When we took walks together the "clever" girls walked in a separate group, and I was obliged to trail along behind with the "stupid" ones. On top of everything, Käthe, true Prussian that she was, despised all Austrians. She is the only person who ever succeeded in awakening a certain counteractive patriotism in me. Then too the antipathy of the "intellectuals" was understandable, for I was the only aristocrat in the entire school, and when parents came to look the school over the fat old proprietress would call me and announce, with pride: "This is our little… Her cousin is the wife of the heir to the throne, Crown Prince Franz Ferdinand." Whereupon, upset and embarrassed, I would make a stupid face and curtsey.

Dutzi, whose room was next to mine, was very beautiful and newly baptized. She reproached me bitterly for sleeping late on a Sunday morning, instead of going to mass. Dutzi was a spoiled little creature who related to anyone who would listen how her mother and the late

Crown Prince Rudolf[38] had well, . . . One evening as I lay in bed reading she knocked on the connecting door and called: "Come into my room."

I obeyed. There stood Dutzi stark naked and beautiful as God had created her.

"Am I not beautiful?" she asked.

I was accustomed to nude pictures and statues and examined her with the eyes of an expert. "Yes, you are very beautiful, but don't put on any more weight." And I turned to go back.

Dutzi glanced at me crossly. "Aren't you going to stay in here with me?"

"I have an interesting book I want to read."

And I left. I never could understand why from that time on Dutzi was angry with me.

The "clever ones" still excluded me from their group, even though I studied like mad and — thanks to the culture I had picked up painlessly at home — often came out ahead of them in school work. Finally, however, I managed to gain admittance to the intellectual clique in a very "goyish" way. Once, when Käthe, with her insufferable superior smile, remarked yet again: "But that's something you can't understand!" my feelings of anger got the better of me and I gave her a good box on the ears.

This obviously made a deep impression on the Berlin girl. From then on we were good friends, and I was one of the "clever ones."

We didn't mind enjoying our own cleverness a little, got up an hour earlier than the others and read books that "improve the mind." My old arrogance returned. I preached socialism and made the others read Henry George's *Progress and Poverty*[39] and, as a "socialistic" book, Stirner's *The Ego and His Own*.[40] Perhaps the girls who did not have a "goyish" head understood more of this than I did.

Käthe was still vexed; she dragged out Schopenhauer in the little Reklam paperbacks and we all had to read *The World as Will and Representation* at six o'clock in the morning on empty stomachs.

Annie, the Finnish girl, was not so heartless. She brought us Tolstoi's *Resurrection*, the conclusion of which I even then found unsatisfactory, as well as the novels of Turgenev. As a matter of fact, as far as I personally am concerned, everything is her fault. I read *Fathers and Sons* and fell in love with Bazarov and Russia. Subsequently I discovered that Turgenev was at bottom a counter-revolutionary; but in those days he excited all my rebellious feelings, and I had but one wish: to go to Russia and join these heroic beings in bringing about the revolution.

I also owe some less agreeable hours to the Finnish girl. She gave me Ibsen's works to read. With one of them — entitled *Nora* in German — I was already familiar. When I was with my parents in Lisbon there was a little cupboard next to the toilet where father stored away books he had already read. Even at that time I seem to have been true to my principle: never waste a moment. At the age of eight, the sub-title of *Nora* — *A Doll's House* — tempted me and I pulled this book out from the pile. It was a bitter disappointment, because I did not understand a word of it. Now Annie gave me *Ghosts* to read, explaining with worldly wisdom: "All men have syphilis."

The play caused me days and nights of utter misery. It seemed to me that I could never be clean again. I washed myself at every opportunity and my body filled me with disgust.

And then: "All men have syphilis." All men — then my father too had had this disease, and I would end up like Oswald, crying for the sun.

Käthe eased my mind finally with one word: "Rubbish!" and as she was the cleverest of us all, I believed her.

On Sunday mornings when the kneeling and rising faithful went to church we "clever ones" gave talks to each other. Annie lectured on tyranny and revolution, Käthe discoursed on the meaning of drama — she wanted to be an actress — and I, naturally, held forth, with the infinite confidence of the ignorant, on social issues.

Meanwhile, my position with the "clever ones" had become more firmly established. I could do something none of them was able to bring off: I could write. I wrote gruesome plays about the injustice of the world and about women's rights, which we performed on Sundays. I always got the best part, because I was so good at "dying."

In the spring a new girl came to the school, who could not get admitted to either clique — a little Jewish girl from Vienna. She proclaimed to all that there was only one poet in the world, Hofmannsthal, and gave us his works to read. I found them boring, but held my tongue, because Mimi was such a nice girl. There were violent literary debates, but Mimi would not let herself be beaten down — until one day there was a sudden change in her. She received a letter from home, and ran around the whole day with tear-filled eyes. That evening she said: "There are other poets besides Hofmannsthal."

It was not till several days later that we discovered the answer to this puzzle. Mimi's poet had become engaged to Mimi's sister instead of waiting for her.

***

When the holidays came I went with grandmother, who was suffering from a heart ailment, to Nauheim.[41]

In August she died, in Switzerland. My youth, and everything that stood for security and freedom from care, was gone. A hostile world lay before me, a world of ill-intentioned strangers. I had no home any more. At sixteen, I had to cope alone with myself and with the world.

The convent

After grandmother's death, I asked Uncle Anton if he would take me in to live with him. He would have done so gladly, except that the conventions of the time formed an insurmountable obstacle. I was a grown girl, and he was not yet an old man. The tongues would have wagged furiously.

After this effort had failed, I announced, much to their relief, that I would not come to live with my parents, but would begin training to become a school teacher; and would do it right in the convent in G. In this way, I could at least remain in the place where grandmother and I had lived together, and I would be able to spend summer afternoons in the villa and the garden. The house was empty, except for Fräulein Marie who was in receipt of a pension, lived in two of the rooms, and was very happy when I came. With her I could talk about grandmother and reminisce about the wonderful time when the house, now so sad and desolate, had been filled with her love and kindness.

The convent had its good points; I learned there to live a perfectly simple life. We all wore the same hideous dark blue, beige-braided uniform, shared the same bad food, and had to clean our own rooms. I did, however, manage to get out of one unpleasant chore, bed-making, by cleaning the other girls' shoes; in return, they made my bed for me.

The two years I spent in the convent were peaceful and quiet. The person I loved most was dead, and I needed a heaven that held out the promise of our meeting again in the future. I got to know the seductive attraction of the mystical: strange nocturnal hours in the dim chapel, lit only by the pale red glow of the altar lamps. Easter-tide came, after the forty days of fasting, during which, with the penchant I then had for doing everything in excess, I almost starved. On an empty stomach and with a giddy head it is not difficult to see visions and feel the overpowering presence of a God. The miracle of faith is the miracle of the great union with a higher power, which is at once past, present, and future, the complete losing of one's own puny self in the mighty whole of which one becomes a part. I have often had the same feeling when at a mass demonstration the "Internationale" was sung. Thousands upon thousands moved by the same world-embracing, barrier-breaking struggle, by the same hope, the same present, and the same future. And one is oneself part of that, no longer something separate, no longer an individual, but only a tiny, evanescent part of a great cause.

I scraped through the exam by the skin of my teeth. I got entangled in traps in math and geometry but I had mastered the other subjects pretty well, and so I managed to slip through.

Father brushed aside my desire to apply for a post as a school teacher: "Nonsense. Such things aren't done."

And so I went to join my parents who were spending the summer in Cernobbio on Lake Como.

Villa d'Este

The hotel, formerly the castle of an English queen, was situated on the lake and had an enormous park. Whenever I went out laden with books in search of an isolated spot, I invariably met a quiet man with glasses, going the same way. This was Professor Henry Thode,[42] also in search of a remote nook where he could work in peace. Although we knew each other we never exchanged a word; but the professor always bowed to me in the most friendly manner, and I was happy that he shared my solitude in a way.

Siegfried Wagner[43] also came to Villa d'Este. With his big nose, the future Swastika-supporter looked quite Jewish. He whistled tunes from operettas, and impressed one as loud and common. Later in Florence I made the acquaintance of another, far more appealing member of the Wagner family, a daughter of von Bülow,[44] who had married a Sicilian and after her husband's death retired to Florence. Here she lived with her three children in rather modest surroundings. In her salon hung innumerable Wagner pictures, and her main topic of conversation was "Father" and "Papa." One got a little confused until finally it became clear that "Father" was Hans von Bülow while "Papa" was Richard Wagner; "Papa" played by far the more important role.

The Marchesa was a pretty, somewhat faded woman, blonde and German. In contrast, her oldest son, who was then attending the Naval Academy, was passionately Italian. He seems to have the same convictions — in Italian translation — as his step-uncle. Very badly written but enthusiastic glorifications of Fascism from the pen of Cosima's grandchild can be read in the *Corriere della Sera* today.

My poor mother suffered a great deal from the proximity of a grown daughter, and so father made the heroic decision to take me along with him to Tangiers, where for a year he had been serving as the Austrian envoy. Mother stayed behind in Europe.

Tangiers

We embarked at Genoa. The sea was rough, and father drove me to despair by entering my cabin and demanding unfeelingly: "Just tell me, how did you contrive to be seasick?" As if I had done it on purpose!

It was in fact only the short crossing from Gibraltar to Tangiers aboard the *Gebbel-Tarik* that was really bad. The little ship with its two funnels — a real one and a wooden one for show only — rolled helplessly from side to side.

The friendly old English captain tried to cheer me up by showing me a canary which turned somersaults on his finger. His effort was in vain. The ship rolled and tossed, and the little yellow downy creature turned and turned until I was quite dizzy.

At last, after hours of torment, the coast came in sight, and we were debarked in small boats. A figure out of the *Thousand and One Nights*, but clad in European style, came to meet us: Abensur, the Austrian vice-consul, a Moorish Jew and one of the handsomest men I have ever seen. Also waiting for us on the wharf were the Moroccan soldiers who accompany all the foreign representatives.

In those days there were still no paved streets in all Tangiers. During the dry season one sank into the sand, and in the wet season the mud came up over the ankles.

I was still shaky from seasickness but instead of going to the hotel in a carriage, as we usually did, I had to let myself be hoisted by a groom on to Ali, a little brown Arab gelding, while father mounted Moghreb, a large black Berber stallion that was a gift from the Sultan of Morocco.

We rode up a steep path to an area of swarming streets, lined on both sides by open booths, and then reached the great city gate, which was closed every evening at dusk.

Behind the gate was the *suk*, the big market-place. Here large dromedaries stood as motionless as if they had been carved out of wood; little grey donkeys raised their shaggy heads and brayed; and snake-charmers crouched on the ground, surrounded by gaping throngs. As they played monotonous melodies on primitive flutes, an enormous snake would uncoil and wave its body in rhythm. In other parts of the *suk*, people were gathered around a story-teller, who, half-singing, half-speaking, told of wonderful things. After the market place came an empty stretch with nothing but sand. Father spurred Moghreb into a gallop, and Ali began to gallop also. As I was sitting on a horse for the first time, I became extremely uncomfortable and clung without shame to the mane of the beautiful animal. So we rode up to the front of the Villa Valentina, the hotel at Tangiers, where we were welcomed by the proprietress in the most beautiful Austrian dialect.

***

To save himself and me the bother of keeping house, father had taken five rooms in the hotel. The legation itself was just across the way, a one-story house in the midst of a tangled garden.

Mother had sent a French maid along with me, because, now that in some degree I also represented Austria in Morocco, my external appearance (to which I was only too happy to pay no attention) had to be taken care of.

Father made me a little speech about my social duties, and cautioned me never to go out unless I was accompanied by one of the Moroccan soldiers, and never to go riding without Sliman, the groom.

It was about a year before the "*Panther* affair,"[45] the country was unsettled, the tribes were in revolt, the sultan was threatened by his one-eyed brother,[46] and through the streets rode, heavily armed and surrounded by armed men, a great man of the future: Raisuli.[47]

For the first few days I was allowed to enjoy my new surroundings for hours on end, always accompanied by the bored, unhappy soldiers; I could stand in the market-place and ride on the beach. But then my social duties made their demands. We were invited to dinner by the French minister.

"Do you know anything about Hippolyte Taine?" father asked me before this event and laid a copy of the *Origines de la France Contemporaine* before me on the table. "Madame St. R. T.[48] is a niece of Taine's, and she never misses a chance to talk about him. Don't disgrace me."

"Sir Arthur Nicholson[49] will be there, too," he continued. "One of the shrewdest diplomats there is. He may even try to pump you. Don't say anything stupid."

The evening came; the maid did my hair beautifully, and I put on my first low-necked dress, in which I thought I looked quite naked. Until dinner all went well, and then, sitting between the French and English ministers I discovered to my horror that I had to blow my nose — and I had no handkerchief.

What was I to do? This was a fine way for me to make my debut. I sniffled violently and lost the thread of the conversation. Father was not within reach. My nose began to run; I looked around at my neighbours: which of them would be the first to understand my need? The Frenchman was grave and solemn, like a priest celebrating mass. I had been warned against the Englishman, but his blue eyes had a smile in them. I whispered to him: "Can you slip me a handkerchief under the table?" He looked at me astonished, and I began to feel dreadfully embarrassed. Then he laughed, father cast me an approving glance, because I was evidently not boring my dinner partner, and Sir Arthur Nicholson passed the handkerchief to me under the table.

In his heart of hearts Sir Arthur Nicholson was no lover of Germans, and the German minister was no match for the artful Englishman. He knew this and always went around with a troubled, anxious look on his kindly face. All his other colleagues liked him. He was a good man, always ready to help, but he was no diplomat. He was happiest when he could be left to himself at home with his beautiful wife and many children, or when he invited the German colony to some celebration.

Only the Germans, English, French and Spaniards had real interests in Morocco. Representing the entirely disinterested Austrian state, father watched with great interest the skirmishings and intrigues and told me about them, so that I was continually *au courant*. The first report received by the Austrian Ministry of Foreign Affairs concerning the activities of Raisuli and the latter's future significance came from my pen. There was to be a wild boar hunt at the time, in which the boars are speared from horses with long lances, and I did not yet ride well enough to go on such a hunt. But as father planned to go, "You might as well write the report," he said. "No one will read it anyway."

He was quite pleased with my work, and sent off the report, though he cut out a few poetical expressions, such as "the brave son of the mountains" and "the falcon-eyed hero."

***

I learned Spanish and also some Arabic, rode a lot, and danced the nights through. We had to go on horseback even to the balls. In the whole of Tangiers there was a single, ancient, musty-smelling sedan-chair; heaven knows from what century it dated, and what *précieuses* had leaned back against its cushions. The chair-bearers were Jews: they did not work on Saturdays and holidays, so that on those days elderly ladies were obliged to ride on donkeys to dinners and receptions. We young girls mounted our horses in our evening dresses, pulled the skirts up high and wrapped our legs in plaids. If it rained we held our umbrella in one hand and the bridle in the other. Soldiers walked in front of the horses carrying lanterns with two candles, which only the *baschador*, the ambassador, was permitted to have. Ordinary mortals had to be content with one candle.

We would ride through the *suk*, the fantastic shapes of dromedaries rising ghost-like out of the darkness, little flickering lights burning in front of the tents, and countless rats running in front of the horses' hoofs.

We would halt at the closed gate. One of the soldiers would knock three times, the signal that a *baschador* wished to enter, then the gate would open with a grating sound and we would pass through. It was all a strange mixture of Orient and Occident. The members of the diplomatic corps were the same people one might meet in the capital of any country, and their dinners and balls could have been given in Vienna, Berlin or any other European city. Then, out of the blue, something happened that revealed the Orient and its barbaric cruelty in a glaring light.

Above all, no complications!

One morning I was riding with Sliman through the town. Suddenly we heard a wild cry. An Arab dashed by us on horseback with a young girl stretched across the saddle. She was trying to get free and screaming desperately. Sliman, who had observed this scene quite calmly, explained: "She is a bad girl, *Señorita*. She worked at the house of some Jews and got involved with one of the sons. Now her brothers have come after her."

"And what will happen to her?"

Sliman drew his hand across his throat in an unmistakable gesture and laughed in a friendly way.

Cold chills ran down my spine; such a thing could not be allowed to happen; the Europeans cannot permit it.

The French legation was closest; I galloped toward it. Monsieur St. R. T.[50] received me cordially and with dignity, but became more and more reserved as I told him my story. He could do nothing, he said, the affair was no concern of the Europeans; if they got mixed up in it there might be complications, and above all: no complications!

I rode on to the German legation; but I experienced the same reception there too; the same thing once again at the American consulate. I stormed in helpless rage; it was as though they were all standing calmly by while a murder took place. In those days I still believed that the purpose of diplomacy was to prevent people from being murdered.

The prison on the Marschan, a hill outside the city, was barbaric too. It was a large building, low to the ground; the barred side was fully visible, and behind the bars you could see the prisoners crammed together, standing or crouching. They were not fed by the state but were dependent upon what friends and relatives brought them. Those who came from the interior were often on the verge of starvation. They pressed against the bars like wild animals, stretching out shrivelled hands to beg a piece of bread, scuffling and beating each other bloody over a bit of bread — and this within five hours of Gibraltar.

Trip into the Rif

Father made me a present of a beautiful brown horse called Said, and poor Sliman complained bitterly, because I rode him so hard.

"The *Señorita* is like a *Semuria*," he told father, who gave me a long lecture to the effect that, even on horseback, a young lady of good society should not bear the least resemblance to the wildest of the Moroccan tribes.

Sliman was a Kabyle from the Rif, a tall, lean, handsome man with a completely shaved head except for one long lock left standing straight up, so that the Prophet might seize him by it one day and take him into Paradise.

He was exceptionally superstitious, and once I gave him a terrible fright. About two hours from Tangiers there was a thick grove which was inhabited, according to the natives, by *djinns,* or evil spirits. Once, while taking a ride, we came to the grove, and Sliman urged me to ride quickly by. I jumped off my horse and headed straight for the wood.

Sliman besought me by his god and mine to stop; he was responsible for me, and what would father do to him if I were to be killed by the djinn? I laughed at him and went into the grove.

The djinn did not harm me. When I came back, there was Sliman, who was afraid of nothing in the whole world, pale as death and trembling, scarcely able to believe his eyes when he saw me appear alive and unscathed.

As soon as we got home, however, he implored my rather to forbid me to tempt the spirits again, otherwise, he, Sliman, could not accompany me any more when I went out riding.

One evening he said to me: "Tomorrow I am riding home into the Rif."

"Take me with you."

At first he did not want to, then he gave in. I had taken the precaution of not saying anything to father about my plan; the environs of the town were not supposed to be safe, and women ought not to venture too far into the countryside.

After a five hour ride we reached Sliman's home village, a group of mud huts so low that one could not stand up in them.

As an unclean Christian, I was put into an empty hut by Sliman. I later learned that the occupant of the hut had died a short time before. Sliman advised me strongly not to venture out of the hut. Here he was the master; I felt this and, somewhat intimidated, I obeyed. Sliman brought me bread and water, and then the whole village came and squatted down in front of the hut to marvel at the "infidel," the first who had ever come there.

Sliman explained to me how shameless they all considered my unveiled face; he did not consider it in the least improper that the heavily veiled women exposed their naked bellies.

It was hot and damp in the low mud hut; I sat on the straw-covered earth floor; the straw was old and mildewed and swarming with fleas. The village had finally seen enough of me, and Sliman had disappeared with his family. I was in a way a prisoner.

Finally Sliman came back, and we rode home. Then there was another big scene with father.

"Really you are impossible! You go out riding all alone with Sliman to his village! You know very well how unsafe the country is. You are a woman, didn't you think what might happen to you."

No, I really had not thought of it; I had simply been charmed and tempted by the unknown. It also seemed to me that father was exaggerating. Not a soul had come near me, and except for the fleas nothing unpleasant had happened to me. From that time on, however, I always had to inform father of my destination when I went out riding.

Slave trade

Yet even when I merely went for an innocent walk about town, accompanied by one of the soldiers, I managed to get up to "stupidities" of one kind or another. In the marketplace there was an old Negro who played the banjo and sang in a cracked voice. He had been in America, spoke English and drawled a sort of song composed of the names of various cities in which he had lived: New York, San Francisco, Chicago-o-o! Beside him, squatting on the ground, was his little grandchild Maimuna, four years old, coal-black and round as a button, with gleaming teeth and shining bright eyes. I could never pass the two without stopping and playing with the child. One day the old Negro, pointing to Maimuna, asked me: "would you like to have her?"

Naturally, I was delighted: "Yes."

"You can have her for one sovereign."

I paid the sovereign and took Maimuna by the hand. The soldier shook his head disapprovingly. He was used to seeing me pick up all the stray dogs I came across and bring them back to the legation garden, but a Negro child — that was too much!

"What will the *Baschador* say, señorita?"

"He will be delighted, Mohammed."

Maimuna, who already knew me quite well, came along willingly. At home I undressed her and put her in the bathtub. That pleased her less and she began to bawl with all her might. Then, wrapping her in my bathrobe, I carried her into father's study which was sunnier than my room, placed her on the large round table and fed her cakes.

The door opened, father came in from his ride, and seeing the naked black child sitting on his newspapers, stood stock still, horrified, in the doorway.

"What is it this time?"

"Maimuna, you already know her."

"What are you doing with her here in my room?"

"I bought her from her grandfather."

"What? What did you say?"

"She only cost a sovereign."

Then poor father lost all patience.

"If that isn't you all over! Now you go out and buy a Negro child so that people will say the Austrian legation is involved in the slave trade. You take that child right back to the old scoundrel!"

Maimuna wept, I wept, but it was of no avail. I had to dress her and take her back to her grandfather. The old fellow was not at all angry; he had earned an easy sovereign. But father threatened me: "You do another stupid thing like that and back you go to your mother. That's quite enough for one week. First my cigars and now this brat!"

***

The incident of the cigars, with which he reproached me, illustrates the dangers of private acts of charity. Not far from the hotel there lived a poor Jewish family with countless children. The oldest son, Abrahamito, a little fellow of about ten, was my special friend. He wore his father's old trousers, which came down over his shoes and which he held up by a rope fastened about his waist, and an old battered hat much too large for him. If I was alone in the house — Abrahamito always seemed to know when that was — he would come to the window and beg for cigars. Moved by the poverty of the boy I would reach into the cigar box and take out some of the prized Virginias which father had sent to him from Austria, and threw them to Abrahamito; he was happy, I felt magnanimous, and everything was just fine until one day my father said: "If only I knew where that little Jewish scamp, Abrahamito, gets the Virginias. Today he sold me ten more."

I turned so red that father noticed it. Abrahamito got no more cigars from me.

Christian customs and manners

One of our soldiers, an old man of perhaps sixty, married a second wife. She was sixteen and extremely pretty. Old Ali seemed very much in love with his young wife. Every time he started to accompany me on my walks the same thing would happen without fail: he would begin to make the most terrible faces, press his hand to his middle and moan that he had a stomach ache. He had to go home and drink tea, he claimed. He was too old to run around with me, I could go on alone, he would meet me at the *suk* — but the *Baschador* must never know.

After a few weeks this stolen leave time did not suffice him, he gave notice and was replaced by a young fellow named Mohammed, who was fresh from the interior and had never before associated with Europeans.

The first time he accompanied us was to a wedding. The manager of the German postal service was marrying the daughter of the German engineer, R. The entire European colony had gathered in the tiny Protestant church. The soldiers from the legations waited in front of the door. A young girl with more good will and expenditure of voice than musical talent sang some wedding song or other. It must have sounded less than happy for when we came out of the church Mohammed asked father in astonishment:

"*Baschador*, what do the Christians do to the bride in the church to make her scream like that?"

But not all their encounters with Christian customs and manners had such a harmless effect on the Arabs. Another Mohammed, the head-waiter in the hotel, had a story to tell about that. Mohammed was a *hadji*, a holy man, who had made the pilgrimage to Mecca — twice in fact. He had been forced by Christians to make the second pilgrimage. Mohammed had a young wife, a beautiful, marvellously developed Negress, Fatma. Fatma had worked with the Perdicarises,[51] a family of rich Greek-Americans, who owned the finest house in all Tangiers and entertained a lot. (Old Mr. Perdicaris was later a victim of Raisuli; he was the first to be kidnapped by the bandit and was only released after payment of a very large ransom.)

Once at a grand ball given by the Perdicarises, Fatma, gorgeously dressed, was supposed to distribute the *cotillion* favours. With true European-American thoughtlessness the Perdicarises insisted that on this one occasion Fatma should go unveiled. Fatma wept, refused, pleaded to be spared this dishonour. In vain. The "master" and the "mistress" threatened to fire her and Fatma knew that she would never be as well paid in any other house. The economically weaker party had to yield. On the evening of the ball Fatma stood in the hall with an expression of shame and despair on her face, not daring to raise her eyes from the floor. From time to time tears ran down her beautiful dark face. Fatma knew well enough what not covering her face meant for her, and her "master and mistress" knew too — but who would be interested in the humiliation of a black servant girl?

From that evening on Fatma was ostracised. No decent Muslim woman spoke to her any more, friends and relatives disowned her. Had the wife of Mohammed, the *hadji*, become a woman of the streets the shame could not have been greater.

Fatma took her misfortune very much to heart, became thin and melancholy and fled the moment she saw anyone coming. Yet Mohammed, who had been wounded in the depths of his honour, still stood by his wife; he was wise enough to know where the blame lay. And finally his love and wisdom found a means of salvation for Fatma.

When it was time for the pilgrimage to Mecca, Mohammed and his wife made the journey to the holy city. Fatma came back purified, cleansed of her sin, and even more — sanctified. Now she no longer had to look away in the presence of others; she was a *hadja*, a holy woman; her sins were all forgiven and wiped away. But Mohammed never forgave the Christians for what they had done to Fatma and to him.

A friend of the Sultan

After two months of rain and constantly howling and raging winds, spring came. Now there were two seas, one with blue waves lapping against the beach, and a second one inland — whole fields of blue irises, gleaming and perfuming the air, rippling like little waves in the wind. Everything was blue as far as the eye could see.

The "foreigners" had been frightened off by the rain. Now new ones came in their place, among them the English writer, Cunningham Graham,[52] who related with great pride that he had been arrested in Hyde Park for having made a socialist speech and that he was descended from the royal house of Stuart. He actually did look a great deal like the Van Dyck portrait of Charles I. He spoke of Bernard Shaw and the Fabians, and I became angry when father called him an unbearable poseur. Father could not endure Cunningham Graham because he was a friend of the *Times* correspondent, Walter Harris,[53] my father's *bête noire*. Harris owned a beautiful Arab house on the beach, which the Sultan had given him. He was a lean, sun-burnt man, and belonged to the type known in Austria as a *Gschaftlhuber* [a self-important "operator"]. He never spoke without mentioning "my friend the Sultan." It was said that he had become rich by making the Sultan the most impossible gifts of articles imported from Europe: cuckoo clocks, wax flowers, music boxes. (At any rate, the Sultan had once proudly displayed a music box to my father and played him his favourite tune — "The Little Fisher Maiden" — on it.) For these worthless European trinkets Harris received in return horses, jewelled daggers, Morocco leather, and many other such gifts.

When things began to go badly for the Sultan and those in the know began to anticipate the rise of his brother, he was left in the lurch by his faithless European friend. I still recall a scene at a daytime reception one day at the Russian legation. The B.'s had no children and Madame von B. asked me to serve tea at her afternoon receptions, and help her see to the material needs of her guests. The whole diplomatic corps was there when Harris in riding breeches, hot and dusty, strode into the salon, self-important as always. He announced the imminent downfall of the Sultan in a loud voice; this time he did not call the Sultan "my friend." When he walked over to greet father, the latter placed his hand ostentatiously behind his back and asked in the inimitable tone of aristocratic superiority he could adopt at will: "If things are going so badly for your friend the Sultan, how is it that you are here, Mr. Harris? Why did you not stay with him?" Whereupon he turned his back on him.

The *Times* correspondent became red as a turkeycock, stammered a few words and walked over to the tea table. But father was already there and said to me in a loud voice: "I forbid you to speak to that turncoat!"

If father never became an ambassador and retired as a minister, such scenes as this were largely the cause. He let his anger get the better of him and did not consider the consequences of such incidents. At bottom he was cynical and believed in nothing. He had a favourite Spanish proverb which I hated in my youth but which often came back to me later as communicating a grim truth: *mismos perros con otros collares*; in other words: nothing changes; everything stays at it always was: it's always the same dogs, only with different collars. But still, he did believe in one thing: that one should stick by one's friends when things do not go well for them. Disloyalty, I think, was the only thing he did not dismiss with mocking laughter.

An anarchist

One day the police in Gibraltar notified the Austrian legation that a notorious Austrian anarchist, Siegfried N., was due to arrive in Tangiers on the next steamer, and that he ought to be closely watched.

Father told me this at breakfast and said, smiling: "What on earth can the fellow get up to here? Such nonsense."

But I was deeply stirred. A real anarchist, a man who — if it was necessary — threw bombs. I had to meet him! First I talked at great length about anarchism — as I understood it — and then slyly veered the conversation around to father's open-mindedness. Finally, after a careful working up: "Come, father, he is certainly an interesting man. Invite him to dinner!"

Had the "notorious" anarchist thrown a bomb at our breakfast table, the effect could hardly have been greater. Father stared at me: "You are really quite mad! The police warn us officially about the fellow and I, the minister, am to invite him to dinner!"

But I insisted, begged and pleaded and — father always had a little sympathy for crazy ideas — at last he promised: "All right. If he isn't altogether impossible I'll invite him, so that your poor soul may have some peace."

Then he went across to the legation.

I could hardly wait for the midday meal: Would father find the anarchist possible or impossible? I went to father's library, pulled out books on anarchy — as there was nothing in which he was not at least casually interested, there were books by well-known anarchists on the shelves — and quickly "boned up" so as to be ready for any eventuality.

Father came back in good humour with the mocking smile I knew so well on his lips.

"So?" I was so excited I could scarcely articulate my question.

"Yes, you shall have 'your' anarchist. He is coming to dinner, but you'll be disappointed."

In general, I was not a vain girl, my beautiful mother had made sure of that with her repeated "Whenever I look at you I can't believe that you are my daughter. You look like a Czech." But that evening I took a long time to dress; I made myself beautiful for "my" anarchist.

What will he be like? Will he even touch the food or will he reproach us for our frivolous life, for feasting while the poor go hungry? Perhaps his sense of justice will be affronted by the beautiful roses which I fetched from the Russian legation and with which I covered the whole table. He will certainly not suspect that the daughter of the Austrian minister, the granddaughter of one of the highest Austrian dignitaries, whose greatest pride was that "his most gracious Lord and Emperor" had once visited him in his villa at G. — a stone tablet in the hall proclaimed this — would be joining him in praising anarchy. And really I ought not have put on my low-cut white silk dress; a high-necked black one would be more fitting. Can one take a girl seriously if she wears a white silk dress and a string of pearls around her neck?

But I did not possess a black dress, so all I could do was put away the pearls.

I could already hear voices in the salon; he is there, he is there!

I knew exactly how one is supposed to behave with ministers, dukes, arch-duchesses and normal mortals: but how do you behave with a "notorious" anarchist? How do you address him? One can't say "Liberator of mankind." And so, quite banally, just "Herr N."? How can that show the respect due to him?

With a violently beating heart I entered the salon. Father introduced me: "Herr N., my daughter."

Herr N. did not wear a red shirt. Herr N. did not appear to have a bomb concealed in his pocket. He wore a dinner jacket and was a rather small, still young Austrian Jew with a high forehead and bushy black hair.

He made no fiery speeches at table. He ate the food he was served without batting an eyelid, and called us not profiteers and blood-suckers, but most politely Count Cr. and Countess.[54]

Whenever father met my glance his blue eyes smiled. The two men conversed chiefly with one another. They talked about — literature. In vain I tried to turn the conversation toward *the* topic: anarchism.

Herr N. looked at me pityingly and turned again to father. He had no idea of the timid awe with which I was waiting to hear an "anarchistic" word. When he had gone my father said:

"You were right. I am glad I invited him. An intelligent, likeable, interesting chap."

To me, however, my acquaintance with my first anarchist was a bitter disappointment.

A little while ago I heard of him through a mutual acquaintance: Herr (or rather "Colleague") Siegfried N. is a minister himself now, and no longer keen to remember the dinner at the Austrian legation in Tangiers, still less the young girl he so deeply disappointed.

Mutton chops

Spring also brought us an attaché, Herr von M.,[55] who later, during the war, became a considerable personage in Austria: head of the press, I think. In those days we little suspected his future greatness; he was tall, thin, shy, and awkward, and he wore what in father's eyes constituted a crime — mutton chops! He arrived on a Sunday. At dinner father moved uneasily in his chair, cast grim looks at the attaché from time to time, and at last could no longer contain himself.

"You are a charming young man, M. . . . , you also speak really excellent French, but if we are going to get along together those mutton chops will have to go!"

Herr von M. looked at my father in astonishment and made a woeful face. I thought to myself: "He will die rather than sacrifice his mutton chops."

Father explained that mutton chops were the symbol of the old Austria, reactionary ideas, stupidity. Herr von M. became sadder and sadder, but about his mouth there was an expression of immovable resoluteness, and I felt that those mutton chops would weather all the storms of existence.

The next day I went dutifully to mass. As I got up to leave after the service, a man was standing near the holy water font, who very gravely offered me some holy water. I looked at him with astonishment and at first did not recognize him. It was Herr von M. — minus the mutton chops.

Such was the power of the *baschador*!

Arab festivities

The Sultan lived in Rabat, where he also held audiences with the foreign diplomats.

There was no court in Tangiers itself, only two Moroccan princes, Muley Ali and Muley Hafid, who gave parties from time to time to which the whole diplomatic corps was invited. When Muley Ali's first son was born he decreed a three-day festival. The diplomats' wives visited the young sixteen-year-old wife in the harem, sat around in utter boredom, listened to monotonous Arabian music, and drank green tea with peppermint leaves. It was considered impolite to decline the cup of tea offered one, and I did much in those days for the sake of the good name of Austria, for I could be offered as many as twenty cups of tea to drink — and I drank them. The music was enough to put you to sleep, always the same five notes. The room was full of heavy oriental perfumes, and it was difficult for the older ladies to keep their eyes open.

Moroccan weddings also lasted three days; during this time neither the unfortunate bridegroom nor the unfortunate bride could get a wink of sleep by night or day. The wedding procession passed through the city, first the bridegroom and the male relatives on horseback and then the bride, likewise on a horse, but enclosed in a sort of cabinet hung with rugs and open only at the top. She was carried around for hours on end in this manner.

The most momentous of all these occasions was the Muslim New Year celebration. In front of a mosque situated on a hill a lamb's throat was cut, then two men seized the dying creature and ran down the hill with it to the nearest mosque in the town. If the lamb was still alive when they reached the mosque, the faithful would have a good year. If it were dead, that was a sign of coming misfortune. (Naturally it always lived until the mosque was reached.)

"Admiral Raschid"

Ramadan came; the look of the town changed. Everything was still, as though paralysed. The faithful, exhausted from endless fasting, sat crouched on the ground, weary and morose; and the Europeans knew that they must be exceptionally careful; during Ramadan, the month of fasting, the natives were especially irritable, and it was very easy for the so greatly feared "complications" to develop.

Raschid, father's servant, made the most of these conditions; for everything he forgot or did wrong he always had an excuse: "Ramadan, Baschador."

Raschid had been a sailor on the Sultan's one warship. He would recall this every time he reported for duty. The longer he remained in father's service, the more exalted the rank he had held became. When father went home to Austria on leave he took Raschid with him, and this turned out to be the Moroccan's misfortune. He had always been a vain fellow, and now he spent all his money on clothes in order to please the European women. He began to drink, too. His greatest pride was the calling cards which he had had made for himself and which read:

Raschid ben Mohammed
Amiral de sa Majesté le Sultan du Maroc

Now he actually himself believed that he had been an admiral, and he recounted wild stories of naval battles, in which he, with the Sultan's one warship, had defeated entire enemy fleets.

In the end his vanity was his downfall. Father was at that time paying court to a pretty woman and sent Raschid with a large bouquet of roses for her. The next time he and Countess S. met, he wondered a little that she did not thank him for the flowers. In the course of the conversation he unraveled the solution of the mystery.

"Your Arab servant is the most charming fellow. Imagine, he brought me the most wonderful bouquet of roses not long ago. Tell me, was the man really an admiral?"

"Admiral" Raschid, who was obviously as attracted to the pretty woman as father was, had removed the latter's card and substituted his own.

Father sent him back to Tangiers. We never learned what became of our admiral.

A battle

One morning we were awakened by shots: two hostile tribes had run up against each other on the beach, and now a sharp battle was raging. Father ordered two horses to be saddled, forbade me to leave the house, and as an extra precaution, himself locked the door of our stable where my good Said stood lonely and forlorn. Then he rode down to the beach with Sliman, who had prepared himself for any and all emergencies by slinging a long, old-fashioned musket around his shoulder.

Naturally I had no intention of remaining at home; still, I could not go on foot to the scene of battle. I tried to open the stable door with every key I could lay hands on — in vain. Said neighed loudly when he heard me fumbling about at the door, but I could not get to him. I became more and more impatient. Then, in the door of the second stall, which was next to ours, I caught sight of Ali, the old groom of the French attaché. I saw that there was still one horse in the stable: Mesrur, a detestable black stallion, constantly rearing and unmanageable. With some nice words and a liberal tip I managed to persuade Ali that Monsieur C. would undoubtedly allow me to ride his horse. My saddle was in the locked stable; but it didn't matter; for this once I could ride in a man's saddle. (In those days that was considered exceedingly improper.)

Somehow I got astride the stallion. The moment we reached the beach and he felt the hard sand beneath his hoofs he threw back his head and gave me a big bruise on my forehead. Then the dear animal bolted.

In the distance there was shooting and a lot of loud shouting; white figures could be seen chasing wildly after each other. I tried to turn Mesrur in the direction of the fighting, but he did not like the noise and galloped off in the opposite direction, toward a rise in the dunes where he saw other horses standing.

On one of those horses sat — of course — my father and on the second Monsieur C, the French attaché, whose animal I had appropriated without his permission!

In the mad ride I had lost my hat, my hair had come undone and hung over my shoulders; I did not look in the least like "a young society lady."

To my astonishment, however, the thing passed off quietly. Deep down, father was delighted by my courage and proud that I had not let the stallion throw me. And the little attaché could not say much, either.

It's true that I did not get to see much of the battle; Sliman took me back home cursing all the way and giving free rein to his outrage at my unruliness.

***

In June father went on leave, and we travelled to Florence where mother had rented a villa.

The antiquarian

It was strange to be transported from the colourful barbarousness and exuberance of the orient to a city where the Middle Ages were still a living presence. I found the old grey stone buildings oppressive; even the Italian sky seemed pale and sad, and I felt extremely ill at ease. For father, Florence was a city from his childhood days in which he felt completely at home. My grandfather, as governor of Tuscany, had lived here with his family; his third son had been born here. To me, all that seemed such ancient history that it had already lost all reality for me, until one day, quite unexpectedly, a figure rose from the past to bring it closer to the present.

I had discovered an old illustrated edition of the *Divina Commedia* in an antiquarian's shop. I would have liked very much to have it, but the little old white-bearded man to whom the shop belonged was asking a price far beyond my means. In Italy in those days it was generally possible to bargain down the price of anything by half, so I went daily to the shop to haggle and bargain for the book. But the old gentleman would not budge. One day I told him that I would not come again; in case he should reconsider the matter he could let me know, and I gave him my name and address.

The old man stared at me for a moment as though he saw a ghost standing in front of him. Then he repeated my name in a trembling voice:

"Is that really your name?"

"Yes."

"Are you related to Count Cr.[56] who many years ago was governor of Tuscany?"

"He was my grandfather."

The little old man reached for the book I wanted to buy, wrapped it up, and handed it to me.

"Take it. It will cost you nothing, nothing at all. And if something else in my shop pleases you, take it, take it!" As he said this, tears coursed down his cheeks.

I was quite alarmed; had the old man suddenly gone crazy?

He came up to me, stroked my hand, and begged me repeatedly to pick out something else in the shop and take it as a gift.

Finally he grew calmer and told me the reason for his strange conduct.

When my grandfather was governor of Tuscany a plot against Austrian rule was uncovered. Among the conspirators were three very young boys, the youngest of them was sixteen years old.

My grandfather was hated and feared because of his inexorable severity; the parents of the three young men thought their sons were lost. But on this one occasion my grandfather exercised mercy; perhaps he felt sorry for the three lads because he himself had three sons: he let them go.

The youngest of them was the son of the old antiquarian dealer, to whose shop chance had led me.

I had to promise to come again and bring father with me. The old man remembered him and spoke of him fondly as a "bel bambino."

Andrea del Sarto

After a few months my mother again found it unbearable to have a grown daughter in the house, and I was sent back to G. to stay with an aunt.

Grandmother's villa was still empty except for Fräulein Marie who occupied her two rooms. I went to my grandfather's villa, a building situated on a hill, constructed in a conglomerate of styles, and bearing the name *Bergschlössel*.

There was something here that was quite to my taste — a large, cool library filled with old and new books. I spent many hours in it. My aunt, the wife of one of my father's brothers,[57] was very kind to me, but at first I could not get acclimated. Everything truly Austrian had become strange to me, I had lived too intensely in another world. But I was young, the summer was beautiful, and after a short while everything became fun, the picnics, the dances — in summer there were no real "balls" — and the excursions on the lake. My aunt would have been very happy to settle me with an appropriate husband and, moved by the most praiseworthy intentions, invited "desirable parties" over to her house. It was not her fault that among the desirable parties there was a single "undesirable" one and that it was that one that appealed to me most. Perhaps it was because the young man was a painter who wanted to accomplish something and could talk of other things besides the usual boring "society" gossip.

When I informed my aunt that we were engaged, there was a huge row and father was summoned by letter to come and stop me from doing "something foolish."

He looked at the matter from a practical angle: "In the first place, one doesn't marry a baron, and in the second, he has only ten thousand gulden a year. You can't marry a beggar, for goodness' sake! From me you won't get more than ten thousand gulden a year either. On that you could starve."

I knew nothing whatever about money; perhaps one really would starve on twenty thousand gulden a year.

"Besides, it was only his grandfather who was ennobled." It was another one of father's aristocratic days. "Out of the question!"

I was nineteen years old and had to yield and — that was perhaps the hardest part — do so with grace.

"Your eyes are red with crying again. Stop making faces. You're not a bourgeoise who doesn't know how to hide her feelings."

With all that, father realized that I was going through a hard time and sometimes he forgot to be angry and tried to cheer me up. Not so my mother. When I got back to Florence, she treated me as though I had committed a crime. How often I took refuge, in those weeks, behind an imaginary headache, just so as to escape the dreadful dinners and no less dreadful hours in the drawing-room afterwards, when my mother would make mean, mocking comments about my distress.

In front of her, father did not dare to protect me. But he brought me his universal panacea: books. I read everything written about Florence in the way of history and history of art, and gradually I came to feel the magic of that wonderful city. The dead became more alive for me than the living: Lorenzo di Medici and, above all, Savonarola. I read the story of the latter's life, as well as his sermons, which I combined with the socialist ideas I had never abandoned.

I spent whole afternoons in the galleries. Sometimes father came with me, but then everything invariably came to a disheartening end. My taste did not please him. We would wander happily enough through the rooms, delighting in special favourites, until we came to some picture by Andrea del Sarto. Then it would start:

"I like him better than all the others put together."

"Don't you see it's kitsch?" father would ask impatiently.

"No."

"Sickly sweet, vacuous kitsch! Just compare him with Masaccio."

Then we would both fly into a rage, and the end was always the same. Father would leave me standing in front of my beloved Andrea and say: "You really are *too* stupid. It's impossible to go to a gallery with you!"

As far as I can recall we never came out of a picture gallery, where there were Andrea del Sartos, together; we were always too angry with each other.

Nevertheless I owe to these arguments one of my most beautiful and loving memories of my father. When I was in Russia, married and very ill, he sent me a big photograph of a Madonna by Andrea del Sarto. I can still imagine today what an effort he must have had to make to buy a reproduction of one of those "horrible" pictures.

Chains

Life with my parents was responsible for many of the difficulties I experienced later in life. My mother's great principle was that everything around her must be beautiful. And truly, from my mother's Empire bedroom to the bright cretonne-covered furniture in the servants' dining-room there was not a single ugly object in the entire villa. In every salon there were flowers that always matched the colour of the room. Everything visible was in unbelievable harmony with everything else. Basic material things were also important. If a new cook was engaged, he was obliged to do some "trial cooking" and prepare the most difficult and delicate dishes, before he was actually hired: an omelette, rice, *vol-au-vent*. Likewise the food that came to the table had to be beautiful. (Poor father had a secret fondness for "ordinary food" — sausage, tripe and onions — but he could enjoy these dishes only in little local restaurants; mother would not tolerate such "common" things at home.) If we had lived sumptuously I would certainly have found that vulgar, but this elegant simplicity — we were proud of the fact that we were driven in a horse-drawn carriage rather than an automobile, like the rich bourgeois — became, unnoticed, part of one's very being, one's flesh and blood, and in the end made trivial things seem absolutely important and thus distorted all values. It is impossible to wear a *decolleté* dress every evening, sit down to a beautifully appointed table, and feel that, for the moment, a well-cooked dinner is the most important thing in the world, without becoming estranged from real life. Once red plush furniture is seen as the epitome of horror, it becomes hard to understand people for whom such furniture is the object of all desire. Of all the kinds of intolerance, aesthetic intolerance is the most difficult to free oneself from, and perhaps the most cruel. It creates necessities without which life is found to be unacceptable, it encourages a kind of cowardice that lets one commit the one unpardonable sin: refusal to acknowledge what every one knows to be true. It creates individuals who because of their convictions are capable of carrying out a great deed, even perhaps sacrificing their lives, but who could never under any circumstances endure a "red-plush-furniture existence." It is the *small* things in life that are truly dangerous and really shackle us, clinging to us like chains that will not be shaken off.

***

Morocco as a "post" was not good enough for mother. For the time being, however, father had no prospect of getting anything else, and so he went into "disposition," which means that he did not give up the career but took an unlimited leave until he could be offered a more acceptable post.

"I got as far as 'honourary Excellency.' That's sufficient for me," he said laughing.

(An ambassador was a real "Excellency," but a minister or an envoy was only addressed in this way as a matter of courtesy — and that was known in Austria as an "honourary Excellency.")

To my sorrow my parents — especially mother — began to tire of Florence. The villa was given up, we spent the winter in Cannes, and in the spring went to Geneva.

Natasha

Father could never travel without his books. Wherever we went we were inevitably followed by case upon case of them. The unpacking and arranging of the books was entrusted to me. Sometimes we only stayed one month in a place, but the books always had to be taken out of the boxes and put in order; only then did father feel at home. It was my custom in packing and unpacking the books, as a sort of reward for my labours, to increase my own library in a rather dishonest manner. (When, later on, father visited me in Russia, he exclaimed more than once as he stood before my bookshelves: "What! Did you steal that, too? Well, now I understand your 'socialism': what belongs to you belongs also to me, but it will be a long time before what belongs to me belongs to you.")

In Geneva my somewhat dormant socialism was awakened to new life.[58] At that time the entire quarter of the city known as Carouge was inhabited by Russian émigrés; wild-looking men and women with short hair and skirts reaching only to their ankles.

I spent a great deal of time in Carouge, observed the strange figures with considerable interest, but never dared speak to one of them, however much I would have liked to. I was ashamed of my well-groomed appearance and my pretty clothes, ashamed of my whole idle, comfortable existence.

On the first of May I succeeded in persuading father to accompany me to the May Day celebration in Carouge. It took place in a large vacant lot. I made poor father march a little way in the procession behind the red flag, but he got his revenge by dragging me to hear the speakers of the various parties and drew my attention to the disagreements among the speakers.

My head was in a whirl; up to that time I had thought socialism one indissoluble whole, but here socialists were attacking one another. As I knew nothing about economic matters, I could understand nothing of it all. The debates were quite incomprehensible to me; the red flag alone was something to which I could cling. Father observed me with a mocking smile; then he discovered a likeable-looking Italian anarchist and began to talk to him.

Weary and disillusioned I wandered over to another tribune where a young man was speaking in Russian.

In the press my parasol was jerked from my hand. I hesitated for a moment to pick it up, for it had a beautifully carved silver handle, and I was embarrassed in this poor, shabby throng to acknowledge that it belonged to me.

A dark-haired young girl of about my age bent quickly down, picked up the parasol and handed it to me with a friendly smile. My confusion disappeared. The young Russian girl spoke good French and we began to talk.

When I saw father appear in the distance I hastily arranged a rendezvous with my new acquaintance and went towards him.

From that time on we met almost every day in a public park beside the lake, known as Mon Repos. I went there as to a lovers' tryst, with beating heart and in constant fear of being caught by my mother.

The young Russian sensed in me a possible proselyte. She discoursed about socialism at great length and brought some order into my confused thoughts; she forced me to consider social problems not simply with my heart but with my head. She was a medical student and planned to return to Russia after she had completed her studies.

We would sit on a bench at the edge of the lake. The waves splashed against the stones. Elegantly dressed people promenaded by us. In the distance the spa band played. And Natasha would speak calmly and even joyfully of Siberia and the prison that awaited her in Russia. She spoke of such things in the way other girls speak of balls and marriage. Only when she pronounced the word "revolution" did her voice take on another tone, like that of a pious Jew, when, carried away by his devotions, he pronounces the mysterious, forbidden name of his God.

I never learned Natasha's family name; nor did I have any desire to know it. She was not a regular human being to me, not a young girl like other girls, but the embodiment of an unattainable ideal: a human being who has sacrificed everything to a Cause.

It was autumn when we met for the last time. The dry leaves rustled on the park paths, the lake was grey and the cold wind howled and whipped up the waves of the lake.

Natasha, who was generally very reserved, kissed me good-bye and said: "You will join us. Promise me that you will join us."

I promised and believed at the time that, notwithstanding everything working against it, I would have the strength and the courage to keep my promise. But the little things of life had me chained. It was ten years before I kept my promise.

I never saw Natasha again.

Return to the Orient

When the first autumn mist shrouds the world in grey and the moaning of the wind announces the approach of winter, I often think back, with a slight feeling of envy, on the autumn days of my childhood and youth. At that time there was no need to fear the gloomy, cold days of winter; it was possible to escape from them.

As soon as the weather began to turn bad, the question "Where shall we go this winter?" was raised. The whole sunny world of the south stood open — all that was necessary was to make a choice.

To be sure, there were always long discussions before my parents could come to an agreement. And so this autumn, too, we bent over maps, deliberated, debated.

The cold weather had set in early, so early that it caught the swallows by surprise. The cruel wind drove the little creatures into our rooms. Others, lashed by the stormy weather, lay dying miserably on the paths.

Perhaps the early winter, which had also caught us unawares, awakened in my parents the desire to go further south this time; perhaps they already knew Italy too well. Whatever the reason, we left Geneva and took ship for Alexandria.

Again the Orient, but a different Orient, an Orient washed, as it were, and neatly combed by the English.

In Cairo, European buildings, European streets and hotels, electric trams. Alongside these, dark veiled women and fellahin riding through the town on their donkeys: a strange mixture.

The bazaar was beautiful and enticing, with narrow lanes lined on both sides by open stalls where you could buy the most splendid oriental objects — some of them manufactured in Birmingham and Pforzheim.

It was a favourite trick of the Arab guides to take innocent foreigners aside in the neighbourhood of the Pyramids and whisper mysteriously to them: "Here is the place to dig; perhaps the Effendi will find something ancient." The Effendi would dig enthusiastically and in a short while bring to light a little scarab, a beautiful, unbelievably well-preserved little scarab — which, in truth, had not been buried in the time of the Pharaohs, but had instead a long journey behind it from the German factory to the Pyramids. But the Effendi did not know that, and the clever guide received an especially large tip.

There are no more charming or adroit liars than the Egyptian guides. That fact was already noted by old Herodotus, and his portrait of these likeable rogues holds good today.

The first time I saw the Sphinx I was disappointed. Then one moonlit night I went again with father and saw the real Sphinx. Before setting out we had coffee at the Mena House, the great hotel de luxe, surrounded by women in *décolleté* and men in dinner jackets; a band was playing and there was dancing; everything was European, everything was of our own time.

Then we went alone across the sand, past the Pyramids, to the Sphinx.

Here everything was very still, the sand gleamed dun-coloured like a massive lion's mane, the moonlight illuminated the stone visage, and the Sphinx leered at us, with a superior and malicious smirk, as if to say: "Poor fools. I have known you and your likes for thousands of years. You vanish, but I remain. I have known everything, seen everything, and I know that nothing that happens in the world deserves more than a scornful grin." The horrible creature crouched in the sand, the very embodiment of cynicism and mockery. The Sphinx was sinister not because she posed riddles and demanded answers to them, like the Sphinx of mythology; but because there were no riddles for her: she already knew everything — and laughed at it all.

I was glad when we got back to the bright lights of the Mena House.

***

My parents had spent a winter in Cairo once before and they were continually visited by old and new acquaintances. Among the former was Sir Rudolf Slatin Pasha.[59] To look at him one would never have guessed that he had become personally acquainted with "fire and sword" in the Sudan. He was a little, lean, modest man who spoke in a soft voice with an unadulterated Austrian accent. He hailed from Upper Austria and had been a clerk in a bookshop until his desire for adventure led him into far-off lands. Now he was already a great man in Egypt. But he made nothing of that and only became a little less quiet and more animated when the conversation turned to the Sudan.

There was also an interesting individual among the German diplomats, a Baron Oppenheim.[60] He spoke Arabic like a native, and would frequently disappear from Cairo for months on end — no one knew where. He lived in a beautiful house set up in the Arab manner, and it was rumoured that he had been converted to Islam. He had no official position in the diplomatic corps, but in fact was a propagandist for the Kaiser. The object of his mysterious trips into the interior was to gain the sympathy of the people for Germany — in anticipation of a possible war one day with England.

At that time Germany was investing a great deal of money in spreading propaganda among the Muslim peoples. Curiously, the latter had a certain admiration for the Kaiser. They liked the noisy, almost oriental parades and spectacles and the grand gestures, for these corresponded very well to the Arab "Fantasia Kebir"[61] or Festival of Aïd el-Kebir, at which also there is much noise and shooting without serious consequences. The German diplomats concluded from this that it might be possible to excite the Muslims to Jihad[62] or holy war. The oriental experts knew better, of course, but was there ever a diplomat willing to learn from an expert?

***

In those days the Egyptian Muslims were true fanatics. A foreigner could safely curse them, after the custom of the country, with an *Inallahbuk* (God damn your father), but woe to the European who employed another current invective, *Inalldinak* (God damn your religion); he would be killed on the spot.

Father, who had already been in Egypt before, when he was a young man, had seen the faithful throw themselves in front of the horses of the pilgrims returning from Mecca; if one of them chanced to be struck to death by a hoof he went immediately to Paradise.

This custom no longer existed, but the departure of the holy carpet for Mecca was still a beautiful and impressive ceremony.

The procession moved slowly and majestically to the great mosque, led by the camel bearing the holy carpet. It was led by an ancient white-haired Negro clad in green, who had already made the pilgrimage to Mecca twenty-five times. Behind came camels laden with water skins, above which large, newly cut palm branches waved in the breeze. From a distance, it looked like a moving forest of palms.

The pilgrims passed the greater part of the night in prayer. In one portion of the mosque dancing dervishes held their services. A strange sight. They began at first to turn very slowly, calling to Allah, then the turning and twisting became faster and faster and the crying and calling out ever louder. At last the room was nothing but a brightly coloured, madly whirling, wildly roaring mass, in which it had become impossible to distinguish a single individual form. Colours blended into each other, voices mingled together, and the room was filled with turbaned heads whirling around like bright little planets.

Before my eyes, too, everything began to turn around; the high shrill hysterical voices tore at my nerves. You had the feeling that if you did not keep a tight grip on yourself, you too would be sucked into that human maelstrom and begin to dance and scream. It was a weird evening. Here, seeing the frenzied dervishes and the pilgrims who next day would set out on the endless road to the holy city, you got a sense of the enormous power of this faith and the utterly alien character of its followers. You understood why the natives seem so strange, so closed off against outsiders, like the doors of their houses which blend into the walls; and you also understood the hostile looks you were constantly met with in the streets. Europeans did not belong in this land. They were intruders and would always remain such.

An adventure

My recklessness and craving for adventure must have been inexhaustible back in those days, for I remember one experience which, though it ended harmlessly, could well have had a quite unpleasant outcome.

I took the tram to the Pyramids, then took a side road and walked on until I came to a village.

There I wandered about among the mud huts and played with the little naked children; I was especially taken by one very young little girl, and I took off a silver Egyptian bracelet and gave it to her, without suspecting for a moment what the consequences would be.

The next instant I was entirely surrounded by the female population of the village. They all wanted me to give them something, and as I did not accede to their wishes, they rushed at me, screaming and crying. They tore my hat from my head, pulled off my clothes and grabbed at my silk underskirt. I already saw myself riding back on the tram to Cairo, clad in nothing but a chemise.

Then I in turn started to scream. Some of the men came running up. The elder of the village realized at once that this event could have disagreeable consequences for his village.

He roared at the women, and he roared at me; I didn't understand a word he said, but the mere expression of his rage was comforting. Without offering the slightest resistance, the women gave up their booty and crept cowed and frightened into their huts.

So I was able to ride back to Cairo, dishevelled and scratched up, but fully clothed all the same.

Garde de la Côte

The Arab Garde de la Côte, positioned at the edge of the desert to combat smuggling, was commanded by a Württemberger, Baron Dummreicher.[63]

It was a remarkable sight, this slender, elegant man, who still kept his Swabian dialect, at the head of a troop of Arab soldiers.

Since they often had to pursue smugglers far into the desert, the Coast Guard rode on camels.

Here, for the first time, I saw that a camel can be a beautiful, graceful beast. The young camels were delightful and very amusing, nothing but long legs and an immense head.

Baron Dummreicher knew every one of his animals. They were as tame and friendly as horses, ate out of his hand, and gently licked his face with their huge tongues.

We rode a little way into the desert. The moment when a camel rises to its feet is extremely disagreeable. Its long legs seem endless and one's stomach starts to churn. Pure-blooded, thoroughbred camels have a fine elastic gait, but the others would shake the soul out of your body. Riding them is never, in any circumstances, particularly pleasant. You sit much too high up, and when a camel bolts, there is nothing you can do. You can only hold on to the saddle as tightly as you can and hope for the best.

The little Coast Guard station lay in a very isolated spot. For weeks at a time its commander did not get a glimpse of a European, and he had settled so thoroughly into the way of life of the natives that he almost never came to Cairo. He no longer cared for Europeans.

Pork tripe

In April it began to get hot; the foreigners who were there for the winter departed; a pleasant inertia took over the entire city.

The Nile shimmered, greener in colour, between the tall trees lining its banks, and in the stillness of the evenings you could hear the sighing and moaning of the old wells as their buckets were drawn up by donkeys.

We embarked at Alexandria and sailed to Beirut. Mother left the ship at Jaffa to go to Jerusalem. Disembarking here was a hazardous affair. There was no harbour at Jaffa. Passengers were brought to land in boats which bobbed up and down on the high waves and tacked between dangerous rocks. The boats were manned exclusively by Jews. They were the only ones who had the courage to brave the danger over and over again.

Father and I continued on to Beirut.

Beirut was very dirty and not especially beautiful. Here the worst of the Occident came together with the worst of the Orient. The Christian Syrians in the city lacked the nobility of the Muslims, and as far as their honesty is concerned, they had as bad a reputation as the Armenians.

We often looked up the Austrian consul, who had been a boyhood friend of father's. Count K.[64] had made himself "impossible" by marrying the once beautiful daughter of a Greek pharmacist. He was always sent to posts where there was no social life. He had been stuck in Beirut for years with no prospect of ever being transferred to a more desirable post.

The beautiful daughter of the Greek pharmacist had become heavy and fat and went about in a dirty dressing gown, her hair unkempt; a number of little, entirely Greek-looking children romped noisily about the house.

Father had described his friend to me as an intelligent fellow, full of *joie de vivre*. He himself scarcely recognized him in the silent, morose man who no longer knew anything of the outside world and no longer cared to. One joy alone was left to him in life, an Austrian national dish: pork tripe. He prepared it himself in the kitchen, and if someone praised it he seemed to come alive and would relate in great detail how pork tripe should be cooked, and how difficult it was to prepare it correctly in this God-forsaken hole. It was a minor tragedy: this man, who was once expected to have a brilliant career, had given up everything for the love of a beautiful woman, but now the beautiful woman was old and fat and all he had left was — pork tripe.

Legends

The Governor of Lebanon was a Pole,[65] charming, elegantly dressed as though about to take a walk in Bond Street, bored, and continually longing for European capitals. He invited us to his castle in Lebanon from the heights of which he could look down upon his subjects, like a prince of olden times. The large, imposing building with its European salons was as incongruous here on the Old Testament mountain as the urbane Pole himself. It was beautifully located on a wooded slope, but I searched in vain for the cedars that are inseparably linked with the name of Lebanon. There were magnificent trees all around, but not a single cedar. What had happened to them? Had Solomon cut them all down when he built his temple?

Once, however, on an expedition into the countryside, I did see a few of them. They were protected by steel railings like wild animals in a zoo. A rarity that could be looked at but not touched. Besides, they were not especially beautiful; apparently the Christian regime had not been conducive to their well-being.

In spite of this, however, Lebanon itself was wonderfully beautiful, with its wild ravines and sunny slopes, its little villages nestled in narrow valleys and its mysterious groves. The entire Old Testament came alive; Rebecca stood slender and sunburned by the well watering the camels; in the distance, barely distinguishable from the blue mists enveloping them, the herds of the patriarchs grazed; and in the evening twilight, you could distinguish, against a purple sky, like a Fata Morgana, the black outlines of the caravans winding their way along the rim of hills towards Damascus.

Mount Lebanon is the land of legend and saga; history and fiction mingle here, spinning a web of enchantment over hills and valleys. This quiet piece of earth has seen much blood flow — idyll and tragedy side by side.

On a lonely peak which may only be reached by steep overgrown paths lies the old half-ruined castle of the robber knight, Emir Bekir.

From here he ruled the land with an iron hand and undertook sallies against the infidels, to whom he was a terror. The forest has made its way into the old castle, strong young trees rise up between fallen walls, and creepers have covered the sad grey of weather-beaten stones with fresh green. Behind the castle, at the edge of a gorge, through which a mountain torrent rushes, there is a little garden. Here in this nook open to the sun and sheltered from the wind grow the most beautiful roses, and among the roses there is an uninscribed marble tombstone.

The same legend that is told of Stenka Razin the Cossack,[66] also flourishes in the rose garden of Emir Bekir. The Emir had brought back a Christian maiden from one of his plundering expeditions and made her his wife, even though she remained true to her Christian faith. However, his followers feared the influence of the Infidel woman and threatened to leave him if he refused to part with her. She understood the danger her presence meant for her beloved and begged him to kill her. The Emir stabbed her with his own hand and buried her in the little garden at the edge of the gorge. But he ordered the most beautiful roses to be brought up from the valley in order that his beloved wife might sleep surrounded by the flowers of her homeland.

***

From Beirut we went on to Damascus. The little train which crosses Mount Lebanon puffed slowly upwards through snow and cold. Then, as though it longed to flee the desolation, it began to run down swiftly into paradise.

A green plain, the Bekaa, nut trees and a sweet-smelling sea of pink blossoms, apricot trees, that is the entrance to Damascus.

The Damascenes say that paradise was once located where their city now rises. One of the streams that pass through the city, the Barrada, also flowed through paradise. They recount a pretty legend about this river:

When Adam and Eve were driven out of paradise they came to a desolate and barren land. Their eyes, accustomed to the beauties of the great garden, beheld with fear and sadness only barren country and desolate rocks. A deathly stillness lay all about them, no bird sang, no beast cried, no water splashed.

They had been rejected by God and were alone in the wilderness, threatened by death. Then suddenly they heard a sound, louder than that of their own desperate weeping: the rushing of water. They looked up and saw a bright stream flowing through the desolate land; it was their old friend from paradise: the Barrada.

The river had been moved by the wretchedness of the two humans; it did not abandon them, but flowed after them. And wherever it passed the wasteland became green and blossomed and bore fruit. All the domestic animals followed the river; the wilderness turned into a second paradise and the children of the first men played with the little waves of the generous river, to which, as to a second creator, they owed their being.

That is why Damascus too is so beautiful; the waters of the Barrada on which it lies, once mirrored paradise and the river has given some of that paradisiac beauty to the city.

Bakshish

The Damascenes were truly quite right to be proud of the city they had built. The slender minarets from which the call to prayer was sounded were superb, as was the great bazaar, which was like a second city in the midst of the city. Under the great dome, in a warm half-light, entire streets were laid out and in each street there were other beautiful things. Circles of light played on swords and daggers. The merchant selling them would take a thin blade in his hand, bend it double and then let it fly back with a light swishing sound. The handles of knives and swords were ornamented with precious and semi-precious stones and gleamed brilliantly. In another street unset gems were being offered for sale. Tiny blue ripples of aquamarine would trickle through the merchant's fingers; during some fairytale night he had plucked down the Milky Way, and now it lay delicate and brilliantly white in a casket of moonstones. Out of a corner great red rubies glittered, full of malice, like evil eyes, and gentle turquoises smiled blue like a bit of northern sky that had strayed down here.

Near the street of the precious stones there was a smell of leather; here were marvellous ornamented saddles and slippers of all colours.

Less salutary for a European stomach was the street of sweets. The candied fruits and coloured sweet drinks sparkled like jewels and looked so beautiful that one constantly had to sample something.

I was always delighted with the "free gift" you received after having made a purchase, or the *bakshish* that the merchant presented to you with such a friendly smile as his "gift"; certainly he had already made enough profit from you. Naturally the *bakshish* was always some utterly worthless little article, yet because it was a "gift" it possessed a particular charm.

When you were invited out you dared not express great admiration for anything, for the host would immediately say: "My whole house is yours. Do me the honour of accepting this small trifle from me."

Father had forgotten to inform me of this custom and, once when we were visiting a wealthy Damascus merchant, in all innocence, I admired a vase and was enchanted when the owner of the house made me a gift of it. On the way home, however, father remarked with some irritation: "That will cost me a gold cigarette case. Don't you know these people always expect a gift in return? It's a blessing that you didn't admire something more expensive!"

The first station on the Berlin-Baghdad railway

The days were not long enough for us to see everything and enjoy everything — the beautiful Arab buildings, the large gardens of the wealthy merchants outside the city gate. We would wander aimlessly through the city, attracted by beautiful things on every side, take our shoes off and put on clumsy slippers before crossing the threshold of the mosques so as not to pollute the holy places. The slippers were always too big and I was continually in fear of losing them and finding myself in my stocking-feet on the sacred marble floor.

The mosque of Omar was not only beautiful but a striking illustration of the tolerance and mutual understanding that prevailed in earlier days. When the Crusaders captured the city they wanted to have a church so that they could pray to their God. And so their "enemies," the Muslims, gave them half of the mosque. An enormous curtain was stretched across the centre: on one side of it the Muslims held their services and on the other the Christians celebrated mass. Allah and the

Christian God got on perfectly well together. To this day a stone tablet in the mosque commemorates this rare example of religious tolerance.

The Muslims despise the Christians, but, with inborn tact, they are careful not to demean their religion. More than once I heard a Muslim, in conversation with father, explain with great politeness that he respects Jesus as a noble prophet, albeit a relatively minor one and in any case not remotely comparable with Mohammed. Of the Madonna, they would speak most respectfully, as the *Sit* ("Lady") Mary.

In those days Orient and Occident met in Damascus. Through the streets rode tall, heavily armed Circassians in their high fur hats; black-robed nuns, always in pairs, all carrying the inevitable umbrella, glided undisturbed through the throng; with their green turbans and shining robes, *hadjis* who had made the pilgrimage to Mecca and little children who had been born there (the greatest good fortune that could befall a Muslim child) stood out from all others in the crowd. And a few hours from Damascus, in a dismal, barren spot, next to the gleaming rails, stood a little house: the first station so far completed on the fateful Baghdad Railway line.

The men from the interior of the country were afraid of the ugly, unprepossessing little stone building and the ugly, snorting monster, black with soot, that could run faster than their best camels. Perhaps it was their instinct that warned them. They would not have boarded the train for anything in the world.

A missionary

In Lebanon we had already noticed women who veiled only half their face. These were Druze women. They seemed less timid and frightened than the Muslim women and the young ones sometimes used one eye very flirtatiously. The men also made an entirely different impression from the Syrian Christians; they were tall and well built with sharp, energetic features.

We learned a number of things about the Druze from a man who had spent many years among them.

We were sitting one evening in the small public room of the one hotel in a little place not far from Damascus when the sound of horses' hooves could be heard coming from the road. A tall, sun-burned man with grey hair came in; he was dressed like an Arab except for the fact that his robe was black and not white. He was followed by a young Arab. We were the only Europeans in the hotel; after a little while the old gentleman came over to our table and asked in beautiful French if he might sit with us.

He introduced himself with one of the oldest aristocratic French names and told us he was a Jesuit and had been living for twenty years among the Druze in Lebanon.

As soon as the conversation turned to the Druze the old Jesuit thawed out; he spoke of them with great affection, you could almost say with enthusiasm.

"They are the most decent people in the world," he declared. "They do not steal, and they do not lie."

Father observed that the Druze were nevertheless notorious for their cruelty, and he reminded the Jesuit father of the Christian massacres. The latter shrugged his shoulders slightly and smiled as though it were a question of some inconsequential trifle.

"The Druze are awaiting the return of their prophet," he told us. "He has already appeared twice on earth. At his third coming paradise will begin on earth — paradise for the Druze. But for their womenfolk too, for, unlike the Muslims, the Druze believe that women too have souls and will be able to enter paradise. The Druze are much more tolerant than the Muslims and the Christians; even unbelievers will not be damned at the coming of the prophet, if they have been decent human beings; they will only become servants of the Druze. With me" — the old Jesuit smiled contentedly — "it will go well. My servant has promised me that I shall be his servant in paradise, and since I am — in his view — a decent human being, my only duty will be to black his boots."

"And have you converted many Druze?" father asked.

The old missionary almost lost his temper.

"Converted? What are you talking about? The Druze will not allow themselves to be converted. They are decent human beings and they hold fast to their own faith. If one of them came to me to be converted, I should know right away that he was not a real Druze but a rogue and a deceiver. I studied medicine, and people come to me to be healed of their sicknesses. I gladly take care of their bodies, but I should never venture to tamper with their souls." Then the conversation turned to France and Europe.

"Six months ago I was in Paris for the first time in many years," said the Jesuit father. "For appearances' sake, one has to go back once in a while. But I couldn't take if for very long. I have been spoiled by living among the Druze. I don't like Europeans, and I don't like Christians either."

The Jesuit father laughed almost defiantly as he pronounced this heresy. Scorn played over his fine old face, which, with its high-arched nose and deep black eyes, resembled that of an Arab.

On the following day he rode back to Lebanon — to the only decent people he knew in the world.

Measles

On a Friday, the thirteenth, we embarked at Beirut. The steamer was supposed to put to sea in the forenoon, but it was midnight before the anchors rattled and the ship slowly got under way. The next day we learned from the captain the reason for this: the sailors had refused to sail on such an unlucky day.

The unlucky day brought misfortune on me anyway. I felt wretched, had a high fever and a bad cough. But, in keeping with the principles of my upbringing, I kept it to myself, secretly swallowing large quantities of quinine which I wheedled out of the ship's doctor. As a result, the entire trip to Constantinople is a blank in my memory. I recall only unbearable thirst, roaring in my ears, dizziness, and the heat. I presumed that I had caught malaria somewhere. It will go away, I thought, provided I take quinine regularly.

As we came into Constantinople, however, I was coughing so much that even my parents realized something was not right. The doctor came and diagnosed a case of measles. Of all the things to do in Constantinople, I had thought of nothing smarter than to get myself sent to the German hospital with measles. I was furious, but I had to submit.

After seemingly endless burning days of high fever I was released from the infectious diseases ward, and much thinner and with shaking knees, permitted to walk in the wonderful gardens of the hospital which stood on a hill overlooking the city.

I made friends with Sister Katherine, a large, energetic woman who was in charge of the men's section of the hospital. That is how I also made my way to that part of the garden where her patients lay or strolled around in the shade of the great trees.

My interest was aroused by a young sailor, who seemed to be in an exceptionally bad way. I went up to him and with a great deal of sympathy asked him what he was suffering from.

To my astonishment the poor devil turned red as a beetroot, looked around in embarrassment for Sister Katherine to help him out, seemed to be cudgelling his brains for an answer, and finally came out, stammering, with: "Rh . . . rheumatism."

Afterwards Sister Katherine told me dryly that young girls were well advised not to ask sailors about their maladies.

The diplomats' summer resort

As soon as I was able to leave the hospital we went to the island of Prinkipo, where we spent a month, and from there to Therapia, the diplomatic summer resort on the Bosphorus. White palaces with marvellous gardens stretching all the way to the water, nothing but green as far as the eye can see, thick groves where so many nightingales sing that it is hard to sleep at night, great Turkish barges and sail-boats passing through the Bosphorus — that was Therapia from the outside. Inside, it was a veritable hornets' nest filled with the malicious buzzing and humming of mutually mistrustful and hostile people.

This was the centre of all the gossip and intrigue of Turkey. Everyone was suspicious of everyone else and at the teas and tennis matches the diplomats kept a sharp eye on each other: who was on especially good terms with whom, who had talked longer than usual with some Turkish dignitary?

One tall, heavy-set, morose-looking man was to be seen at all the diplomatic receptions and parties, generally in conversation with influential Turks. This was Freiherr v. d. G.,[67] the German ambassador, of whom it was said that he had a hand in everything that happened in Turkey. The Young Turks[68] did not like him; they spoke of him with a strange smile and a peculiar gesture of the hand. Sometimes Count Széchenyi[69] appeared, as lively and energetic as a young man. He was the organizer of the Turkish fire brigade, which had the reputation of being one of the best fire brigades in the world. Certainly it never got out of practice, for there was an extraordinary number of fires in this part of the world. Red flames were continually leaping up into the night sky, the air was filled with the smell of burning and the silence was shattered again and again by the rattling of fire engines heading to the scene of a fire. The merry old Hungarian, who generally commanded the fire brigade himself, had — in contrast to most Europeans — not harmed the "Asiatics" but rather helped them; he had brought them a bit of genuine civilization.

Diplomats are like women, they cut each other up mercilessly, and rarely and only unwillingly concede any superior knowledge or understanding to their esteemed colleagues. It gives them much greater happiness than it does ordinary mortals to think of everyone as "really quite stupid." In Therapia, however, there was one man whose superior knowledge and understanding were universally acknowledged. He seems to have been better and more accurately informed about Turkish affairs than all the diplomats put together. "You must ask Paul Weitz,[70] he will know for sure," they would say, and the moment the cheerful, somewhat overweight correspondent of the *Frankfurter Zeitung* appeared he was surrounded by people who listened carefully to his every word.

There was also a great figure in finance to be seen in Therapia, one Herr Gutmann;[71] I believe he was from the Deutsche Bank. I was impressed by one fact only: that so young a man should understand something about banking, which is incomprehensible to me to this day. What Paul Weitz did not know, Herr Gutmann did — the two of them were the oracles of the Europeans.

Father had become very friendly with one of the Young Turks, an energetic young man who played an important role in the Young Turk Revolution. The Young Turk never came to see us until late in the evening; it was dangerous to have anything to do with Europeans openly, and the Turkish espionage system was as good as that of czarist Russia. The Young Turk always came with his collar turned up high, and always made sure that no one was listening at the door.

His precaution was not exaggerated; the place was swarming with secret police; servants, door-keepers, beggars on the streets — you could never be sure that any one of them might not be a spy. The Turks sold and betrayed each other, and the Armenians were even worse. The Albanians were the most trustworthy, but they in turn could make your life miserable with their fidelity — it was impossible to get rid of them. When father had first come to Turkey many years before, a strange little episode with a tragic ending had taken place in Constantinople.

A European diplomat had an excellent Albanian servant whom he prized highly and of whom he was very fond. He was deeply grieved when the servant, an old man, became ill one day and, in spite of the most careful treatment, died.

One morning a few days later a young Albanian appeared in the diplomat's bedroom. When the diplomat in astonishment asked him what he wanted, he said:

"I am the nephew of your servant. My uncle has left you to me. From this day on I am your servant."

The young Albanian was a worthless and dishonest servant, but the diplomat could not get rid of him. He tried to dismiss him, but each time he sent the Albanian away the fellow came back and said: "You cannot send me away. My uncle left you to me. You have to keep me."

Finally the diplomat lost patience and had the embassy soldiers throw the man out of the house. Two days later the diplomat was found dead in the street with a dagger in his heart. The servant was arrested. He did not deny the deed; it was his conviction that he was in the right. His uncle had bequeathed the diplomat to him and the diplomat had in a sense become his property; he could not be permitted to pass alive to anyone else.

Father also liked to tell another characteristic story from the same period in his life. "Wild" *pashas* from the interior used to appear at diplomatic soirées in those days — barbarians little versed in social usages but endowed with practical sense, for they believed in always "taking away" something with them. One of them, with especially refined tastes, after having eaten his fill at the buffet, slipped an entire lobster into his pocket. A young *attaché* noticed it and in a fit of exasperation seized the sauce bowl and poured the contents into the pasha's pocket with the polite remark: "Votre Excellence a oublié la sauce."

The young attaché was not destined to go very far in the "career."

The *Loreley*

In Constantinople and on the Bosphorus whenever the conversation turned to the subject of the warships of the various European nations, which lay at anchor there as a reminder of the power of their respective countries, the Austrians would become embarrassed and quickly talk of something else. It was really impossible to cut much of a dash with the old tub that represented Austria's power; it was a screw steamer that might possibly have been new fifty years before, a miserable, clumsy, insignificant monstrosity, in the wretched appearance of which you could read the shame if felt in the company of its ally, the beautiful little *Loreley*.[72]

The *Loreley* was lean and graceful, as snow-white as a preened swan, and spotless from the smallest screw to the guns. It was a pleasure to view the ship and take tea or lunch on its shining white deck. Yet for me personally the time spent on the ship was the source of various unpleasantnesses. When I think back on these, I still experience a feeling of aversion.

Two days after our first lunch on the *Loreley* father called me and explained that the commander had asked him for my hand; as he was a charming man and everything else was also in order, I should think the matter over.

I was anxious to get away from home. I liked Constantinople and I liked the *Loreley* — but I did not like the commander. I said no, much to my mother's annoyance. To my mother's annoyance but to my own good fortune, as well as to that of the commander, who is today one of the leading lights of the German Nationalists.

After this episode the atmosphere at home became distinctly uncomfortable; father, who was always eager to avoid any unpleasantness, decided to make a trip into Asia Minor and took me with him.

In Asia Minor

Led by two soldiers on horseback we travelled across wild stretches of country, over the roughest roads imaginable. Out of their swampy edges giant tortoises poked their heads. We got to Tarsus and saw the ruins of Paul's house and from there we went to Eskisehir, where the inhabitants, using primitive techniques, made all kinds of objects out of meerschaum.

As it was summer, we travelled at night in order to avoid the heat of the day. I remember particularly one journey by moonlight through a lonely stretch of forest country. It was deathly still all around; only the hoof-beats of our escort echoed through the night. There was a full moon. Father had warned me: "Wear a thick veil, the moon burns."

I didn't believe him and didn't follow his advice. The next morning I was burned quite brown and my whole face hurt.

Once we spent the night in a little place where there was no inn. I stayed in the mayor's house where I was given a fine big room. In the lower part of the door leading into the adjacent room there was an opening about three centimeters wide. This did not bother me, for no one was staying in that room.

In the middle of the night, however, I was awakened by a mysterious sound: a loud sound of nibbling and scratching. My flesh began to creep. What could it be?

I lit a candle and saw big horrible-looking worms crawling into my room through the opening in the door. I jumped out of bed and opened the door leading into the next room; the floor in there was alive with innumerable worms crawling around and nibbling noisily on mulberry leaves. They seemed to be completely at their ease — certainly more so than I was. The mayor, it turned out, was the biggest silk-worm grower in the area. I was very happy that I did not have to spend a second night in these disagreeable surroundings.

We stayed in Bursa for a short while, and I spent many hours at the wonderful Turkish baths. In the marble halls there were pools and baths and douches at every temperature from cold to hot. One walked around there quite as one had been created by God — except for the Armenian women who wore, as their single article of clothing, a cross around the neck. The slim, brown forms of beautiful young girls were like fine bronzes; but there were also hideous, bulbous old women — they were not usually over thirty — who looked like caricatures. After one had gone through all the rooms and immersed oneself in all the different waters, one had one's hair washed with henna by Negresses, and this was followed by a massage. (During this procedure I was always told: "You will never get a man, you are much too thin.")

After the massage one lay on a sofa, drank black coffee, smoked, and felt very much at peace with the world.

I had my fortune told in the market-place at Bursa. I still remember one thing from what was foretold: "You will marry shortly and go to live in the coldest land in the world."

I laughed; how improbable that a creature who loved the sun and the warmth of the south above all else should move, of all places, to the coldest land in the world.

Return to Europe

After we came back to Therapia father began to be bored. He already knew Turkey quite well from earlier journeys, and felt a desire to return to Europe. Good-natured as he was, he took me with him so as to spare mother and me the unpleasantness of living together.

***

We took passage through the Dardanelles with the Austrian Lloyd.

At a certain spot every steamer had to fire a cannon to indicate that everything on board was in order. As an Austrian minister to foreign countries, father was an important man on an Austrian ship, and so the captain invited me to fire the cannon.

Before the shot was fired, I felt very important. Afterwards, however, there was such a tremendous ringing in my ears that I thought my eardrums would burst. I had not drawn back in time.

It was a wonderful trip. The sea was as smooth as a lake, dolphins played in the blue water, and at night the little waves gleamed like molten silver.

The ship put in at Piraeus, and we took the road to Athens.

I had expected to find Homeric figures, and the modern Greeks were a great disappointment to me. On top of that father dragged me to the Acropolis in the noonday heat and then was vexed at my lack of enthusiasm. He was a great venerator of the Greeks and even then could still recite whole passages in Greek from the Iliad and the Odyssey.

Athens was too European for me, and I began to feel nostalgic for the Orient. I was very happy when at last we left Athens and went on to Corfu, where an uncle of mine was consul.

Here everything was still and green and beautiful. My uncle's wife, whom I had not met before, was charming to me. I was thoroughly at ease and very happy.

Soon afterwards my uncle lost this beautiful post — in a very strange manner. He was a talented, genial man who, however, from time to time would go off the deep end or throw a fit in anger. To his great misfortune he had one of those fits while my aunt was in Vienna, where she went periodically to take care of her affairs. A reforming zeal was not unconnected with my uncle's fits. In this case the issue was the reform of the *maisons publiques*. My uncle fumed with rage over conditions in the bordellos of Athens and Corfu and the mistreatment of the prostitutes. Unhappily his rage was not confined to spoken words — he vented his wrath in newspapers and magazines, he was merciless in his attacks on the proprietors of the *maisons publiques* and he assuredly thought that some good would come of it all.

The result, however, was a note from the Ministry of Foreign Affairs transferring him to a much less desirable post.

My uncle had not taken the precaution of finding out who the proprietor of most of the brothels was. On his passage through Austria to his new post he discovered that most of them belonged to the Greek Minister of Foreign Affairs.

***

We left Corfu, took ship to Trieste, and from there went on to Vienna.

At first father was happy to see old acquaintances again, but after a few days he began to complain that they were boring and said he could not stand Vienna any longer.

He too missed the colours of the Orient; everything seemed to him pale, monotonous, dead.

We took the train to Frankfurt-am-Main. Here father pointed out to me, as a remarkable curiosity, a hotel near the station. A sign on the door read: "No dogs and Jews admitted."

At that time such a thing was still a curiosity in Germany.

However we also saw something in Frankfurt that was more in keeping with my ideas of culture — even though it came from a barely civilized country and was foreign to the "innermost being of the German people." We saw Saharet[73] dance.

I have seen a great many dancers since that time, including the entire Russian ballet, but I have never again seen such completely natural grace and charm, the expression, simultaneously, of a little wild animal and a beautifully refined woman.

Frankfurt was the first big German city which I got to know well as a grown woman. I liked the handsome, noble buildings and the many oases of green — as well as the antipathy of its inhabitants to the Prussians. Like good tourists we made pilgrimages to the original home of the Rothschilds and to Schopenhauer's house. We took in Dannecker's[74] fat *Ariadne*, and in the Palm House celebrated seeing tropical plants and flowers again with melancholy joy. One night when there was a full moon we wandered about on the Römerberg. The Middle Ages appeared before our eyes, the magnificent old houses seemed to tell of dark secrets. Here father was able to indulge in "ordinary food" to his heart's content. He dragged me along to tiny restaurants and consumed innumerable Frankfurter sausages. On one such occasion he almost frightened a poor waiter to death. The city of wealthy merchants seemed to have reawakened strongly aristocratic feelings in him — this happened time and time again. True to his Austrian ways, he gave the waiter a — by German standards — extremely large tip. "Thank you very much, Herr Baron!" the fellow said. In the city of the Rothschilds that was indeed the highest title of nobility by which a person could be addressed. But father, deeply insulted, replied quickly and in a loud voice: "Call me Victor if it will make you happy, but for God's sake don't call me Baron!"

The poor waiter thought he was dealing with a madman; he gave father a terrified look and rushed away — without having called him Victor.

Little did I then suspect that Frankfurt would again play a role in my life, and that, after I had finally broken with my old world, it would become a kind of home for me.

***

Father had gone into "disposition" too early. As much as he had grumbled about the "career" in the past, he now missed it. He was pursued everywhere by an inexorable grey spectre, which he could never get rid of for long: boredom. He tried to run away from it, but it always caught up with him and would not let him go. How often in the morning I would leave him content and cheerful, at peace with the world, enthusiastic about the place where we happened to be at the moment and then come back at lunch time to find him sitting in his room, surrounded by newspapers, looking years older, wearing a desolate expression, and muttering: "Really, it's too unbelievably boring here. Even the people are dull and stupid. Pack your things, we are leaving tomorrow."

On the train or aboard ship he would become cheerful again; he was blessed with indestructible optimism, always expected something good to happen, and was always happy when he was "on the road." He was bored only when the destination was reached.

On the train, he used an excellent trick to get disagreeable fellow-travellers to leave our compartment. He would sit with a lowering expression and stare threateningly at the intruders. Then he would begin to mutter strange sounds, wave his arms wildly and behave generally like a lunatic. That was my cue; I had to assume a frightened expression and whisper to the passengers that my father had just been released from a mental hospital and had to be protected from any excitement.

If the trick worked and the fellow-travellers speedily left the compartment, father would laugh like a schoolboy and be in a good mood for hours.

From Frankfurt we took a trip on the Rhine. I compared it with the Nile and longed to be back in the Orient. At first father was enthusiastic about the "German River" — especially about the vineyards on its banks. He tormented me with talk of the Nibelungen, scolded me because, unlike him, I could no longer recite entire passages in middle-high German, praised German orderliness and efficiency, and was generally content. Then we came to the Niederwald monument[75] and, as he hated everything ugly, that immediately spoiled his good humour. All at once the Rhine with its "gingerbread castles" became a miserable river; the wines, in the long run, were undrinkable; even the orderliness and efficiency of the Germans left much to be desired. Now, casting angry looks at the patriots gathered around the monument, he recited Musset's "Nous l'avons eu, votre Rhin allemand"[76] and began loudly and ostentatiously to lament the fate of poor Alsace, which had come under the rule of a country capable of producing such a horror as the Niederwald monument. I was glad when the Rhine trip at last came to an end. We zigzagged back and forth through southern Germany and saw all manner of beautiful things, but father became more and more out of sorts and more and more regretted having returned to Europe. I was also ill-humoured, for I had again found a suitor who, both on aristocratic grounds — he was a baron — and on financial grounds, did not please father. I had a singular talent for setting my heart on someone my parents considered a "poor sucker." The result: family scenes, arguments, irritation on all sides. Then I was shipped off to Merano[77] for the winter with a lady companion as chaperone.

The eight-hour working day

I came to Merano irritable and in a bad mood. The teas and balls bored me; I now found the usual chatter about Mitzi and Baby and Putzi hard to take. Among all the people I met, there was only one I liked — old Herr von Pribam.[78] Years before he had been tutor to my father and his brothers and had subsequently filled a rather high post in some ministry. Now he lived with his wife and son in a pretty, tastefully furnished villa.

I was flattered that the old gentleman, who avoided all his wife's other guests, enjoyed chatting with me, and I was always delighted when his son would whisper to me at one of her teas: "Papa is in his study. You are to be sure to drop in on him."

Surrounded by his books, the old man led a solitary existence, writing up his memoirs. He could speak interestingly about many aspects of the old Austria; he did not like the "new times." He did not agree with my reading newspapers: "They are not for young girls." But he encouraged my reawakening literary ambition, and patiently read two horrendously bad novels and many equally bad short stories that I had concocted.

That winter I appeared in print for the first time, in the *Meraner Zeitung*, under a fine pseudonym. I shall never forget the friendly, sandy-haired editor, Herr Ellmenreich. I have rarely felt so grateful to someone. The tiny editorial office lives on in my memory as an impressive, awe-inspiring room and I still have warm feelings for the *Meraner Zeitung* in which two *feuilletons* by me appeared.

I hardly noticed that I received no honorarium. It was honour enough simply to have been published.

After this good fortune (and after the well-intentioned editor had sent back both my novels), I suddenly discovered that every decent person should learn a trade, and I apprenticed myself to a book-binder. At first the honest Tyrolean thought I was mad, but later he got used to me and yelled at me as much as he yelled at the other apprentices when I cut a book crooked or spoiled the gold lettering. For months I applied myself diligently and learned everything I could in the little work-shop. Then I decided that for one week I would try to work the eight-hour day that was the still unattained goal of the labour movement.

After the first two days, however, I had already made the discovery that the eight-hour day was a most remarkable ideal. My back and shoulders ached as though they were going to break, my hands trembled, I cut myself with every one of the knives, bruised my fingers with the paper-mill and upset the lime-pot. After work I could not eat, and at night I could not sleep. I could not get the smell of lime out of my nose and it made me nauseous. But I did not give in and held out for the entire week. Then, when, at last, on Saturday, our day off was about to come, I startled the entire shop by falling to the floor half dead and beginning to weep uncontrollably. I was very ashamed of myself, but I could not help it.

That one week taught me more about social problems than a dozen heavy tomes.

Marriage

In the meantime father had retired, and my parents had to decide where they wanted to settle. This was not a simple matter. Father wanted to go to Switzerland and become a naturalized Swiss. He had always had a strong liking for Switzerland and the Swiss. But mother was against it; she did not like "hotel places." Finally they agreed upon Baden-Baden where we spent a completely uneventful summer as far as I was concerned.

In the autumn my parents went to India, and I again went to Merano with a lady companion.

I was now twenty-four years old and, according to Austrian law, no longer a minor. I did not in the least enjoy living with my parents, and I had all sorts of wild schemes to make myself independent; but what could I actually do? In practical matters, I was as inexperienced as a child; all my life everything had been there for me and everything had been done for me, as though that was part of the natural order. I did not even know how one checks baggage at the station. But I wanted to get away from my parents at all costs. One of my aunts advised me to become a canoness, and I spent a considerable amount of time drawing up my family tree; for at that time anyone who aspired to become a canoness was required to demonstrate sixteen "incontestable" ancestors on both the paternal and the maternal sides. I could have spared myself this tedious task, for just at the point when I had successfully collected all my ancestors, I met a young Balt[79] at a ball, and three weeks later I was engaged to be married.

Had the two of us searched the whole world over it would have been impossible for either of us to have found anyone less suited than we were to each other. There was nothing about which we did not have opposing opinions. My future husband related with pride and enthusiasm that he had spent most of his time in the previous two years shooting revolutionaries; I, on the other hand, dreamed of an estate run as a co-operative, in which all the workers had a share. Neither of us made a secret of our convictions, but the young Balt, accustomed to the submissive German women of his homeland, assumed that after the first two or three children my "madness" would automatically disappear, while I, for my part, was convinced that it would be an easy matter for me to "convert" him.

For that matter, we had little time to argue; ten days after our engagement he went back to Russia in order to be home for the *Saat* — the Sowing.

I knew nothing about the *Saat*, could scarcely distinguish between barley and rye, and had never lived in the real country. But everything, as I imagined it, was very beautiful: the endless Russian steppe, the solitude and quiet, the many animals. The Russian cold did not alarm me in the least: "One goes south in the winter, of course." I had occupied myself with social questions practically since childhood, but I could not conceive of an existence in which one did not spend the winter in warmer climes and in which everything was not designed to enhance one's comforts and satisfy one's taste for the beautiful.

***

When my parents returned from their Indian trip they were not exactly enthusiastic about my engagement. Father came to Merano to meet his future son-in-law; he found him pleasant and likeable, but — the misalliance! First the barons and now a Herr von. A Protestant too, on top of that.

"I will not try to dissuade you," father said. "You are old enough to know what you are doing. But has it occurred to you that your sons can never become chamberlains or your daughters ladies of the Order of the Star and Cross?"

I had not thought of it, nor did the revelation now worry me in the least. My sons and daughters would fight for the liberation of humanity, and for that they did not need to be either chamberlains or ladies of the Order of the Star and Cross.

I went with father to Baden-Baden. Mother was already there. "You'll see how disagreeable it will be when people only call you *'gnädige Frau'*" she said scornfully. But she was glad to get rid of me at last and with great eagerness helped me prepare my trousseau. We were married in June, but not in Baden-Baden: that would have brought the grown daughter, whom my still beautiful mother preferred to keep a secret from people, too conspicuously into the limelight. She suffered enough from the grievous fact of my existence, even though father, in order to make things easier for her, had found a charming way of saving her youth. He always introduced me to strangers as: "My daughter from my first marriage." Thus without lying, as he always proudly insisted, he succeeded in getting people to take me for my mother's step-daughter. In order to heighten the illusion, I also had to call her by her first name.

For these reasons, therefore, the wedding was not to take place in Baden-Baden, but in Frankfurt. Two days before the ceremony we discovered that the civil marriage had to be in Baden-Baden. We went back in all haste and experienced an amusing scene in the city clerk's office. I was wearing a tailor-made dress, while father, my fiancé and his two brothers were in lounge suits. The clerk wrinkled his forehead when we appeared before him and said sternly:

"Why have you come here dressed in everyday clothes? A marriage is a festive occasion in a person's life. Go home and put on the proper clothes, and then I will marry you."

Our trunks were in Frankfurt, and we had no other clothing with us. But we were so intimidated by the clerk's strictness that we rushed to tailor and dressmaker to have ourselves fitted out with the "proper clothes." I came off easiest; my white lace dress was put together with a few stitches and some pins, but my father and my fiancé were most extraordinary looking in their ill-fitting frock coats. Still, they were indeed frock coats, and the clerk was content. Father was so angry about the makeshift coat and stared so furiously at the official during the whole ceremony that I could scarcely keep a serious face. Also, during the clerk's long, unctuous speech he kept up a steady stream of facetious remarks; it was a very jolly wedding.

The next day the church wedding took place. I do not remember now in what church; since then I have looked for it in vain. For me, however, the ceremonial aspect was marred by the fact that I had never been to a Protestant wedding before and did not know how to act.

The leave-taking from my parents was not especially moving. Poor father found my father-in-law, who had come to the wedding, an unmitigated bore and had but one wish — to get rid of us all. By way of farewell, mother said: "I know that you would now like to have no more to do with us. Just remember, however, that it is very *mauvais genre* to break completely with one's family when one gets married. Don't forget it."

I kissed our little fox-terrier Jack, took his sister Gilly, whom I had begged from father, under my arm and went with my husband to Berlin, where we planned to remain for a week.

An Austrian woman in Russia

It was a wonderfully beautiful summer, hot and dry, and I could not believe my husband when he said that "at home" it was still freezing on the moors at night. I did not like Berlin and was happy when one evening we boarded the train that was to take me to Russia.

The long trip began. At the border my heart began to beat wildly: Russia — what experiences lay in store for me in this mysterious and dangerous land? How would it change me?

The trains ran more slowly now, in broad, comfortable rocking movements. The locomotive spewed big glowing sparks out into the night.

"The trains run on wood," explained my husband. "In our distillery too we use only wood. It works out much cheaper than coal."

In all the stations there were enormous hissing samovars. Even at small whistle-stops you could get wonderful tea.

We were already at the beginning of the great plain — endless fields and great forests which cast fantastic shadows. Night came but it did not get dark. A pale, ghostly light gave everything an air of unreality. The uncanny white light crept through the curtains of the compartment and kept one from sleeping. Outside, the vast plain slipped past the windows, cold and dead; not a village, not a house to be seen, nothing but endless fields.

***

After a forty-eight hour journey we at last came to our station. A dismal grey stone building, and behind it, in the morning light, a tiny village.

A carriage with four horses was waiting in front of the station, as well as a cart for the luggage. I was greeted by the driver and I replied politely but sleepily: "*Terre, terre,*" the only word of Estonian I knew; it means "good day."

I was dead tired. The carriage had hardly begun to move before I fell sound asleep. Whenever I was awakened by a jolt, I caught the same view of endless fields, with the rough road stretching ahead of us. For all I could tell, the carriage might not have moved at all while I slept.

"How far is it to the estate?" I asked, drunk with sleep.

"Seventy kilometers."

A thought that was hardly appropriate to someone on her honeymoon shot through my mind: Good God, seventy kilometers! How shall I ever get away from here if I can't stand it?

My mother had once said: "The ideal of country life for me is the Hotel St. ... in Baden-Baden." How far that kind of "country life" was from that in the Baltic provinces! For miles and miles nothing but meadows, fields, the occasional "big house" of an estate, and vast forests. (In the

"Punishment Expedition"[80] that followed the 1905–1906 Revolution the villages were all destroyed and their inhabitants sent to Siberia.)

Siberia — the word weighed on the whole land like a nightmare. Article §1 in the Russian legal code proclaimed that anyone was subject to punishment who by deed, word or *thought* came too close to the person of the Czar. You were sent to Siberia if you were caught reading a forbidden book, sent to Siberia if you taught peasant children without the government's permission, sent to Siberia if you belonged to a temperance society; for in the eyes of the authorities every sports club, every temperance society was a potential band of conspirators. Every great estate had its own *uriadnik*,[81] or country gendarme, and evidence brought by any one of these was sufficient to get you sent on the long journey.

And what did not threaten the sacrosanct person of the Czar and the no less sacrosanct regime! The *Neue Freie Presse*, to which I subscribed came to me so blacked out by the censor that almost nothing remained except the "Court and Society News"; most of the time nothing at all was left of Harden's[82] *Zukunft*. Even in my encyclopedia, which was sent after me along with other books, whole sections of "Russia: history" had been blacked out.

The Baltic barons, German to the core and wildly antagonistic to everything Russian, found this regime very much to their liking; they were not harmed, and with its assistance they could get workmen for almost nothing.

They were absolute masters on their own estates; it was up to them whether their workers' children could go to school or not (there was no obligatory school law in Russia). And woe to the worker who subscribed to the one progressive newspaper published in Estonian; as the workers' mail was delivered in big black sacks first to the proprietor of the estate, the worker never got his paper, and was categorically forbidden ever to subscribe to it again.

The attitude of the local people to the Baltic barons was understandably not especially cordial. Whenever one encountered a little farm cart on a country road the peasant would shout angrily: "*Kurrati-sax!*" (German devil!), and my husband impressed on me that I should never go for a long walk without my revolver; there was no knowing what "these animals" might do. As I was far more afraid of the little Browning[83] he had given me as a "suitable" wedding present than of the entire population of "animals," I did not follow his advice. Besides, despite my ignorance of the language, I was soon on good terms with all our workers. They said: "The master has married a blonde gypsy; she is crazy, but a good sort."

***

In Austria I had been familiar with the amiable arrogance of the aristocrats, which became disagreeable only when it was directed at the "bourgeois," and which, in any case, did not exclude a grain of good-humored doubt about the aristocrats' own godlike superiority. Here in Estonia there was no doubt; the smallest baron's child was convinced that he had been created by a Protestant God, who was particularly well disposed toward him, of quite different material from that of the Estonian "animals." The bourgeois, whatever their profession, were termed "literati," and, so long as they spoke German, were treated with condescending politeness.

"Literati," God knows, the Baltic barons were not. When I arrived at the big house on my husband's estate, where he had lived for six years, I found, after a thorough search, two books: the Bible and a pornographic work, *The Memoirs of a Singer*.[84] And when I went to Dorpat[85] for the first time and bought four hundred rubles worth of books and subscribed, on top of that, to magazines in various languages, my husband was genuinely dumbfounded, and my mother-in-law asked in astonishment: "What do you need all those books for? A good house-wife has so much to do taking care of the house that she hardly has time to read."

The "Austrian woman" quickly came to be regarded with horror by the good "Baltic housewives." When at my first breakfast at home I asked in surprise: "Where is the jam?" my husband stared at me in even greater surprise and then announced: "Only whores eat jam." And my poor mother-in-law, horrified, asked: "You bathe twice a day? No decent woman does that!"

My clothes, and especially my underwear, which my mother had bought in Paris, also scandalized the family. One did not have lace on one's underclothing, and one did not wear transparent nightgowns! The only thing that would have reconciled them to my sinful underwear — the coronet marking our aristocratic status — was missing. Coronets were much favored in the Baltic provinces, and at my parents-in-law's there was a beautiful chamber pot with a magnificent five-pointed coronet on the bottom. (I always asked for it whenever I visited them, but that had nothing whatsoever to do with aristocratic feelings.)

I would not do an injustice to the people among whom I lived for six years. They truly believed in aristocracy and in their own place among the elect. It never occurred to them, at any moment in their lives, that other people were also human. And the "literati" — doctors, teachers, and pastors — encouraged them in this belief.

***

I sought in vain for the culture of these German "bearers of culture" in "barbaric" Russia. On our own estate I found miserable workers' huts without floors, where from seven to twelve people lived crowded together in one room. My husband once came home with his cane broken and when I asked him in astonishment what had happened, he replied: "I broke it over the back of one of the labourers."

He could not understand when I cried, half weeping, half in anger: "Have the carriage hitched. I am leaving. I am getting a divorce!"

***

He was equally dumbfounded by my response when once, coming up from the farm, he exclaimed in triumph: "I've given that fellow Tönnies the hiding of his life. The rascal dared to whistle the Marseillaise."[86] I went to the piano, which was by the open window, and played the Marseillaise over and over again the whole day long. The workers laughed: "The master can't handle that gypsy."

When my husband was out at farms several hours away, they came directly to me, partly because I gave them French cognac when they complained to me of suddenly feeling faint — and it was remarkable how often these great strong men seemed to suffer from this — and partly because, having taken out a subscription for several copies of the prohibited Estonian newspaper, of which I understood not a word, I used to distribute those copies among them. The servant girls too were astonished because I did not beat them but was polite to them. We paid calls on other landowners; the "Austrian woman" had to be introduced. You drove for hours in the carriage and four and arrived dead tired.

And then you had to talk for more hours with the good women of the house. They would chat about their children and their servants — like characters in a novel of small town life. After the meal the sexes would separate, the men going into the smoking-room, while the women remained in the salon. There would then be more talk of the children and the servants; it was desperately boring. The women would give me advice about housekeeping; little good it did. The men would ask me questions about farming to which I would give the most fantastic replies. On the way home my curiosity would be aroused: "What did your friends say about me?"

My husband would laugh: "A charming woman but not very useful for breeding purposes. Much too delicate. How will you ever get children from her?"

That was the general view of women in a country in which a family of under five was called "childless." Here in the Protestant north, in a strange way, the oriental and the Baltic world views merged. A married woman was still nothing but a mother. She was not to dress in bright colours any more, was not to wear *décolleté* dresses, and was not to look pretty. She had attained her goal — a husband.

"Why don't you wear black instead?" my mother-in-law asked me when I appeared in one of my prettiest Paris dresses. "You are a married woman now, for goodness' sake."

And every Sunday, which we always spent at my husband's parents' house, I was asked the same question: "What, not yet? You should ride less and above all not bathe so much." And a disapproving glance would be directed at my narrow hips.

***

In spite of everything the first summer was beautiful. I loved the birch woods and the broad moors where one could wander for hours. At sundown the brown heath glowed rust-red all the way to the far-off horizon. It was glorious to ride across the estate in the early morning, to stop and play with the colts in the paddock, to go to the kennels where the English hunting dogs belled. Along the river that flowed through the park there were lovely secluded spots. Silvery willows trailed their branches in the water and shone pale in the midday sun. Sometimes I would drift along in the canoe and jump into the water, warily keeping out of the way of the big old crayfish with their threatening claws.

Autumn came, the maples flamed red, and the rowanberries glowed. Grey mists rose up from the river towards the house and swathed it in an impenetrable veil. Huge oak logs crackled in the fireplace, and the oil lamps spread their friendly light. A great silence settled over everything, except for the distant whirring of the threshing-machine, like some monstrous purring cat.

Now came days of solitude. My husband went hunting on neighbouring estates; I had become ill and had to remain at home. In addition, I had to "watch over the farm." I was not a good manager. When I was in the threshing-room I let the people steal as much as they wanted; heaven knows their pay was miserable enough. Once only, when one of them dragged a whole sack away right under my eyes, I asked him politely to please do it in a less obvious manner.

***

The stables for the work horses were located about five minutes from the house, and my husband had asked me to keep an eye on the head stableman, because, my husband said, he was quite untrustworthy. One evening when it was already quite dark, I felt a sudden dutiful urge and went to the stalls. I found the stableman lying on the cold ground groaning in a frightful fashion. I was horrified, ran back to the house and returned with the universal panacea: cognac. I raised the sick man as well as I could and poured the cognac down his throat. It seemed to do him good, and I was much pleased with my medical knowledge, when suddenly our estate manager appeared, took in the touching scene, and quite dumbfounded asked: "What are you doing there, *gnädige Frau*. The fellow is dead drunk already!"

***

The nearest doctor lived in a little village about three hours away; so even in the most favourable conditions, it was six hours before he could be at the estate. Hence the workers, their wives, and their children came to me with all their little ailments. In Florence I had worked for several months at the infirmary of the Sisters of Mercy and was therefore able to deal with minor illnesses.

One day one of the old workers came running up to me and said, rather unemotionally: "I think my wife is dying. She has been in labour for six hours. Please, will you come and take a look at her."

I sent the coachman at once for the doctor and ran to the hut. There lay the woman in labour, groaning on the filthy floor, surrounded by loudly jabbering old women, each one giving a different piece of advice.

"Why isn't the woman in bed?" I asked in horror.

"She will dirty the bed-clothes."

"I will give you some more."

"Will you give us a new mattress, too?"

"You can have a whole new bed as far as I am concerned; only don't let her lie any longer on the dirty ground."

They shook their heads at my mad ideas, but they did what I said. The woman herself was the most vociferous in her objections; she had given birth to six children on the floor, why should she be put in a bed for the seventh?

The woman was forty-four years old; she should have left it at six children. The hours that went by before the doctor arrived were like a horrible dream. My experience at the infirmary was completely inadequate here; the only thing I could do was drive away the old women who kept wanting to touch the woman in labour with their dirty hands. It was hot and stuffy in the small space. The animal-like cries of the woman filled the entire room. The pale half-light of late afternoon fell on her pain-racked face. Death lurked in the corners. Children came running up and gaped at the woman, unmoved, with astonished eyes. The old women did not understand why I became angry and chased the children away. "We all have to go through this," they said. "Why shouldn't the children see it?"

Finally the doctor came. He approached the bed and with a look of indifference on his face drew a pair of forceps from his bag. He glanced at me questioningly. "Do you think you can stand to stay here? It won't make you faint?" He seemed far more concerned about the *"gnädige Frau"* than about the woman screaming and writhing in pain on the bed.

When finally, after an eternity of pain and anxiety, the child was born, the doctor came up with me to the house and ate his supper, contentedly and with a good appetite.

He was a remarkable type, that Doctor Hasenjäger [hare-hunter]. He fully lived up to his name, for his main interest in life was hunting. How often was he called to see a patient only to quite overlook the object of his visit the moment he heard my husband say: "Wouldn't you like to take a gun and come into the woods first, doctor?" Sometimes he would forget to bring his instruments, but he always brought his shot-gun. He was more feudal than the most feudal baron, and his poor patients did not interest him in the least. He always approached the sick bed with a lighted cigar in his mouth, until one day, when he had been called to see a child with a pulmonary inflammation and did it again, I lost patience.

"But it smells so bad in the huts," he said. "Why shouldn't I smoke?"

"It is not good for the child."

He shrugged his shoulders: "There are so many of them. If one dies there is always a new one next year."

I saw red: "All right, you can go into the huts like that, but on one condition. If you are ever called to see me you shall come into my room also with a lighted cigar in your mouth."

The little hard blue eyes in his weather-beaten face stared at me uncomprehendingly. I was trembling with anger. "You'll soon get over your sentimentality with this pack, my dear lady," said Doctor Hasenjäger and with a sigh of regret threw away his cigar.

That evening my husband asked me: "What on earth went on between you and the doctor? He told me you were extraordinarily nervous and that it would be a good idea if you had a child soon."

The doctor was not the only one with whom I had serious spats. One day while my husband was away a friend of his, whom I did not know as yet, came to see him. We chatted about all sorts of things, and finally got around to politics. The guest became extremely lively, praised the Russian regime, and finally said: "We have a wonderful method for treating political prisoners. It works better than any rack. For a week they get nothing to eat but herring and not a drop of water to drink." He grinned. "Believe me, *gnädige Frau*, after a week of this diet they all come around."

The good man was most astonished when without a word I rang for the servant and said: "Have the Baron's horses hitched at once. And if he comes back again he is not to be received." He never came back again.

Family gathering

In the late autumn a family gathering took place in Dorpat. It was to be a most festive occasion. Two new members of the family were to be "displayed" — I, the Austrian woman, and a young man from St. Petersburg who had become "Russianized" and was visiting the Baltic province for the first time. In addition, judgment was to be passed on a black sheep of the family.

The gathering took place at Aunt Lilly's house. Aunt Lilly was a widow and very rich. (Strangely enough, money made a great impression on the Baltic aristocracy, and my husband was most astonished when I explained that that was "bourgeois" and that money was something of quite secondary importance.)

Aunt Lilly was famous because she had a blue salon; a genuine "period" salon. To the solid housekeeping women of the family with their plain tastes this seemed almost immoral.

The "blue salon" and the adjoining rooms were full of people. My first thought was: "How on earth did a family that seems to be mostly made up of old maids get so many children?" The women wore black jet-trimmed silk dresses, cut high but very full about the bosom and hips. At first glance they all looked exactly alike; it was impossible to tell one from another. That is how I came to say nice things about their children to the real old maids among them, which affected them painfully. Aunt Lilly held court on a big blue sofa to a circle of people surrounding her. In a corner, anxious and bored, sat Grischa, the "Russianized" cousin who only spoke French and Russian; which seemed as outrageous to the assembled family members as the *décolleté* Empire dress and high-heeled gold shoes of "the Austrian."

I was presented to one old lady after another. And each one asked: "How do you like our dear Baltic land? Do you find running a house with our terrible servants very difficult?"

Smoking was not permitted in the blue salon, as a married woman I was not supposed to sit with the younger members of the family, and everyone looked disapprovingly at me. It was deadly. However, there was one other person there who felt as I did. That was Uncle Max,[87] my father-in-law's brother. Because he was poor and had scientific interests — I discovered later that the dear old gentleman was a well-known ichthyologist — he was treated with condescension by the rest of the family. For me, however, he was soon the best and most tolerant friend I had in all the Baltic provinces. He came up to me with his kindly smile and rescued me from a bunch of old ladies.

"Come, you poor child, you must be bored to death. Sit down by Grischa. He will be so happy to have someone to talk French to."

And so we, the prime exhibits at this family gathering, who of all the people there could at least speak French, sat down together and quietly made malicious comments.

The gathering had begun at three o'clock. It was now six; Grischa and I were surprised that there was nothing to eat.

"What are we waiting for now?" we asked Uncle Max.

"Bruno."

Bruno was the black sheep upon whom judgment was to be passed today.

"What did he actually do?"

"He stole a forest."

"Stole a forest?"

Uncle Max laughed at my astonishment — the thing seemed less incomprehensible to Grischa — and enlightened me. Bruno had been the manager of some Russian prince or other's estate, had sold a forest belonging to the prince and pocketed the money. The prince did not seem to make too much of it, for he did not bring suit — but the family, on the other hand, did not want the dishonour to fall on it.

At about half past six the servant opened the door; everyone immediately became stiff and solemn, and the whole blue salon breathed severity and pitilessness. Bruno entered, followed by his mother and sister whose black clothes, because of their grief and shame, seemed even blacker than those of the rest of the family.

Bruno was a disappointment. He did not look in the least like a brazen thief who had stolen a whole forest, but was an ugly, frightened little man who pressed his fingers together in embarrassment and did not lift his eyes from the floor.

No one shook hands with him. Only a stiff, formal nod of heads greeted him.

The men came out of the smoking-room. Then Aunt Lilly rose majestically, and everyone followed her into the dining-room and sat down at the big table.

Bruno sat at the end of the table between his mother and his sister, who cast beseeching glances at the others and wiped their eyes.

The oldest male member of the family stood up and made a long speech in which a great deal was said about the family honour and about Bruno, the "shameful blot" on it. After that the accused defended himself as best he could, but a Russian forest is too big an object to be gainsaid, and as most of the members of the family themselves possessed forests which might have been stolen from them, they could appreciate the enormity of the crime. The head of the family rose again and announced that Bruno was to be cast out of the family for "dishonourable conduct," that he was no longer part of it, and that he could no longer count on it for help and support of any kind.

As Bruno and his family withdrew like a pack of whipped dogs, three of those present shook hands with him: Uncle Max out of kindness of heart, I out of contrariness, and Grischa because he thought that far too much fuss had been made about a trivial matter. Grischa did not own any forests and was a Russian *tchinovnik*[88] (civil servant).

The sentence had been pronounced, but there was still nothing to eat, and the boredom became more acute. It was impossible to continue to be indignant for hours over the unfortunate Bruno. Finally Grischa and I discovered two bridge partners and withdrew to the smoking-room to play cards.

The old ladies observed this with strong disapproval and said to my husband: "Your dear wife has much to learn before she becomes a proper Balt wife." And my poor husband offered the by now standard excuse for my shortcomings: "My wife is an Austrian and doesn't understand all that."

Winter silence

The first snow fell, and darkness hung down over the land. The petrol lamps burned until eleven o'clock in the morning and had to be lighted again at three in the afternoon. The paths in the park were covered with snow, and you sank in over your knees the moment you left one that had been shovelled out. Our little river was frozen over with ice — it no longer gurgled; and everything else fell silent along with it. Nothing moved; the snow deadened every sound. The silence surrounded the house like a wall... and the sun had disappeared. Grey sky, grey silence, grey solitude.

Dreadful evenings and dreadful nights followed. My husband was away a great deal elk hunting, and because of my health I was obliged to remain alone at home. Until dinner time it was still bearable. I could hear the servants moving about the house; foremen came by; I had to telephone my husband about this and that; from time to time you could hear the soft but audible sound of a sleigh passing. Somewhere, there was still life in the world.

At nine o'clock the samovar was brought into my little salon. "Does the *gnädige Frau* need anything?" "No, thank you." "Good night." "Good night." The servants betook themselves to the lower floor; I called all the dogs to me — six dachshunds, two setters, and my Gilly, and then the endless night began.

Silence, oppressive, nerve-wracking silence. The hissing of the samovar gradually ceased. The dogs, sated with cakes, fell asleep. The world had disappeared; there was only the snow-bound house, in which I was alone, alone with the deathly silence. From the fireplace came the gentle ticking of the little Empire-style clock — very faint. Sometimes I could hardly hear the ticking. My God, if it stops, I shall forget my upbringing, I shall forget that one is not a bourgeois woman and that one must exercise self-control. I stare at the clock; if it stops, if its ticking ceases to be the only thing between me and dead silence, I shall begin to scream like a madwoman!

Dear, good little clock, with your blue medallions reflecting the yellow light of the standard lamp, you never did stop. You never struck terror into me like your rival, the dining-room clock, when one eerie night it struck thirteen. I could have hugged you when your fine silver chimes sounded eleven, twelve, one, two o'clock, and gave me comfort. "I am alive," they said. "My little clock-heart is beating next to yours. You are not all alone."

I surrounded myself with books, read, did needlework, shook the dogs to wake them up. They would wag their tails in a friendly and reassuring way and then go back to sleep. The big standard lamp would begin to hiss and flicker — the oil had been used up. Quickly, light the other lamp before that one goes out, just don't let yourself be left in the darkness, alone with the silence that has its claws at your throat.

Steps in front of the window. God be praised, the night-watchman is on his rounds and is checking the house. The good old man. Quickly, pour a glass of cognac for him and open the window. "Good evening, nightwatchman. Won't you have a schnapps to warm you up?"

Icy air swept into the room. I shivered in my teagown but scarcely noticed it. There was a human being out there, speaking with a human voice; I was no longer alone.

The old night-watchman was pleased to get the cognac and quite willing to chat with me a little.

He had only one topic of conversation: the depravity of the younger generation. I listened enthusiastically, agreed with him on everything, no matter how much he ranted and raved about the immorality of the old cabinetmaker on the estate who in a state of drunkenness had fathered a son by his own daughter — naturally the girl was to blame. Let him say the most terrible things about the young workgirls; just so long as he stays there and doesn't go away; just so long as his hoarse, boozy voice saves me from the silence.

But after three glasses of cognac, swallowed down very slowly, the old man had had enough: "Otherwise I'd fall asleep while walking on my rounds."

"Come back again, night-watchman. It is so cold. You must drink something or you'll freeze."

"I have to make the big round now, *gnädige Frau*."

The window was lowered. The steps faded away in the distance. Roughly and without mercy I shook the dachshunds from their sleep. "Schnauz, wake up. Little Kutz, big Kutz! Gilly, come here! Jacko, you've slept enough. Can't you bark, just once?"

Sleepy dog eyes, yawning dog muzzles. I crouched down on the floor next to Jacko, the black-haired Gordon setter, and laid my head against his soft fur. How warm he was, how alive. Give me your paw, Jacko, or I'll go out of my mind.

Little Empire clock, you are crazy. It has to be more than two o'clock. I've been sitting here an eternity. Look how many oak logs have been burned in the fire-place. What, only two? Are you sure? Shall I go into the dining-room and make certain? No, the big salon and the study are so dark, and in the darkness the silence feels even worse. I believe you, I shan't go."

Sometimes the silence was broken, but not agreeably. One of the hounds in the pack would wake up and find his surroundings so gloomy that he would begin to howl. Then the whole pack would join in. The black night was filled with howling and whining. It was as though the end of the world had come and lost souls were crying out in anguish to an avenging heaven. Then I too, holding fast to Jacko, who was a philosopher and let nothing upset him, would begin to weep in helplessness and despair.

As soon as dawn began to break I would chase all the dogs into my bedroom, entice them on to the bed and then lie down myself, dead tired but with my nerves all unstrung. No wonder I grew pale and thin during those winter months. My husband did not understand why, and I was ashamed to tell him of my fear of the lonely nights, for when he came into my bedroom one evening and, finding me crying my eyes out, asked what was wrong, and I replied: "There is no more sun, no sun anywhere," he only laughed at me and said, "Of course the sun doesn't shine at night, you little sheep!" He would never have been able to understand my fear of the silence.

Neighbours

The winter was endless. On both sides of the road, which had been shovelled out, stood walls of snow as high as a man. Everything was covered with ice, and if I went in the open sleigh my hairpins got so cold that they burnt my head like flames. I sat by the fire-place the whole day long. When we went to pay our usual week-end visit to my parents-in-law my husband would have a *reggi* (hay-sled) hitched up. I would wrap myself up in furs and crawl under the straw, leaving only the tip of my nose outside so as to breathe. I made the entire journey in that condition. Whenever we took the ordinary sleigh, I would curl up under the fur covers and squat on the floor. Forty below, along with a bitter wind, was no light matter for someone who had spent every winter of her life in the warm south.

My husband was a justice of the peace and had to travel to the little town of Fellin, about five hours away, to carry out his duties. On the eve of one of his trips, a neighbouring landowner came to see him.

"I have a problem with a peasant," the neighbour said in the course of the conversation. "It's about a piece of land I have got to have. The peasant says it belongs to him. You'll make a judgment in my favor of course?"

Both men were disagreeably startled when I said in my most "aristocratic" tone of voice: "How much are you offering as a bribe, Baron Taube?"

Even the excuse that, being an Austrian woman, I had no understanding of such matters failed to appease the old baron. Yet strangely enough — it must have been extremely awkward to have a wife like me — the peasant won his case.

In Fellin we were visited by an elderly landowner whom everybody in the whole district made a fool of. He was an ill-kempt, thoroughly dirty old gentleman, with a long grey beard. By this time I had got used to the way the "neighbours" spoke of nothing but farming matters, and I did not expect anything else. But, quite abruptly, the old gentleman asked, as if he were talking about potatoes: "Have you read Anatole France's new book?"

As a result of this question, a warm friendship developed between the old gentleman and myself. He would come to the estate for a three-day hunt, bringing only a toothbrush with him, and generally stayed three weeks. We went out hunting together but we never brought anything home. We chatted about books and other countries and let the deer get away. The old gentleman had, in the eyes of the Baltic barons, a dark past. As a young man he had made the customary "educational tour" and had gone to Naples where he fell in love with a fisher girl. The Neapolitan beauty would not listen to him, and to the horror of his family the young Balt stayed ten years in Naples, ceaselessly trying to win the girl over. Finally, his parents stopped sending him money, his beautiful fisher maid married a Neapolitan, and he returned home, sad and constantly yearning for the south. His family married him to a "capable" woman who ran his estate for him. He, however, took refuge in books, where he found something of the life he had been robbed of. The good landowners looked on him with contempt, and it was touching to see this somewhat bungling, morose man awaken to new life on finding someone who knew Naples and modern literature.

There was also a reading group: each estate contributed two books, which could be kept for one month. I aroused great indignation when I contributed Sombart[89] and François Coppée.[90] Sombart was condemned as revolutionary and Coppée as — indecent. The others brought to the circle, as modern writers — Stratz[91] and Rudolph Herzog.[92] One "intellectual" woman, who was said to have had an affair twenty years before with the revolutionary tutor of her son, dared to contribute Gerhart Hauptmann's[93] works, but no one ever read them: "So depraved we are not!"

Hunt

Yesterday it had still been winter, but today a real sun was shining, the ice was melting on the river, the big ice blocks were banging against each other and cracking, the snow was vanishing as if by magic, the winter wheat was putting out its green shoots, and, in front of the house, an overpowering scent was coming from the black alders. The northern spring arrives overnight; it comes with a gentle, warm wind that smilingly drives away all the misery of winter, with fragrance and blossoms and tender new leaves on the slender silver birches.

Everything awakens from its winter sleep, kissed back to life by the blessed sun. The cows become restless in their stalls, the young colts frisk wildly in the paddock, the sheep bleat joyfully, and work begins in the fields. The earth gives off a wonderful smell, a promise of fertility and triumphant Life.

In the fields, the cries of peewits filled the air — their eggs, so expensive in the cities, rotted here; the bright blue spring sky suddenly darkened as a flock of cranes passed over. In the dense grove near the house the moor hens sounded their mating calls; you could hear them from the house.

As dusk fell, it was a special treat to wander through clearings in the woods, following the flight of the woodsnipes. Through the trees the sun could be seen sinking slowly below the fields; gradually the wood fell asleep and no more birdsounds were heard. Evening wrapped itself around the world; the cries of screech owls pierced the air. Then a lightning-like flash, a sudden rush, a flight of feathers, and a snipe fell to the ground.

It was no pleasure for my poor husband to go hunting with me. He was a good huntsman, and I became sentimental over every deer or hare he brought down and called him a murderer (which never kept me from eating roast venison or hare). Once he wounded a roebuck, and the dogs leapt upon the beautiful dying animal.

"Shoot it dead, for God's sake, shoot it dead!"

"I can't. I'd hit the dogs! Stay where you are. Watch out!"

But I ran up and pulled one of the dogs away. Only "little" Kutz had gotten such a hold that I couldn't get him loose.

"Shoot!" I cried: "It's too awful, shoot!"

My husband fired, the roebuck was dead, little Kutz fell to the ground, stunned. And now I was angry because something had happened to him. I carried him home in my arms; on the way he revived and bit my hand. That was the last deer hunt I ever took part in. For a long time afterwards I was haunted by the tortured look in the eyes of the dying buck.

St. Petersburg

In the summer my husband was obliged to report for military duty and I insisted on going with him. One year of country life was enough; the prospect of going to St. Petersburg was extremely enticing.

There was a good deal of tension and excitement at the time. Austria had annexed Bosnia and Herzegovina, and the Russian capital was in an uproar about it.

We arrived just as dawn was breaking; the Neva gleamed silver-grey; as we passed over the bridge, a dark gloomy building with towers and ramparts loomed up before us — the Peter and Paul Fortress, the prison for political offenders. The Nevsky Prospect stretched into the distance, with the Admiralty Tower at one end of it. Little *droshkies* tore along the streets. If a man and a woman were in one together, he would hold her about the waist, without any *arrière-pensée*, but simply to keep her from being thrown out.

On the first evening we dined in the big *Myedvyed* restaurant.[94] Two days before a very exciting scene had taken place here. A grand-duke had had dinner with a little actress and had offered her a thousand rubles if she would take off her clothes and walk through the big room naked. A thousand rubles was a lot of money, and besides it was dangerous to displease a grand-duke. The little actress slipped behind a screen, removed her clothing and began to walk naked through the restaurant. The guests were outraged, but they dared not say anything; they knew that the instigator of the affair was a grand-duke. The actress walked embarrassed among the tables, until a waiter had the presence of mind to throw a table cloth over her and get her to withdraw behind the screen again. The little actress fled from the restaurant; not so the grand-duke.

***

At that time a terrible epidemic of cholera was raging in St. Petersburg, there were kettles of disinfectant in all the streets, innumerable hearses rattled by, and huge posters forbade, in the name of the Czar, the drinking of water from the Neva. At first it felt very uncanny, but one quickly got used to it. It was more difficult to get used to the tense atmosphere which enveloped the whole city. The revolution of 1905 had been suppressed with much bloodshed, but even the most dyed-in-the-wool reactionaries knew well that they had only won a breathing spell. The universal feeling was that "In ten or twelve years it will break out again." These people already foresaw their downfall even then; their ferocity sprang from deadly fear. Everything was dangerous. Every book, every word, even colours. An Austrian vaudeville troupe was playing at the Summer Theatre; their last number was the then new Apache dance. When the dancers, a man and a woman, appeared on the stage a chill swept over the house, you could almost hear the people hold their breath: both dancers were dressed in flaming red. All chatter stopped. You were no longer aware of the strong perfume Russian women wear — there was a smell of horror. Wide-eyed, the audience stared at the stage, and although it was summer, the women drew their cloaks closer about their shoulders.

"That's the revolution dancing on your heads," I whispered to my husband, and he replied: "Will you be still!" But his eyes, too, were fastened spellbound on the red figures dancing wildly on the stage.

When the dancers went off there was a deathlike silence. Not a hand moved. Then the high society of St. Petersburg drew a deep breath, and returned, its limbs still quaking slightly, to its usual elegant life.

***

In other European capitals wealth and poverty, the well-to-do parts of town and the working class sections are kept strictly separate from one another; in St. Petersburg, in contrast, everything was thrown together. Next to an elegant palace there was often a wretched low wooden hut, next to a de luxe restaurant a dirty pub.

Summer was not the best season in St. Petersburg. "Society" had for the most part gone off to country estates or summer resorts. Nevertheless at the big restaurant on the "Islands" the display of luxury, of women in *décolleté* almost to the navel, of quantities of priceless jewels was astounding. Mixed in among all that were traders from Nizhny Novgorod and other cities inland, big, burly, bearded, dirty men who came into the restaurant in high boots and riding breeches, drank heavily, made a lot of noise, shouted a lot, spat with abandon on the floor, and left the waiter a hundred ruble tip. In the evenings on the "Islands" a band of Russian Gypsies played music that is even more furious and rousing than that of the Hungarian Gypsies. And here too the white nights lent to the scene an air of unreality — the whole thing felt like a dress rehearsal in a theatre lit by daylight, not like the last act of a tragedy advancing slowly but surely toward its end.

It was not only countless hearses that rolled over the wood-paved streets of St. Petersburg; a far more sinister impression was created by police wagons escorted by mounted soldiers, or in the midst of a crowd two men handcuffed together, accompanied by policemen on either side.

"Political types," said my husband as I stopped in the street to stare at two very young boys being led away in this manner. No one showed any concern. It would have been too dangerous to utter a word of pity.

Just as the conversation at teas and dinners in other cities is about tennis matches and who is getting engaged to whom, here it was about "conspiracies." Here one had been uncovered, there a whole nest of conspirators had been eliminated. In Krasnoye Syelo,[95] in Peterhof[96] the police had "suspicious" characters under observation. The breeding ground of all evil was Finland, and the Secret Police was not doing a very good job any more; the Duma[97] was a disaster for the country. The ground was already quaking in Russia at that time, but the foreign diplomats did not notice it. They encountered the same affable, well-bred men here as in Paris or Rome; at most they thought that the

Minister of Foreign Affairs was too clever by half and that the *Novoye Vremya*[98] was a despicable nationalist propaganda rag.

"You haven't the slightest idea of the way things really are and the mood of the people," I remarked — with my then customary arrogance — to Count Berchtold,[99] the Austrian ambassador, next to whom I was seated at a dinner. "Why do you only frequent drawing rooms? I advise you to visit the districts where the workers live."

"Oh, but please, dear Baroness — that wouldn't do at all. That would be taken very badly here. Anyway, I have no interest in the internal politics of this country. I have a hard enough time of it as it is." He complained about the hostility with which Austria was regarded, about the heavy responsibilities he bore.

"Every day I read Bismarck's *Thoughts and Reminiscences*. That is my Bible. One always learns something new from it."

But the wife of a Russian minister said to me with a fine ironical smile: "A charming man, the Austrian ambassador. An excellent *causeur*. And he knows so much about the Pre-Raphaelites!"

***

The ambassador gave a dinner in my honour, as a former compatriot.

"I am inviting the Germans for you. They are nice people. And the Englishman who was once at the same post you were. He would like to see you. A likeable fellow, Nicholson."

Sir Arthur Nicholson had changed very little. He was still the good diplomat to whom no one was too insignificant to be pumped for information. After dinner he led me into a corner and began a regular cross-examination about the Germans in the Baltic provinces. Were they loyal subjects of the Czar or were their sympathies entirely with Germany? In case of war should Russia fear treachery in the Baltic provinces? What were the relations between the population and the barons?

A strange feeling of uneasiness came over me. When one is subjected to questioning like that, one is obliged to lie. Something odd now happened to me: I firmly believed I was lying when I told him of the absolute loyalty of the Baltic barons to the Czar — but what I told him was in fact the pure truth. It had been too long since I had stopped moving in diplomatic circles.

***

It was unbearably hot in St. Petersburg, and my husband sent me to Peterhof, an old residence of the Czars. The great park, laid out in the manner of Versailles, with many fountains, sloped down to the sea. There were pretty villas in all the most beautiful parts of the place. Everything was well tended, clean, un-Russian.

We were frequent guests in the house of General Keller,[100] and when the great *smotr* (parade) was about to be held, he said to me: "Bring your Austrian friends along with you. The ambassador also, if you like." The blond Russian giant looked at me with a smile — of the kind we in Austria call a *Malefizlächeln* [a malicious smile]; but I did not notice anything and thought only that he was most obliging.

Count Berchtold came to the *smotr*; he saw regiment after regiment march and ride by. The Cossacks performed equestrian feats; their shaggy little horses were trained like dogs, they could be made to do anything. Artillery exercises followed. The Austrian ambassador was standing near me; he grew more and more wide-eyed, and there was a tense look on his face. Finally he whispered to me with a sigh: "My God, how those Russians can shoot! I never would have thought it of them! No — how those Russians can shoot!"

The whole *smotr* seemed to make a deep impression on him. He became silent and meditative.

A few years later, however, that day on the great dusty plain had apparently faded from his memory; he had forgotten "how those Russians can shoot."

Visit

That autumn my father, who had been in Japan and China, crossed with the Trans-Siberian into Russia to visit us. For the first few days he thought everything was wonderful. He went about the estate with my husband, offered him bits of "good" advice, which fortunately for the estate were not followed, and declared that a simple healthy life in the country had always been his ideal.

On the third day he was already very discontented because there was no mail. (The mail had to be fetched from the station, and when my husband did not expect any important business letters we often went five or six days without mail.) Furthermore he wanted to go to a barber's for a shave and was horrified to learn that the nearest one was three hours away.

"One shouldn't exaggerate the benefits of country life," he remarked somewhat mournfully.

He had planned to stay three weeks, and he did; but he was probably never in his entire life as utterly bored as during those three weeks.

We took him to visit other estates, but that did not turn out to be of much help.

"Tell me," he asked angrily after one of those visits, "are there no pretty women at all in this damned country? How can the men stand it?"

Every dinner was a catastrophe. My father would try a bit of the food and become more and more depressed.

"You always were a barbarian in culinary matters, dear child — but how can one eat such awful stuff!"

He declared that he would starve to death here and walked gloomily about the vegetable garden, digging up onions, which, according to him, were the only edible thing we had to offer. Then he had the groom bring him cookies from the nearest village. Whenever I went into his room I found him sitting there, bored to death, behind a five-days-old newspaper, nibbling cookies.

He also found himself in an annoying dilemma. Without my having said a word to him, he noticed how hard life in the Baltics was for me. So, not wanting to excite longings in me, he decided not to talk to me about the real wide world outside. If, on occasion, he let himself go and spoke disparagingly about our way of life, he would stop all of a sudden, horrified, and change his tune: "You always wanted to live in the country. All this is great for you. Just see to it that there is an heir soon. Then you'll be completely happy."

Everyday matters

My husband was as little aware as the other great landowners of an enormous contradiction in their lives.

On the one hand, luxury: innumerable servants, riding and carriage horses, vast sums spent on hunting, old wines, and food. And on the other, a total lack of all the little things that make life attractive. Drawing-rooms in which the truly quite beautiful old furniture was covered with dark rep — so that the dirt would not show so much, bathrooms with no windows and no running water. (In any case, the custom was to take only one "general bath" a week.) No books, no magazines — or at most: *Sport im Bild*[101] and, once in a while, *Die Woche*.[102]

Their passionate devotion to all things German made these people look on foreign cultures with disdain. Young girls, out of patriotism, did not learn Russian, and being able to speak good French or English was almost immoral. In general, it was not good form to be educated — that was left to the "literati."

All this was easier to accept in the old than in the young people. A few of the old gentlemen were — in a primitive way — *grands seigneurs*, who had been transplanted from another century into the age of the telephone and the telegraph. The telephone and the telegraph were in any case used mainly for the entertainment of the landowners' wives. Telegrams were received at the county seat by fat Fräulein Paulson, who would telephone the message to the estate; the same method was used to send a telegram. If a telegram contained an interesting item of news Fräulein Paulson telephoned the various estates: "Did you know that Fräulein v. Y. has become engaged?" or "Baron X. has become a father." Once I sent my mother a telegram to Japan for her birthday. It was in English, which Fräulein Paulson did not understand, and half an hour later my mother-in-law rang me: "Is someone ill at your place? Did you send a telegram to Japan?"

There were two railway stations near us — that is to say, one was thirty, the other seventy kilometers away. The little train that stopped at the closest one made fifteen kilometers an hour and in winter regularly got stuck in the snow. According to one story, it once ran off the rails, but neither the engineer nor the passengers noticed the difference. Still, speed itself is a relative matter. Once we went to a cattle market and took our head drover with us. He was a man of about forty, and he had never been on a train before. As we boarded the train, he already looked dubious, and when the train stopped at the first station, he came to our compartment, pale, his knees trembling, and said, almost in tears: "I won't go any further, *gnädiger Herr*. Not even if you fire me this minute. The little devil runs like a mad thing, and there's bound to be an accident. One ought not to tempt God like this."

In spite of all our assurances he got out and walked the whole of the long way back.

Even my father-in-law preferred driving twenty hours in a carriage to riding in the train, albeit for a different reason. "I will not travel in the same conveyance with the common herd." Nor would he drive with fewer than four horses, and in general he preferred six. His carriage raced along; Jan, the coachman, continually threatened with the prospect of being dismissed because he was thin (and a "gentleman's coachman" should be fat), drove like the very devil.

Gradually automobiles appeared, but they could not move very fast on the bad roads and continually had to stop to allow frightened horses and scarcely less frightened peasants to pass.

A charming story was told about one of the old landowners. His nephew had bought an automobile, and the old gentleman let himself be talked into taking a drive in it. The speed pleased him, and when he got out he went up to the driver with a friendly smile and in the palm of his hand offered him a lump of sugar. It was his custom to do this with his horses when they made good time.

***

A trip to town was always an exciting affair, for the train ran only every twenty-four hours. If you missed it, you had to take the post coach, which almost broke your bones. The Balts, who would let their coachmen wait for hours in the bitterest winter cold — the horses were always well covered — could not get used to the idea that they had to be punctual. When we went to town it was always the same story: "Hurry up. We'll miss the train."

"I still have to shave."

"There isn't time. Come along."

Then my husband would go to the telephone and ring the stationmaster: "Herr Wilms, I am taking the train. We shall be a little late. Please see to it that we don't miss it."

"Certainly, Herr Baron."

And so indeed, when we arrived at the station half an hour late, there was the train patiently waiting for us, and Herr Wilms received us with a broad smile. Each year my husband made him a present of a cow.

***

Cows played an important role on the estate. They lived far better than the workers, and if anything went wrong with *them*, the weather was never too bad to fetch the vet. I was a little afraid of the cows and kept out of their way; only the yard where the calves were raised appealed to me. The little creatures were soft and gentle and came to know one. But that too had its dark side; if one of the calves with which I had made friends was slaughtered, I would eat no meat for days. This greatly irritated my husband to whom it was "stupid sentimentality."

Twice a year Herr Meischtke, the cattle dealer, a little red-headed Jew, came to the estate. Sometimes he came in a carriage and four, sometimes with two horses, now and then with one, and once, indeed, on foot. But he recovered from every one of his business failures, and managed to swim up to the surface again. As soon as he had enquired about our health and asked if there was still no son and heir, the trading and haggling would begin. Herr Meischtke had nothing to teach my husband in this regard; the one was as crafty as the other. My love of truth was outraged — how can one, as an aristocrat, try to pass off inferior goods on a poor man who has to struggle so hard to earn his living? I made a face and then finally burst out: "Don't buy that cow, Herr Meischtke. It has been sick for months and will not get any fatter!"

From that day on, the moment Herr Meischtke arrived at the farm he always asked: "Where is the *gnädige* Frau Baroness? The *gnädige* Frau Baroness is a good business woman; she should be here when we strike our deal."

My husband had his revenge when I tried to sell my gelding, Charmant, to one of his friends for a very good price. The deal was almost closed when he asked in a friendly way: "Did my wife tell you that the gelding limps as soon as it strikes pavement?"

When the visitor had gone, without having bought Charmant, I reproached my husband bitterly.

"The fellow has so much money! And when I think of the way you always try to get the better of poor Herr Meischtke!"

"One does not cheat one's equals," he replied sternly.

The "Russian soul"

An Austrian relative went home after spending two weeks with us and raved in all the salons about the "unfathomable soul of the Russian people." She had met two Russians: the excise officer who came at regular intervals to check on the brewery, and the judge from the closest county seat. For us, neither the excise officer, Alexander Tichonovitch, nor Judge Vladimir Stepanovitch was in the least unfathomable; nor in the matter of their souls was there much to remark. Alexander Tichonovitch always announced his arrival the day before — it would have been unpleasant for all if he had had to discover an irregularity in the brewery.

"Is there enough *Astchistchinoye* (vodka)?" asked my husband hanging up the telephone receiver. "Alexander Tichonovitch is coming tomorrow."

He drove up in the forenoon. Hearty greetings all around; I sputtered a few words in broken Russian and led him to breakfast in the dining-room. His little eyes shone as they glanced over the table. He sat down and drank clear, colourless spirits out of a water glass. As far as the effect was concerned, he might just as well have drunk water. He spent two hours in this way. Then he went with me to the paddock; he was a great horse fancier.

At luncheon he again drank quantities, and over coffee poured down one liqueur after another. His grey face did not become in the least flushed; he only talked a little more volubly, and his little grey eyes had a moist gleam. At last, at about five o'clock he said lazily: "Really I must go to the brewery now, but I'll be back for tea."

I looked at him affectionately. "Alexander Tichonovitch, I should so like to make schnapps, but I haven't any alcohol."

"Ah, what a good *Hausfrau*!" he cried enthusiastically. "What a dear, noble soul, always thinking of her guests! She shall make schnapps, the dear Baroness, she shall indeed."

And so, although it was strictly forbidden to take alcohol from the brewery, he came back from his inspection with three enormous bottles of "ninety degrees." Sometimes he came back from the brewery with a wrinkled brow and a troubled expression on his face. On such occasions, my husband would tell me in the evening: "Poor Alexander

Tichonovitch, he again has so many worries. His wife is not well, and his son's education costs so much. He told me all about his troubles."

In our brewery everything was always in order.

Vladimir Stepanovitch was a different type, tall and thin with the face of a hungry wolf. He came every year for a week to go hunting; it was advisable, in order to be prepared for any eventuality, to be sure to stay on good terms with him. As a passionate Russian he actually hated Germans, but he loved hunting more than anything. He was an exceptionally fine shot, and no wonder, for he was invited to hunt on all the estates in the neighbourhood.

It was not altogether impossible to touch his judicial heart; you had only to find the right "words." How my rather taciturn husband managed to do this, I once saw for myself. We were at the horse fair at Fellin and were just about to have dinner when my husband was called to the telephone. He came back half laughing; yet at the same time irritated: "Can you imagine, Kubias Tönnison (the foreman) is being sent to Siberia!"

"What? Why?"

"Yes, our estate manager just telephoned. The *uriadnik* has reported Tönnison. Yesterday when they were weeding in the potato field Tönnison said to the workers: 'Do your work well. There will be war next year with the Germans, and then we'll have a revolution, and the land will belong to us.' Today the gendarmes came and took Kubias to O. Tomorrow morning he will be sent on."

"The *uriadnik* only did that because Tönnison stole his girlfriend from him. What are you going to do?"

"Nothing."

"But poor Tönnison!"

"Poor Tönnison is a rotten apple, and if he says things like that he has it coming to him."

There was no getting around my husband with sentimental arguments; the only way to reach him was through his feudal feelings and his strong sense of being German.

"But you are not going to let that miserable *uriadnik* take away one of your best workers! It was an impudence on his part to go ahead with this without first informing you."

"That is true."

"And surely you're not going to let a miserable *Russian* judge tell you how to manage the estate. All this is a lot less about Tönnison than about your authority."

My husband got up. "I am going to telephone Vladimir Stepanovitch."

He was angry when he came back. "Impossible to get anywhere with that stupid fool. He says we can't talk about such serious matters over the telephone."

"You see how that Russian is snapping his fingers at you."

My husband laughed: "I know very well what your aim is. I don't care about Kubias, but I won't let Vladimir Stepanovitch get the better of me. Tönnison is to be taken away at four in the morning. We just have time. Get changed, quickly. We are going to O."

The last train had left long before; we made the first part of the trip with our own horses, the last by post-coach. It was pouring cats and dogs, a howling autumn wind was blowing. The post-coach rocked from side to side on the road like a ship in rough seas, but I was too worked up to notice it.

"Tell him we won't invite him to hunt again if he doesn't release Kubias."

"That won't be enough."

"I'll chip in two hundred rubles myself."

"It will cost five."

"All right. I'll pay half."

At four o'clock in the morning we arrived in O. Vladimir Stepanovitch was awakened, and disappeared into his study with my husband.

Half an hour later the two men emerged, looking very pleased.

"An unfortunate error, Germinia Viktorovna," said the judge amiably. "I'm so sorry you have had to make this long journey in the middle of the night. The *uriadnik* lied to me shamefully. He shall hear from me; it's unpardonable to arrest an innocent man."

He turned to my husband.

"Tönnison can go back with you, if you like." We shook hands with the judge.

"Come to our place next week for some hunting, Vladimir Stepanovitch," I said affably. "We haven't seen you in such a long time."

"Thank you. With pleasure."

When the carriage at last got under way with the liberated Tönnison on the box, my husband made a face: "These fellows are getting to be absolutely shameless. That little joke cost me seven hundred. But I'll be taking Tönnison in hand myself now."

The one who came off worst in the whole affair was the *uriadnik*. Three days later, as punishment for his bare-faced lie he was transferred to a less desirable post. In his place came a fat friendly man whose age was a safeguard against any mix-up with women, and who was interested only in crimes against property.

Not all functionaries made as high demands as Vladimir Stepanovitch — sometimes one got off for very little. Once, coming home from Reval, I sat alone smoking in a "non-smoking" compartment. A conductor appeared, called my attention to the "no smoking" sign and went away.

After a little while, assuming that he would not come back, I lighted another cigarette, only to be caught again by the conductor. This time he spoke more sternly and said something about a fine.

He came back a third time and found me again with a lighted cigarette. Very dignified, raising himself to his full height, every inch the inexorable *tchinovnik*, he closed the door behind him and came over to me. "It is forbidden…"

The devil got into me. I held out my cigarette case to him: "Do you smoke?"

The conductor was speechless. Words stuck in his throat. But a moment later he was sitting opposite me, grinning, and praising the quality of my cigarettes. In the course of the ten-hour train ride, he came many times to my compartment and smoked my cigarettes. "So long as I am here," he declared, "you will not get into trouble for smoking."

"Crazy" ideas

I had now been three years in the Baltic provinces. My husband's friends and acquaintances shared, to a certain extent, the view of our workers: the woman is not only an Austrian; she is totally mad. It was so easy to come by a reputation for madness; it was enough to ask a guest: "At what time would you like to take your bath?" A look of astonishment; then the outraged response: "Do you find me so dirty that you have to offer me a bath?" Finally, a slight shaking of the head. I had been forgiven similar faux-pas: the *décolleté* dress at dinner, the little silk candle-shades on the dining-table lights, even the Paris skirts which came down only to my ankles. But my political position, my conviction, bordering on insanity, that an Estonian worker deserves the same respect as a Baltic baron was unpardonable. And who would ever have dreamed of asking a Baltic nobleman to sit down to dinner with an Estonian veterinarian?

One of our most frequent guests was a Baron Wolff; he was a wild fellow, the type of the born lansquenet. He had served six months for firing a load of buckshot into the behind of a postillion who was not driving fast enough. Before that, he had fought on the side of the Boers in the Transvaal. He was an even more accomplished drinker than Alexander Tichonovitch, and in his hip-pocket he carried a loaded Browning which he whipped out on the slightest provocation. Along with that he was uncannily, almost pathologically arrogant. On one occasion, he had come to us again to go hunting on the estate, when by a stroke of misfortune we were obliged to call in the veterinarian in the morning to attend to a thoroughbred dam in labour.

"The veterinarian can't eat with us today," my husband declared. "Wolff would get up and leave the table if you expected that much of him."

"The veterinarian is better educated and far nicer than all of you put together. If he doesn't eat with you then I won't either."

"Be reasonable, for goodness' sake. You know that at the very best Wolff would only be rude to the man."

"But if I get him to be polite?"

"Your speeches about the people won't go down well with him."

"I shan't make any speeches," I promised.

"Do as you like, but I won't have any scenes at the table, do you understand? And my guest is not to be offended."

I went to our guest.

"Baron Wolff, is it true that you will not sit down to eat at the same table with the veterinarian?"

"Naturally, with that filthy Estonian, certainly not!"

I gave the "Baltic nobleman" a searching look. "You come to see us almost every month, Baron Wolff. Have I ever refused to sit down to table with you?"

The Baltic baron was speechless.

"Don't you think," I said smiling amiably, "that if I condescend to sit down to table with a lowly baron, you might be happy sitting with the veterinarian?"

Strangely enough this argument seemed to hit home. The luncheon passed off peacefully and merrily, in spite of the veterinarian's presence. It is true that Baron Wolff later said to my husband: "If I had a wife like yours, I would see to it that she got shipped off to Siberia as soon as possible."

Later I lost the Baron's friendship for good, and his visits became more infrequent. He was a wild anti-Semite, and could spend hours badmouthing the Jews. That irritated me. My father had brought me the first edition of the Semi-Gotha[103] in order to show me that I had a Jewish relative — Saint Ignatius Loyola,[104] whose cousin was an ancestress of mine on my mother's side. (This edition was subsequently suppressed because the Romanoffs were in it too.) To my great delight, I discovered that the great-grandmother of the Jew-hating Baron Wolff was a Jewish woman. So the next time the Baron came to visit us I placed the Semi-Gotha, with the section about his family underlined in red, on the night table in the guest room. From that day on, he absolutely could not stand me.

"On the gentle art of making enemies"

My father sent me Whistler's book, *On the Gentle Art of Making Enemies*[105] and wrote: "Actually you have no need of this. Still, you might just discover a way of making yourself disliked in it that you hadn't thought of before."

I don't want to boast, but in this art — for as long as I lived in the Baltic provinces — I was more than a match for Whistler.

What was one to do, after all, when small-pox broke out among the workers on my father-in-law's estate and not a thing was done to combat the epidemic?

"The seventh child died today in one of the families," my mother-in-law telephoned to tell me. She was a pious Protestant and an exemplary mother.

"Have you had your people vaccinated?"

"No, Doctor Hasenjäger is away and father will not call another doctor, but God will help."

My mother-in-law had once asked me, "Do you Catholics also have the commandments: thou shalt not steal, thou shalt not kill, thou shalt not commit adultery?" and I had answered: "On the contrary: our faith exhorts us to do all those things." Consequently, she was not in the least surprised that the Catholic woman had more faith in vaccination than in God. What was more surprising was that the Catholic woman translated her faith into action by ringing up Vladimir Stepanovitch.

"Vladimir Stepanovitch, people are dying like flies of small-pox on the W. estate. This is criminal. See to it that a doctor is sent out there at once to vaccinate the workers. Otherwise, I shall telegraph the Governor. Yes, certainly, you should feel free to say who demanded this."

The Governor was like God to these people, and the crazy Austrian woman was capable of anything. The doctor appeared on my father-in-law's estate, accompanied by two gendarmes, and the workers were vaccinated along with their wives and children.

To tell the truth, mass vaccination of this kind was not such a simple matter, as I had to learn for myself when I insisted that it be done on our estate. All our people were summoned, I bared my arm, and the doctor approached with his needle, so that everyone might see that there was absolutely nothing to be afraid of. Yet in spite of this, the women were terror-stricken and started to weep, and one of the workers, a fellow as strong as an ox, fell down in a dead faint after witnessing the "operation." He collapsed right into my arms, and almost bowled me over. The blacksmith's wife took her three children, fled into the forest, and was not seen again until five days later.

My husband was triumphant: "Now you see that it's impossible to get anywhere with this herd."

"Because no one teaches them anything. Let me build a school, then you'll see soon enough. We have about a hundred children here. Please let me set up a school; I will pay the teacher."

I was pregnant at the time; at last there was the prospect of an heir; and my husband was in a gentle mood.

"Very well, but on one condition — the wealthy peasants in the neighbourhood must pay a part of the cost. See if you can persuade them."

Did anyone ever succeed in persuading a wealthy peasant to do anything? I did not, at any rate. They scratched behind their ears and announced unanimously: "We don't want a school. When children get a bit of education, they go off to the city and don't want to work on the land any more. No, we won't pay anything."

That was the end of the school project. It was the last public improvement plan my husband showed at least some willingness to co-operate on. A few months later his hopes for a son were dashed for the second time; and after a serious operation, I was nothing more than a fragile woman with eccentric ideas, in need of constant care, good for nothing.

Marriage and politics

Things had now come to such a pass that my husband and I were no longer good-humouredly scornful of each other's opinions or hopeful of bringing the other around to our own position. When the mail bag arrived whoever opened it handed the other his newspaper with the fire-tongs so as not to dirty his hands on it.

More and more frequently I heard the words: "I will not allow such a thing to be said in my house!"

"Where am I to speak the truth, then? Among strangers? I must have a neutral spot somewhere where I can speak as I wish."

I became obsessed by the idea of a "neutral" spot. Finally I bought a wood near the house from my husband with the intention of being "the master" there at least. Yet even this fell short of achieving my goals. If my husband was out riding, he would give it a wide berth whenever he knew I was there, and even when he did enter it on one occasion, I was more preoccupied with the threat of the venomous snakes that inhabited it than with starting a discussion.

Had it not been for politics we might have got along quite well together; I had become so attached to country life that I loved even the silence and solitude of the winters. My husband for his part forgave my "eternal reading" and "stupid obsession with culture" and no longer hoped to make "a real Baltic housewife" out of me. But the conversation always veered towards politics, and scarcely a day passed without our getting into a "purely political" row.

I experienced the worst of all of these on the way home from my parents-in-law's estate. The newspapers had arrived during dinner, bearing news of a failed attempt on the life of the king of Italy.[106] All evening I had listened patiently to repeated expressions of indignation at the "villainous" anarchists and had held my tongue. But family dinners rarely put one in a good mood. When at last we were in the sleigh going home and my husband began to speak again of the assassination attempt, I lost patience: "Stop, please, I implore you. I prefer the man who tried to do that to all of you. He risked something for the sake of his convictions."

"Be quiet!"

"I can say what I like. I am truly sorry that the attempt failed." (I was in no way a supporter of individual acts of "terror"; equally, I was not going to allow myself to be terrorized.)

"I will not permit you to say such things in my presence, do you understand?"

"I am more than sorry that the attempt failed."

"Joseph!" my husband called out to the driver. "Stop!"

The coachman obeyed. My husband took me gently in his arms and carefully lifted me out of the sleigh.

"Drive on."

There I was with my convictions and my anger, standing in the deep snow in low, open shoes and an evening dress with a long train under my fur coat, with nothing to do but walk the still considerable distance home in the darkness. Such incidents did not make me more favorably disposed toward reactionaries and autocrats.

The "business" with Sviderski

There were hours when we stared at one another like two mistrustful animals, each one of us thinking, in despair: "The other means well enough. If I only treated him with more understanding, he would really be a very good person. But it's impossible to penetrate the wall of prejudices he has built up around himself."

My husband discovered a curious explanation for my convictions. "You only side with the mob out of cowardice. You believe it will soon come to power, and you think that by siding with it now you will be all right when that happens. Strange, because you are not a coward in any other respect."

I justified myself. "You know I am not afraid. Just remember the affair with Sviderski."

The "affair with Sviderski" was one of the high spots of my life and had earned me high praise from the male members of the family. Sviderski, the new manager of the estate, was an unbearable, brutal East Prussian who beat the workers and was always telling everyone that his sister was married to a baron. Between us there was bitter enmity; I dubbed him *Sigasax* (German swine), and soon that is what all the workers called him. One afternoon when I was alone in the house, I heard a shot, and a moment later the cook came running in to me. "Oh my God, Sviderski is blind drunk; he is standing in the kitchen shooting with his Browning."

Crack — a second shot, and then a third.

The cook was weeping: "What shall we do, *gnädige Frau*, for God's sake, what shall we do?"

"No one is to go into the kitchen. I shall go down to him myself."

"No, no, he will shoot the *gnädige Frau* dead."

I was much too furious with Sigasax to feel any dread. In the hall I took down a riding whip — what I expected to do with a whip against a revolver, I do not know — and ran to the kitchen. There stood Sigasax near the door, grinning idiotically. He raised his big Browning and aimed at me.

I shall probably be dead in a moment, I said to myself, but then a saving thought flashed through my brain: the fellow is a Prussian, has seen service, has the military in his bones, and he is too drunk to know who is standing in front of him. In as military a tone as possible I yelled: "Right about face! Forward, March!"

He was a Prussian of the true Wilhelminian school. His body stiffened, and he came to attention. Then he marched past me, as though I were a sergeant-major, through the other kitchen door into the open. With military commands I drove him across the court into his room where I locked him up. My husband laughed so much over my clever idea that he quite forgot to send Sigasax away. It was only months later that I managed to get rid of him.

Freedom from care

A great deal of alcohol was consumed in the Baltic provinces. In winter the work days were short, and the workers drowned out the boredom of their dreary homes with schnapps. The steward in charge of our dairy-farm, a responsible, hardworking man, got drunk four times a year. On those occasions he filled the milk-wagon with empty cans, hitched up two horses, and galloped over the whole estate. The cans rattled about making an infernal din, while the steward sat on the box with a blissful expression on his face, singing at the top of his voice, and driving the horses as hard as he could. The god of drunkards was good to him. Nothing ever happened either to him or to his horses; only milk cans strewn along the road marked the path taken by the cart.

The Estonian peasants were not satisfied with schnapps; they were drawn to a more deadly drink: ether. At the pharmacy in the county seat you could get anything you wanted — ether, cocaine, morphine — without a prescription. The estates purchased medicaments in large, wholesale quantities. In our huge medicine cabinet there was enough poison to send the whole estate to a better world. There were dreary days when I would stand in front of the shelf where the morphine and hypodermic needles were stored and have to call on every ounce of willpower I possessed, in order to resist the temptation to make my life easier with the help of these dangerous remedies. The ether-drinkers one ran into did not shout and stagger about like the brandy-drinkers. They had fixed expressions and seemed totally oblivious of their surroundings; this made a far more disturbing impression than ordinary drunkenness. It was heart-rending to see human beings destroying themselves in this manner.

The Baltic barons drank quite as much as their "vassals," but — with the exception of certain notorious drinkers — only on special occasions. On many of the estates there was only milk on the table when the family was alone. (The water was undrinkable.) At dinners and hunts, however, most of the "bearers of culture" got roaring drunk. The next day the salons looked like the scene of a battle. In the mahogany table-leaves there were huge holes burnt by cigars, sofa cushions with their stomachs ripped open lay all around, broken glass was everywhere. My piano was completely out of tune, one of the guests having poured a whole bottle of wine on the strings. In the circles in which I had formerly lived it was unheard of for men to get drunk in the presence of women — the worst that ever happened was that a Hungarian diplomat became sentimental and paid court more passionately than decorum allowed to some pretty woman or other, or sadly announced that nobody loved him. But here the men were frequently blind drunk, and their ever so moral wives thought nothing of it. "Our poor menfolk, they have so many worries with the farms. They have to relax once in a while."

When they went into "town" they amused themselves in the same primitive and uncivilized manner as the merchants from Nizhny Novgorod, for whom they had such disdain. The women stayed irreproachably with relatives and saw to it that there was herring and mineral water to deal with the inevitable hangover of their menfolk. I was the first respectable woman in Livland[107] to get the men to take her along with them to a honky-tonk.

The superflous bunch of keys

The Estonian peasant and worker was a good sort, intelligent, industrious, upright, a good friend and an equally good enemy. The dishonesty of the people was not an inborn trait; they were poorly paid, their working conditions were harsh — they were obliged to steal.

"I tell you, dear child," my mother-in-law often said to me, "that will not do. You must lock up the sugar and marmalade. You know well enough that the servants steal like ravens."

"Not at my house."

And that was not an exaggeration. After having made life miserable for myself during the first few months by continually leaving the enormous bunch of keys around, I tried another method. I called the servants together and in bad Estonian but with much emotion made them a fine speech, in which I told them that they were to feel at home in my house and that they should live as well as I did. If they wanted something they were to tell me, and as good friends do not secretly take things from each other, I begged them not to either.

The people looked at me in astonishment, and then there was general hand-shaking. So I was able to rest easy, lay aside forever the hated keys, and proudly tell my neighbours: "At my house nothing is stolen."

Hatred in the land

There was something even more exciting in Dorpat than the honky-tonk — a visit to the book-seller. Old Herr Krüger, a German from Germany proper, had taken me straight to his heart; the fact that I was his best customer may well have strengthened his affection for me. I spent long hours browsing among his books, generally in the forenoon when the shop was empty. As soon as the clerks had gone to lunch, he would give me a knowing smile and then roll down the iron shutter in front of the shop. A candle was lighted, and like two conspirators we tiptoed down into the cellar, one part of which was separated from the rest by an iron door. Herr Krüger looked around nervously, then pulled away the boxes piled before the iron door, took a key out of his pocket, opened the door without making a sound, and led me into the dangerous space where "forbidden" books were kept. A strange assortment. Stepniak,[108] Kropotkin,[109] Kennan's work on Siberia,[110] Rütten & Loening's series on "Society",[111] works by Sombart and Bebel.[112] Any one of these books would have been sufficient to send Herr Krüger to Siberia. Down here in the cellar, in the infectious atmosphere of forbidden writings, a change came over the old man. He no longer spoke in the third person; he did not say: "Here is a book which might interest the Baroness," but: "Look at this, this is an interesting work, but the people here don't understand anything. They are barbarians." Then, to his heart's content, he would vent his contempt for the barons, the reactionaries, the whole country. In his damp, musty book catacomb the respectable little old man became a revolutionary. Here all his hatred of the arrogant aristocracy, all the anger he had had to keep bottled up for months, spilled out. For a brief moment, down there in the cellar of his book shop, he was a free man.

Such sudden transformations were not unusual. I studied Russian with a young Estonian girl who had graduated from the Russian Gymnasium. Her brother had been exiled to Siberia after the 1905

Revolution, and her father, a small farmer, was still being subjected by the police to repeated house searches and other forms of harassment. At first Linda Must was distant and reserved. She gave me my hour and never spoke a word that did not pertain to the Russian lesson. Slowly I managed to gain her confidence and later even her friendship. She let herself be persuaded to stay for tea after the lesson was over. I was happy to have some one with whom I could talk openly. Linda was a pretty girl, lively and clever. Once we were chatting happily of a hundred different things, when in astonishment I noticed that a change had come over my little friend. She was again sitting up stiffly, her face quite expressionless, as though she had put on a mask, and her eyes were cold and hard. In the doorway of the salon stood my husband — the enemy, the aristocrat. For as long as he was there, not a word was to be got out of her. An oppressive, icy atmosphere of hatred filled the entire room.

Friends

This hatred of the landlords smouldered throughout the whole land, suppressed, but ready to break out at any moment. The Baltic barons, unabashed fighting men and rowdies, did not mind at all being surrounded by enemies; it added zest to their primitive *joie de vivre*. Besides, they despised their opponents and were convinced that they would always be able to handle them. I, in contrast, was depressed by my awareness of the general hostility, though I personally was never an object of it. The workers on our estate felt that for some reason or other the "foreign baroness" was on their side; they liked me, and they were good to me. The herdsmen neglected the other animals so as to take special care of my sheep. When I let the cook persuade me that it was possible to cross a hen with a pheasant the forester caught me a beautiful pheasant cock and the foreman planted a whole wood in the chicken run so that the pheasant would feel at home. The crossing did not work out, for although the hens were willing the pheasant refused to perform his marital functions. The wood, however, flourished in the chicken run and was a source of much happiness to me, as a sign that the people of whom I was genuinely fond did not look upon me too as an enemy.

The workers, male and female alike, never lost an opportunity of demonstrating their friendship for me. I remember a certain potato harvest; my husband had gone off to hunt and I was to see to it that none of the potatoes were stolen. I was ashamed to stand idly in the fields among all the people working, and so I worked along with them as best I could. Now and again a worker came up to me and, using the familiar "du" form they used among themselves, said: "Don't tire yourself out. The basket is too heavy for you, don't lift it." And when it began to get cool, one of the workers suddenly stepped up holding my leather jacket; without a word he had run to the house, half an hour away, to fetch the jacket for me." Our lady is not to catch cold." The good fellow was most bewildered when I suddenly began to cry because I was so touched by his goodness.

I also think back upon one gloomy winter evening, when after a nasty scene with my husband I lost my head and ran wildly out into the snow. I had no idea where I was going, I only wanted to get away, far away — perhaps I would freeze to death, and then everything would be all right.

My husband, who knew how much I feared the cold, thought: "She will come back as soon as she gets cold," and sat down calmly at his desk. The house servants were of another opinion, however. They set out with lanterns to hunt for me.

I ran into the forest, where the snow was very deep. I was dead tired; I sat down on the ground and tried to go to sleep — that was the easiest way to freeze to death. In the distance I heard voices calling: "*Praua! Praua!* (Lady!) Where are you?" But I let them call; I did not want to go back. I was beginning to be overcome by a pleasant weariness. How good it would be to go to sleep, to forget everything, and never be sad again. I felt my eyes closing.

Someone shook me awake. Standing above me, a lantern in her hand, was Kaje, the washerwoman, who could hold her own with any man when it came to drinking and fighting. Her face, hard as if carved out of wood, beamed with joy because she had at last found me.

"Come back at once."

"I don't want to, Kaje. Go away and let me die."

She laughed. "Nonsense!" Then she picked me up like a child, placed me on her shoulders, and carried me back to the house, scolding me all the way, but now and again interjecting gently in her hoarse, boozy voice:

"You poor child! You poor child!"

I had dreamed of helping these people to a better, easier life, and now I was for them a "poor child" who needed to be helped and cared for.

A worker's holiday

There came a broiling hot summer. The fields dried up, clover and grass turned yellow. The sky was a relentless blue. Sometimes a little cloud would pass overhead and all eyes would be turned upward: Will it bring rain? The land was dying of thirst: the cows dragged themselves feebly around the parched meadows; all night long you could hear the mournful sound of an accordion; the fear of a crop failure lay heavy in the air. Now and again a hot breeze rose and drove clouds of smoke up as far as the house. A forest was on fire! Anyone driving through the country would come across veritable oceans of flame. The forests burned like match-wood, giant trees fell crashing to the ground, and for miles around there was a smell of smoke and soot. The horses were afraid and raced like mad past the flaming torches that had once been trees.

On St. John's Eve, the summer solstice, other fires burned. This one night was the workers' lupanar — in an honourable sense. On this one night in the entire year all class distinctions were erased. The festivities took place in a large clearing not far from the house. There were rivers of schnapps and beer. No one could refuse to drink when invited. A worker came up with his glass: "Drink, Praua, to your health and mine and to the harvest!" Before the celebration of St. John's Eve I used to take lots of aspirin for I had discovered that this was a way of forestalling the effects of the alcohol. St. John's Eve was the only time when I did not take pleasure in the friendship of the workers. At one of the fires a certain Kubias was reciting a long poem of his own composition about an Estonian who left his home and went to a foreign land. There were thirty stanzas to the poem, and Kubias stopped at the end of each one to ask me if I liked it. At other fires, the game was to leap over them. The women laughed: "Our lady is not a real woman, she can leap like a young girl." They came up to me. "What about that son, dear lady? It is really time now. But you are a gypsy, and gallop about the fields on a horse. You are a good woman; we would like you to give us a son for the estate."

I glanced nervously at my husband. He too wanted a son; I had gradually become in his sight the most useless creature in the world — a woman who cannot have children.

At another spot I was seized by the workers, lifted up high and tossed through the air to another group. This was a most respectful act, a proof of their friendship, but it was not particularly pleasant. The people were accustomed to their own hefty women and did not reckon with my lightness; they threw me much higher than they expected, and I was happy when I landed in the arms of the second group without mishap.

Still, it was a beautiful night; people forgot their enmity; the red moon lit up happy faces; and the workers, masters for one night, were friendly and full of good will.

Female harvesters and colonists

At harvest time female workers came over from the Island of Moon.[113] They wore red kerchiefs on their heads and were strong-willed women, who did not let themselves be pushed around. But each one of them could do the work of two men.

The Moon girls had a house to themselves and set great store by cleanliness and neatness. They were always dissatisfied with everything, but the most tyrannical landlords yielded to their demands in all matters. These girls were extremely chaste, and no man was allowed into their house. In the evenings they walked about in pairs, like wandering poppies with dark red heads.

In the autumn Russian women were brought in for the potato harvest. The moment they saw me, they would again ask: "Have you a son now? What, not yet? Well, why haven't you a son?" They would scold me, sit down on the ground near me, and give me all sorts of good tips to help me finally have a child.

The Russian women were the despair of the manager and the foremen. They would work very industriously for a certain time and then all sit down in the field and sing songs. No amount of scolding or threats affected them. Not until they had had their fill of singing would they return to work.

The German colonists who were being hired on many of the estates were dangerous competition for the Estonian workers. One autumn my father-in-law too decided to employ German colonists. Stocky, sturdy peasant types with long blond and red beards, they arrived with their whole kit and caboodle. Strangely enough these Swabian peasants, who for generations had only married among themselves and still spoke in Swabian dialect, were very Jewish in appearance. The colonists were not packed together in some hole like the Estonian "herd of animals." They were given decent, clean accommodations; they also got better pay and more allowances.

"It is a real pleasure all the same," my father-in-law opined, "to deal with people who speak our own language and who have honesty written all over their faces."

And my mother-in-law chimed in enthusiastically: "They are so God-fearing, they have asked me to read a sermon to them every Sunday and sing hymns with them."

"Isn't the service for the 'common herd' good enough for them?" I asked spitefully.

In the various Lutheran churches scattered widely over the countryside there were in fact two services on Sunday — one, very early in the morning, for the "people" and one, later in the morning, for "gentlefolk." No "common" person was permitted to attend the latter. I myself once saw the sexton shut the door of the church in the face of an old peasant woman who had the audacity to want to attend the "gentlefolk's" service.

On Sundays the colonists streamed into the big salon. They asked for a "nice, long sermon" and could not get enough of hymns; they always had to sing "just one more."

"There is something really touching about the piety of these simple people," said my father-in-law, who was not easily touched.

"What about their work?" I inquired somewhat indelicately. I did not like these cunning peasant types with their nauseating religious zeal.

"They haven't got used to things yet. But you'll see — as soon as they feel more at home they'll get twice as much done as the Estonians."

The labour contracts were, as a rule, for one year. For that entire period, a worker did not have the right to leave the job and equally the landlord did not really have the right to fire a worker, though that stipulation was not taken too seriously. As wages were paid half-yearly in cash, it was impossible for a worker to leave. The German colonists were craftier than the Estonians; they insisted on being paid monthly. When winter came all those good people, except for one tall, thin, red-haired fellow, cleared out without saying a word, in the dead of night. The following morning their houses stood empty, and my father-in-law was left to manage as best he could. I was triumphant, for with much effort I had kept my husband from hiring colonists and so taking the bread out of the mouths of our Estonian workers, and he had finally agreed to wait and see "how the folk at W. turn out"

The "one faithful colonist," tall red-haired Ulrich, now became an important person on the W. estate. My father-in-law made him assistant manager and trusted him blindly; my mother-in-law gave a long sermon every Sunday for him alone, and then all the other members of the family had to come and sing hymns with him. Being of "another faith," I was generally excused from this domestic religious service, though I "went along" with it when my two youngest brothers-in-law were at home. With them it was always possible to get something amusing going. We agreed to come to the service if we were permitted to select the hymns. So one fine day, to the horror of the God-fearing Ulrich, we sang a Moravian hymn which I had discovered in an old scrap book, and which — among other beautiful verses — contained the following:

> I am an evil carrion, A wicked child of sin, Whose sins like Jewish usuries Consume themselves within. Lord take this sinful dog to You, Throw out the bone of grace, And bring this poor benighted one Unto Your Heavenly place.

As it turned out, red-haired Ulrich was indeed himself, in the depths of his heart, a child of sin. Just before the half-yearly pay-day my father-in-law sent him to the nearest town to pick up the money for the wages — a very considerable sum — at the bank. Ulrich disappeared with the money, leaving no trace. My mother-in-law warned me over the telephone: "When you come to see us on Sunday, dear child, please don't ask father about the 'last of the Mohicans'; he is certain to fly into a rage."

No more German colonists were given employment on the W. estate.

A father-in-law's ways

My father-in-law held fast to the old German principle: "I am master in my own house." The whole family, even his grown sons, trembled before him. He was a handsome, unbelievably young-looking man, a first-rate horseman and hunter, and thoroughly convinced of his likeness to God. If anyone contradicted him he flew into a rage. Since his twenty-first year when he had married and come into possession of the estate, his will had been law.

As a child I had been so afraid of my mother that merely hearing her step was enough to make my knees shake; I understood a child's fear. But that grown men should tremble before another man I could not comprehend. So it happened that in his fifty-second year, for the first time in his life, the universally feared and detested master of W. encountered an individual who dared to contradict him, who would not allow herself to be roared at, and who — when it came to the "explosion" so much feared by all the others — was capable of being every bit as disagreeable as himself. At first his astonishment was boundless. He would stare at me as though he thought I had lost my mind, then he would roar louder than ever: "If I were your husband I should beat you to a pulp."

"If you were my husband I should either have murdered you a long time ago, or else you would have learned how to behave like a gentleman."

"You forget that I am your husband's father."

"The poor fellow can't be blamed for that."

"When I speak, you are to hold your tongue!"

"Can you explain to me why I should?"

The "explosion" would drag on. My poor mother-in-law would sit trembling in the next room. There would be an anxious expression on my husband's face, but my small sisters-in-law would have a hard time concealing their glee.

The battle would end mostly with my father-in-law's saying, "It's impossible to get anywhere with you" and leaving the room.

Strangely enough, in spite of everything, he felt a certain fondness for me, mixed with fear. He was the only one who did not reproach me continually for being childless. In the two last years we almost never quarelled, and in a weak moment he once admitted, "It is impossible to get the better of that thin little woman."

A weary summer

The all-powerful tyrant did not know that at that very time I had come to a point at which the Baltic provinces and life itself had just about done with me. I was ill a lot of the time, could no longer ride or swim or take long walks, spent half the day lying on a chaise-longue, and had ample time to think about things.

The thoughts that went through my mind were not particularly happy ones. I knew very well that my whole life was a betrayal of the cause in which I believed — in which, in fact, I believed more strongly the more I observed the injustice and oppression all around me. As a decent, self-respecting human being, I had to go away, begin a new life, work, serve the movement. But I was so tired that I longed only for rest, and I was afraid of the difficulties and the cares of an independent life, for which I felt I was quite unprepared.

My mother came on a visit and said: "I really don't see how you can live in such primitive, inelegant surroundings." But when I compared my existence and my surroundings with those of our workers I was ashamed and could not understand how it was possible for me to act so much against my conscience.

My little friend Linda had gone to St. Petersburg; everyone I came in contact with had different convictions from mine. What could I hope to achieve all alone against all of them?

Somewhere far away, there was a larger world where people were fighting for justice, but here I lay in the garden under the tall pines, reading, knitting warm clothes for the workers' children, and thinking as the sun went down behind the mournful silver willows: the end of another useless day. Will there ever be anything but useless days in my life?

My poor husband was pleased that I had become "quiet and gentle"; but he could not understand why my buoyant good spirits had so completely disappeared. Still, a gentle, boring wife was better than a merry, loud-mouthed one.

What I remember of these last two summers is above all the great silence. The little flower garden that I had laid out on the model of an old Italian convent garden was filled with the scent of roses; through the silver leaves of the willows the vast wheat fields were visible, bathed in a golden glow; the house gleamed white in the sunlight; and the dogs lay in the shade near my deckchair snapping lazily at the flies. Never before had I loved the house, the garden, the whole wonderfully beautiful estate as I did now that I was telling myself: I have to give it up, I can't allow myself to live off the labour of others any longer. But my cowardice was always finding a way out, a reason to delay: I was ill, I was tired, I would be incapable of doing anything constructive. Not yet. Just a few more months, another year of ease and security.

A murder

As summer drew to a close, a great anxiety came over the entire countryside. All sorts of strange things had been happening. One peasant's barn was burned down, another found his cows dead in the meadow one morning. "Revolutionary" activities were clearly not involved, because the big landlords were unscathed; the mysterious evil had not touched them. Those affected were certain peasants who had a "bad reputation," and who were said to have belonged, years ago, to a band of house burglars.

One beautiful summer night there was loud knocking at the heavy house door, which was locked. My husband opened it, and on the steps stood a woman weeping, the wife of a tenant who lived about ten minutes away from us: "My husband has been murdered! A half an hour ago. Some one knocked at the door, and when he went to open it he was shot in the head with a bullet. It killed him at once."

Murder, a murder in the still of the summer night, and only a short distance from us. My husband took his revolver.

"Telephone at once to Vladimir Stepanovitch, and have him send the gendarmes. And telephone to Fellin for the police bloodhound. Have the groom saddle the horses at once and get the peasants out to help with the man-hunt. Are you afraid?"

"No."

"Then go down to the river. He might have tried to escape that way. Is your revolver loaded?"

"Yes."

"If you catch sight of the fellow down there, try to hit him in the leg. Don't aim too high. I'll be along in a few minutes."

Standing at my post by the river was not exactly reassuring. In the bright moonlight the bushes cast strange shadows which moved like living beings, and the branches cracked and creaked. I drew Jacko, the setter, close to me. We stood there motionless. Let the man please not come this way. He is a murderer, that's true, but to shoot at a human being! And anyway, I'm such a bad shot, I'm bound to hit him in the stomach instead of the leg.

At last one of the foremen, armed with a shot-gun, took over from me. The entire farm was awake now; figures rose up everywhere out of the shadows. The men were furious, totally intent on capturing the murderer, while the women moaned, frightened to death. The last to show up was the fat *uriadnik* who came over from the next farm. Half asleep, he declared that it was a mean trick to commit a murder in the middle of the night and frighten people out of their sleep. My husband distributed guns to the men and sent them out in different directions. Then the horrific gave way to the prosaic.

"Have the cook make coffee and butter some bread so that the peasants can have something to eat. And put some schnapps on ice for the captain of the gendarmerie."

Gradually silence again settled over the farm. Down in the little hut, which was visible from the upper stories of the house, lay a dead man, and somewhere not very far from us, the murderer was trying to get away. The moon leered mockingly, and in the east the sky was beginning to be coloured pink.

Clip, clop — the sound of hoofs on the highway. Strange hard knockings like the approach of a threatening fate. The pack in the kennels began to howl. A command shouted in Russian, and the gendarmes came to a halt in front of the house.

The captain declared that he could do nothing until the police dog arrived, and sat down to eat his breakfast in comfort. In the yard the horses champed at the bit, and the young workgirls joked around with the gendarmes until the big bell sounded the call to work.

A loud murmur of voices, the sound of heavy steps; the peasants are coming. I looked out of the window; it is a scene from the Peasant War. That is how "Poor Konrad"[114] might have marched his men out. At their head an old white-haired peasant with a scythe in his hand; following him, peasants armed with ancient flint-locks, axes and flails, sickles, and heavy oak clubs. Faces twisted in anger, raised, threatening fists: "We'll tear the fellow to bits."

Breakfast calmed them slightly, but they would not wait for the police dog. They divided up into four troops and marched off again.

At last the police captain had his fill of coffee and bread and butter; he began to drink schnapps and eat herring. Then the sound of rolling wheels; the Doberman arrived in a little peasant cart, escorted on both sides by mounted gendarmes, like a prisoner.

The other gendarmes came out; the dog was led away ahead of them all to the hut of the murdered man. (As in a detective story, the murderer had dropped his leather belt in front of the hut.)

The dog sniffed about for a while, then picked up the scent. He raced like mad across a great swampy meadow and plunged into the pine wood that lay along the highway. The gendarmes, my husband, and some armed men from the estate followed him.

It was as though a a pack of hounds had been set loose on the trail of a hare. Somewhere a human being was trying to get away, creeping low behind bushes, anxiously avoiding every open space, wading across brooks to wipe out his tracks. Behind him the dog, the gendarmes, the furious peasants — a man hunt.

About noontime a peasant from the neighbourhood rode up and asked to speak to me alone.

"I have just received a threatening letter. Probably from the murderer. He is threatening to set fire to my farm. Phone the police in O. for me, and tell them to send me two gendarmes."

"You can phone yourself."

"No chance. He also threatens to shoot me or anyone else who informs the police. You phone."

I gathered that the peasant would rather have me be shot than himself, and so I phoned.

In the afternoon the Russian examining magistrate arrived, an innocent-looking, still quite young man with a round face and round eyes behind spectacles. There was nothing about him that corresponded in the least to my idea of an examining magistrate; he chatted away innocently and amiably and drank unbelievable quantities of tea.

Slowly the peasants came home; they had not found the murderer.

The hearing

Darkness began to fall and the endless day gradually drew towards evening. A gendarme rode up to the house and announced to the magistrate in a military manner: "We have him. He was about four hours from the estate. We found him in a pasture. He was running around a hay-stack like a madman."

The expression on the magistrate's face changed. His round eyes lit up behind the glasses. He wet his lips with his tongue and took on the look of a cat that has just spied a mouse.

"When will he be here?" he asked.

"In about an hour."

"Have him sent in to me at once."

"At your service, your honour."

The magistrate smiled amiably at me. "Now you will soon see me at work, Germinia Viktorovna."

He walked through all the rooms to choose the one best suited to his "work."

"The Baron's study will be best." He arranged the table lamp. "I shall sit here, and we'll put the fellow over there in the light."

The posse returned; chained between two gendarmes was a pale frightened little man who seemed anything but a murderer. The gendarmes had found no weapons on him. The magistrate did not give him time to draw a breath. The prisoner was taken immediately into the study and seated on a stool directly in the brilliant light of the desk lamp. The magistrate leaned back in his arm-chair. Nothing was to be seen of his entire face except the lenses of his spectacles, which reflected the light from the lamp.

Then the hearing began.

At first the prisoner protested his innocence; he had indeed heard the shot; but he had been on the scene by accident. The murderer had met him and forced him to go with him. Yes, he knew who the murderer was, but he did not dare tell his name.

Questions rained on him like hail-stones. Every statement he made was dissected, torn to pieces, twisted this way and that. A plump, threatening finger shot out of the shadow. The magistrate's voice was sharp as a knife and cold as ice. From time to time he asked in an almost friendly tone: "Ah, so that was how it happened, eh? I see — ee — ee."

Then suddenly his round head seemed to roll out of the dark like a ball straight towards the accused man, the spectacles flashed, and the dreadful cold voice drawled: "You are lying."

Somewhere behind the drawn curtains silence and peace lay over the fields, somewhere people fought honourably with the same weapons, but here one man was boring a screw into the brain of another, boring deeper and deeper and smiling as he did it.

The prisoner became entangled in contradictions; he began to stammer; sweat ran down his face; his hands trembled. Once he pleaded: "Water."

I got up at once, but a gesture from the judge kept me back. "Not now, Germinia Viktorovna. Later, after he has confessed, he may have anything he likes."

My hands were trembling too, and there was perspiration on my forehead. Vainly I tried to tell myself: "The man is a nasty murderer. He shot some one who had been one of his friends; he doesn't deserve better." Yet I wanted to hurl myself at that perfectly functioning machine, the examining magistrate, and force it to shut up.

After a two-hour hearing the little Estonian peasant confessed to a murder — which, as it afterwards turned out, he had not committed. He could no longer stand the torture. If that judge had questioned me in the same way I would also have confessed to the murder.

At last the prisoner was allowed to eat and drink. Then he was put in the cart and taken by the gendarmes to O.

The investigating magistrate was a well-bred gentleman. As we left the study he asked with an amiable smile: "May I brush up a little before dinner, Germinia Viktorovna? This kind of work is pretty exhausting."

As the police cart with the prisoner in it was being driven out of the yard, the magistrate, combed, washed, and smelling of Russian eau de Cologne, sat down to table with a good appetite and spoke enthusiastically about St. Petersburg.

Traitors

The eerie atmosphere surrounding the tenant's hut since the murder had not yet begun to wear off when there was a murder in St. Petersburg that sent shock waves through the whole country.

It was early autumn. We were having dinner at the estate of the Czar's Grand Master of the Horse. The master of the manor himself was in St. Petersburg, but his American wife and two pretty daughters were spending the summer on the estate.

Dinners in the autumn were always jollier than at other times; the harvest, including the potatoes, was in, the hunting season was approaching, and the estate owners were contented and good-humoured. During this particular dinner the lady of the house was called to the telephone — a telegram from St. Petersburg.

She came back pale and extremely upset: "Stolypin[115] has been assassinated!"

For a moment a deep silence fell upon the table. People looked at each other; their faces pale and strained. No one uttered a word, but everyone had the same thought: "The first sign. It's breaking out again!"

Then one of the old estate owners laughed loudly. The sound of his voice had a strange ring as it broke the complete silence.

"We will defend ourselves as we did the first time!" he cried out resolutely. "We will soon bring the herd to order!"

I glanced at the men sitting around the table — yes, they will defend themselves, they will fight to the last, they are not afraid, they are almost glad to engage their enemy. They are men who have somehow been transported from the time of the robber barons to our present age, fighting is their element. And they will fight well because they have an unshakable belief in their cause, and because there are no "traitors" among them. In the first revolution there had been two "traitors," two elderly sisters who had always sympathized with the workers on the land. When the revolution broke out they raised the red flag over their castle and supplied the revolutionaries with guns. The Baltic barons seized the castle in "self-defence," and the two women were brought to the nearest village. Here, on the village square, in front of everybody, their clothes were torn off and they were whipped with riding whips on their bare behinds. These were "social equals"; one can imagine how the other prisoners fared, those who were not social equals.

While the others at the table were again beginning to engage in conversation, I kept thinking of the two "traitresses." They had been typical Baltic women, modest and prudish. For as long as they did not know what was going to happen to them they had kept their courage up; but then they had broken down and, weeping, implored their captors: "Shoot us, but do not inflict this shame on us!"

My husband who was sitting across from me, gave me a long, searching glance; he knew on which side I would stand if it "broke out again."

After dinner the men divided up into small groups. They spoke of "arming," "self-defence," "headquarters" and of how at the first sign of insurrection the women and children would be sent abroad, so that they, the men, "could have a free hand."

But the assassination of the minister was only a flash of summer lightning. The land became quiet once more, and routine existence again took its course.

***

The following autumn the doctor ordered me to Davos. For months I had been running a fever and coughing. The climate was now too much for me.

I wept desperately when I bade farewell to the familiar house and all the dogs; I knew that I should never see them again, I knew that fate had at last come to my aid by tearing me away from my life of comfort and security. The first step had been taken for me; if I did not go on now it would be sheer cowardice.

Manoeuvers

As the train approached the Russian border, lots of soldiers were to be seen, nothing but soldiers, on foot, on horseback, with artillery. Uniforms everywhere. It created an uncanny feeling in the autumn peacefulness, caused a tightness around the heart. My God, what are all those soldiers doing so close to the border? The country is at peace after all. Can the rumour that the Czar has decided to avert the imminent danger of a new revolution by starting a war be true?

The sun sank beneath the horizon, the fields were bathed in red, blood seemed to be streaming over them, and in the distance — the soldiers. Was it war? "

"Manoeuvers" said a fellow traveller reassuringly, and in Berlin, when I ran across a friend, who was the German Empress's head chamberlain, and asked: "For God's sake, tell me the truth, will there be a war?", he too laughed reassuringly: "Of course not. Don't get all worked up. Germany doesn't want war. And Russia knows very well that she can't get the better of us."

He spent his entire life at court, he certainly had to know. But for months I was pursued by that vision of Russian uniforms near the frontier.

When the Austrian crown prince was assassinated I saw these uniforms again, and the sunset and the plain with the blood streaming over it, the blood of innocent men who, on both sides, did not know what they were dying for.

When the war broke out, I was still in Davos. It was not difficult for me to be "unpatriotic." I knew the various peoples engaged in the war too well — there was hardly one of them of which I did not have some blood in my veins — to give any one of them preference over the others. All I could see was poor devils being driven pointlessly and uselessly to death; I also saw the one thing that is capable of putting an end to imperialist wars.

Being a "Russian" woman in Austria

I was to have one more glimpse of my old world before I took the leap into the new one.

In 1915 my parents were in Karlsbad, and my father who had not been able to recover from a heart attack was very eager to see me. But how was I, the citizen of an "enemy" country,[116] to travel to Austria?

"Write to Count Berchtold," my father wrote me. "He will give you an entry permit for sure."

In the old Austria everything was possible. I received the permit, and now I had the experience of being the "Russian woman" in Austria after having been for so long the "Austrian woman" in Russia.

"Just be sure not to make pacifist speeches," acquaintances in Davos warned me, and my father also wrote: "For God's sake don't talk about bomb-throwing, and don't say that all governments should be hanged."

Thus provided with good advice I entered "enemy territory."

On the border the first "incident" occurred. Among other books I had brought a volume of Shakespeare and Plato's *Republic*. The two books aroused the suspicion of the customs officers.

"That's an Englishman," said one of them eyeing the Shakespeare fiercely. "You can't take that over the border with you."

I remarked demurely that the author had been dead for several hundred years.

"He is an Englishman all the same. You can't take the book with you."

Plato was examined from every angle; the officials were not sure about him. Finally one of them discovered the publisher's name: Georg Müller, Munich. He turned to his assistant: "The writer is a Bavarian. She can take that book with her."

The volume of Shakespeare was left on the Swiss side of the frontier; the "Bavarian" Plato was allowed to accompany me into Austria.

Shortly after we had passed the border a detective came into the compartment. "Which of you is the Russian woman?"

I revealed my identity. He made me a long but friendly speech about what my conduct should be and then explained comfortingly: "I shall keep an eye on you, Countess." (Good-hearted, as Austrians can't help being, they immediately gave me back my old title.)

At the next station a Turk got on the train. The detective immediately approached the "ally," who, however, knew only Turkish and French, and so the two were unable to communicate. Then a brilliant idea came to the simple detective: the "Russian woman" certainly knew French. So the "enemy woman" acted as interpreter for the two "allies," while our fellow passengers eyed the Turk just as suspiciously as they did me.

Russian prisoners were working along the railway track. I gave them my cigarettes and spoke to them in their own language. It was moving to see the joy on their faces at hearing a few words of Russian. The friendly detective did not interfere. "I take it you're not going to do any spying," he said in a relaxed tone. "The Russians are good people, they don't give us any trouble. Did they really have to declare war on us?" The other passengers remained neutral, except for one German, a citizen of the Reich, who declared rudely: "I'll have you know, *Fräulein*, that martial law is in effect here."

There was a stirring of the old Austrian in me: "So what about it!"

From that moment on, the German punished me with his contempt. In Linz the train pulled out right under my nose; there would not be another for seven hours. The detective turned me over to an old police officer: "You've got a Russian here, but she's not dangerous."

An uncle of mine was governor of the city; I asked the police officer if I might be allowed to go and spend the hours I had to wait with him.

"So," he said good-humouredly, "Count Ch. is your uncle? Don't you see that anyone could say that? You stay right here."

"And if I go into town anyway?"

"Then we'll shoot."

"And will you also hit me?"

"What do you think? We have a reputation as good marksmen. You had better not put us to the test."

"May I at least phone my uncle?"

"No."

The old fellow was adamant; I had to stay at the station.

I had caught cold in the train and had exhausted my supply of handkerchiefs. I turned to the police officer for help. He called a porter: "Go into town and buy the lady a dozen handkerchiefs, but bring them to me first."

When the porter came back he took each one of the hideous, brightbordered handkerchiefs separately and shook it. Not until this operation was completed did I finally get them. The old officer was a friendly man and a strong opponent of the war. "The whole thing is a piece of madness," he declared. With him I could comfortably "talk pacifism." But when I said that I wanted to spend the night in Pilsen, he stiffened: "I imagine you would find the Skoda works interesting. No, you'll go only as far as Budweis. And report at once to the station master there."

I was dead tired when at about three o'clock in the morning I reached Budweis and knocked on the door of the officer on duty. A sleepy voice answered: "What is it now? Can't one have any rest at all?"

"I have to report to the station master."

"Why so?"

"I am a Russian citizen."

"What did you say you are?"

"A Russian citizen."

A very sleepy, half-dressed man came out of the door.

"What are you?"

"A Russian citizen," I repeated patiently, and held out the document signed by the Minister of Foreign Affairs.

"What are you doing here then, if you are a Russian citizen?"

I explained the object of my trip.

He grabbed the document.

"Well, why are you a Russian citizen?"

"Because I am married to a Russian."

"So? But why did you marry a Russian?"

He studied the document. "I see, Berchtold. Well then, if you were formerly an Austrian citizen... It's all right. You can go. But tomorrow you must report to the district prefect." He heaved a deep sigh, "There's not a minute's peace here. Now it's a Russian woman coming in the middle of the night. You can go now. Have a pleasant journey."

The porter I had blindly entrusted myself to in my weariness led me to a terrible inn where the wash-basins were chained to the wall and the people spoke only Czech. I wanted just one thing: a cup of tea, but the owners refused to understand me. I decided to speak Russian: either I will be arrested or I will get my tea. I had scarcely uttered the word *tchai* when the expression on the faces of the proprietor and his wife changed. I immediately became an honoured guest. I was given tea and cake and even a jug of hot water to wash with — something which certainly no other guest in that inn ever requested. The innkeeper and his wife could not do enough to show how well disposed they were towards me.

When I reported to the prefect he wrinkled his forehead: "You will have to stay here twenty-four hours, Countess. I must make inquiries at the Ministry of Foreign Affairs."

"Look, tomorrow is my father's birthday, and I do so want to be there in time for it."

He was an Austrian; and so he let me travel on without making inquiries.

***

I had been a little fearful of the patriotism of the Austrians, but in 1915 it had already faded away completely. I encountered only two patriots. One, a Frau H., the wife of the biggest candy manufacturer in Austria, came to see my mother about an "entertainment" that had been organized for the benefit of wounded soldiers. A pretty, very elegant young woman with a wonderful string of pearls about her neck. "We shall stick it out," she said enthusiastically.

After her visit my mother asked me in astonishment: "You say you're a socialist, so why were you so high and mighty with Frau H.? The poor woman was quite disconcerted."

I said nothing; mother would not have understood my explanation.

The second was a woman of the aristocracy. From her came this beautiful phrase: "And when I think of all the dead whose names are in the Gotha[117] . . . !"

***

On the way back to Switzerland I got into a difficult situation. A hotel-keeper in Innsbruck — he must have been an excellent judge of people's character — asked me to take a check made out to someone in Italy with me to Switzerland and from there send it on to a bank. He had to make a payment to an Italian business associate; the war could not last forever; and he would lose a considerable sum of money if he did not make the payment now.

I had no interest in either the hotel-keeper or his business associate, but the adventure was tempting.

"I must tell you, Countess, that you will be interned if the check is found on you," the honest hotel-keeper warned me.

"So be it. I'll take it with me." When our train reached the frontier only three people got out besides me. We had a two hour wait.

"This could turn out pretty interesting," I thought. The dangerous check was in my handbag. "With all that time for customs' examination the check is bound to be found."

A great, shaggy sheep-dog lay on the station platform. I had always been passionately fond of dogs, and so even now I forgot the danger I was in and bent down to play with the dog. He saved me from an Austrian internment camp. The officer in charge identified himself as the owner of the dog; he had brought it from Serbia. A point of connection had been found, and so I talked and talked and talked for two hours, without stopping, about dogs, war, Serbia, Russia — until at long last the train came in and we four passengers were able to board, without ever having been examined.

The old Imperial Austria disappeared into the shadows of the night, and I never saw it again.

"Zdravstvui Revolyutsia!"

Moissi[118] was giving a guest performance of *The Living Corpse* in Davos. At the end of the first act a telegram came that provoked great agitation all around: "Revolution in Russia!" The citizens of the Central Powers pricked up their ears, and the Russians fell upon each other madly. "Zdravstvui Revolyutsia!" (Hail to the Revolution!) In the second act Moissi's art was completely wasted. What did a corpse matter, alive or not, when over there in the East there was resurrection, new life! A nightmare had been lifted from the people; in the East a light had blazed up, promising peace, bread, and freedom. Revolution in Russia!

Women are child-like; I took my wedding ring from my finger and bought myself a new plain gold band to mark my marriage to the Russian Revolution. But behind the childish gesture there was a serious intent: I have remained faithful to the Revolution.

Now it was easy to take the final step, to sever the last link binding me to that useless, comfortable life. I broke with my old world and dared to leap into the new. I learned to work, to stand on my own two feet. (My husband made this easier for me by refusing, on various pretexts, to part with my dowry and my jewels even after our divorce. I had become a "class enemy" and, as a Baltic nobleman, he was not only entitled but obligated to cause me harm.) I was no longer a single individual struggling senselessly against overpowering opponents, but a tiny part of a great whole which I could serve, in however modest measure, to the best of my ability.

It had been a long road from the carefree life of a diplomat's daughter to where I stood now. Others might perhaps have covered the ground more quickly.

Behind me lay a dying world of privilege, before me a new, vital world, still, as yet, in the throes of birth.

My path had been unwittingly predicted in the Gotha. After the name of my great-grandmother in the Gotha stand three magic letters: K.P.D.,[119] meaning *Kaiserliche Palast-Dame,* Lady-in-Waiting to the Empress. I can also attach these three letters to my name, but they now stand for something very different from what they meant in the case of Empress Marie Louise's playmate.

The End.

No, the Beginning.

2. Supplement to
*The End and the Beginning**

by Hermynia Zur Mühlen

Editor's note: For a serialized republication of her memoir in the socialist women's magazine "Die Frau" (October 6, 1949 — April 20, 1950⁺) Hermynia Zur Mühlen removed the final chapter entitled "Zdravstvui Revolyutsia" in the original and substituted the following pages after "The old Imperial Austria disappeared into the shadows of the night, and I never saw it again."

This book was written twenty-two years ago. It has thus reached a respectable age — one by which many of its contemporaries have already vanished from the scene. Had it been a product of the "good old days" (which, whatever century we ascribe them to, were in all likelihood held by those who actually lived in them to be the most terrible and most dangerous of times), it would have been easy, with the help of a little make-up, to restore a certain youthfulness to it. But the history of the last two decades has made any such innocent swindle impossible.

A woman friend advised me to write a continuation of the book and I went along with her suggestion without giving the matter much thought. In order to find out whether the book still had some life in it and was more or less deserving of being sent out into the world again, I reread it for the first time since correcting the publisher's proofs. With mixed feelings, pleasure being still the strongest of them, I was able to

---

*   Reprinted in *Nebenglück: Ausgewählte Erzählungen und Feuilletons aus dem Exil von Hermynia Zur Mühlen*, ed. Deborah J. Vietor-Engländer, Eckart Früh and Ursula Seeber (Bern: Peter Lang, 2002), pp. 243–55.

Translation © Lionel Gossman, CC BY 4.0   https://doi.org/10.11647/OBP.0140.02

ascertain that, like most of my books, it had little prospect of finding a publisher, and that it was, therefore, still very much alive. I realized with far less pleasure, however, that I could no longer write a continuation of it in the same vein as that in which the final chapter had originally been written. That could be due, among other things, to the fact that until 1917 everything in my life was a personal experience and was therefore easy to portray. In contrast, the second half of my life has not been rich in purely personal experiences. The world of the impersonal has left almost no space for these, and such personal experiences as there are seem quite insignificant.

After I had made several unsuccessful attempts to earn my living by sewing, language teaching, and typing, someone suggested that I should take advantage of the knowledge of foreign languages I had acquired painlessly in my youth and use it to translate books into German. I would never have hit on this idea by myself. I had always disliked translations, and besides I did not know that translators were paid. Still, aside from my distaste for reading books in anything but their original language, the idea appealed to me. I could not remember any time when books had not been the most important and satisfying thing in my life. Add to that the fact that I had come to know the other side of life chiefly through books and that these, especially the New Testament and the novels of Turgenev, had had a very strong influence on my development. As a result, I overestimated the effectiveness of books and was thoroughly convinced that through the work of translation I might help to make the world a better place. The desire to do so seems to have been always very strong in me. I still recall the childlike megalomania that inspired me, on the eve of my fifteenth birthday, to write in my diary: "Tomorrow I shall be fifteen and I have still done nothing to improve the world." Today I must unfortunately acknowledge that a good part of my passion for improving the world has to be attributed to a very strong and still lively contrariness.

My father — I still cannot make up my mind whether he was a disillusioned idealist or a hopeless cynic — used to reduce me to despair in my youth when he would counter my admittedly excessive optimism with a bitter Spanish saying about dogs that change only their collars but otherwise remain the same. Unfortunately, having developed a passion for history books at an early age, I often had to concede that he was right, for indeed much of what I read confirmed the view he held: it was always so and, with certain modifications, will always be so. Nevertheless, with the impatient and insufferable assurance of youthful converts I believed that in a not too distant future a peaceful, better, and more just world would come about. In this unshakable conviction, I began my work as a writer.

My first substantial piece of work was a translation of the Russian anti-war novel, *The Yoke of War*, by Leonid Andreyev.*[120] This appeared in 1917, first in the feature pages of the *Neue Zürcher Zeitung* and then with the Rascher publishing firm in Zurich. At the time, this publisher was bringing out a series of anti-war books — by Andreas Latzko,[121] Leonhard Frank,[122] Henri Barbusse,[123] Rudolf Jeremias Kreutz,[124] and others. After this first translation there followed further translations of books by Upton Sinclair, Galsworthy, Zangwill and then, as the first major work of my own, the fairy-tale collection *Was Peterchens Freunde erzählen*. This work was written in Frankfurt am Main, where by 1919 my second husband and I were living.

On our arrival at the Frankfurt Railway Station, with two dogs and very little money, the red flag was flying over it, heartwarming and full of promise. When we left the same station again on April 1, 1933, once more with two dogs and very little money, the flag flying over it was the Swastika.

I knew Frankfurt well from an earlier time in my life. It had been one of my father's favourite cities. But how different the city I was now living in was from that of the past. Not only because the city itself and its inhabitants had changed so fundamentally, but because in the past we used to stop off here in order to break a journey and stayed only a few days, naturally in a good hotel. We visited the sights of the city and were in the pleasant position of going round the then famous fine stores of Frankfurt and making purchases without having first to ask anxiously: "How much does it cost?" Now, however, I was simply a tolerated individual whose bobbed hair provoked disapproval in many. Now, I belonged in that class of persons who are told, in a not particularly friendly tone of voice: "Wait" or "I don't have time today. Come back tomorrow." I had to learn, here and later on in other places too, that cities and people are quite different according as one drives through the streets or goes on foot (not by choice but of necessity).

They are not less interesting or worse, but one does get to know them better, and that does not always redound to their advantage. But that is also how it is in our relations to other people, especially in politically uncertain times, when you so often have to hear the excuse: "What can be done? We are going through a time of transition." Or, "You have to get on with your life."

And the years after 1919 were indeed, as can be seen now with the wisdom of hindsight, a time of transition. Looking back on them, we can now discern the signs that foretold the horrors to come — and we can see how easily the latter could have been avoided. But how many really wanted to recognize the signs? It was a time of slogan phrases and, if I may coin an expression, slogan thoughts — one of the most dangerous things that exist. There were those who explained that one had to let Hitler have his head and that after him would come… About what would come afterwards there was no agreement. A large part of the German people held the view, as I just said, that "one has to get on with life" and above all that "Auch Hitler wird mit Wasser kochen" ["Even Hitler will cook with water" — i.e. will have to acknowledge reality and act pragmatically — L.G.] Later the excuses were far less innocuous, and Hitler did not cook with water but with blood, and millions who had let everything happen because, after all, one needs to get on with one's life, had to die.

As I had no intention of making any concessions and as my husband, who was Jewish, was in particular danger, we seized the first opportunity to cross the frontier, with two dogs, yet again. Even if one lives a rather secluded life, after fourteen years one has acquired many friends, like-minded companions, and acquaintances, albeit their number had been shrinking noticeably, in the last years, with every passing week. At the station, where drunken hooligans were rampaging around, only two people showed up to take leave of us: a young (Christian) worker, who was later slaughtered in a concentration camp, and a young (Jewish) actor, who disappeared without trace after the Germans occupied Belgium.

I often see the troubled faces of these two young men in my mind's eye. I feel I share responsibility for their death and reproach myself with the dullness of my feelings at the time. Everything else, the entire fourteen years spent in Germany, is now shrouded for me in thick mist.

***

Every railway station in Germany had been hit by a snowstorm of pamphlets urging boycott of Jewish stores, and it was a relief when we finally crossed the bridge with the two crazy-looking Bavarian lions and got to the other side of the border. We continued to travel through the same countryside, but it looked quite different. The sky seemed more blue and the sun more golden. The first leaves were sprouting on the trees, fresh, delicate, and green. The conductor did not bark at one — not, at that time, yet — but encouraged us to go and get ourselves some coffee and cake.

In Vienna, which I had not seen for twenty-seven years, I received the same welcome as in Frankfurt. From the station we drove in a rickety taxi with an ancient driver, not to the charming little town palace, in which almost half a century before I had come into the world, but to a flea-ridden boarding-house on Alserstrasse. Still, even though I hate fleas and they love me, not even they could destroy the feelings of hope we experienced after crossing the border. (My husband was convinced that it was only thanks to the dogs that we had crossed so easily, for who could have suspected that a couple with two dogs were refugees?) Now we were driving through a city where there were no swastika banners, past people who did not have the fixed expression of the Germans on their faces but had the appearance of being real people. We had seen so many horrific things on the other side of the border that everything on this side made a deep impression on us and I immediately got the idea that the people here had to be warned. We had to write the truth about National Socialism. We had to do it day and night, when it was convenient and when it was inconvenient. Somehow we had to get the indifferent to open their eyes to the frightful truth — and to the terrible danger threatening Austria. But I was not very successful in this enterprise. Only very few newspapers — among them the *Arbeiter-Zeitung*[125] —agreed from time to time to publish an anti-Nazi short story. Most wanted humorous stories. When one features-page editor explained that he did not want anti-Nazi things and that I should bring him entertaining little sketches that would make readers split their sides laughing, I flew into such a rage, that I went home, sat down at my desk and in three weeks wrote my anti-Nazi novel *Unsere Töchter die Nazinen*. It took a good deal longer to find a publisher for it. This novel had a strange fate: every publisher who was given a copy to consider, declared he was willing to publish it — on condition that certain passages were altered or eliminated. Each one of them was bothered by something different. But I was unwilling to make the equired changes, since I believed they would give a false representation of the way things truly were. Then I took the novel to the Socialist Schiller Marmorek,[126] who with his infinite helpfulness and genuine friendship did much to make our lives easier. (In my first youthful enthusiasm for socialism, I had imagined all Socialists to be like him.) I shall always think of him with love and gratitude. He read the novel and recommended it to Julius Braunthal.[127] Braunthal did not let himself be put out by certain esthetic shortcomings, which must have marred the book from his point of view, and he agreed to publish it. Naturally, I was delighted, but our correspondence took place at the end of January 1934. February came,[128] and the manuscript disappeared without a trace. After the assassination of Dolfuss, the book was finally put out by the publishing house of Gsur,[129] without any changes, only to be banned two weeks later at the behest of Von Papen. Proceedings were taken against me, the only effect of which was that from that time on I received a monthly visit from a detective, who inquired in a friendly manner how I was getting along, said: "You haven't gotten up to anything, have you?", politely kissed my hand, and left. The good man must have been very well informed, moreover; about a month before the *Anschluß* he advised us to move to Czechoslovakia where the climate, he said, might well be healthier for us. Even after the Liberation the unfortunate little book still could not find a publisher. Although the spirit of National Socialism is by no means dead, publishers once again prefer humorous novels.

I had always loved the city of Vienna: the gentle light that somehow was able to make even ugly buildings seem beautiful, St. Stephen's Cathedral and the Church of Maria am Gestade, the Danube (when you could catch a glimpse of it), the lilacs, which bloom more beautifully here than anywhere. If I think back on it now, however, I see only strange figures and scenes — the feature-pages editor who, when the whole land already lay under the shadow of the swastika, asked me to provide him with humorous sketches that would make readers split their sides laughing; February 1934; community halls that had been destroyed; a man being carried on a stretcher to be executed; I hear a voice on the radio: "And now, ladies and gentlemen, we will play the Horst-Wessel song"; I see the first episodes of looting in the Mariahilf district of the city, but also the old driver who made the sign of the cross every time we passed a church and shook his fist at every swastika banner. He was taking us to the railway station, once again with the two dogs, on the day marked for Hitler's entry into Vienna. Perhaps it was thanks to them that we were able to drive unimpeded on the same street along which, an hour later, Hitler's grand entry parade was to pass. I can still hear the cries of *"Sieg Heil"* that poisoned the air. Now the swastika flag was flying over the Vienna railway station too and a frenzied, no longer human mass of people — the women were the most feral — was behaving even worse than the crowd in Frankfurt-am-Main.

Once again, for me, as for countless others, a world had collapsed. The personal was no longer of any interest whatsoever. I remember only a grey landscape and a grey train travelling through it, without hope, into a grey world.

***

It was late at night when we arrived in Bratislava. The town was already overflowing with refugees and we were told at the train station that there was not a room to be had anywhere. We called several acquaintances, but they were all so alarmed and suspicious that they pretended not to know us. There was nothing for it but to wait, with the two dogs, in the miserable railway station. For what exactly, we ourselves did not know. But, as always, I was convinced that something would turn up. The something soon appeared in the form of an anything but confidence-inspiring man who, for an appropriate payment, offered to find us a room. He took us to a quite remarkable hotel. The following morning, when I opened the door to the hallway a young woman came by wearing only a cross and boots and singing merrily. The detective who appeared shortly afterwards could not get over his surprise at our staying in that hotel.

He did not disclose the reasons for his surprise, but found a room for us a few days later, albeit in a hotel opposite the railway station which, rumor had it, would be immediately bombed and shelled if war were to break out. On a small hill opposite, stood a lone tree, which I immediately considered my friend. It stood quite alone there, vulnerable, helpless, destined to be struck by the first bombs. For the moment, however, it was being struck only by the first rays of the sun and by a wind out of the North. Whenever I hear the name Bratislava, I immediately see that lonely tree on the hill.

The more threatening the situation became, the more the hotel became transformed into a kind of barracks and the more the entire city took on the air of a besieged fortress. All those who could leave left and as most of the inhabitants, even the poorest, had relatives in the country, almost nobody remained behind. A city suddenly deserted has something uncanny about it, something ghostly, as though the plague has swept through it and destroyed every living thing. The stores were all closed, in the better parts of town at least; the trams were no longer running. Trenches were dug in the fields beyond, and on the Danube embankment there was no sign of life except here and there poor, frightened-looking women pushing prams and abandoned dogs with labels round their necks saying that the owner had been drafted and could someone please take care of them. The only heartening thing in those days was that most Slovaks were ready to fight against National Socialism, partly in all likelihood out of nationalist sentiment, but still, they were ready to fight. But then there was Munich, and demoralization set in.

I fell ill and the doctor insisted that I not remain in the city. We moved to Piestany, where, as luck would have it, our lodging was directly opposite the "Brown House." Piestany and its neighborhood had always been a focal point for the Hlinka movement[130] and at that very moment — Hacha[131] had already taken over the Czech government — an armed Slovak uprising broke out and was spreading rapidly. Moreover the Hlinka leader Tuka[132] had settled in Piestany, after his release from prison, as the guest of the Jewish operator of the spa, who, incidentally, had also provided accommodation free of charge for Tuka's wife while Tuka was in prison.

The villages lying within three or four kilometers of the Austrian border were occupied by the Germans. As the soldiers came in, some of the officers ostentatiously carried copies of the *Deutsche Allgemeine Zeitung*,[133] clearly intending to demonstrate that they were not Nazis. As most Slovaks still refused to speak German at that time, you could see how the Germans, time and time again, turned for help to Jews. The

SA, however, crossed over from Vienna and in broad daylight stopped Jews on the street and dragged them away. Some were able to buy their release, others disappeared without trace. At first the Slovaks would not allow Jewish women to be forced into sweeping and cleaning the streets, on the grounds that the Mother of God had been a Jewish woman, and when an old Jewish woman, who had been a Socialist, died, half the place lined up behind the coffin and the red flag. Jewish businesses were protected from looters and in the church the priest delivered a sermon against National Socialism. In contrast, dark and sinister like an embodiment of evil, the priest in the neighboring community went about only in the uniform of the Hlinka Guards, delivered wild, rabble-rousing, anti-Semitic sermons, and had Jews shut up in the cellars of his vineyard. They were released by other Slovaks. In those terrible times there were always exemplary demonstrations of simple humanity. But the border was too close and the resistance to evil, even of the good, was too weak. Within a few months, Slovakia too was a lost land, dragged into the witches' cauldron in which the Germans were brewing the ruination of a world. I tried to portray all this in my novel *Came the Stranger*. That book is really a piece of reporting and almost all the characters that appear in it are people I knew or at least observed, like the priest in SS boots and the true heroine of my novel, Marianka.[134] The events recounted in it were in part witnessed by me personally, in part told me by eyewitnesses. Let me emphasize that I *tried* to portray all this. My literary talent is not sufficient to make the reader feel the horror or to communicate the indescribable coarseness and meanness fascism unleashed in people. If it was hard for me to do so in a novel, how should I be able to do it here, in a few pages.

Friends who were more worried about our fate than we were ourselves arranged for us to get an entry permit for England. This time the journey was longer; it took us by way of Hungary, Yugoslavia, Italy, Switzerland, and France. In these incredibly beautiful summer days, the countries through which we travelled by train gave an impression of peacefulness. The corn was ripening and would soon be ready for harvesting. What kind of harvest would it be, we asked ourselves anxiously. The whole journey was a farewell to a world that was condemned to death. Our awareness of this cast a shadow over everything and made the most beautiful landscapes nightmarish. There was a quality of unreality about everything. The brilliant, flower-bedecked pastures of Yugoslavia seemed to belong to a fairy tale: everything in them was still in bloom, but within a moment a curse could fall on them and the flowers would all wither. And there was something else besides, something that concerned us personally. There was a time when we would simply get off the train whenever a village or a little town seemed especially charming and spend a few hours or even days there. Now everything was subordinated to the need for haste. "Keep going, keep going, keep going," the wheels seemed to say. The only purpose of the journey was to get to the next frontier, for today it was still open, but who was to say what would be tomorrow. And we had only transit visas, we could not stop anywhere.

We stopped off for a while — two weeks — only in Paris. The dog's papers — alas, there was only one dog now — were not in order. For me, certainly, each day that we were able to spend there was a gift. The sky arched so high over the city that one could breathe again. Wherever we went, we came upon something especially beautiful, and everything had its own particular charm. It seemed amazing that anything like this still existed. We also met up with old friends and acquaintances, who had been in Paris for some time and were already completely at home there. But then the papers came and we had to get on the road again.

After having had to hoof it in many cities where once I had been able to drive or take taxis, I had real anxiety about finding myself in London again. Hadn't I always been told by my parents that it is impossible to live in London unless you have a lot of money and that we, for instance, were not rich enough! In addition, my memory of a winter's stay in that city was of stone, stone, and more stone. For some reason I had apparently forgotten about all the beautiful parks. But when we finally arrived in London, it wasn't so bad after all. With few exceptions, the people we had to deal with were friendly and helpful; neither the police nor the authorities gave us any trouble; and we had the same rights as every Englishman. Almost nobody seemed to assume that refugee meant the same thing as thief or robber and murderer. And in the British Museum, that wonderful island of calm, that treasure-house of the mind, one was entrusted unquestioningly with the most precious books. There was also so much here that strengthened one in the conviction not, to be sure, that man is good by nature, as youthful idealists since

Rousseau's time have maintained, but that he *can* be good. The basic decency of people, unmarred by arrogance, unimpaired by cowardice, together with humor and good manners, which even the war failed to alter, seemed like a miracle. There were so many examples of it. I was most impressed by the fact that German airmen who had been shot down — and who only a few moments before had been trying to set cities on fire and destroy them — were treated no differently from their injured victims. Here they were not mistreated or murdered. In the country the farmer's wife would bring them the inevitable comforting English cup of tea and arrange for medical help even if her husband or son had to travel a long way to get hold of the nearest doctor. In a gesture that is infinitely characteristic of this land, the downed airmen would also be given cigarettes. In the city too, of course, the enemy airmen were treated like human beings. (We spent the entire period of the war in London, including the eight months when the city was being bombed virtually day and night.)

When I think back on the war years, I can barely understand those people who, as long as they were here, did their best to outdo each other in loud expressions of admiration for England and the English, but as soon as they returned to their homeland completely forgot that Hitler and his henchmen would be lords of all Europe had England not resolved, without a moment's hesitation, to continue the fight after the collapse of France. It goes without saying that they were also fighting for their own freedom and their own very existence, but because of that, they saved Europe and made amends for much of what they may have done wrong. That ought not to be so easily forgotten.

Our last stop, for now, is a small English village, odd and charming at the same time, as only English villages can be. Fourteen miles from London, it is truly the country. I could not ask for a better place to spend the time that remains to me. For years now, I have no longer been seeing the world through the eyes of some one who walks around in it, but only through my window. Still, in the country, this is not so bad. I have always been moved by the desire to see what lies on the other side of things and now, in our modest quarters it has been vouchsafed to me to do that. On the one side, through the window of my study, I see a large meadow in the middle of which there is a little cluster of holm-oaks. Three horses graze and take their rest there. A stream, which with the spring rains becomes a river and announces that fact loudly and with much beating of waves, flows by in front of the window. In spring it is alive with waterfowl of one kind and another, in summer with lovable little English rascals who wade in it and dirty their clothes to their heart's content. A steep bank rises on the other side of the stream. Many trees grow on it and in these are the nests of those strange English birds, which have something to sing about all winter long and are so tame that they come right into your room, or would do were it not for the cat.

On the other side of the house stands the monument to the fallen of the First World War. Many names are inscribed on it, heartbreakingly many names. On our way here we saw similar monuments in every village. One does not like to think how many such monuments there are in the entire country, for there are only thirty small villages in all England with no dead to mourn from the First World War. The monuments to those who fell in the Second World War will carry even more names. And the monuments to the fallen of the Third...

On moonlit nights, the monument gleams white and ghostly, a silent warning, a silent reproach. What have we done, what are we doing to combat the criminal madness that is already, once again, talking of war, provoking war? What have we done, what are we doing to awaken, finally, respect for humanity in people, to make it clear to all that other human beings are not there to be dragged off, tortured, humiliated, deprived of their freedom in every possible way — no matter what the cause in the name of which these things are done?

In this struggle, every person of good will will be needed. And it will end in victory, if all Europe, indeed the entire world is not to be enslaved.

As I write these words, a wild storm is raging, the trees are swaying and groaning, the stream is roaring louder than ever. And the clouds are scurrying across the sky. A storm of ruin swept over the world, but there are also spring storms that announce new growth and development. In these I place my hope and faith as ardently in my old age as I did in my youth. Everything can be different, everything can be made good, if only we truly will it.

And then it will not be the end that comes, but the beginning.

Radlett, early February 1950

3. Notes on Persons and Events Mentioned in the Memoir

by Lionel Gossman

1 Dehm

Properly Deym. Franz de Paula, Graf Deym von Střtež (1838–1903), a large landowner in Bohemia, was Austro-Hungarian Ambassador in London, 1883–1903. At an early stage in his own diplomatic career, Zur Mühlen's "Onkel Anton" (Christoph Anton Maria, Graf von Wydenbruck) served under him in the Legation in London, where Wydenbruck's daughter, the writer Nora Wydenbruck, was born in 1894. The family mockery of Deym suggests that the young diplomat did not get on with his chief.

He was apparently not the only one. Another diplomat, Franz, Graf Lützow, who had also served under Deym in London and had since retired from the service, had married a lady reputed to have once been the mistress of Prince Batthyány, a Hungarian residing in England, where he bred horses. To get his new wife accepted in good society, Lützow asked Deym if, as a favor, he would arrange for the ambassadress to introduce the lady in question at one of her receptions. Deym refused point blank, probably in disrespectful terms, for Lützow immediately challenged him to a duel. Apparently it did not have a fatal outcome for either party. The fall-out from the affair did not enhance Deym's reputation as a diplomat, however, since Lützow was soon writing and speaking out in England in favor of independence for the Czechs and in terms very unfavorable to the dual monarchy.

(Source: Edwin Marsch, ed., *November 1918 auf dem Ballhausplatz. Erinnerungen Ludwigs Freiherrn von Flotow* [Vienna/ Cologne/ Graz: Hermann Böhlau Nachf., 1982], p. 363).

2   Uncle

The Uncle in question, who asks the provocative question about his niece's father (i.e. his brother-in-law), is Onkel Anton (Christoph Anton Maria), the eldest son of Ferdinand, Graf (Count) von Wydenbruck, and the latter's wife — Zur Mühlen's beloved grandmother Isabella Blacker. A diplomat like his father and like Zur Mühlen's own father, Christoph Anton "first went to school in America," during the two years when Ferdinand von Wydenbruck was Emperor Franz Joseph's Envoy Extraordinary in Washington, D.C. (1865–1867) — a circumstance that resulted, in the view of his daughter, the writer Nora Wydenbruck, in his "democratic predilections" and "violent disapproval of Austrian society and its Byzantine class distinctions." (See Chapter 6 below, "Remembering Hemynia Zur Mühlen.") His diplomatic career, according to one modern scholar, was that of "a mediocrity who made little mark on his contemporaries." After stints in a subaltern position in London, as ambassador to Japan from 1893 until 1899 (not, probably a much desired or prestigious posting at the time), and as head of the Austro-Hungarian legation first in Denmark (1899–1907), then in the Netherlands (1908–1911), his "comfortably mediocre career ended as ambassador in Spain" (1911–1913). This was not his wish, however, nor is the judgment of his career a fair one, in the view of his daughter. He had been promised the post of ambassador to Washington, she recounts, and "he would have been eminently fitted for this appointment: not only had he spent part of his schooldays in the United States, he had democratic sympathies, a realistic outlook and a grasp of world politics which must have been almost unique among Austrian career diplomats." For instance, "his dispatches from Tokyo had been such that when the Russo-Japanese war broke out and an astonished world realized that the country of geishas and cherry-blossom had produced a nation to be reckoned with from a military point of view, it was murmured on the Ballhausplatz [where the Austrian Foreign Office was situated] that 'Wydenbrook had been right after all,' though previously everyone had made fun of his alarmist reports."

On his return from Madrid Onkel Anton found himself less and less at home in his native Austria. "He already had at that time a liking for solitude and a certain timidity with people," according to Zur Mühlen, "and he was finally driven to live all alone in an old castle in the country," where he died in 1917. In addition, Nora Wydenbruck writes, "in his loneliness he [had become] a sad and solitary drinker" whose "main weapons against the outside world were irony and sarcasm." Just as Zur Mühlen's paternal grandfather, Franz de Crenneville, was probably a distant model for the figure of the young heroine's great-uncle Franz in the novel *Reise durch ein Leben*, a solitary who has devoted his retirement to writing a book against the death penalty in order to make amends for the many death sentences he signed while governor of one of the provinces of the Empire, Onkel Anton was probably the model for the same heroine's great-uncle Emanuel, who, we are told, was sometimes referred to as *"der rote Graf"* [the red Count] — a solitary who likes to talk down his own class and its prejudices but who does not expect rule by the bourgeoisie or the popular masses to be any better and who thus remains socially and politically isolated and ineffectual.

(Sources: William D. Godsey, Jr., *Aristocratic Redoubt: The Austro-Hungarian Foreign Office on the Eve of the First World War* [West Lafayette, Indiana: Purdue University Press, 1999; Nora Wydenbruck, *My Two Worlds: An Autobiography* [London: Longmans, Green, 1956], quotations from pp. 3, 39–40; http://en.wikipedia.org/wiki/List_of_diplomatic_missions_of_Austria-Hungary).

3 Father

Victor, Count Folliot de Crenneville-Poutet (1847–1920), Zur Mühlen's father, was the oldest of the three sons of Franz, Count Folliot de Crenneville-Poutet (on whom see below under "Paternal Grandfather"). He had a less distinguished career than his father. After being appointed Secretary of the Austrian Legation in Washington, D.C. in 1889, he served in the consular corps as Consul-General in Tunis and in various other positions. He was the author of a small book on the island of Cyprus, *Die Insel Cypern in ihrer heutigen Gestalt, ihren ethnographischen und wirtschaftlichen Verhältnissen* (Vienna: Faesy und Frick, 1879). He married Isabella, Countess von Wydenbruck in 1882. In addition to the portrait she presents of her father in her memoir, Zur Mühlen drew a fictionalized portrait of him as the father of the young heroine of her 1932 novel *Das Riesenrad* [*The Wheel of Life*]; see "Remembering Hermynia Zur Mühlen: A Tribute" in the present volume, Chapter 6, note 8.

4 Paternal grandfather

Franz Maria Johann, Count Folliot de Crenneville-Poutet (1815–1888), Hermynia Zur Mühlen's paternal grandfather, had a distinguished career, first as a general in the Imperial Austrian army, and then, later in life, at the court of Emperor Franz Joseph, where as First Chamberlain (*Oberstkämmerer*), he oversaw the Imperial art collections.

"With the benefit of a cosmopolitan education and wide interests," he started out at age 25 as a gentleman-in-waiting (*Dienstkämmerer*) to the epileptic and severely handicapped Emperor Ferdinand I, but soon followed in the footsteps of his father, Ludwig Folliot de Crenneville — an *émigré*

French aristocrat who had become a cavalry general in the service of the Austrian Emperor — and embarked on a military career. He quickly rose to the rank of colonel and aide-de-camp of the Emperor. After Ferdinand's abdication in favor of his nephew Franz Joseph (December 1848), Crenneville took part in the Austrian campaign to quell nationalist revolts in Italy and in 1850 was appointed Governor of Livorno and commander of the Imperial forces in Tuscany. His zeal in combatting revolutionaries and supporters of Garibaldi was remarked upon in a communication from Carl von Hügel, a seasoned diplomat then serving as Austrian *chargé d'affaires* in Florence, to Foreign Minister Schwarzenberg (15 January 1850): "Livourne est la seule ville de la Toscane où la population des basses classes est animée d'un esprit d'insubordination et de révolte. Le colonel comte de Crenneville y est parfaitement à sa place et il se sert admirablement de la force que lui donne l'état de siège pour maintenir et punir les mauvaises passions et actions qui s'y montrent continuellement."

By July 1850 Crenneville had been promoted to the rank of general. During the Crimean War he was sent on a special mission to Napoleon III; in 1854 he played a leading part in putting down revolutionary unrest in Parma after the assassination of Duke Carlo III; and at the battle of Solferino (1859), at which the French and Sardinian armies under Napoleon III and Vittorio Emmanuele II defeated the Austrian army under Franz Joseph I, his horse was killed under him and he himself was wounded. For his bravery in battle, he was awarded the Cross of the Order of Leopold and soon afterwards made Privy Councillor and First Adjutant-General of the Emperor. In this capacity, he helped to carry out important reforms in the army. His strong military bearing and his forceful way of expressing his opinions, both in public and in conversation with individuals, made him enemies, however, and probably led to his being held responsible in some quarters for the army's failures in the 1866 war with Prussia. Further honours were heaped upon him. He was promoted to the rank of Field Commander (*Feldzugmeister*) and in 1867 appointed First Chamberlain. In 1876, Franz Joseph charged him with the design and execution of what has been called "an elaborate program" intended to "enhance the Emperor's prestige through glorification of Habsburg cultural achievements."

Himself the owner of a notable library and collection of medals, Crenneville set about reorganizing the Imperial collections. He had them thoroughly inventoried, oversaw their transfer to the new museum on the Ringstrasse, recruited first-rate staff for the new museum, and arranged for the preparation of catalogues and guides. One of these, *Die hervorragensten Kunstwerke der Schatzkammer des österreichischen Kaiserhauses*, received a long and glowing review in the French *Gazette des Beaux-Arts* (16ème année, 2ème période, vol. XI, pp. 209–32), in which special praise was reserved for "M. le comte Folliot de Crenneville, dont aucun des exposants français de 1873 [at the Vienna International Exhibition] n'a oublié la courtoise obligeance." In 1880–82 a two-volume facsimile edition of *Freydal: des Kaisers Maximilian I Turniere und Mummereien*, edited by Quirin von Leitner, with over 250 heliogravures, was published by Holzhausen in Vienna "unter der Leitung des K.K. Oberstkämmerers, Feldzugmeister Franz Grafen Folliot de

Crenneville." Finally, the Count initiated and supervised the publication of the *Jahrbuch der kunsthistorischen Sammlungen des allerhöchsten Kaiserhauses* (Vienna: A. Holzhausen), the first volume of which, dated 1883, was immediately hailed as a major event in the art and museum world. This annual publication has continued to appear for well over a century, albeit with a few interruptions during wartime, and to enjoy the reputation for impeccable scholarship that had been a key objective of its founder. In 1884, however, depressed by the death of his wife and of his best friend, Count Bigot de St. Quentin, Crenneville asked the Emperor for permission to retire and spent the last four years of his life working on the history and art treasures of the little lakeside city of Gmunden, where in 1867 he had acquired a villa known as "Bergschlössl."

Though we can only surmise from the published evidence that Hermynia Zur Mühlen's paternal grandfather, with all his talents, held extremely conservative political views, we do know what those of his "best friend," Karl, Count Bigot de St. Quentin, were, since Bigot chose to make them public. Like Creneville, Bigot (1805–1884) was the son of a French aristocrat who had emigrated to Austria at the time of the French Revolution. The author of several works, including the frequently republished *Von einem deutschen Soldate* (1843), he "had a highly conservative conviction of the domestic stabilizing function of the army," according to one recent scholar, and had nothing but contempt for the lower classes (*der Pöbel*) "which," he declared, "lust only after well-paid idleness, acts of violence, nights spent at the barricades, and that sanctioned debauchery that comes with the erosion of the bonds of order." Nor was the bourgeoisie spared. He scorned the self-interest allegedly motivating it as much as he scorned the greediness of the revolutionary masses. "The ideas of the people should never be permitted to follow a path that diverges from that of the upper classes," he asserted. "It should be emancipated only to the extent that is necessary at any given time, and it should never be allowed to get to the point that it itself loosens its iron collar, because, like a raging tiger, it will not stop until it is completely unfettered." The paternal grandfather of the so-called *"rote Gräfin"* [red Countess] has given posterity no reason to believe that his opinions were different from those of his "best friend."

She, however, made an attempt to redeem him, from her point of view, in her fiction. Though she could not have known him well personally (she was five years old when he died), she used him, in all likelihood, as the model for the figure referred to in the novel *Reise durch ein Leben* as "Exzellenz" — the heroine's great-uncle Franz, who, as governor of one of the provinces of the Habsburg Empire had had to sign many death sentences, and is now, in his solitary retirement, making amends for his actions by writing a massive scholarly critique of the death penalty. Zur Mühlen also attributes to this figure an old, exalted idea of what it means to be an aristocrat: "The young people today, like your father," he tells Erika, the heroine of the novel, "do not understand that they have more obligations than others. They only enjoy the privileges of rank. And that is why they are headed for ruin. For them, being a member of the aristocracy is only something that provides comfort and ease, not something that obligates them to live an honest, simple, honourable life." (*Reise durch ein Leben* [Bern and Leipzig: Gotthelf, 1933], p. 73)

(Sources: Oscar Griste in *Allgemeine deutsche Biogaphie*, 48, pp. 614–16; Erwin M. Auer in *Neue deutsche Biographie*, 5, p. 287; *Fonti per la Storia d'Italia pubblicate dall'Istituto Storico Italiano; Le Relazione diplomatiche fra l'Austria e il Granducato di Toscana, III Serie 1848–1860*, ed. Angelo Filipuzzi [Rome: Istituto Storico Italiano per l'Età Moderna e Contemporanea, 1967], vol. 2, pp. 47–48, 216, 366, 411; Erika Esau, "Imperial Cultural Policy and the Jahrbuch der kunshistorischen Sammlungen in Wien," *Journal of the History of Collections*, 8 [1996], pp. 193–200; Günther Kronenbitter, *"Krieg im Frieden." Die Führung der k.u.k. Armee und die Großmachtpolitik Österreich-Ungarns 1906–1914* [Munich: Oldenbourg, 2003], p. 125; Karl August, Graf Bigot de Saint Quentin, *Cancan eines deutschen Edelmanns* [Leipzig: F.A. Brockhaus, 1842–1845], 3 vols., vol. 1, p. 256).

5   Great-uncle

Ludwig, Count Folliot de Crenneville (1813–1876), brother of the better known Franz. He was a cavalry general, commander of the fortress in Mainz, and at one point (1861–1867) Governor of Transylvania, just before it was incorporated into Hungary. In a letter to his daughter Leontine (11 September, 1848), Metternich tells of having lunch "chez les Crenneville, à Mayence." (*Mémoires, documents et écrits divers laissés par le Prince de Metternich*, 8 vols, [Paris: Plon, 1880–1884], vol. 8, p. 294; the originals of Metternich's letters to his daughter are in French).

6   His wife

Ernestine, Gräfin (Countess) Kinsky zu Wchinitz und Tettau (b. 1827). She married Ludwig Folliot de Crenneville in 1852. Like both her brother-in-law Franz and Countess von Wydenbruck, Zur Mühlen's grandmother, she settled in the small lakeside city of Gmunden.

7   Sophie Chotek

Daughter of Bohuslav, Count Chotek von Chotkova, chief equerry at the Imperial Court, onetime Austrian envoy to Russia and Spain, and his wife Wilhelmine, Countess Kinsky zu Wchinitz und Tettau, sister of Zur Mühlen's great-aunt, Ernestine, Countess Kinsky zu Wchinitz und Tettau. As a young woman Sophie became lady-in-waiting to Archduchess Isabella of Pressburg. She met Franz Ferdinand, the heir to the Imperial throne, at a ball in Prague in 1888 and the two fell in love. When Franz Ferdinand began paying frequent visits to the Archduke and Archduchess of Pressburg, it was assumed that he was interested in one of their daughters, Marie Christine. After it finally became known that he was pursuing not Marie Christine but her mother's lady-in-waiting,

Countess Sophie was dismissed and the affair created a public scandal. The Emperor made it clear to his heir that he would not be permitted to marry Sophie. An eligible partner for a member of the royal family had to be descended from the House of Hapsburg or from one of the ruling dynasties of Europe. Archduke Franz Ferdinand, however, insisted that he would not marry anyone other than Countess Sophie. After various European monarchs intervened on Franz Ferdinand's behalf, Franz Joseph agreed in 1899 to a morganatic marriage (which meant that no child of Sophie's could succeed to the throne). He himself did not attend the wedding. Nor did Franz Ferdinand's brothers or their families. The judgment of Sophie by her aunt — Zur Mühlen's great-aunt — thus reflects the view of Sophie generally held in conservative circles. At the time about which Zur Mühlen is writing here, Countess Ernestine could not, of course, know the tragic events that were to ensue some fifteen years later.

In June 1914 the Governor of Austrian-ruled Bosnia-Herzegovina, invited Archduke Franz Ferdinand and Sophie to observe his troops on manoeuvers. Immediately after the royal couple arrived in Sarajevo a carefully planned attempt was made by a nationalist, pro-Serbian group to assassinate the Archduke. The attempt failed, but two occupants of the car behind that in which Franz Ferdinand and Sophie were travelling were seriously wounded. Later the same day, after the official welcome at the Town Hall, Franz Ferdinand expressed a desire to visit the wounded men in the hospital. It was generally agreed that such a visit was dangerous and that Sophie should stay behind, but she refused. This time, due to a driver's error, the assassination succeeded. Franz Ferdinand and Sophie were both hit and died from their wounds soon after. The stage was now set for the First World War.

These events were, of course, known to Zur Mühlen herself, writing in 1929.

8 Neue Freie Presse

The successor to and for a time rival of *Die Presse* (founded in the so-called Year of Revolutions, 1848), the *Neue Freie Presse*, launched in 1864 by two editors who had seceded from the older newspaper, represented the political and economic liberalism of the educated and cultivated upper bourgeoisie in the Austro-Hungarian Empire. Despite the early deaths (1872 and 1879) of the two founding editors, the paper continued to flourish under a new editor, Eduard Bacher, and his brilliant lead article writer, Moritz Benedikt — both from liberal Jewish families in the Czech provinces of Bohemia and Moravia. Known throughout Europe as the Austrian *Times*, the paper had a staff of over 500, including 80 foreign correspondents. It was stylish in the upper bourgeoisie to be a subscriber and the paper was often critical of the aristocracy. "In contrast to London where (even before our time) the Iron Duke bowed before Peel who was a weaver's son, the aristocracy here is sterile and sequestered," the paper declared in December 1888. "Forty years ago, Mrs. Trollope spent a winter in Vienna and was quite astonished by the caste-like separations of the various social levels. She had never met more graceful ladies than those in bankers' houses, yet these were not admitted to aristocratic circles." Though some members of the bourgeoisie "try to deny their origins," the article continued, and "are indolent in all questions of bourgeois freedom, we are not. The bourgeoisie must contend with the aristocrats, but it is sure of victory." (Quoted in Frederic Morton, *A Nevous Splendor: Vienna 1888/1889* [Boston and Toronto: Little, Brown and Company, 1979], p. 167) Nevertheless, the paper was supportive of the multi-ethnic Empire and opposed to nationalist movements in its constituent parts, though not to some increased local autonomy. At the same time it sometimes sounded a note of elegiac pessimism about the viability of the Empire in a continent overwhelmed by vehement nationalism.

9   Fremdenblatt

A daily paper published in Vienna from 1847 until 1919. From about 1852, it was virtually a mouthpiece of the government and especially of the Ministry of Foreign Affairs.

10   Grandmother

Isabella Luisa, Countess von Wydenbruck (1829–1900) was one of two daughters of St. John Blacker of Merrion Square in Dublin, a member of the Anglo-Irish gentry, a sometime British Envoy to the Court of Persia, and a lieutenant-colonel in the First Regiment of the Madras Native Army. Her mother was Welsh and her grandmother half Scottish. She and Ferdinand von Wydenbruck (1816–1878), an Austrian diplomat, were married in London in 1854. She bore him three children: Christoph Anton (b. 1856), August Wilhelm (b. 1857) and Isabella Luisa Alexandrina Maria (b. 1862), Zur Mühlen's mother. For more information about her, see Chapter 6, "Remembering Hermynia Zur Mühlen," in the present volume.

11   Moritz Benedikt

A baptized Jew from Moravia, Benedikt (1849–1920) joined the staff of the Vienna *Neue Freie Presse* as a journalist at the age of twenty-three. In 1880 he became editor-in-chief of the paper as well as its co-publisher. His lead articles were celebrated for their intelligence and wit. His liberalism was not incompatible with strong support for the multi-ethnic Empire and opposition to minority nationalist movements, including Zionism — which led in 1896 to a falling-out with Theodor Herzl, then one of the journalists who worked for him. Benedikt and his paper later became a favourite target of Karl Kraus in *Die Fackel*.

12   Great-uncle

This was Julius, Graf von Falkenhayn (1829–1899), who in 1857 married Zur Mühlen's great-aunt, Viktoria Eugenia, Countess Crenneville (1816–1900), fourth child of the original French émigré and cavalry general Ludwig Folliot de Crenneville and widow of Johann, Graf Keglevich von Buzin, her first husband. Falkenhayn was himself the son of a cavalry general and began his career in the military but then turned to managing his estates in Upper Austria. He was elected to the Upper Austrian *Landtag* or regional parliament as a representative of the conservative federalist and ultramontane party. His interest in financial questions led to the publication of two books on the finances of the Austrian state in the 1870s. In 1879 Franz Joseph appointed him Minister of Agriculture, in which capacity he served for sixteen years. He was known as an extreme conservative in politics.

13   G.

G. is the town of Gmunden on the Traunsee, a lake in the Salzkammergut, a hundred and some miles west of Vienna where Zur Mühlen's grandmother had a villa, and where other members of her family also lived or had summer homes. It is where the author of *The End and the Beginning* claims she spent the happiest years of her childhood and it is also evoked in at least two of her main fictional writings, *Das Riesenrad* and *Reise durch ein Leben*.

It was a resort much favored by the titled nobility of the German-speaking lands. Albrecht, Duke of Württenberg, had an estate there, mentioned on p. 9 of Zur Mühlen's memoir, and George V of Hanover, expelled from his kingdom, after it had been annexed by Prussia for having sided with Austria in the Austro-Prussian War of 1866, settled there with his family. Hubertus, Prinz zu Loewenstein, a Bavarian nobleman of about the same age as Zur Mühlen and subsequently a friend and ally in the fight against National Socialism, was another resident of Gmunden in his youth. "Gmunden in Upper Austria," he wrote in his Memoirs, "… a little town of about six thousand inhabitants, on the banks of a wonderful lake… was looked upon as the refuge of impoverished Austrian and German aristocrats. It used to be said that if you accidentally trod on the toe of an unknown man in the street, it was perfectly safe to say, 'I beg your pardon, my dear Count,' for you would be sure to be right." (*Conquest of the Past: An Autobiography* [Boston: Houghton Mifflin, 1938], p. 33)

Neither Zur Mühlen's grandfather, Count Franz de Crenneville, who acquired the villa known as "Bergschlössl" in Gmunden as early as 1867, nor her grandmother, Countess Isabella Luisa von Wydenbruck, who, in 1888, bought the Villa Elisabeth (so called after its previous owner, Elisabeth Franziska Maria, Archduchess of Austria, Princess of Hungary and Bohemia), appears to have been in the least impoverished before World War I, though Countess von Wydenbruck may well have lived more modestly than other members of the family. Sigmund Freud spent his first vacation in the little town in the year of Zur Mühlen's birth and wrote glowingly of it to his fiancée Martha Bernays. Artists, apparently, were as drawn to it as aristocrats — Moritz von Schwind earlier in the century and, as Zur Mühlen herself tells us, the composer Karl Goldmark, the painter Heinrich von Angeli, and the writer Peter Altenberg in the 1890s and early 1900s. Altenberg in particular wrote often and affectionately about the town, beginning with a piece about the deposed Queen Maria, the wife of George V of Hanover, in the celebrated art nouveau journal *Jugend* (16 April, 1900). The most famous historical event in the history of Gmunden — the defeat and massacre, in 1626, of "hundreds of peasants fighting for their rights and their daily bread" by the forces of Maximilian I — is adroitly evoked in Zur Mühlen's novel *Reise durch ein Leben* (the chapter entitled "Das heilige Brot," pp. 118–19; "Holy Bread" in the English translation, *A Life's Journey*, pp. 98–99]) as a social and political learning experience for the heroine.

14   Countess Szapáry

Widow of the Hungarian-born László Szapáry of Muraszombath (1831–1883), a decorated cavalry general in the Imperial Army who had fought with Radetzky's army in Italy. A favourite of both Franz Joseph and Empress Elisabeth, Szapáry died of a stroke at age 51. His widow, born Marianne, Countess Grünne in 1835, was the daughter of Carl, Count Grünne, First Adjutant-General of Franz Joseph from 1848 to 1859. She died in Gmunden in 1906.

15   Friedericke Grossmann

A popular actress of the time, Grossmann is listed among the leading living actors and actresses of Germany in Albert Ellery Berg, *The Drama, Painting, Poetry, and Song* (New York: P.F. Collier, 1884), p. 256. In her biography of her brother, Elisabeth Förster-Nietzsche tells of the philosopher's enthusiasm for the theatre and for Friederike Grossmann in particular: "He took advantage of his stay in Bonn to attend as many theatres and concerts there and in Cologne as he could possibly afford. And he was very lucky, for he heard the most famous singers and actresses of the period... He saw Seebach in a series of her most beautiful parts, and finally Friederike Grossmann in several little comedies. 'We Franconians, he writes, 'were naturally in love with her to a man, shouted her songs of an evening at the beer table, and would drink general toasts in her honour.'" (*The Life of Nietzsche by Frau Förster-Nietzsche*, transl. Anthony M. Ludovici, vol. 1: *The Young Nietzsche* [New York: Sturgis and Walton, 1912], p. 130) *Die Grille* or *The Cricket* was a popular German adaptation for the stage of George Sand's *La petite Fadette*.

Anton Prokesch von Osten, to whom Friedericke Grossmann was married, was the son of the internationally celebrated soldier, diplomat, scholar and writer of the same name (1795–1876).

16 Pauline Lucca

Born in modest circumstances in Vienna in 1841, Pauline Lucca, "the greatest singer that Germany has produced in recent times" (Albert Ellery Berg, *The Drama, Painting, Poetry, and Song* [New York: P.F. Collier, 1884], p. 256), made her debut as the Second Boy in Mozart's *Zauberflöte* at the Komische Oper. Her first major role was as Elvira in Verdi's *Ernani* in the provincial city of Olmütz in Moravia. She came to the attention of Meyerbeer who brought her to Berlin to sing Selica in *L'Africaine*, a role she repeated in London, where she enjoyed great success, returning regularly in 1863–68 and 1870–72, with a brief interruption in 1871 when she came back to Germany to nurse her husband, Baron von Rahden, who had been injured in the Franco-Prussian war. In 1868–69 she performed in Russia, and in 1872, to great acclaim, in America. From 1874 until 1889 she was a member of the Vienna Opera. Meyerbeer and Auber considered her unequalled, and the latter was so struck by her interpretation of the part of Zerline in *Fra Diavolo* that he made her a present of the pen with which he had written the opera. Her most celebrated roles were Carmen, Selica in *L'Africaine*, Zerlina in *Don Giovanni*, and Leonora in Verdi's *Trovatore*. Her Carmen, in particular, is said to have caused a sensation — "as did her appearances offstage with Bismarck: Cosima Wagner, lamenting their public familiarity, wrote: 'Such things do no honour to the Crown or to art.'" (*Oxford Dictionary of Opera*, 1992, p. 420) In 1889, she retired to Gmunden, where she gave voice lessons. She was a potential purchaser of the *Villa Elisabeth* just before it was acquired by Zur Mühlen's grandmother.

17 Fritzi Massary

Born in Vienna to Jewish parents, who encouraged her to take singing lessons, Friederike Massarik (1882–1969) got her first engagement, under her new stage name Fritzi Massary, in a minor role at the Landestheater in Linz in 1899/1900. After another similar engagement in Hamburg, she returned to Vienna to a stint, lasting until 1904, at Danzer's *Orpheum*, a summer theatre. Meantime she gave birth to a daughter — the father was Karl-Kuno Rollo, Graf von Coudenhove, whose family threatened to have him shut up in a mental institution if he dared to marry an actress — and was baptised a Protestant. While performing at the *Orpheum*, she was discovered by a Berlin theatre director and brought to the Geman capital, where she mostly performed in revues. Soon the cheeky soubrette, "the Massary," had become the idol of a generation. A major breakthrough in her career occurred in 1911, when she appeared as guest artist in Jacques Offenbach's *La Belle Hélène* at Max Reinhardt's *Künstlertheater*. In 1917 she married Max Pallenberg (1877–1934), the leading comic actor of the German stage.

Among the works created especially for her was the operetta *Die Kaiserin* (The Empress) by Leo Fall (1915). She sang the title role in Franz Lehar's *The Merry Widow* and that of Adele in Johann Strauss's *Die Fledermaus* under Bruno Walter. She had a close association with Oscar Straus, creating roles in six of his operettas, notably *Der letzte Walzer* (1920). Massary first nights were a highlight of every season in Berlin. According to her friend and mentor Alma Mahler-Werfel, the intelligence she brought to the stupidest operettas "made the impossible credible." Her recordings include excerpts from Oscar Straus's *Eine Frau, die weiß, was sie will* (*A Woman Who Knows What She Wants*), in the premiere of which she starred in 1932, and from *Madame Pompadour* by Leo Fall.

Being non-Aryan, neither she nor Pallenberg had opportunities to perform in Berlin after 1933. The couple returned to Vienna, then moved to Switzerland. Pallenberg was killed in a plane crash shortly afterwards. Finally, after a brief guest appearance in London, where she was befriended by Noel Coward and played the role of Liesl Haren, the fading Viennese operetta star, in his not very successful musical play *Operette* (1938), Massary moved to the United States. Along with her daughter and her son-in-law, the author Bruno Frank, she settled, like other exiles, such as Elisabeth Bergner and Max Reinhardt, in Beverly Hills, California, in what was known as the "New Weimar" on the Pacific. Once idolized, she lived a quiet, withdrawn life. "The Massary of the stage no longer exists," she said. "Some people can remember her, if they wish, but I don't want to any more." She died in Los Angeles on January 30, 1969.

In a little book dedicated to her art as a stage performer in 1920, Oscar Bie — the author of a classic study of the piano — emphasized both her many-sidedness and the diligence with which she worked to make the most of her talents as actress, singer, and dancer. "It is almost as though I had never seen her in a work that was worthy of her," he wrote of her career as an operetta star. "She remains, while the works she plays in vanish. […] Her art makes me dream of the possibilities a future operetta might open up, an operetta different from anything yet written, an operetta that would fully realize the essence of the genre. Every time I saw her in the imperfect works to which her art provides support, that dream was transformed for me into a living and complete image that bore her name." (Oscar Bie, *Fritzi Massary* [Berlin: Erich Reiß Verlag, n.d.], p. 33)

18   Goldmark

The composer Karl or Karoly Goldmark, one of the many children of a Jewish cantor, was born in Hungary in 1830. He entered the Vienna Conservatoire in 1867, played in various theaters as a violinist, and had his first major success as a composer with the opera *Die Königin von Saba* (*The Queen of Sheba*). First performed at the Vienna Opera in 1875, it remained in the repertoire until 1938.

Other operas followed: *Merlin* (1886, revised in 1904), *Die Kriegsgefangene* (1890), *Götz von Berlichingen* (1902), *Ein Wintermärchen* (1908). Goldmark also composed symphonies, symphonic poems, concert overtures, a violin concerto, chamber music, piano music, choral music and Lieder. Much influenced by Wagner, he is generally considered a late Romantic. He died in Vienna in 1915 and was clearly at a mature, productive stage in his life when the young Zur Mühlen would run into him on the lakeside promenade in Gmunden.

19   Peter Altenberg

Pseudonym of Richard Engländer (1859–1919). Born into a middle-class Jewish family in Vienna, he first studied law, then medicine. When both proved uncongenial, his kindly and understanding father provided him with an allowance, thanks to which he set himself up (for life, as it turned out) in a room at the Hotel Graben in the heart of Vienna, took up writing, assumed a new name, and quickly became part of *Jung Wien*, the lively fin-de-siècle avant-garde artistic movement that had put Vienna on the map in music, literature, and design. A *flâneur*, he did most of his writing on scraps of paper or on the backs of postcards in cafés, nightspots, and bars. His first publication, a volume of extremely short, fragmentary sketches and poems entitled *Wie ich es sehe* (1896), with an emphasis on the moment and on everyday, seemingly insignificant characters, conversations, gestures, and events, created a sensation in Germany as well as Austria. Twelve collections of sketches, aphorisms and poems followed. (The little town of Gmunden figures in several of these and was clearly a place to which he was strongly attached.) All were published, with one exception, by the highly respected S. Fischer Verlag in Berlin and all went through several — up to twenty — editions. Hugo von Hofmannsthal admired the young writer's ability to make the ordinary into something special and to discern magic in the quotidian. Always eager to be enchanted, Hofmannsthal explained, Altenberg saw the world as a scene of enchantment. To Thomas Mann, the young Viennese combined the childlike, magical vision of Hans Christian Andersen with the talent and penchant for the short form and for aphorism of Nietzsche. Among Altenberg's admirers, in addition to Hofmannsthal and Thomas Mann, were Karl Kraus, the sharp-tongued Viennese commentator and satirist, the playwrights Gerhart Hauptmann and Arthur Schnitzler, the critic Hermann Bahr, and the novelists Heinrich Mann and Robert Musil, to say nothing of his close friends, the noted architect and designer Adolf Loos and the composer Alban Berg, who set some of his work to music. (The first performance of Berg's

Five songs on picture postcard texts by Peter Altenberg in 1913 caused an uproar and had to be halted — a complete performance was not given until 1952! — but the unfavorable reception was most probably due to the music rather than to the text.) Another friend, the well-known cultural historian Egon Friedell, devoted a book to him (*Ecce Poeta* [1912]), the aim of which was to present him, with his disdain of conventional rhyme, meter, and subject-matter, and his choice of the fragmentary in place of sustained, elaborated forms like the epic and the novel (about which he sometimes wrote disparagingly), as the prototype of the modern writer. After Altenberg's death Friedell again produced a book in his praise: *Das Altenbergbuch* (Leipzig, Vienna, Zurich: Verlag der Wiener graphischen Werkstätte, 1921) with selections from his work, numerous photographs and caricatures, a moving tribute from Adolf Loos, and testimonies from Heinrich Mann, Thomas Mann, Hugo von Hofmannsthal, Georg Kaiser, and others. "If one may speak of 'love at first hearing,' that is what happened to me," Thomas Mann wrote in this book (p. 72), "when, early on, I came across this poet in prose."

In an age of violence, oppression, and injustice, Brecht once said, it becomes almost a crime to write about trees. Peter Altenberg wrote almost exclusively about "trees." It might be argued that, though he was not politically active or engaged, his emphasis on the moment (*carpe horam* became his motto), on spontaneity, on immediate experience, on the everyday and seemingly insignificant, his contempt for convention, social prejudice, cliché ideas and feelings, everything that blurs or distorts the purity and immediacy of perception and experience, and his Diogenes-like advocacy of the simple life, together with his constant critique of what he saw as a culturally implanted desire for luxury and excess, were in themselves subversive in an age of hypocrisy, class and ethnic prejudice, exploitation, and dangerous jingoism. The limitations of Altenberg's form of protest and celebration became clear, however, with the outbreak of the First World War. He became despondent; his writing began to flag; and after breaking both wrists in a fall at his hotel, he was bedridden for months and began to slowly poison himself by taking vast quantities of sleeping pills. "I find myself completely abandoned, isolated, put away into a corner" [Ich finde mich vollkommen verlassen, vereinsamt, in die Ecke gestellt], he noted on August 3, 1918. When he died in 1919 — Karl Kraus spoke the eulogy at his graveside — he was already, in a sense, *passé*. As a contributor to *Das Altenbergbuch* wrote, "A poet who understood, loved, and revered the world, died because he could not survive the folly and evil of the World War." (Dr. Genia Schwarzwald, p. 383)

There has been a strong revival of interest in Altenberg and in his fragmentary writing in the last twenty years or so, both in the German-speaking world and in the English-speaking world. Most of his work has been republished; several books have been written about him in both English and German; and hitherto untranslated works have been translated into English.

20 Angeli

The son of an innkeeper in Hungary of Venetian origin, Heinrich von Angeli (1840–1925) studied art at the academies of Vienna, Düsseldorf, and Munich. Though he painted genre scenes in his early years, by the early 1870s he was well launched on a highly successful career as a court painter in Vienna, London, Berlin, and St. Petersburg. There are numerous portraits by him of members of the European royal and princely families, including Emperor Franz Joseph, Frederick III of Prussia as Crown Prince, as well as his wife Princess Victoria, Queen Victoria's daughter. He was a great favourite of Queen Victoria herself, as well as of Prince Albert. He made portraits of her for the various royal residences. She also had him make portraits of other members of the royal family and, as a mark of her special regard for Slatin Pasha (see below) and her Indian servant Abdul Karim (the "Munshi"), had Angeli make her portraits of them. In addition, Angeli was much in demand in English and German aristocratic circles.

21 Hans Blum

Hans Blum (1841–1910) was the son of Robert Blum (1804–1848), a combatant in the 1848 Revolution in Vienna, whither he had gone to bring a message of solidarity with the Viennese revolutionaries from the left wing of the Frankfurt Parliament — in which he represented Leipzig. When the revolutionaries were defeated by the Imperial troops, Robert Blum was taken prisoner. On November 8, he was tried and condemned to death and, a day later, executed. He immediately became a hero and martyr in the cause of freedom for the entire German democratic movement. Ferdinand Freiligrath, the popular poet of the Revolution (see note below), published a poetic tribute to him as a proletarian hero. His son Hans Blum, however, was no revolutionary but an ardent German nationalist. In 1867–70 he was a representative from the National Liberal party, Bismarck's chief parliamentary support, in the North German Confederation Reichstag and its expanded version, the so-called "Zollparlament," to which the South German states were pressured by Bismarck to send representatives after Prussia's victory in the Austro-Prussian War of 1866. A war correspondent in the Franco-Prussian War of 1870, he continued his career in journalism by serving as editor of *Der Grenzbote* from 1871 to 1878. All his historical writing was directed to the German *Volk* and to German youth and aimed to promote patriotism and national pride in both. In the richly illustrated book on the 1848 Revolution referred to here by Zur Mühlen (*Die Deutsche Revolution 1848–49. Ein Jubiläumsausgabe für das deutsche Volk* [Florence and Leipzig: Eugen Diederichs, 1898], Blum gave a clear hint where his political sympathies lay when he wrote that the work he is undertaking is one for which he is ill equipped, since he is "not at all in full sympathy" with the political tendencies he has to discuss.

Zur Mühlen might have discovered that "Blum's son had actually written a reactionary book" sooner than she did had she also read Blum's biography of his father, written thirty years after 1848, when Germany was basking in the glory of Prussia's victory over France and the establishment of the Second German Empire. In it Blum relates that on May 23, 1870, "after a session of the Reichstag in which I was attacked by 'die Herrn Socialisten' because, by my vote, the criminal code [*Strafgesetzbuch*] had come into existence, Count Bismarck, then *Bundeskanzler,* invited me into his study. He stretched out his hand and said, 'Let us make an alliance at this hour, which I regard as one fraught with blessings for Germany.' I was startled. 'An alliance,' he continued, with a subtle smile [*feinem Lächeln*], 'not for the benefit of either one of us, or of any living man, but of the dead. Do you understand what I mean? Should *Messieurs les Socialistes* entertain the idea of degrading your father by claiming him as one of themselves, then you are at liberty to make use of my power, in the press, to keep that picture clean. Your father was very advanced [*sehr liberal*]. Even to-day he would be regarded as very "liberal." But he was also a good patriot [*gut national*] — that is, a supporter of the government.'" After quoting this passage in his massive, four-volume *History of the German Struggle for Liberty* (New York and London: Harper and Brothers, 1896–1905), Poultney Bigelow comments: "Thus we see, as in 1864 with Lassalle [founder of the *Allgemeiner deutscher Arbeiterverein*, the forerunner of the German Social Democratic Party], for the sake of weakening the Socialists, the strongest single party in the state, Bismarck claimed Blum as his fellow-partisan — and the son capitulated to Bismarck" (vol. 3, p. 306). In 1903, to cap his career, Hans Blum published a book celebrating the statesmanship of Bismarck (*Bismarck: ein Buch für Deutschlands Jugend und Volk* [Heidelberg: C. Winter, 1903]).

22   Uncle Anton

See Note 2, 'Uncle.'

23   "Where do the aristocrats belong?"

The reference is to the famous French Revolutionary song, the *Ça ira*:

> Les aristocrates à la lanterne!
> Ah! ça ira, ça ira, ça ira.
> Les aristocrates, on les pendra.
> Le despotisme expirera.
> La liberté triomphera.
> Ah! ça ira, ça ira, ça ira...

24   Lenau

Hungarian-born Nikolaus Franz Niembsch, Edler von Strehlenau (1807–1850), studied law, then medicine, but after receiving an inheritance on his grandmother's death was able to devote himself to writing, under the pseudonym Nikolaus Lenau. A major figure in German Romantic literature, his reputation as the author of a body of lyric poetry suffused with melancholy has remained high. His first volume of *Gedichte* appeared in 1832. Lenau also wrote verse epics and dramas (*Faust*, 1836, *Savonarola*, 1837, *Die Albigensier*, 1842, *Don Juan* — begun in 1844 and published posthumously). His melancholy was no doubt partly due to a dark vision of human existence in general but it was also not unrelated to a negative judgment of the society and culture of his time, which led him, in 1832, to set sail for the New World in the hope of finding more congenial conditions in what he took to  be an unspoiled wilderness. He landed in Baltimore and settled briefly on a farm, then in the community known as *Economy* (now Ambridge) on the Ohio River, about 16 miles North-West of Pittsburgh, which had been founded by the mystically inclined Württemberger Georg Rapp and his chiliastic followers. Duke Bernhard of Saxe-Weimar, who visited "*das freundliche und werktätige* [friendly and hardworking] Economy," reported that while "Rapp's intention is almost the same as Mr. Owen's [Robert Owen, the early British socialist, who purchased Rapp's settlement of New Harmony, Indiana in 1825 and reformed it according to his own principles] — i.e. communal ownership and co-operation of each member of the community for the good of all — *Herr* Rapp also holds his community together by the bonds of religion, which is totally absent from Mr. Owen's community." Lenau did not stay long in Economy. Disillusioned by America and what he judged to be its materialist culture, he returned to Europe after a year. The experience led him to distance himself radically from his earlier political liberalism and to identify with the downtrodden and oppressed, represented by American Indians and Gypsies. Never very stable emotionally, Lenau had a severe nervous breakdown in 1844 when he jumped out of a window and ran down the street shouting "Revolt! Freedom! Help! Fire!" He spent the last years of his life in a mental asylum on the outskirts of Vienna. The young Zur Mühlen's attraction to him is understandable in light of her own outlook at the time.

(Source for information on Lenau's American journey, commonly and erroneously said to have included a stay at New Harmony, Indiana: Roman Roček, *Dämonie des Biedermeier: Nikolaus Lenaus Lebenstragödie* [Vienna, Cologne, Weimar: Böhlau, 2005, pp. 135–241]).

25 Freiligrath

Ferdinand Freiligrath (1810–1876) had a successful career as a popular poet and journalist, interrupted by stints of activity in the world of commerce. His first volume of poems, *Gedichte* (1839), was such a success that he was able to give up his job as a bookkeeper in Barmen. On the recommendation of Alexander von Humboldt, he was awarded a pension by Friedrich Wilhelm IV of Prussia in 1842, which he renounced, however, in 1844 when he aligned himself unequivocally with the democratic opposition to the established order. His next collection, *Glaubensbekenntnis* (1844), established him as the poet of the struggle for freedom and social justice of the middle years of the nineteenth century and was an even greater success than the 1839 volume. The revolutionary content was unmistakable. The following are some sample lines from the poem "Mit raschen Pferden jagt die Zeit":

> Mit raschen Pferden jagt die Zeit
> Ein heißes Weib, nach Freiheit lechzend...
> Ein Gottweib! Ernst verehr' ich sie,
> Und geh' ihr nach mit Schwert und Schilde,
> Und jauchz' ihr zu; - doch nun und nie
> Entweih' ich sie zum Götzenbilde!

> [On speedy steeds, Time, a woman hot with passion and thirsty for freedom, leads the hunt... A divine woman! I adore her with all my being and follow her with sword and shield, and sing her hymns of praise — but neither now nor ever will I turn her into a sacred idol!]

Feeling that he was no longer safe from arrest in Germany, Freiligrath moved to Belgium, where he came into contact with Karl Marx. In 1845 the provocatively titled *Ça ira! Sechs Gedichte* appeared. The verse was marked by even stronger, almost military rhythms and clear, memorable rhymes. The tone was now outspokenly revolutionary. Two samples, the first from "Von unten auf," the second from "Wie man's macht":

> "Du bist viel weniger ein Zeus, als ich, O König, ein Titan!
> Beherrsch' ich nicht, auf dem Du gehst, den allzeit kochenden Vulkan?
> Es liegt an mir; - Ein Ruck von mir, Ein Schlag von mir zu dieser Frist,
> und siehe, das Gebäude stürzt, von welchem Du die Spitze bist!"

> ["You are far less a Zeus, O King, than I am a Titan! Do I not control the ever rumbling volcano on which you walk? It is up to me; One push from me, one blow from me at this point in time, and behold, the whole edifice of which you are the summit collapses!"]

> So wird es kommen, eh' ihr denkt: — Das Volk hat Nichts zu beißen mehr!
> Durch seine Lumpen pfeift der Wind! Wo nimmt es Brot und Kleider her?
> Da tritt ein kecker Bursche vor; der spricht: "Die Kleider wüßt' ich schon!
> Mir nach, wer Rock und Hosen will! Zeug für ein ganzes Bataillon!"

> [And so it will come before you think: — The common people have nothing more to chew! The wind whistles through their rags. Where

are they to get bread and clothes? A bold young fellow steps forward and says: "I know where to get clothes. Let whoever wants a coat and stockings follow me! There is stuff for a whole battalion!"]

"Von unten auf" continues with the people storming an army storehouse and taking not only clothes but weapons.

In 1848 Freiligrath returned to Germany to take part in the Revolution, was quickly arrested, released shortly afterwards, and accepted Marx's invitation to join the staff of the *Neue Rheinische Zeitung*, of which Marx was general editor. When the paper was banned in 1849, however, Freiligrath was again out of a job. With a warrant out for his arrest, he moved from one city to another until in 1851 he again left Germany, this time for London. After working for a few years for a commercial firm he was appointed director of the London branch of a Swiss bank. In 1865 the branch was closed and two years later, after the announcement of an amnesty for everyone charged with political crimes, Freiligrath returned to Germany. Like several others, who had once been revolutionaries of the Left, he rallied to the nationalist cause and on the outbreak of war with France, on 25 July 1870, produced the jingoist poem "Hurra, Germania!" which won general applause and was immediately set to folksong-like music:

Hurra, du stolzes, schönes Weib,	[Hurrah! thou lady proud and fair,
Hurra, Germania!	Hurrah! Germania mine!
Wie kühn mit vorgebeugtem Leib	What fire is in thine eye as there
Am Rheine stehst du da!	Thou bendest o'er the Rhine!
Im vollen Brand der Juliglut,	How in July's full blaze dost thou
Wie ziehst du frisch dein Schwert!	Flash forth thy sword, and go,
Wie trittst du zornig frohgemut	With heart elate and knitted brow,
Zum Schutz vor deinen Herd!	To strike the invader low!
Hurra, hurra, hurra!	Hurrah! Hurrah! Hurrah!
Hurra, Germania!	Hurrah! Germania!
Du dachtest nicht an Kampf und Streit:	No thought hadst thou, so calm and light,
In Fried' und Freud' und Ruh'	Of war or battle plain,
Auf deinen Feldern, weit und breit,	But on thy broad fields, waving bright,
Die Ernte schnittest du.	Didst mow the golden grain,
Bei Sichelklang im Ährenkranz	With clashing sickles, wreaths of corn
Die Garben fuhrst du ein:	Thy sheaves didst garner in,
Da plötzlich, horch, ein andrer Tanz!	When, hark! across the Rhine War's horn
Das Kriegshorn überm Rhein!	Breaks through the merry din!
Hurra, hurra, hurra!	Hurrah! Hurrah! Hurrah!
Hurra, Germania!	Hurrah! Germania!

Da warfst die Sichel du ins Korn,
Den Ährenkranz dazu;
Da fuhrst du auf in hellem Zorn
Tief atmend auf im Nu;
Schlugst jauchzend in die Hände dann:
Willst du's, so mag es sein!
Auf, meine Kinder, alle Mann!
Zum Rhein! zum Rhein! zum Rhein!
Hurra, hurra, hurra!
Hurra, Germania!

Da rauscht das Haff, da rauscht der Belt,
Da rauscht das deutsche Meer;
Da rückt die Oder dreist ins Feld,
Die Elbe greift zur Wehr.
Neckar und Weser stürmen an,
Sogar die Flut des Mains!
Vergessen ist der alte Span:
Das deutsche Volk ist eins!
Hurra, hurra, hurra!
Hurra, Germania!

Schwaben und Preußen Hand in Hand,
Der Nord, der Süd ein Heer!
Was ist des Deutschen Vaterland--
Wir fragen's heut nicht mehr!
Ein Geist, ein Arm, ein einz'ger Leib,
Ein Wille sind wir heut!
Hurra, Germania, stolzes Weib!
Hurra, du große Zeit!
Hurra, hurra, hurra!
Hurra, Germania!

Mag kommen nun, was kommen mag:
Fest steht Germania!
Dies ist All-Deutschlands Ehrentag:
Nun weh dir, Gallia!
Weh, daß ein Räuber dir das Schwert
Frech in die Hand gedrückt!
Fluch ihm! Und nun für Heim und Herd
Das deutsche Schwert gezückt!
Hurra, hurra, hurra!
Hurra, Germania!

Down sickle then and wreath of wheat
Amidst the corn were cast,
And, starting fiercely to thy feet,
Thy heart beat loud and fast;
Then with a shout I heard thee call.
Well, since you will, you may!
Up, up, my children, one and all,
On to the Rhine! Away!
Hurrah! Hurrah! Hurrah!
Hurrah! Germania!

From port to port the summons flew,
Rang o'er our German wave,
The Oder on her harness drew,
The Elbe girt on her glaive;
Neckar and Weser swell the tide,
Main flashes to the sun,
Old feuds, old hates are dash'd aside,
All German men are one!
Hurrah! Hurrah! Hurrah!
Hurrah! Germania!

Swabian and Prussian, hand in hand,
North, South, one host, one vow!
"What is the German's Fatherland?"
Who asks that question now?
One soul, one arm, one close-knit frame,
One will are we to-day;
Hurrah, Germania! thou proud dame,
Oh, glorious time, hurrah!
Hurrah! Hurrah! Hurrah!
Hurrah! Germania!

Germania now, let come what may,
Will stand unshook through all;
This is our country's festal day;
Now woe betide thee, Gaul!
Woe worth the hour a robber thrust
Thy sword into thy hand!
A curse upon him that we must
Unsheathe our German brand!
Hurrah! Hurrah! Hurrah!
Hurrah! Germania!

Für Heim und Herd, für Weib und Kind,	For home and hearth, for wife and child,
Für jedes teure Gut,	For all loved things that we
Dem wir bestellt zu Hütern sind	Are bound to keep all undefiled
Vor fremdem Frevelmut!	From foreign ruffianry!
Für deutsches Recht, für deutsches Wort	For German right, for German speech,
Für deutsche Sitt und Art-	For German household ways,
Für jeden heil'gen deutschen Hort!	For German homesteads, all and each,
Hurra! zur Kriegesfahrt!	Strike home through battle's blaze!
Hurra, hurra, hurra!	Hurrah! Hurrah! Hurrah!
Hurra, Germania!	Hurrah! Germania!
Auf, Deutschland, auf, und Gott mit dir!	Up, Germans, up, with God! The die
Ins Feld! der Würfel klirrt!	Clicks loud, — we wait the throw!
Wohl schnürt die Brust uns, denken wir	Oh, who may think without a sigh,
Des Bluts, das fließen wird!	What blood is doom'd to flow?
Dennoch das Auge kühn empor!	Yet, look thou up, with fearless heart!
Denn siegen wirst du ja:	Thou must, thou shalt prevail!
Groß, herrlich, frei, wie nie zuvor!	Great, glorious, free as ne'er thou wert,
Hurra, Germania!	All hail, Germania, hail!
Hurra, Viktoria!	Hurrah! Victoria!
Hurra, Germania!	Hurrah! Germania!]

(Source of English translation: Theodore S. Hamerow, ed., *The Age of Bismarck: Documents and Interpretations*. New York: Harper & Row, 1973, pp. 96–97).

It is a fair bet that the poems by Freiligrath "published" in the *Anchor Society*'s monthly bulletin were not those of this later period in the poet's career.

26   Anastasius Grün

Anastasius Grün was the pseudonym of Anton Alexander, Graf von Auersperg (1806–1876). He achieved celebrity in the *Vormärz*, the period leading up to the 1848 Revolution, as an aristocratic supporter of liberal ideals and demands. Born into a noble German-speaking family in Laibach (present-day Ljubljana, Slovenia), then the capital of a province of the Austrian Empire known as the Duchy of Carniola (Krain in German), he studied law at the Universities of Graz and Vienna and in 1830 published a volume of harmless lyric poems, *Blätter der Liebe*. Another collection, *Der letzte Ritter*, published later the same year, while celebrating the chivalry and bravery of Kaiser Maximilian I in verses of the same form as the *Nibelungenlied*, already showed signs of the rhetoric of freedom which was to characterise the poems of the succeeding years and on which the poet's reputation as a champion of liberal principles was based. One of the poems in the collection, for instance, the lively ballad entitled "Ritter und Freie" [Knights and Free Men], is an eighty-stanza paean to Switzerland as the land of the free.

> Was treibt euch wohl, ihr Fürsten, stets in die Schweizergaun?
> Wollt einmal doch im Leben ein freies Land ihr schaun?
> Wollt ihr das Zepter tauschen um einen Hirtenstab?
> Ha, oder wollt ihr finden in freier Erd' ein Grab?
>
> Seht auf das Land hernieder von hoher Alpenwand!
> Da liegt's, gleich einem Buche, geschrieben von Gotteshand,
> Die Berge sind die Lettern, das Blatt die grüne Trift,
> Sankt Gotthard ist ein Punkt nur in dieser Riesenschrift.
>
> Wißt ihr, was drin geschrieben? O seht, es strahlt so licht!
> Freiheit! steht drin, ihr Herren; die Schrift kennt ihr wohl nicht,
> Es schrieb sie ja kein Kanzler, es ist kein Pergament,
> Drauf eines Volkes Herzblut als rothes Siegel brennt.
>
> [What drives you constantly, you Princes, to invade the Swiss lands? Do you want, for once in your life, to see a free country? Do you want to exchange the sceptre for a shepherd's staff? Or do you want to find a grave in free soil? Look down on this land from the high wall of the Alps! There it lies, like a book written by the hand of God. The mountains are the letters, the green pastures are the page. The Saint Gotthard is but a period in this gigantic text. Do you know what is written in it? Oh, look, it shines out so clearly! Freedom! is what it says, my lords. You do not know this script. No chancellor wrote it; it is not written on parchment. The red seal burned on it is the blood of a people's heart.]

The two heroes of the ballad, a brave and faithful knight on King Max's side and an equally brave free Swiss, are both killed in battle. The narrator laments their death, then asks rhetorically in whose place the living would rather sleep the eternal sleep.

> Schlaft sanft, ihr Zwei! Ihr aber, die ihr noch jetzo wacht:
> An wessen Stelle lieber schlieft ihr die ew'ge Nacht?
>
> (Sleep softly, you two! But you who are still awake, in whose place would you rather sleep the eternal sleep?)

Two further collections, *Spaziergänge eines Wiener Poeten* (1831) and *Schutt* (1835), created something of a sensation on account of their criticisms of political conditions in Germany and Austria (then still led by Metternich). In subsequent works — *Nibelungen im Frack* (1843) and *Pfaff vom Kahlenberg* (1850), criticism was expressed by means of ironic humor. Auersberg also translated Slovenian folk poems into German and wrote a series of ballads on the theme of Robin Hood.

In the meantime, he had succeeded to his ancestral estate and two years later, in 1832, became a member of the upper house of the *Landtag*, or assembly, of the Duchy of Carniola. Here too he made a name for himself by criticising political conditions in Austria and leading local opposition to the exactions of the central government in Vienna. After the 1848 Revolution he represented the district of Laibach in the Frankfurt Parliament but failed to persuade the Slavic Slovenians, who desired independence, to send representatives to the German parliament. Within a year the violent turn taken by the Revolution led him to resign his seat and withdraw into private life. In 1860, however, he was summoned to the remodeled *Reichsrat* by Franz Joseph and the following year was appointed a life member of the Austrian upper house (*Herrenhaus*). His evolution from idealistic champion of freedom to a moderate position within the political establishment is not untypical, but to the young editor of the "Anchor Society" bulletin, he doubtless stood out as a model aristocrat who rose above the prejudices of his class and used his literary talent to advance the cause of progress.

27 Daschynski

Ignacy Daszyński (1866–1936), born in a Polish province of the Habsburg Empire, was one of the founders of the Polish Republic after the defeat of the Central Powers in 1918. Having helped to organize the Social Democratic Party of Galicia (1890), the forerunner of the Polish Social Democratic Party, he entered the lower house of the *Reichsrat* (the parliament established by Emperor Franz Joseph in 1861) as a deputy from Galicia in 1897 and quickly made a name for himself as a brilliant public orator. It was in this role that he made an impression on the young Hermynia Zur Mühlen. Much later, on the night of November 6, 1918, after the occupying Austrian army had withdrawn, he led a group of Galician socialists in forming a Provisional People's Government of the Polish Republic in the city of Lublin, south-west of Warsaw, with himself at the head of it as Prime Minister. On November 18 General Josef Pilsudksi, also a socialist and a founder, in 1892, of the Polish Socialist Party (with which the Social Democratic Party merged in 1919), but above all a Polish nationalist and long-time fighter for Polish independence, entered Warsaw and entrusted Daszyński with the task of forming a new cabinet. The Polish Right objected so strongly, however, that Daszyński was replaced by a more moderate socialist before he ever got to serve. In 1926, when Pilsudski, who had retired as chief of state four years earlier in accordance with the constitution, staged a coup that returned him to power, Daszyński at first supported him, along with the Socialist Party, but soon led the opposition to him. To Pilsudski's annoyance, the Sejm or Diet, elected not his candidate for the position of marshal or speaker, but Daszyński.

In 1929, Daszyński had his moment of glory — of which Zur Mühlen cannot have been aware since it occurred after her memoir had appeared. In an attempt to intimidate the Sejm, Pilsudksi sent a large group of army officers to take up positions in the vestibule and hallways on the day of the opening session. Ushers asked the officers to leave, but they refused. In his office Daszyński had a violent interview with his one-time friend and fellow-combattant, Pilsudski; it ended with Daszyński refusing to open the session. "Is that your last word?" Pilsudski is said to have demanded. "Yes," Daszyński replied. "I refuse to open the session under the threat of swords, bayonets, carbines, and revolvers." This reply became famous. In his autobiography Trotsky quotes a similar dramatic retort of Daszyński's on the same occasion: "To this day I remember the phrase which Daszyński flung in the face of the police when they entered the house of parliament. 'I represent thirty thousand workers and peasants of Galicia — who will dare touch me?' We pictured the Galician revolutionist as a titanic figure. The theatrical stage of parliamentarism, alas, cruelly deceived us." To Trotsky, in the end, the fiery Daszyński turned out to be just another ineffectual socialist in the Social Democratic ranks, a man with the gift of the gab, but no revolutionary commitment.

28   Tried for high treason

Zur Mühlen was charged with high treason in Germany, where she was then living, after the publication of her novella *Schupomann Karl Müller* (1924), in which the policeman hero breaks ranks and sides with the revolutionaries he is supposed to defend "society" against. The charges were dropped for lack of evidence.

29   Trotzkopf

Der Trotzkopf was a celebrated, widely read German girls' story by Emmy von Rhoden (pseudonym of Emilie Friedrich) that first appeared in 1885. Its lesson was essentially that marriage is a girl's main aim in life, and that she cannot therefore be headstrong or wilful, but must learn to be meek, pliant, and amiable; she should also acquire appropriate domestic skills like sewing and cooking. This is the lesson that the unruly 15-year old heroine of the story, Ilse Macket — the "Trotzkopf" or contrary spirit — has to be taught in the course of von Rhoden's novel. The penalty for not getting a husband and remaining a spinster is having to work. Marriage and work are thus opposites, the former the reward of good behaviour, the latter the punishment for bad behaviour. In general, pursuing a career of any kind is viewed in the novel as a sign of a woman's failure in the most important business of her life. The novel spawned several sequels, three of them by von Rhoden's daughter, Else Wildhagen, in the 1890s and early 1900s. It is still in print and has also been made into a movie and a TV series. *Der Trotzkopf* is a classic of the so-called *Backfischroman*, novels for young girls, the aim of which was to prepare their readers for a place in the conservative social order ot the Wilhelminian age. Zur Mühlen's hatred of the *Backfischroman* was deep and enduring. Several of her own fictions can be read as anti-*Backfisch* novels (as can her memoir, which, even though it purports to be non-fiction, still has the form of a *Bildungsroman*) and she also criticized these novels directly in an article of 1919, "Junge-Mädchen-Literatur," published in the leftwing *Die Erde*. See the article "'Fairy Tales for Workers' Children': Zur Mühlen and the socialist fairy tale" in the online supplement to this volume.

30 Aunt Maria, aunt Vicky, aunt Steffi

Aunt Maria might be either Maria, Countess von Esterhàzy (born in 1859), the wife of Zur Mühlen's mother's brother, August Wilhelm Maria von Wydenbruck, or Maria Countess Fugger zu Babenhausen (born in 1858), the wife of her mother's other brother, Christoph Anton Maria von Wydenbruck, the "Onkel Anton" of Zur Mühlen's memoir. However, even if one or the other was "little and roly-poly," neither is likely to have been considered "old" at this point in Zur Mühlen's life, even in those days. They were barely 25 years older than Zur Mühlen herself.

The Hungarian Teréz Brunszvik, Countess von Korompa (1775–1861), to whom Aunt Maria was related, is sometimes said to have been the "ferne Geliebte" of Beethoven's celebrated song cycle. "Korompa" was the name Zur Mühlen gave to the estate in Slovakia of the fictitious aristocratic family, the Herdegens, whose destinies from 1815 to 1848 and from 1938 to 1939 are the subject of her two late novels, *We Poor Shadows* (London, 1943; original German, 1939) and *Came the Stranger* (London, 1946). The real Korompa (in Hungarian; Krompachy in Slovak) is actually quite far from Vienna. It lies in Eastern Slovakia, near Kosice.

Aunt Victoria was probably Victoria Eugenie, the sister of Zur Mühlen's grandfather Franz, Count Crenneville. She was indeed old. Born in 1816 and married twice — first to Johann, Graf Keglevich zu Busin and after his death to Julius, Graf von Falkenhayn — she outlived her second husband by one year and died in Vienna in 1900.

Aunt Steffi could unfortunately not be identified.

31 Prater

The celebrated green area and amusement park established in the Leopoldstadt district for the benefit of the citizens of Vienna by Emperor Joseph II in 1766. It was the site of a universal exhibition in 1873 and figures famously in Carol Reed's 1949 film, *The Third Man*, the screenplay of which was written by Graham Greene.

32 Herr Habert

Zur Mühlen's piano teacher was in fact a distinguished musician, musical scholar, and composer. Johannes Evangelista Habert (1833–1896), born in Bohemia and trained in Linz, settled in Gmunden in 1860 and was appointed municipal organist there in 1861. He edited musical compositions by earlier composers of church music (Stadlmayr, Fux, Führer)`and was a prolific composer, in his own right, of masses, litanies, and motets, as well as of orchestral and chamber music, piano pieces, and songs. In the context of the Cecilianist movement in German Church music in the nineteenth century — the aim of which was to free church music from the theatrical and operatic style of the baroque and rococo and return to the simplicity of the fifteenth and sixteenth centuries — Habert used his position as editor of the *Zeitschrift für katholische Musik*, which he founded in 1867, to argue in favor of retaining instrumentally accompanied liturgical music. Thus he wrote an extremely favorable review of Bruckner's Mass in E minor and became one of Bruckner's staunchest champions.

A multi-volume complete edition of Habert's works was begun under his own direction two years before his death and published by Breitkopf and Härtel in Leipzig (1894–99), with four volumes devoted to his theoretical writings alone (*Beiträge zur Lehre von der musikalischen Komposition*). His Mass in B Minor was republished by Breitkopf and Härtl (now in Wiesbaden) as recently as 1989, his Mass in C Major for two voices and organ by Edition Musica Rinata in Ditzingen in 2007.

(Sources: Matthias Schmidt in *New Grove Dictionary of Music and Musicians*, ed. Stanley Sadie [London: Macmillan, 2001], vol. 10, p. 637; James Garratt, *Palestrina and the German Romantic Imagination* [Cambridge: Cambridge University Press, 2002]).

33   Aunt Agnes

Almost certainly a relative of Zur Mühlen's Anglo-Irish grandmother. Hence Aunt Agnes's friendship with May Crommelin, whose family was also prominent in Northern Ireland.

34   May Cromelin

Maria Henriette de la Cherois Crommelin (1849–1930), known as May Crommelin, was a descendant of a Huguenot refugee family that had settled in Great Britain in 1690, one of her ancestors having been invited by William III to establish the linen industry in Ireland. Her family's Irish connection — May Crommelin herself was born on the family estate of Carrowdore Castle in County Down, Northern Ireland — probably explains her relation to Aunt  Agnes, who was in all likelihood, like Zur Mühlen's grandmother, from the family of the Blackers of Carrickblacker, County Armagh. Completely forgotten now, Crommelin was a prolific and in her time popular author. Between her first novel, *Queenie*, published in 1874, when she was 25, and her last, published in 1924, when she was 75, she wrote over two dozen novels and collections of short stories, in addition to children's books and travel books. One of a long line of intrepid British women travellers (*Over the Andes from the Argentine to Chile and Peru* appeared in 1896), she was a Fellow of the Royal Geographical Society. When Zur Mühlen met her, she was at the height of her popularity.

35   Jerome K. Jerome

Jerome K. Jerome (1859–1927), best known as the author of the still widely read *Three Men in a Boat (To Say Nothing of the Dog)* (1899) and *Idle Thoughts of an Idle Fellow* (1886), produced a number of novels as well as plays and collections of short stories and essays. A contemporary and friend of J. M. Barrie, H. G. Wells, Rudyard Kipling, Arthur Conan Doyle, Thomas Hardy, and Israel Zangwill, he was probably one of the English-language authors read to Zur Mühlen by her grandmother. He quickly became one of her favourites. She translated several of his stories and also wrote his obituary for the *Frankfurter Zeitung* (1927, no. 437A, p. 649), two years before *Ende und Anfang* appeared in instalments in the same newspaper.

36   Kürenberger

Most likely not "Der von Kürenberg" or "Der Kürenberger," an Austrian poet of the mid-twelfth century, but Ferdinand Kürnberger (1821–1879), a child of working-class parents, who became one of Austria's leading journalists. His *feuilletons* were famously critical of the old Habsburg Empire in general ("Asiatic, retarded, lazy, and stupid") [*"asiatisch, zurückgeblieben, faul, dumm"*] and of Viennese society in particular: "In the shadow of a scepter whose sway extends from Donauschingen to Smyrna, Vienna is developing relentlessly into a world-city, but while we have become inhabitants of a world-city, we have acquired none of the urbanity of world citizens." Kürnberger also wrote plays, novellas, and novels. Karl Kraus, the famous Viennese critic and satirist of the next generation, sometimes referred to him as his most important predecessor.

Kürnberger was already writing for various newspapers when the October 1848 Revolution broke out in Vienna. Having taken part in it, he fled to Germany after it was suppressed, but soon landed in prison anyway for having allegedly participated in the Dresden uprising of the following May. In 1855 he published *Der Amerika-Müde*, based on Nikolaus Lenau's American experience. Ostensibly a novel, it was also a critical study of modern democratic and capitalist societies through the eyes of its idealistic hero Moorfeld, who, arriving in New York full of enthusiasm for a New World he expects to be radically different from Old Europe, discovers that "the crowning blossom of human progress," "the savior that one day will redeem us all," while certainly different from Old Europe, is a land where all are equally grasping and obsessed with gain and where the first lesson one is taught is indeed "not German metaphysics" but that "time is money" and that "wasting" it in unremunerated activities is equivalent to throwing money away. (*Der Amerika-Müde. Amerikanisches Kulturbild* [Frankfurt a.M.: Meidinger Sohn & Cie., 1855], in the series *Deutsche Bibliothek, Sammlung auserlesener Original-Romane*, vol. 8, pp. 1, 2, 19)

Kürnberger's way of looking at his world — unblinkingly, without illusion, and with provocative realism — can be gauged from the cynical observation of one of the characters in *Der Amerika-Müde*: "Long live the freedom of the press! Yes, yes, my dear Sir, the freedom of the press is the jewel of our enlightened and happy land. An enslaved press is an excellent instrument of emancipation, for then the public forms its own judgment. But a free press is an invaluable instrument of tyranny. The mob believes it and parrots what it is told." (p. 190) "Press freedom and press abomination are directly connected," the narrator had already noted at the beginning of the novel (p. 8). Usually accounted a liberal, Kürnberger did not shrink from unmasking liberal hypocrisy and attacking liberal shibboleths. Hence the press itself, for which he worked on and off for most of his life, became a prime object of criticism in as much as it served to disseminate political clichés. For the political slogan [*"die politische Phrase"*], he declared, "is a dangerous toy" [*"ein gefährliches Spielzeug"*]. In the 1860's when he served as General Secretary of the Schiller Foundation, what he picked out from Schiller's writings (and paraphrased in his own way) was almost the opposite of the idea people usually associated with the most loved and admired poet of German neo-classicism. Literature should not restore wellbeing to people, Schiller held (according to Kürnberger), but should "destroy their sense of wellbeing," it should *"inkommodieren"* them [cause them discomfort]. Likewise Revolution should never allow itself to become institutionalized in a new order. In phrases reminiscent of Stirner, Kürnberger warned that "the avenger whom the people itself awakens, can never hold an office and incur obligations; he can never be engaged, patented, privileged; he can never be a subscriber to anything; he can only be totally free and he can never act except of his own free will." The critic did not allow himself any illusions about his own activity. "I have been enlightened about the Enlightenment itself," he once remarked. Criticism and satire are not effective in themselves, he added. They change nothing. Power will not yield to truth, but only to the pressure that will follow widespread recognition of the truth.

While the corrosiveness of his criticism doubtless appealed to Zur Mühlen's father — and to the rebellious young Countess herself — it is unlikely that either endorsed his German nationalism, which manifested itself in contempt for the multi-ethnic Habsburg Empire and, in particular, for its Slavic ("Asiatic") components and which culminated in enthusiastic celebration of the Prussian victory over France in 1870. Germany has long been despised and the German worker treated like a domestic animal, the revolutionary of 1848 wrote — without irony — in August 1870, but "Now our Messiah has come! Nothing on earth is greater than the German name." To Zur Mühlen, in contrast, as her novel *Ewiges Schattenspiel* (*We Poor Shadows*) makes especially clear, the multi-ethnic character of the old Austro-Hungarian Empire was a positive quality, while in the novel *Reise durch ein Leben* (*A Life's Journey*), the patchwork quilt is a symbol of the only unity individuals and nations can or ought to strive for.

(Sources: Karl Riha, *Kritik, Satire, Parodie* [Opladen: Westdeutscher Verlag, 1992]; Andrea Wildhagen, *Das politische Feuilleton Ferdinand Kürnbergers* [Frankfurt, Bern, New York: Peter Lang, 1985]; Wolfgang Klaubacher, "Ferdinand Kürnberger und Adolf Fischhof: zwei ehemalige `Märzkämpfer` in deutschnationaler Euphorie," in Klaus Amann and Karl Wagner, eds., *Literatur und Nation* [Vienna, Cologne, Weimar: Böhlau, 1996]).

37 "Gojicher Kopf"

A Yiddish expression, meaning "mind or brain of a Christian." While in this case the narrator is simply quoting, Zur Mühlen did like to use the occasional common Yiddish expression, as in one of her letters to Nathaniel Asch — a Jewish-American writer, whose work she had translated — where she refers to herself as one of the anti-Nazi "gojim" (Christians), whom even the Jewish publishers in Vienna are afraid to publish. (See the essay "Remembering Hermynia Zur Mühlen" in this volume.) This was obviously a way of making her opposition to anti-Semitism public.

38 Crown Prince Rudolf

Archduke Rudolf, Crown Prince of Austria, Hungary, and Bohemia (1858–1889), the well-educated, thoughtful, and relatively liberally inclined son and heir of Franz Joseph I was rather unhappily married and had apparently many affairs. In 1889 he was found dead, along with his latest mistress, a girl of seventeen, at Mayerling, his hunting lodge. What actually happened at Mayerling is still the subject of much speculation and many books. With Rudolf's death, Franz Joseph's younger brother Karl Ludwig became heir to the throne. He, however, renounced his succession rights in favor of his son, Franz Ferdinand, who was assassinated in 1914 at Sarajevo. (See Note 7, "Sophie Chotek.")

39 Henry George

An American politician and political economist, George (1839–1897) was a proponent of a land value tax, also known as the "Single Tax" on land. According to the economic line of thought he inspired, everyone owns the product of his or her labour, but everything found in nature, above all land, belongs equally to all humanity. George supported state ownership of telegraphic communications and municipal ownership of the water supply. He was strongly opposed to private monopolies. His most famous work, *Progress and Poverty* (1879), deals with inequality and the cyclic nature of industrial economies and proposes possible remedies. A well known speaker and public figure, George ran for Mayor of New York City in 1886 and came in second, ahead of the Republican candidate, Theodore Roosevelt. 100,000 people attended his funeral. Now almost forgotten, he influenced the thinking of George Bernard Shaw and Leo Tolstoi on economic matters, and of Silvio Gesell, an unconventional economist, near-contemporary of Zur Mühlen, and author of *Die natürliche Wirtschaftsordnung* (1916; originally two volumes under different titles [1906, 1911]; French translation 1916, English translation 1929), who is likewise almost forgotten now, but was well regarded by Keynes.

40   Stirner

Max Stirner (1806–1856) studied under Hegel in Berlin and was one of the group known as the "Young Hegelians." These students of Hegel — they included, besides Stirner, Bruno Bauer, David Strauss, Ludwig Feuerbach, and Karl Marx — diverged in important respects from the master and also engaged in polemical debates with each other. Stirner is usually seen as one of the founders of anarchism. He was also an influence on modern existentialism.

Rejecting revolution in the usual sense as inherently statist and fated simply to replace one repressive system by another, he advocated instead freeing oneself from any fixed standpoint and from all dogmatic presuppositions, those of the Left as well as those of the Right, those of modern atheists as well as those of traditional Christians, "nature" no less than God. His writing style and mode of argumentation were distinctive and disconcerting. He relied a good deal on word play and on exploiting words with related etymologies, since he claimed that language and rationality are themselves products of human culture that have come to constrain and oppress their creators. *Der Einzige und sein Eigentum* (1844; English transl. *The Ego and Its Own*, 1907) was the most important statement of his radical philosophical views.

41   Nauheim

Bad Nauheim, about 20 miles from Frankfurt-am-Main, was a world-famous health resort, noted for its salt springs, which were used to treat heart and nerve diseases. President Franklin Delano Roosevelt's father underwent the water cure here for his heart condition and brought his son along with him.

42   Henry Thode

Thode (1857–1920) was one of the most prominent art historians of the turn of the century. From 1884 he co-edited the prestigious art-history journal *Repertorium für Kunstwissenschaft* with Hugo von Tschudi, who was later to become director of the Berlin Nationalgalerie. In 1889, on the recommendation of Wilhelm Bode, then Director of the Kaiser Friedrich Museum in Berlin, Thode was offered the position of Director of the Städelsches Kunstinstitut in Frankfurt, one of the greatest German art museums. He resigned two years later, however, because of disagreements with the administration. After three years as an untenured professor of art history at Heidelberg, he was appointed to the Chair of Art History in 1896. In 1886 he had married Daniela, the daughter of Cosima Liszt and the conductor Hans von Bülow. This brought him into close contact with the Wagner family and the Wagnerites. (Cosima had begun living with Wagner in 1866 and, after getting a divorce from von Bülow, married him in 1870.) As an art and cultural historian, Thode rejected Burckhardt's widely accepted view that the Italian Renaissance marked Western humanity's emancipation from the Middle Ages and the emergence of modern individualism. He emphasized instead the continued importance of Christian values and ideas. A longtime friend of the painter Hans Thoma, he also opposed the "alien" influence of French Impressionism on contemporary German art, attacking in particular its leading representative at the time, the Jewish painter Max Liebermann, and the "commercial interests of a small clique in Berlin," by which he meant the — largely Jewish — Berlin art dealers who were promoting Impressionism. This did not prevent Thode from living a high-profile social life. He and Daniela ultimately moved to a villa on the Lago di Garda in Italy where they maintained a lavish lifestyle.

43 Siegfried Wagner

The son of Richard Wagner and his second wife Cosima — and thus the grandson of Liszt — Siegfried Wagner (1869–1930) followed in his father's footsteps after briefly contemplating a career as an architect. Between the late 1890s and the 1920s he wrote both the music and the libretti for over a dozen operas, none of them much performed now, though several have been recorded. He also wrote orchestral works and Lieder. He made his debut at Bayreuth as assistant conductor in 1894, became associate conductor two years later, and in 1908 succeeded his mother as Artistic Director of the Festival. He was often held to have inherited his father's anti-Semitism — hence Zur Mühlen's remark about his nose, written from the perspective of 1929 — and his wife Winfried certainly maintained the anti-Semitic climate that enveloped the entire Wagnerian enterprise. (This did not, of course, prevent the use of an occasional Jewish singer or musician when the success of the performances required it.) It has been argued, however — most movingly by his daughter Friedlinde, who emigrated in 1939 first to England, where she wrote anti-Nazi columns for the *Daily Sketch*, then in 1941 to the United States, where she took part in anti-Nazi radio broadcasts, in her memoir *Heritage of Fire: The Story of Richard Wagner's Grand-daughter* (New York and London: Harper Brothers, 1945) — that Siegfried did not share his father's or his wife's anti-Semitism.

44   Daughter of Bülow

Blandine von Bülow (1863–1941), the younger of two daughters of Richard Wagner's wife Cosima (herself the daughter of Franz Liszt) and her first husband, the musician Hans von Bülow, who conducted the premieres of *Tristan und Isolde* (1865) and *Die Meistersinger von Nürnberg* (1868). She was married to Biagio, Conte di Gravina, who died in 1897 at the age of forty-seven, a year after the birth of the couple's fourth child. The oldest son, referred to here as a Fascist in the late 1920s, was Manfredi (1883–1932). From 1929 until his death he was the League of Nations' High Commissioner for the then Free City of Danzig.

45   "Panther affair"

The *Panther* was a German warship. Zur Mühlen may be confusing two incidents involving it. In the first, which took place in 1905 and is usually referred to as the "*Panther* affair," the ship was deployed to the Brazilian port of Itajahy, where her crew conducted an unauthorized search on Brazilian soil and kidnapped a German dissident. This "*Panther* affair" had obviously nothing to do with Morocco. In the second incident, which took place in 1911 and is usually referred to as the "Agadir Crisis," the *Panther* was sent to Agadir in Morocco, ostensibly to signal German support for a French plan to send troops to Fez, where the Sultan of Morocco was holed up in the midst of a revolt. By "saving" the Sultan, the French would in effect establish themselves as colonial masters of Morocco. The presence of the *Panther* was apparently intended to remind the French that their colonial designs in Morocco, recognized by the British in return for French recognition of Britain's designs in Egypt, also depended on German acquiescence, and thus to promote a Franco-German alliance. It so alarmed the British, however, who read it as a challenge to their naval power, while at the same time alienating the French, that it had the effect of cementing the Entente between Britain and France against Germany. As her father held the post in Tangiers from June 1901 until June 1904, Zur Mühlen's stay there ended just a year before the Brazilian "*Panther* affair." A year before the "Agadir Crisis" in Morocco, she was a married woman and was well established at Eigstfer in Estonia, on the estate of her husband, Viktor von zur Mühlen. Tension among the great powers over their competing colonial ambitions in Africa and the Near East, was already running high by 1904, however, and the recollection of this may have led Zur Mühlen to advance the date of the second "Panther affair."

46   The Sultan and his one-eye'd brother

Presumably Abdul Aziz bin Hasan, Sultan from 1894 to 1908, and his older half-brother Abdul Hafiz bin Hasan. Abdul Aziz, whose attempts to modernize Morocco and whose personal extravagance and infatuation with Western luxury products had made him unpopular, was forced to abdicate in 1908 and yield power to his half-brother. For a time, both claimed the throne, the one "ruling" from Rabat, the other from Marrakesh, with Fez in dispute.

47 Raisuli

Mulay Ahmed ben Mohammed Raisuli — the name is sometimes transcribed as Raisuni — was the Shereef (i.e. leader, claiming direct descent from the Prophet Mohammed) of the Rif Berber tribe at the turn of the nineteenth and twentieth centuries. His dates of birth and death are uncertain: circa 1870 to circa 1925. The American historian Barbara Tuchman describes him as "the renowned Berber chief, lord of the Rif and last of the Barbary pirates, whose personal struggle for power  against his nominal overlord, the Sultan of Morocco, periodically erupted over Tangier in raids, rapine, and interesting varieties of pillage." ("Perdicaris Alive or Raisuli Dead," in *Practicing History: Selected Essays* [New York: Ballantine Books, 1982], pp. 104–17) Though considered by some the rightful heir to the throne of Morocco, he had no pretentions to the Sultanate, according to Walter Harris, the correspondent of the *Times* of London, who spoke Arabic and came to know him well. (*Morocco That Was* [London and Edinburgh: William Blackwood, 1921], p. 212) His struggle seems to have been that of a traditional local warlord against a ruler who, in his view, was trying to exercise a degree of power and authority to which he was not entitled. "The whole situation in Morocco was seething," Harris writes about the first decade of the twentieth century (p. 211). "The tribes had become to all intents and purposes independent, and many threw off all pretence of obeying the orders of their Governors." At the same time, Raisuli sometimes represented himself as a leader engaged in a *jihad* to rid Morocco of foreigners and Christians (mostly French), who, because of the dependence on them of the reigning Sultan Abdul Aziz bin Hasan, were rapidly coming to be masters of the Muslim country. In addition to constant skirmishes with the forces of the Sultan and incessant raids and cattle robberies resulting in not a few murders (for which he was imprisoned at one point for several years in the dreaded dungeons of Mogador), Raisuli used kidnappings as an instrument in his struggle for power, financial resources, and recognition.

In 1903, he kidnapped Harris, who had gone into the countryside on a hunting expedition at the time. Because of Harris's kindness and hospitality to tribespeople at his home in Tangiers, no money was demanded for his release, only the freeing of a number of tribesmen in government detention. This was successfully negotiated by the British Minister, Sir Arthur Nicolson. Harris later described his captor as a handsome, chivalrous, well educated, and intelligent tribal chief with a keen sense of honour, even if he shrank from no act of violence. A more notorious kidnapping took place the following year, when Raisuli boldly abducted a wealthy Greek-American named Ion Perdicaris and his British stepson Cromwell Oliver Varley from Perdicaris's villa in Tangiers — "'Aidonia,' 'the place of nightingales,' a comfortable house," as Sir Arthur's son, Harold Nicolson, later described it, "with green shutters, an open fore-court, red candles on the dining table, a large telescope on the terrace, and groves of myrtle, roses and arbutus falling to the sea," where "he lived a cultured and retired life with his wife, his stepson…, his daughter-in-law Mrs. Varley, some grandchildren, some tame pheasants, a demoiselle crane, and several monkeys." (*Sir Arthur Nicolson, Bart. First Lord Carnock: A Study in the Old Diplomacy* [London: Constable], 1930, p. 151) In return for their release, Raisuli demanded the dismissal of the Governor of Tangiers, a distant relative and bitter enemy, and his own appointment as Governor in his place, the withdrawal of government troops from "his" territory, the arrest and imprisonment of personal enemies, the release from prison of personal friends, and a ransom of $70,000. The kidnapping of Perdicaris caused an international incident. The Sultan was pressured by Britain, France, and the United States to intervene, but was powerless to do so. President Theodore Roosevelt then ordered four American warships with a detachment of Marines to Tangiers. In the end a settlement was negotiated, with most of Raisuli's terms being met. He got his $70,000 and he was appointed Pasha of Tangiers — though the appointment was revoked in 1906. Like Harris, Perdicaris came to admire his captor, describing him later in a talk at the New York Library Club (April, 1905) as "a true patriot who is leading his people in the fight for independence."

Raisuli caused yet another sensation in 1907–1908 — some time after Zur Mühlen and her father had left Tangiers — when he kidnapped Colonel Harry Maclean, known as Caïd Maclean, a British army officer who had been charged with training the Sultan's army and was a well liked figure at the Sultan's court. Maclean had been authorized by the Sultan to negotiate a settlement of some outstanding issues with Raisuli in a remote place half way between Tangiers and Fez. Raisuli took him prisoner, held him for several months, and finally, after lengthy negotiations, obtained £20,000 sterling and the status of a British protected subject in return for his release.

In the struggle between Sultan Abdul Aziz and his brother Abdul Hafiz, Raisuli threw in his lot with the latter. The two swore an oath on the Koran to drive the foreign Christians out of Morocco. (Charles-André Julien, *Le Maroc face aux impérialismes 1415–1956* [Paris: Editions J.A., 1978], p. 46) Abdul Hafiz's reign did not last for long, however, and Raisuli himself was ultimately displaced in the guerilla war against the foreigner by a rival tribal leader, the celebrated Moroccan "freedom fighter" Abdelkrim, whose guerilla tactics are known to have inspired Ho Chi Minh and Che Guevara.

In addition to Harris's book (cited above), of which a 100-page chapter on Raisuli takes up about a third, and the essay by Tuchman (also cited above), Raisuli is the subject of a romantic biography by Rosita Forbes, one of a number of intrepid British women adventurer-writers around this time (*El Raisuni:*

The Sultan of the Mountains. His Life Story as told to Rosita Forbes [London: T. Butterworth, 1924]). A heavily fictionalized film, *The Wind and the Lion* (1975), in which Raisuli is played by Sean Connery, focuses on the Perdicaris kidnapping. Ion Perdicaris himself wrote an account of his kidnapping in the *National Geographic Magazine* in 1906 and in an autobiographical memoir, published in London in 1911, *The Hand of Fate* (reproduced in John Hughes, ed., *House of Tears: Westerners' Adventures in Islamic Lands* [Guildford, CT: The Lyon Press, 2005], pp. 103–26). Raisuli's relation to Spain, which he tried to play off against France, is treated in Stanley G. Payne, *Politics and the Military in Modern Spain* (Stanford: Stanford University Press, 1967). He is situated in the context of the history of terrorism in Jeffrey D. Simon, *The Terrorist Trap: America's Experience with Terrorism* (Bloomington, IN: Indiana University Press, 1994).

48   Madame St. R. T.

Madeleine Marie Louise Chevrillon Saint-René Taillandier (1875-?), the wife of the French Minister in Tangiers, and a niece of the eminent French historian Hippolyte Taine, went on to have a considerable career as a writer in her own right, specializing in books about personalities of the French 16th, 17th, and 18th centuries (*Henri IV avant la messe; Racine; Madame de Maintenon; Madame de Sévigné et sa fille; La Tragédie de Port-Royal; La Jeunesse du Grand Roi: Louis XIV et Anne d'Autriche; Le Grand Roi et sa cour; Du Roi Soleil au roi Voltaire*, among others). Most of her elegantly and concisely written books appeared with leading publishers, such as Plon, Grasset, and Hachette in the 1920s and 1930s, when historical biographies that read like novels were in great vogue, but she continued to publish until the early 1950s and several of her works were translated into English. In 1942, the publisher Plon put out a book by her about her uncle, *Mon Oncle Taine,* and in 1947 the same publisher brought out her charmingly written *Ce Monde disparu: Souvenirs*, the entire second half of which is devoted to the events and personalities of the years she and her husband spent in Morocco. Madame Taillandier's narrative confirms what, according to Zur Mühlen, her father said about the insignificance of the post the Austrian government had given him in Tangiers. Of the great powers, Austria alone had no interests in a country where Germany, France, Great Britain, and Spain all had competing interests, and Madame Taillandier never mentions it. Nor, though she devotes many pages to Nicolson, Lady Nicolson, and their children (for all of whom she had great affection), writes at some length of the German mission and its then chief, Baron de Menzingen ("Ce Badois n'était pas prussianisé: un excellent homme, père de six enfants"), and offers brief accounts of the Russian, Spanish, Italian, and Belgian representatives, does she once mention Crenneville. In fact, Austria maintained neither an embassy nor a legation in Tangiers, but only what was called a "diplomatic agency" ("*diplomatische Agentie*") and even it was shut down in 1913 after being in existence for under twenty years. Though he was a member of the diplomatic corps (and was referred to by the Moroccan servants as "Baschador" or Ambassador), Crenneville bore the official title only of diplomatic agent, not ambassador or minister.

49   Sir Arthur Nicholson

Nicolson (1849–1928), consistently misspelled by Zur Mühlen as "Nicholson," the son of an Admiral, began a wide-ranging career in the British Foreign Office in 1870. From 1872 to 1874 he was Assistant Secretary to the Foreign Secretary, George Granville; from 1874 to 1876 Third Secretary in the Embassy in Berlin; from 1876 to 1878, Second Secretary in Peking. He then returned briefly to Berlin before being posted to Constantinople (1879–1882), Athens (1884–1885), Teheran (1885–1888), Budapest, where he was Consul-General from 1888 to 1892, Constantinople again (1893), and Sofia (1894). In 1895 he was appointed British Minister in Tangiers, a position which he held for almost ten years and in which he finally got a chance to show his mettle as a diplomat. According to a colleague, a Secretary of State for India, writing in 1907, Nicolson was "the best man of his day in his own trade. He is quiet, steady, full of ready resource, not making difficulties, not delighting to put the other man into a hole." Appointed Ambassador to Spain in 1905, he returned to Morocco in 1906 as British representative at the Algeciras Conference and that same year took on the key role of Ambassador to Russia in St. Petersburg, where Zur Mühlen met up with him again. In 1910 he returned to London to be Permanent Under-Secretary to Edward Grey, the Foreign Secretary, in which capacity he did his best, against opposition from many liberals unfavorable to close association with the oppressive regime of the Czar, to promote a strong British-Russian-French alliance as a means of holding Germany in check. He played an important part in the diplomatic negotiations and manoeverings that preceded the outbreak of the First World War, urging Grey to make it very clear to Germany that Britain would support France and Russia in the event of war. The German ambassador to Britain, Prince Lichnowsky, described him as "not a friend" of Germany (this was also Zur Mühlen's view), but unfailingly courteous and eager to avoid war.

During his 1874–1876 stint at the Embassy in Berlin, Nicolson published *A Sketch of the German Constitution and of the Events in Germany from 1815 to 1871* (London: Longmans, Green, 1875), a thoughtful little book on the development of the German Constitution from the time of the German Confederation in 1815 to the Imperial Constitution of 1871. Informative, objective, and fair, while at the same time pointing to important features of the 1871 constitution that left the executive free of responsibility to elected, representative bodies, it gives a good sense of the quality of the author's mind and of his political values. Nicolson was the subject of a fine biography — *Sir Arthur Nicolson, Bart., First Lord Carnock: A Study in the Old Diplomacy* (London: Constable, 1930) — by his son, the prolific and elegant writer, essayist, and scholar, Sir Harold Nicolson. Nicolson's important role in Morocco at a time of increasing tension among the three major powers with interests there — France, Great Britain, and Germany — occupies three chapters of the book (chapters V to VII, pp. 108–99). Nicolson emerges from his son's narrative as cautious and suspicious of German intentions but, contrary to the assertion of Zur Mühlen's father, not ill-disposed to the German Minister in Tangiers, Baron Schenk von Schweinsberg, who was appointed soon after Nicolson himself arrived in 1895 and whom Nicolson describes as "an old friend of mine [doubtless from his time at the Embassy in Berlin] and a great improvement on his hot-headed predecessor. He is mild and conciliatory." Nicolson himself resisted efforts by, among others, "Caïd" Maclean, a retired British army officer in charge of training the Sultan's troops, to get him to promote British power and influence in Morocco by establishing close relations with the Moroccan court. Such an aggressive stance, Nicolson felt, would alienate the other interested European powers and would not, in the end, be to Britain's advantage. "I do not know whether it would be desirable for us to obtain a very intimate and powerful footing at Court," he wrote to Maclean. "We should thereby incur certain responsibilities which I think it would be wiser to avoid. The future is very uncertain in this country, and I should like our hands to be quite free and not to encourage these people to imagine that we were their sole support and advisers. I do not think this would be fair as they might expect more than we should probably perform. I am anxious to be on the most friendly terms and do what I can to help them, but not to strive for a specially predominant position. The consequences might be awkward."

Madame Saint-René Taillandier, wife of the French Ambassador to Morocco, traces an engaging portrait of her husband's colleague and, for a time, rival, in the sense that, as she herself explains with great clarity, while Great Britain had no designs on Morocco, it also sought — until the two countries worked out an agreement giving France a free hand in Morocco in exchange for France's recognition of Britain's control of Egypt — to prevent French dominance there. The passage is quoted in French to give a sense of Madame Saint-René Taillandier's writing: "C'était un homme charmant, il pouvait avoir passé la cinquantaine: très mince et de structure simple et légère, un peu voûté, mais comme un coureur qui va prendre son élan, le visage coloré de cette carnation britannique qui semble se ressentir de la mer et du vent: l'oeil bleu, très clair, pénétrant, à tous moments pétillant de malice et tout à coup adouci en une expression de confiance affectueuse. C'était l'Anglais qui ne ressemble qu'à lui-même; il gardait, à travers une expérience déjà longue, une simplicité de jeunesse: sympathique à tous, de vieille race écossaise, protestant naturellement, mais assez réservé sur le sujet religieux pour qu'on pût le croire détaché ou indifférent, il avait probablement contre le monde catholique en général, contre l'obédience romaine, le préjugé héréditaire des Ecossais, les fils de Knox. Il avait la culture générale de l'Anglais qui doit plus à l'expérience, au contact des hommes qu'aux livres et cette pointe d'humour qui invente une expression imprévue, fait rire et surprend. Avec cela, des attentions affectueuses; j'avais perdu un volume d'un de ces romans anglais dont j'ai toujours nourri mes loisirs. Deux semaines plus tard, Sir Arthur avait fait venir ce volume de Londres et s'excusait de ce qu'il fût rouge et son pareil vert. Il me fit rire un jour qu'il me raconta que, lors de sa première audience avec la reine Victoria, on lui avait dit qu'il devrait s'agenouiller pour lui baiser la main. Cette révélation l'avait consterné et il l'était encore quand il se rappelait son mouvement de protestation: *No, must I really.*" (*Ce Monde disparu: Souvenirs* [Paris: Plon, 1947], pp. 159–60) The Anglo-French agreement altered the terms of the official relations between the British and the French ambassadors — though not their personal relationship, which had always been warm. Basically, Nicolson had been told to give his French counterpart a free hand. "Ce que je me rappelle avec sympathie," Madame Taillandier writes, "c'est l'attitude si noble, et de *fair play* de Sir Arthur Nicolson: il s'associait d'une âme élevée à la politique de grande envergure du cabinet de Londres, il ne manifesta aucun dépit et ne rencontra chez son collègue français aucune vanité de succès. Tous deux se serrèrent les mains, et mieux que jamais en amis." (p. 215) Saint-René Taillandier himself confirms his wife's view of Nicolson. Having great personal regard for each other, he relates, and regularly exchanging information and consulting with each other on day-to-day practical matters and events in Morocco, the two, as if by common consent, avoided "useless" discussions about the long term future of the country, since decisions on that score had to be taken in London and Paris. One day, however, on the eve of Saint-René's departure for a six-week stay in France, Nicolson broached the fenced-off topic: "It's obvious that everyone needs the people here to carry out reforms and it's equally obvious that they won't do so themselves. Helping them to do so is decidedly not our business. But it could well be yours." Saint-René Taillandier had already received a telegram from Paris indicating that negotiations with London appeared to be going well but it was Nicolson's comment that made it clear to him. "Ce mot par où, après une vive et traditionnelle rivalité de deux années, mon adversaire et ami mettait bas les armes, s'est fixé dans mon souvenir comme un bien élégant et généreux exemple de ce que nos voisins appellent le *fair-play*. Il était d'un beau joueur et d'un galant homme." (*Les Origines du Maroc français: Récit d'une mission, 1901–1906* [Paris: Plon, 1930], p. 150)

50 Monsieur St. R. T.

Georges Saint-René Taillandier (sometimes spelled Tallandier) (1852-?), appointed French Minister in Tangiers in 1901, played a major role in defending French interests in Morocco. He was in correspondence in the 1880s with Hippolyte Taine — whose niece he subsequently married — about Taine's *Origines de la France contemporaine,* the first volume of which appeared in 1875.

Taine had taken a dim view of the French Revolution. Taillandier defended the Revolution, claiming that it had resulted in the sweeping away of the Old Regime all over Europe. Taine replied that the way this occurred in England (under the influence of Locke) and in Germany (under the influence of Stein) was far preferable to the way it occurred in France (under the influence of Rousseau). Taine's letters to Taillandier, dated July 20, August 6 and November 21, 1881, are in print. Taillandier subsequently wrote an account of his activity in Morocco: *Les Origines du Maroc français; récit d'une mission 1901–1906* (Paris: Plon, 1930).

51 See under 'Raisuli'.

52 Cunningham Graham

Robert Bontine Cunninghame [note the final 'e'] Graham (1852–1936), though born in London, was of old Scottish stock, with a dash of Spanish nobility on his mother's side. This aristocrat was an adventurer, a prolific writer, a combative socialist, and a Scottish nationalist; he was the first ever avowed socialist to be elected to the British House of Commons, a founder of the Scottish Labour Party, and first President of the Scottish National Party. His political positions were what nowadays would be called "leftist," however, rather than consistently left. Probably he is best described as an anarchist, opposed to all authority. "Much has been said about the badness of the Government of Morocco," he wrote in *Mogreb-el-Acksa: A Journey in Morocco* in 1898. "Most governments are bad, the best a disagreeable institution which men submit to only because they fear to plunge into the unknown, and therefore bear taxation, armies, navies, gold-laced caps, and all the tawdry rubbish which takes from themselves, to furnish living and employment for their neighbours, under the style and title of national defences, home administration, and the like. In countries like Morocco, where men still live under the tribal system, all government must be despotic; witness Algeria, Afghanistan, and Russian Tartary. The unit is the tribe and not the individual, and what we understand by freedom and democracy would seem to them the grossest form of tyranny on earth. No doubt no man in all Morocco is secure in the enjoyment of his property; but then in order to be amenable to tyranny, one must be rich, and as most tribesmen own but a horse or two, a camel, perhaps a slave, some little patch of cultivated ground or olive garden, it is not generally on them the extortion of Government descends, but on the chief Sheikh, Kaid, or Governor, who, if he happens to be rich, can never sleep secure a single day." (London: Heinemann, 1898; quoted from the 1930 ed., New York: Viking Press, p. 53)

Mogreb-el-Acksa: A Journey in Morocco, one of Cunninghame Graham's first books, is chiefly an account of his adventures as, in the guise of "Sheikh Mohammed el Fasi" and claiming to be a Sheerif (i.e. directly descended from the Prophet), he attempted to reach the forbidden city of Tarudant. Zur Mühlen and her father both certainly knew of this journey and they may well also have read Cunninghame Graham's narrative of it.

It would be impossible to do better here than quote from the excellent Introduction to the *Selected Writings of Cunninghame Graham* (East Brunswick, London, Toronto: Associated University Presses, 1981) by Dr. Cedric Watts, a scholar who has studied Cunninghame Graham closely and written a substantial biography of him:

> Robert Bontine Cunninghame Graham was born in 1852 and died in 1936; in the interim he became a celebrity, a notoriety, a living legend; and in the aftermath he has become, gradually, a forgotten figure, his achievements neglected. Those achievements were many, the most notable (as John Lavery [a Scottish painter and friend of Cunninghame Graham] observed) being 'his masterpiece — himself.' He was a colourful, swaggering, protean adventurer: journalists called him 'a cowboy dandy,' 'the Uncrowned King of Scotland,' 'the modern Don Quixote.' He was variously traveler, cattle-rancher and horse-dealer, sword-fencer, Liberal M.P., pioneer Socialist, demagogue, convict, Mohammed el Fasi of Morocco, prospector for gold, begetter of Sergius Saranoff in Shaw's *Arms and the Man*, political columnist, essayist, critic, story-writer, historian, biographer, translator, leader of the Scottish nationalists, 'the curly darling' to factory girls and an expert with the lasso and with pistols. The list of his friends and acquaintances reads like a bizarre *Who's Who*. On political platforms he campaigned alongside William Morris, Friedrich Engels, Prince Kropotkin, Keir Hardie, H.M. Hyndman [...] Eric Linklater and Hugh McDiarmid; he was admired by figures as diverse as Wyndham Lewis, George Bernard Shaw, Jacob Epstein, G.K. Chesterton, Ezra Pound and Theodore Roosevelt; his correspondents included H.G. Wells, Henry James, Thomas Hardy, Oscar Wilde, Lawrence of Arabia and John Galsworthy; and his closest literary friendships were with Joseph Conrad, W.H. Hudson and Edward Garnett.
>
> He was born into the Scottish landed gentry [...]; his ancestry was three-quarters Scottish, one quarter Spanish. On his father's side he could trace his descent from Robert the Bruce, King Robert I of Scotland; another ancestor had fought and died beside William Wallace in 1298. [...] At the age of seventeen he went to South America to seek his fortune. During the subsequent years he frequently travelled in Central and South America, living among *gauchos*, *llaneros* and cattle-ranchers, making repeated attempts to prosper as a cattle- and horse-dealer — attempts which failed partly because of his youthful rashness, and partly because of Indian raids and the revolutionary upheavals in those regions. [...]
>
> Back in Scotland after his father's death [...] he was elected to Parliament as Liberal member for North-West Lanark [a Scottish constituency near Glasgow] in July 1886 and remained an M.P. until 1892. His Liberalism was nominal: he was attentive to the left-wing ideas of H.M. Hyndman and William Morris; the *People's Press* (26 April 1890, p. 30) regarded him as 'the only member of Parliament who can really be called a Socialist'; and indeed he was in practice the first Socialist in the House of Commons. [...] [His] scornfully ironic and uncompromising maiden speech set the tone for his subsequent parliamentary appearances, during which

he condemned British imperialism, profiteering landlords and industrialists, child labour, corporal and capital punishments, the House of Lords, and religious instruction for schoolchildren; and he advocated the eight-hour working day [...], free education, Home Rule for Ireland and Scotland, and nationalisation of mining and industry generally. [...]

His notoriety increased with his part in the 'Bloody Sunday' demonstrations of 13 November, 1887, when huge crowds of radicals, socialists, and workmen were involved in fights with police at Trafalgar Square and were not scattered until the Grenadier Guards appeared on the scene with fixed bayonets. Graham, arrested after a rush at the police, was subsequently found guilty of "unlawful assembly" and was sentenced to six weeks' imprisonment at Pentonville. His experiences as a convict did nothing to diminish his campaigning ardour: in 1888 he helped to found the Scottish Labour Party, becoming its President, with Keir Hardie as Secretary. At demonstrations on behalf of the dockers and in the campaign for the eight-hour day he appeared alongside Kropotkin, Engels, H.M. Hyndman and John Burns, and he travelled to Paris with Hardie and William Morris to speak at the Marxist Congress of the Second International. [...]

After 1900, as the Labour group in Parliament gathered strength, he turned increasingly against it: he felt that once Labour Members arrived there, they became too 'respectable,' too eager to compromise. [...] He [...] became increasingly the champion of extreme militancy, his rhetoric approaching advocacy of violent revolution. [...]

After the war, in his later years he turned increasingly to the cause of Scottish Home Rule [...] He became President of the National Party of Scotland and of its successor, the Scottish National Party, and was still head of the movement when he died in 1936.

There were good reasons why, in his lifetime, he had become known as "the modern Don Quixote." He had the style and swagger of a Spanish grandee, he admired Cervantes's hero, and on horseback, with his lean erect bearing, his upswept hair and his pointed beard, he bore some resemblance to Quixote; and his friends affectionately addressed him as Don Roberto. It is also the case that in his chivalrous impetuosity, in his concern for the underdog, and in his contempt for so much that passed for modern progress he could be seen as quixotically anachronistic. Yet this "champion of lost causes" was also ahead of his times. Many of the causes for which he fought so zealously were eventually to succeed. [...] They included, as we have seen, the eight-hour working day, militant trade-unionism, the end of sweated labour, the emergence of a Labour Party and free education; he championed the cause of feminist emancipation from the 1890s onward, and urged greater concern for oppressed racial minorities. [...]

Just as Graham's political career has received inadequate attention from historians,... so Graham's literary work seems today to have been forgotten by the general public and academic critics alike. Yet, in his lifetime, he was regarded as a master. [...] His works were customarily reviewed in tones ranging from the respectful to the gleeful. He impressed authors as diverse as Edward Garnett, Ezra Pound, Arthur Symons and John Galsworthy. [...] Joseph Conrad's tributes, in his correspondence with Graham, [...] are generous almost to the point of sycophancy. [...] Even when he is not writing at his best, he is distinctive, original, provocative. The texture may be thin, but it is wiry; [...] he always has an eye for the telling detail. [...] His tales form an extended and complex autobiography; and though it is the autobiography of a man who had a large stock of vanity and egotism, we also learn of a man who had magnanimous sympathies and indignations, and a capacity to see human efforts in multiple perspectives.

Probably Victor de Crenneville did not like Cunninghame Graham for the same reason that he did not like the similarly flamboyant Walter Harris, who, as it happens, was a friend of Cunninghame Graham's. If we can judge by Hermynia Zur Mühlen's portrait of her father, he was too cynical and *désabusé* to appreciate the energy and histrionics Graham brought to everything he did. Though she is not very forthcoming, Zur Mühlen herself could well have felt differently. She turned out to be more practical, realistic, and consistent than Graham, but she could well have recognized some of her own impulses in the rage and indignation, the anti-bourgeois stance, and — not least — the chivalrous concern for the oppressed and downtrodden of the leftist Scottish aristocrat.

53   Harris, Walter

Walter Harris (1866–1933), the son of a prosperous London businessman, educated at Harrow and (briefly) Cambridge, visited Constantinople, India, Egypt, Yemen and South Africa before settling in Tangiers in 1886 at the age of twenty. He continued to travel in and write about many areas of the Middle East, but Tangiers, where he occupied a handsome villa, was his home for the next thirty-five years. Though the interior of Morocco was largely closed to foreigners at the time, Harris was an intrepid and clever explorer and got to see and describe areas hitherto unvisited. In addition, as the correspondent of the London *Times* in Tangiers, an Arabic speaker, and the intimate of at least three of the ruling Sultans, he had many opportunities to observe every aspect of Moroccan life. After he was captured by the mountain chieftain Raisuli one day when he was out hunting, he not only succeeded in securing his own release — with the help, generously acknowledged, of Sir Arthur Nicolson, the British Minister in Tangiers — he won the respect of his captor, of whom he in turn wrote admiringly. Harris is the author of many books describing the places and societies he visited: *The Land of the African Sultan: Travels in Morocco* (London: Sampson Low, Marston, Searle and Rivington, 1889); *A Journey through the Yemen* (Edinburgh and London: William Blackwood, 1893); *Tafilat: The Narrative of a Journey of Exploration to the Atlas Mountains and the Oases of the North-west Sahara* (Edinburgh and London: William Blackwood, 1895); *From Batum to Baghdad by way of Tiflis, Tabriz and Persian Kurdistan* (Edinburgh and London: William Blackwood and Son, 1896); *Morocco that Was* (Edinburgh and London: William Backwood and Sons, 1921); *France, Spain and the Rif* (London: Arnold, 1927); *East for Pleasure: The Narrative of Eight Months' Travel in Burma, Siam, the Netherlands East Indies and French Indo-China* (London: Arnold, 1929); *East Again: The Narrative of a Journey in the Near, Middle and Far East* (n.p.: Butterworth, 1933). His books were generally favorably reviewed and deemed "most entertaining." He also published a collection of short stories, *Danovitch and other stories* (Edinburgh and London: William Blackwood and Son, 1895), as well as articles, mostly about North Africa and the Middle East, in magazines, such as *Blackwood's*, *The Independent*, and *The Geographical Journal*.

The editor of a recent re-edition of *Morocco That Was* describes Harris as "an eccentric" about whom "it is hard to distinguish the truth from the legend," a man who "loved to tell stories, especially about himself," and "loved to make his own part in any yarn he was telling into a hymn about his own cleverness, cunning, bravery, popularity, and importance. All his geese had to be swans."

Madame Saint-René Taillandier, the wife of the French envoy in Morocco, remembers him as "un petit homme vif, agile, amusant, hospitalier, se classant volontiers lui-même avec sa demeure, parmi les curiosités à montrer aux étrangers." At the same time, it is said, he was "throughout his life a trusted and valued correspondent of *The Times*, and that august journal, especially in those days, would not tolerate any divergence from strict accuracy." As with Cunninghame Graham, it would seem that Harris's vanity, self-importance, and flamboyance outweighed, for the courteous and aristocratic Victor de Crenneville, whatever virtues he might have had.

(Sources: Walter Harris, *Morocco That Was*, with a new Preface by Patrick Thursfield [London: Eland Books, 1983; orig. Edinburgh and London: W. Blackwood an Sons, 1921]; Mme Saint-René Taillandier, *Ce Monde disparu. Souvenirs* [Paris: Plon, 1947], pp. 164–65 *et passim*).

54   Count Cr.

I.e. Count Crenneville. "Graf Crenneville" was the usual short way of referring to the male members of the Folliot de Crenneville family.

55   Herr von M.

Probably Karl, Freiherr von Macchio (1859–1945), an Austrian career diplomat who was to see service in Constantinople, Bucharest, and St. Petersburg, before becoming Under-Secretary to Foreign Minister Berchtold. He spoke in Berchtold's name whenever the Foreign Minister was not available at the Ballhausplatz, the headquarters of the Austro-Hungarian Ministry of Foreign Affairs. In August, 1914 he was sent on an important special mission to Rome to support the ambassador and the embassy staff there in their efforts to delay for as long as possible an Italian declaration of war against Austria-Hungary. The episode described here by Zur Mühlen obviously occurred early in his career.

56   Count Cr.

In this passage, "Count Cr." refers to Zur Mühlen's paternal grandfather, Franz, Count Crenneville. As Governor of Livorno and Commander of the Imperial forces in Tuscany from about 1850 until 1855, Crenneville was zealous in the execution of his assignment to root out revolutionary movements in the Duchy of Tuscany. (See above under 'Paternal Grandfather'.) His own three sons were Victor (Zur Mühlen's father, born 1847), Heinrich Otto (born 1855) and Franz (born 1856). He is represented in the novel *Reise durch ein Leben* in the figure of the heroine's uncle (referred to as "*Exzellenz*"), who in his retirement from public service, has withdrawn to an old castle, where he lives alone, except for a manservant, receives no one, and spends his days and nights writing a massive history and critique of the death penalty in order to make amends for all the death warrants he signed while in the Emperor's service as governor of an Italian province.

57   My aunt, the wife of one of my father's brothers

Either Rosalie Mathilde Edler von Glaser, born 1860, married to Heinrich Otto, Count Crenneville in 1888, or Hermine, Countess Zichy zu Zichy und Vasonykeö, born 1866, married to Franz, Count Crenneville in 1895.

58   Geneva

Geneva as a gathering-place of socialist exiles from czarist Russia is also the scene of Joseph Conrad's 1911 novel *Under Western Eyes*.

59   Sir Rudolf Slatin Pasha

Rudolf Carl Slatin (1857–1932), the fourth of six children of a Jewish merchant who had converted to Christianity, was born in what is now Vienna's XIIIth District of Ober-Sankt-Veit. After a period of study at the Vienna *Handelsakademie* (commercial school), he took a job, at the age of seventeen, with a German bookseller in Cairo. He boarded ship at Trieste (then part of the Habsburg Empire) for the five-day voyage to Alexandria, set out for Khartoum soon after his arrival in Cairo and began exploring, on his own, the mountainous Dar Nuba region of the Sudan. On the outbreak of a rebellion of local Hawazma Arabs against the Egyptian government, however, being in his own words "merely a traveller" (i.e. tourist), he "received a summons to return forthwith to El Obeid, the chief town of Kodofan," whence he went back to Khartoum. There he met Mehmet Emin Pasha, a.k.a. Izaak Eduard Schnitzer, another converted Jew (in this case from Silesia) who had studied at Breslau, Königsberg and Berlin, qualified as a doctor, opened a practice in Khartoum, and attracted the attention of General Charles George Gordon, then Governor of the Equatorial Provinces of Egypt. Gordon appointed him chief medical officer of the provinces and also sent him, on account of his language skills, on various diplomatic missions. Slatin asked Emin Pasha to take him to meet Gordon, but in the meantime he was recalled to Austria to fulfill his required military service. Emin Pasha, however, did recommend the young Slatin to Gordon for employment in the Sudan, and in 1878, while serving as a lieutenant in Crown Prince Rudolf's regiment in the Bosnian campaign, Slatin received a letter from Gordon, inviting him to the Sudan, where Gordon had become Governor-General.

As soon as the Bosnian campaign was over, Slatin obtained permission to go to Africa, arriving in Khartoum in January 1879. Soon after, Gordon appointed him, at the age of twenty-two, "Mudir" or governor of Dara, the south-western part of Darfur, a post he held until early 1881, when he was promoted to be Governor-General of Darfur and given the rank of "bey." While administering Dara, Slatin conducted a successful campaign against one of the Darfur princes who was leading a revolt, and as Governor of Darfur, he endeavoured to remedy many abuses, particularly in the slave trade — even though he asserted that black Africans "do not deserve to be treated like free and independent men." (When she learned of his views on slavery, Queen Victoria, whose friendship he later enjoyed, was apparently not amused, and he was told to mind his words.) However, he soon had to confront, as Governor, the rising power of the Mahdi, Muhammad Ahmed. Early in 1882, the Arabs in southern Darfur rose in rebellion. Though victorious in over 20 engagements, Slatin kept losing ground, and as his followers attributed this to his being a Christian, he converted nominally, but publicly, to Islam (1883) in the hope of rallying his troops. All possibility of maintaining Egyptian authority vanished, however, with the almost total destruction, at the battle of El Obeid, of Colonel William Hicks's army of Egyptian *fellahin*, which had been sent to combat the Mahdi. In December 1883 Slatin surrendered, seeing it as his duty not to sacrifice lives unnecessarily in a hopeless cause. He considered taking his own life in order to avoid captivity, but "I was young," as he wrote later, "my life during the past four years had been one of anxious responsibility, but of stirring adventure as well, and I had no particular desire to bring it to a close, even with the dark prospect in front of me." (*Fire and Sword in the Sudan* [London and New York: Edward Arnold, 1896], pp. 259–60) He was therefore taken prisoner. When, a little over a year later, he rebuffed the Mahdi's efforts to get him to persuade Gordon to surrender, he was placed in chains and on January 26, 1885, within hours of the fall of Khartoum, the severed head of Gordon was brought to the camp and doubtless shown to him. On the death of the Mahdi the same year, Slatin remained as the prisoner of his successor, Khalifa Abdullahi. Obliged to serve in the latter's personal retinue, and to act as his interpreter and adviser, he was treated alternately with cruelty and comparative indulgence. In fact, Slatin tried to maintain his contacts with the Khalifa and other Mahdists, even after he had regained his freedom, in the belief that for the purposes of intelligence-gathering and negotiating, these contacts could be useful.

After over eleven years in captivity, during which, among other things, the Mahdi had provided him with two concubines, one of whom gave birth to a child by him, Slatin succeeded in making his escape, with the help of Major Sir Reginald Wingate of the Egyptian Intelligence Department, in a dangerous 600-mile three-week journey across the desert. (Wingate was a cousin of the father of Major-General Orde Wingate, the dedicated British supporter of a Jewish state in Palestine.) A year later he wrote *Fire and Sword in the Sudan*, which was not only "a Personal Narrative of Fighting and Serving the Dervishes," as stated in the subtitle, but a comprehensive account of the Sudan under the rule of the Khalifa. "By permission humbly dedicated" to "Her Most Gracious Majesty, The Queen of Great Britain and Ireland and Empress of India, who has ever shown deep solicitude for and gracious sympathy with the European prisoners in the Sudan," "by Her Majesty's most devoted and faithful Rudolf C. Slatin," the book was published simultaneously in German and in an English translation heavily edited by Wingate. It was translated into French and Italian and became a Europe-wide bestseller. Raised to the rank of Pasha by the Ottoman Khedive or Viceroy of Egypt, Slatin was made a CB (Companion of the Order of the Bath) and shortly afterwards a KCMG (Knight Commander of the Order of St. Michael and St. Geoge) by Queen Victoria in recognition of his services. In Austria, he was given an audience with Franz Joseph who made him a baron with the title "Freiherr von Slatin." In 1899, he was knighted by Queen Victoria and made a Brigadier-General in the British army; in 1900 he was appointed Inspector-General of the Sudan, a title which no one had held before or was to hold after him and which he held until the outbreak of war in 1914; and in 1907 he was made an honorary Major-General in the British army. He was a favourite and a frequent guest, at Windsor and Balmoral, of Queen Victoria, who had a portrait of him painted for her own collection by one of her personal portrait-painters, Heinrich von Angeli. He was also a guest at other European courts.

By the time Zur Mühlen met Slatin in Morocco, therefore, he was a European celebrity. Hence her surprise and delight at finding him modest and unassuming.

As Inspector-General of the Sudan, Slatin pursued a policy of strengthening "orthodox" Islam as a barrier against what he saw as Sufi and Mahdist fanaticism. He tried to limit Christian proselytizing and to reinforce tribal leadership and family bonds. The outbreak of war between Great Britain and Austria-Hungary in 1914 was particularly painful for him. His entire career had been in the service of the British monarchy. Now he had to give up his position and separate from some of his closest friends. (He and Wingate were especially close, worked together in the administration of the Sudan, and had complete trust in one another.) Returning to Austria, he settled in the villa at Traunkirchen (only a few miles from Zur Mühlen's beloved Gmunden) which he had purchased in 1897 and where he had been host to many noted personalities, including King Edward VII. He took no active part in the war but instead headed the Prisoners-of-War section of the Austrian Red Cross, which allowed him to intervene on behalf of British prisoners-of-war, and he is said to have been involved in attempts to work out a separate peace between Great Britain and France on the one hand and Austria-Hungary on the other. In 1919, he was a member of the Austrian delegation that negotiated the peace treaty between the new Republic of Austria and the victorious allied powers. In recognition of his having secured food supplies for the starving population of Vienna in 1918, he was made an honorary citizen of Vienna. After the death, in 1921, of his wife, Baroness Alice von Ramberg, whom he had married in 1914 and by whom he had a daughter, he moved to Merano, formerly in Austria, but Italian since the end of the war. In June 1932, a couple of months before his own death following a cancer operation in Vienna, he and his daughter, Anne-Marie, were received by King George V in London.

A movie about Slatin, entitled *Slatin Pascha* was produced in 1967 by the German TV channel ZDF and and a 90-minute documentary about him was completed in 2012 by the Austrian company Fischer Film.

60 Baron Oppenheim

Max von Oppenheim (1860–1946), an internationally renowned orientalist and archaeologist, known to the British in World War I as "the Kaiser's spy," was born into a wealthy Jewish banking family in Cologne. The private bank known as "Sal. [i.e. Salomon] Oppenheim," founded in 1789, exists to this day, though its headquarters were moved to Luxembourg in 2007. It is said to be the largest such bank in Europe, with about 3,100 employees.

The Oppenheims are first mentioned as silk merchants in Frankfurt in the 16th century. In 1740 a Salomon Oppenheim moved to Bonn where the Oppenheims became court factors of the Elector Clement August. The founder of the modern banking business of Sal. Oppenheim Jr & Cie was a younger Salomon (1772–1828) who transferred it in 1798 to Cologne. His sons, Simon (1803–1880) and Abraham (1804–1878), together with their mother Therese, who had taken over the management of the firm on her husband's death, transformed it into a powerful engine of modern commercial and industrial capitalism in Germany. Linked by marriage to other Jewish banking families — the Rothschilds, the Habers, the Foulds — the Oppenheims were involved in the financing of Germany's first industrial firms: they promoted railroad construction, river transportation, insurance, and corporate banks in Germany and abroad, and they helped to finance the up-and-coming heavy industry in the Ruhr, including the Krupp company. In the first half of the nineteenth century Simon and Abraham identified themselves as Jews and sought to advance the cause of Jewish emancipation. In 1841, for example, they submitted "a humble petition" for emancipation of the Jews to the King of Prussia. Twenty years later Abraham helped to fund the construction of a handsome new synagogue in Cologne. Along with a third brother, Dagobert (originally David, 1809–1889), the brothers also supported general cultural and philanthropic ventures in Cologne. They were among the founding members of the Cologne Kunstverein [Art Association] in 1839; they immediately joined the Zentral-Dombau-Verein, set up in 1842 to ensure preservation of the fabric of Cologne's great cathedral; and in 1859 Dagobert and his son Eduard (1831–1909) played a major role in the establishment of the Cologne

Zoo and the "Flora" Horticultural Society. In 1875 Simon and Abraham, along with Dagobert's sons Eduard and Albert (1834–1912), provided funding for the Cologne Music Conservatory. In 1867, "for services in railway financing," Simon was ennobled by Emperor Franz Joseph of Austria with the hereditary title of baron (*Freiherr*); Abraham received the same honour from the Prussian monarch a year later. In 1856, on the occasion of his marriage to the daughter of a prominent Catholic family in Cologne, Dagobert's son Albert — who was to be a major art collector — embraced the Roman Catholic faith; his brother Eduard converted to Protestantism the following year. As they were the only male heirs, the family's and the firm's Jewish connections were thereby ended. Max von Oppenheim was the son of Albert.

It was intended that Max should enter the firm and prepare to take it over when the time came. Max, however, had developed a keen interest in the Islamic world and dreamed of devoting his life to the study of the peoples and cultures of the Middle East and North Africa. After he obtained a law degree in 1883, his father permitted him to undertake a journey to the Orient. In the winter of 1883–1884 he accompanied an uncle to Athens, Smyrna and Constantinople. In 1886 he spent six months in Morocco in what he describes as a *Forschungsreise* [research trip], and he learned Arabic. He himself recounts the subsequent development of his career in the first volume (1939) of his book on the Bedouins:

> In 1892 I was able to begin pursuing my scholarly activities in the Orient on a larger scale. With the ethnographer Wilhelm Joest, a fellow-citizen of Cologne, I travelled from Morocco right across North Africa. At the end of the trip I stopped for some months in Cairo, where I lodged in an Arab house in the native quarter. Here I lived exactly as the local Muslims did in order to develop my fluency in the Arabic language and to study thoroughly the spirit of Islam and the customs and manners of the native inhabitants. My plan was to prepare myself in this way for further expeditions that would lead me into the Eastern part of the Arab world. In the Spring of 1893, my path led to Damascus. From here I set out on my first truly major research trip in the Near East. It is narrated in my two-volume book *Vom Mittelmeer zum Persischen Golf durch den Haurān und die Syrische Wüste* [1899–1900]. [...]
>
> As early as this 1893 trip I was able to collect much material on the Bedouins. This is laid out in the second volume of the aforementioned book. In the course of this expedition I came to love the wild, unconstrained life of the sons of the desert. [...] In Cairo I had already become accustomed to eating with my fingers (one may use only those of the right hand), as was still then the practice in the Cairene middle classes, instead of with a knife and fork. [...] That is naturally how I ate with the Bedouins, both when I was their guest and when they were my guests. By sharing their way of life in the saddle and in the tent, I acquired ever greater knowledge of their ways. They felt that I was well disposed towards them and that I understood their customs and peculiarities. Hence, they were also well disposed towards me and readily answered any question I put to them. [...]
>
> The return journey from Mesopotamia took me by way of the Persian Gulf and India to our then young and beautiful colony of East Africa. I made an expedition into the interior, in the course of which I acquired an extensive tract of land in Usambara, which was later turned into plantations by the *Rheinische*

Handel-Plantagen-Gesellschaft, which here successfully cultivated first the coffee bean, and then, after the coffee worm made its appearance, sisal — until this flourishing plantation was lost to Germany as a consequence of the World War. [...]

From there I returned to Cairo, where in early 1894 I met Zuber Pasha who, by hunting for men to sell as slaves, had succeeded in establishing a large principality. As he began to become too strong, however, Khedive Ismail enticed him to Cairo where he detained him in a beautiful palace, that was like a gilded cage. From Zuber Pasha, I obtained extraordinarily interesting information about one of his former generals named Rabeh, who had refused to capitulate to the Egyptians and had moved westwards from the Nile valley with a large number of his former soldiers and their families.

Back in Germany, I wrote up a report on this, as well as on other things I had learned in Cairo about the area around Lake Chad and about the Muslim order of the Senussi, which was of great importance not only from a religious but also from a political standpoint. This report led the Foreign Office to ask me, in the context of our rivalry with France and England, to lead a German expedition into the hinterland of the Cameroons in order to acquire the area up to Lake Chad for Germany. [...]

Our expedition plans had to be abandoned however. In the competition involving France, England and Germany the aforementioned Rabeh had moved faster than the European powers. Starting out from the Egyptian Sudan he had led his army from victory to victory, like a black Napoleon, and had seized all the lands south of Wadai [a former kingdom situated between Lake Chad and Darfur] together with the large kingdoms of Bagirmi and Bornu. Still, his reign was of short duration. He fell in a battle with the French and the empire he founded collapsed. When his lands were divided up by the European colonial powers, my expedition, which was all ready to go, became part of the bargaining process. Germany received the so-called "Caprivi-strip" of our Cameroons colony, namely large parts of Bagirmi and Bornu and thereby access to Lake Chad.

From then on I was employed by the Foreign Office and attached to our diplomatic legation in Cairo. From there I was in a position to observe closely all the affairs of the Islamic world. No place was better for this than Cairo. The Egyptian Press, published in the Arabic of the Koran, was of decisive importance for the entire Islamic world from the Atlantic to China. Whereas in Turkey Sultan Abdul Hamid wielded absolute power and did not tolerate the free expression of opinion in the newspapers, Cairo was the resort of all Muslim political refugees, especially those from the Ottoman Empire.

But I also managed to establish excellent relations with Sultan Abdul Hamid [...] [who] asked me to call on him whenever I was in Constantinople, which I regularly did.

Oppenheim goes on to tell of the "excellent relations" he established through the Sultan with the family of Emir Faisal, who was to become King of Iraq — and a personal friend, with Abdul Huda, the Sultan's astrologer and the head of the "widespread Muslim brotherhood of Rifa'ija," and with many other personalities of the Muslim world.

With a few interruptions, when he was attached to the Embassies in Washington and Paris or was employed by the Foreign Office in Berlin itself, Oppenheim spent the years from 1896 until 1909, he relates, in Cairo, where his house "was on the border between the native and the European quarters" and where he entertained many Egyptians and other Muslims. It was during this period that Zur Mühlen and her father met him.

It seems clear that Oppenheim's scholarly interest in the world of Islam cannot be dissociated from the politics of the time and in particular from the intense rivalry among the European powers for influence in Africa and the Middle East. It is not surprising therefore that the scholar was approached by Georg von Siemens, the Director of the Deutsche Bank, about prospecting and giving advice on the best route for the Berlin-to-Baghdad railway on the stretch between Aleppo and Mosul. Though the German Foreign Office would not allow Oppenheim to accept this commission openly, for fear that the participation of a Foreign Office agent in the project would be viewed with displeasure and suspicion by the British, the scholar was able to give Siemens the requested advice privately. It seems, moreover, that Oppenheim and his scholarly associates sometimes lodged in the same buildings as the engineers of the Berlin-to-Baghdad railway.

Oppenheim's role in German national politics went considerably further than establishing contacts with leading Muslims and providing Berlin with useful information. In the decades preceding the First World War Kaiser Wilhelm II was actively pursuing an Ottoman-German alliance to counter British and French influence in the Middle East. He had even re-affirmed his friendship with the Ottoman Sultan after an 1896 Turkish massacre of Christian Armenians had shocked most of Europe. Oppenheim's profound knowledge of the region, the voluminous notes he had taken, the countless maps he had drawn, and not least his contacts with Muslim tribal chieftains and leaders were clearly of immense value to the German government and it is hardly to be wondered at that he was soon engaged directly in working for it. What Zur Mühlen reports in her memoir about him and his activities reflects the general opinion of the time, especially in British and French diplomatic circles (but also, thanks to John Buchan's popular spy thriller *Greenmantle* of 1916, in the English-speaking public at large). Oppenheim, in the words of one recent historian, "travelled extensively throughout Mesopotamia and Syria, [...] mapping and taking meticulous notes on everything. [...] It was not long before the British guessed that he, and other scholars, were working for the Kaiser's intelligence services."

Oppenheim's great journey of 1899 from Cairo by way of Aleppo and Urfa to the Khabur, which resulted in his main claim to scholarly fame, the discovery of Tel-Halaf in Syrian Kurdistan, with its rich treasure of Neolithic artefacts from 4,000–5,000 B.C.E., was not, as we have seen, unconnected with prospecting the route of the Berlin to Baghdad railway. A year earlier, shortly before a projected visit of the Kaiser to Constantinople, the scholar had sent a memorandum to Berlin from Cairo, dated 5 July, 1898, in which he reported on pan-Islamic movements in the Middle East and suggested that *jihad* or Muslim holy war could be a mighty weapon if Muslims could actually be made ready and willing to engage in it. Were *jihad* proclaimed, he wrote, volunteers and money from all over the Islamic world would arrive for the Sultan, as happened in his 1877–78 war against Russia. Since Germany, of all the Christian nations, was considered by Muslims to be their best friend, according to Oppenheim, the message of the memorandum was clear: prepare to use the Sultan to call for *jihad* in the colonial territories of potential enemies. Despite some disagreement about how effective it actually was, there is general consensus among modern scholars that the "Holy War strategy," which the Kaiser did in fact adopt in the 1914–1918 War, was "mainly Oppenheim's idea" and that, as its "principal architect" and "mastermind," he was also largely in charge of its execution. It may well be, for instance, that his advice influenced the Sultan's decision in the summer of 1915 to persuade the head of the Senussi religious brotherhood, the Grand Senussi Ahmed Sharif es-Sanussi, to order his tribesmen to attack British-occupied Egypt from the west, raise *jihad*, and foment an insurrection within Egypt against the British. The so-called Senussi revolt turned out to be a serious challenge to the Allied war effort. As Oppenheim himself recalled in the Introduction to his 1939 book on the Bedouins, he had submitted a memorandum to the German Foreign Office in the 1890s on the Sanussi brotherhood, and the military leader of the revolt, Jaafar Pasha al-Askari, a Kurd from Mesopotamia and a former Ottoman army officer, had been trained in Germany.

Around 1909 Oppenheim withdrew from the Foreign Service to devote himself fully to the excavations at Tel-Halaf, having been advised by the Turkish government that he must act immediately on the right to excavate, which he had obtained ten years earlier from the Sultan, since the English were now requesting permission to explore the site. On the outbreak of war, however, he was summoned to Berlin by the Kaiser to head the newly created Oriental News Department at the Foreign Ministry, for which a dozen German academics had been recruited, and the aim of which was to spread propaganda among Muslims. Soon after, in October 1914, he submitted a top secret 136-page report to the Kaiser entitled "Die Revolutionierung der islamischen Gebiete unserer Feinde" ("Fomenting Revolution in the Islamic territories of our enemies"). The report recommended that the Sultan proclaim a *jihad* against the French, the British, and the Russians and that he receive support from Berlin in the form of money, experts, and matériel. The targets of the propaganda effort were to be Muslims in British India, French North Africa, and Russian Asia. In 1915 Oppenheim was sent to head the News Department of the German Embassy in Constantinople. Among other measures, he initiated and oversaw the production of thousands of propaganda leaflets and booklets for distribution in Muslim countries, started a film company to produce newsreels and other short propaganda movies, and created a network of 70 reading halls (*Nachrichtensaale*) in major population centres where his guidelines for *jihad* were to be communicated and spread.

With the defeat of Germany, Oppenheim's nationalist dreams for his country also collapsed. He took up the excavations at Tel-Halaf again and published accounts of the findings, of which he had to give half over to the Syrian authorities. To house and exhibit his share of them he established the Tel-Halaf Museum in Berlin in 1930 and at the same time set up a Foundation, the Max-Freiherr von Oppenheim Stiftung, to promote research into all aspects of the societies and cultures of the Near East, from prehistoric times to the present. The Foundation had a library of 40,000 books and a large collection of Islamic manuscripts and artefacts.

Despite his Jewish origins — after all, though his mother was Christian, his father was a converted Jew and he was therefore, by Nazi standards, half-Jewish — Oppenheim was not molested by the Nazis and continued to live freely in Berlin. Perhaps he was too useful to them. In December 1935 he still professed optimism that, as he wrote in a letter to a nephew, by the time the 150th anniversary of the Oppenheim Bank came around in 1939 "the current unfriendliness with regard to the Jewish origins of the Oppenheims will have faded." Marjorie Veronica Seton Williams, the Australian-born archaeologist, tells of visiting the Tel-Halaf Museum in 1937 and being shown around it by Oppenheim himself, followed by a manservant, who poured the pair a glass of wine every time they stopped. In 1939 Oppenheim made a further final expedition into the Middle East. A report in the New York Times, dated Istanbul, April 7 1941, tells of "three Reich plotters," of whom Oppenheim, "a distinguished archaeologist and astute propagandist" was one, who "after gains in Iraq," had sought support in Syria "for Hitler as 'Protector of Islam,'" and had made "fantastic pedges" to the Arab population. Oppenheim was apparently willing to go to great lengths to ensure his survival, if that is how we are to interpret his active participation in propagandizing for the Third Reich.

The first, richly illustrated and handsomely produced volume of his scholarly study of the Bedouins was published in Leipzig in 1939, under his own name. "Max, Freiherr von Oppenheim." The second volume appeared in 1943, still under the Oppenheim name, even though, as early as 1887 that name had been deemed so "obviously semitic" by a Foreign Office official that he considered a regular diplomatic career impossible for anyone bearing it. The year 1943 also saw the publication with De Gruyter of Berlin, likewise under Oppenheim's own name, of the magnificent first volume of his study of Tel-Halaf. In the Foreword, the author thanks the *Deutsche Forschungsgesellschaft* for financially supporting the publication of his work.

Hoping perhaps to demonstrate his family's continued devotion to what he called, in the letter to his nephew, "das Deutschtum," Oppenheim even revived his earlier anti-British *jihad* plan. In July 1940 he sent a shortened version of it to the German Foreign Office. As France had by then been neutralized, the revised plan focused on provoking uprisings against the British in Iraq and Saudi Arabia, blocking the Suez Canal, and fomenting revolution in India. He recommended co-operation with the Palestinian leader Mohammed Amin al-Husseini, the Grand Mufti of Jerusalem from 1921 to 1948, the setting up of a

Palestinian state under al-Husseini, and the expulsion of all Jews who had not been residents of Palestine before the outbreak of war.

Max von Oppenheim remained in Berlin until he was bombed out of his elegant apartment there toward the end of the Second World War. He moved to Dresden, where he survived the massive destruction of the city. His Tel-Halaf Museum in Berlin was also destroyed in a bombing raid, however. What remained of the collection was subsequently moved to Cologne. Oppenheim retired to Landshut in Lower Bavaria, not far from Munich, where he died in November 1946.

Zur Mühlen's account of the man she and her parents met or at least heard stories about more than two decades before the composition of her memoir appears to reflect some knowledge gained after her visit to Cairo. One cannot help wondering what she may have known, later still, of the last stage of his extraordinary career.

(Sources: Max Freiherr von Oppenheim, *Vom Mittelmeer zum persischen Golf*, 2 vols. [Berlin Dietrich Reimer, 1899–1900]; id., *Die Beduinen*, 4 vols., vol. 1 [Leipzig: Otto Harrassowitz, 1939], vol. 2 [Leipzig: Otto Harrassowitz, 1943]; id., *Tell Halaf*, 4 vols., vol. 1 [Berlin: Walter de Gruyter, 1943]; *Die Revolutionierung der islamischen Gebiete unserer Feinde* [Denkschrift, Berlin, 1914, in Jäckh papers, microfilm 11747, Princeton University Library]; Werner Caskel, "Max Freiherr von Oppenheim, Nachruf," *Zeitschrift der Deutschen Morgenländischen Gesellschaft* [1955], 101: 3–8; Peter Hopkins, *On Secret Service East of Constantinople* [London: John Murray, 1994], pp. 19, 78, 132; Donald M. McKale, "'The Kaiser's Spy': Max von Oppenheim and the Anglo-German Rivalry Before and During the First World War," *European History Quarterly*, 27 [1997]: 199–220; R. L. Melka "Max Freiherr von Oppenheim: Sixty Years of Scholarship and Political Intrigue in the Middle East," *Middle Eastern Studies* [1973] 9: 81–93; Lothar Rathmann, *Stossrichtung Nahost 1914–1918: Zur Expansionspolitik des deutschen Imperialismus im ersten Weltkrieg* [Berlin: Tütten & Loenig, 1962], pp, 28–30, 107–108, 189–93; Wolfgang G. Schwanitz, "Euro-Islam by 'Jihad Made in Germany'," in Nathalie Clayer and Eric Germain, eds., *Islam in Inter-War Europe* [New York: Columbia University Press, 1998], pp. 271–301, especially pp. 275–81, 293; M.V. Seton Williams, *The Road to El-Aguzein* [London: Kegan Paul International, 1988], pp. 71–72; Hew Strachan, *The First World War* [Oxford: Oxford University Press, 2001], vol. 1, pp. 694–712, 770–72; Gabriele Teichmann in *Neue Deutsche Biographie*, 19, p. 559; Michael Stürmer, Gabriele Teichmann, and Wilhelm Treue, *Wägen und Wagen: Sal. Oppenheim, Jr. & Cie. Geschichte einer Bank und einer Familie* [Munich: Piper, 1989], pp. 371–73 *et passim*; Gabriele Teichmann and Gisela Völger, *Faszination Orient: Max von Oppenheim, Forscher, Sammler, Diplomat* [Cologne: DuMont, 2001]. In addition: http://www.oppenheim.de/deen/about_us_at_a_glance/history. A somewhat dissenting view of the importance of Oppenheim's role in the jihad strategy is offered by Marian Kent, *The Great Powers and the Late Ottoman Empire* [London: George Allen and Unwin, 1984],

p. 121). See also Lionel Gossman, *The Passion of Max von Oppenheim: Archaeology and Intrigue in the Middle East from Wilhelm II to Hitler* (Cambridge: Open Book Publishers, 2013), https://www.openbookpublishers.com/product/163.

61   "Fantasia Kebir"

Aïd el-Kebir, the Festival of Sacrifice, is a Muslim holiday celebrated worldwide to commemorate Abraham's willingness to sacrifice his son as an act of obedience to Allah. A lamb, representing the lamb or ram that was sacrificed in place of Isaac, is traditionally slaughtered on the day of the festival. German travelers and archaeologists in the second half of the nineteenth century refer to Aïd el-Kebir as "Fantasia Kebir." During the night, it seems, there was much noisy celebration, music, and dancing.

62   Jihad

"Dschehad" in Zur Mühlen's text. The topic was in the air at the time. For more on Imperial German plans to incite the Muslim subjects of Britain, France, and Russia to Holy War against the infidel, see under 'Oppenheim' and 'Paul Weitz.' A most readable — and in the year 2018 — chilling account of these plans is given by Henry Morgenthau, American Ambassador in Constantinople at the time of World War I, in his book *Ambassador Morgenthau's Story*, first published in 1918.

> In the early days, Wangenheim [Hans Freiherr von Wangenheim, German Ambassador to the Ottoman Empire, 1912–1915] had explained to me one of Germany's main purposes in forcing Turkey into the conflict. He made this explanation quietly and nonchalantly, as though it had been quite the most ordinary matter in the world. Sitting in his office, puffing away at his big black German cigar, he unfolded Germany's scheme to arouse the whole fanatical Moslem world against the Christians. Germany had planned a real "holy war" as one means of destroying English and French influence in the world. "Turkey herself is really the important matter," said Wangenheim. "her army is a small one… But the big thing is the Moslem world. If we can stir the Mohammedans up against the English and Russians, we can force them to make peace."
>
> What Wangenheim evidently meant by the "Big thing" became apparent on November 13, when the Sultan issued his declaration of war; this declaration was really an appeal for a *Jihad*, or a "Holy War" against the infidel. Soon afterward the Sheik-ul-Islam published his proclamation, summoning the whole Moslem world to arise and massacre their Christian oppressors. "Oh, Moslems," concluded this document, "Ye who are smitten with happiness and are on the verge of sacrificing your life and your goods for the cause of right…, gather now around the Imperial throne, obey the commands of the Almighty, who, in the Koran, promises us bliss in this and in the next world; embrace ye the foot of the Caliph's throne and know ye that the state is at war with Russia, England, France, and their Allies, and that these are the enemies of Islam. The Chief of the believers, the Caliph, invites you all as Moslems to join in the Holy War!"
>
> The religious leaders read this proclamation to their assembled congregations in the mosques; all the newspapers printed it conspicuously; it was broadcast in all the countries which had a large Mohammedan population — India, China,

Persia, Egypt, Algiers, Tripoli, Morocco, and the like; in all these places it was read to the assembled multitudes and the populace was exhorted to obey the mandate. The Ikdam, the Turkish newspaper which had passed into German ownership, was constantly inciting the masses. "The deeds of our enemies," wrote this Turco-German editor, "have brought down the wrath of God. A gleam of hope has appeared. All Mohammedans, young and old, men, women and children, must fulfil their duty so that the gleam may not fade away, but give light to us for ever. How many great things can be accomplished by the arms of vigorous men, by the aid of others, of women and children!... The time for action has come. We shall all have to fight with all our strength, with all our soul, with teeth and nails, with all the sinews of our bodies and of our spirits. If we do it, the deliverance of the subjected Mohammedan kingdoms is assured... Allah is our aid and the Prophet is our support."

The Sultan's proclamation was an official public document, and dealt with the proposed Holy War only in a general way, but about this time a secret pamphlet appeared which gave instructions to the faithful in more specific terms. [...] It was printed in Arabic, the language of the Koran. It was a lengthy document [...] full of quotations from the Koran, and its style was frenzied in its appeal to racial and religious hatred. It described a detailed plan of operations for the assassination and extermination of all Christians — except those of German nationality. A few extracts will portray its spirit: "O people of the faith and O beloved Moslems, consider even though but for a brief moment, the present condition of the Islamic world. For if you consider this but a little, you will weep long. You will behold a bewildering state of affairs which will cause the tear to fall and the fire of grief to blaze. You see the great country of India, which contains hundreds of millions of Moslems, fallen, because of religious divisions and weaknesses into the grasp of the enemies of God, the infidel English. You see forty millions of Moslems in Java shackled by the chains of captivity and of affliction under the rule of the Dutch. [...] You see Egypt, Morocco, Tunis, Algeria, and the Sudan [...] groaning in the grasp of the enemies of God and his apostle. [...] Wherever you look you see that the enemies of the true religion, particularly the English, the Russians, and the French, have oppressed Islam and invaded its rights in every possible way. We cannot enumerate the insults we have received at the hands of these nations who desire totally to destroy Islam and drive all Mohammedans off the face of the earth. This tyranny has passed all endurable limits; the cup of our oppression is full to overflowing. [...] In brief, the Moslems work and infidels eat; the Moslems are hungry and suffer and infidels gorge themselves and live in luxury. The world of Islam sinks down and goes backward, and the Christian world goes forward and is more and more exalted. The Moslems are enslaved and the infidels are the great rulers. This is all because the Moslems have abandoned the plan set forth in the Koran and ignored the Holy War which it commands. [...] But the time has now come for the Holy War, and by this the land of Islam shall be for ever freed from the power of the infidels who oppress it. This holy war has now become a sacred duty. Know ye that the blood of infidels in the Islamic lands may be shed with impunity. [...] The killing of infidels who rule over Islam has become a sacred duty, whether you do it secretly or openly, as the Koran has decreed: 'Take them and kill them whenever you find them. Behold we have delivered them unto your hands and given you supreme power over them.' He who kills even one unbeliever of those who rule over us, whether he does it secretly or openly, shall be rewarded by God. And let every Moslem, in whatever part of the world he may be, swear a solemn oath to kill at least three or four of the infidels who rule over him, for they are the enemies of God and of the faith. Let every Moslem know that his reward for doing so shall be doubled by the God who created heaven and earth. A Moslem who does this shall be saved from the terrors of the day of Judgment, of the resurrection of the dead. [...] The time has come that we should rise up as the rising of one man, in one hand a sword, in the other a gun, in his pockets balls of fire and death-dealing missiles, and in his heart the light of the faith [...]"

Specific instruction for carrying out this holy purpose follow. There shall be a "heart war" — every follower of the Prophet, that is, shall constantly nourish in his spirit a hatred of the infidel; a "speech war" — with tongue and pen every Moslem shall spread this same hatred wherever Mohammedans live; and a war of deed — fighting and killing the infidel wherever he shows his head..." The Holy War," says the pamphlet, "will be of three forms. First, the individual war, which consists of the individual personal deed. This may be carried on with cutting, killing instruments, [...] like the slaying of the English chief of police in India, and like the killing of one of the officials arriving in Mecca by Abi Busir (may God be pleased with him)." The document gives several other instances of assassination which the faithful are enjoined to imitate. Second, the believers are told to organize "bands," and to go forth and slay Christians. The most useful are those organized and operating in secret. "It is to be hoped that the Islamic world of to-day will profit very greatly from such secret bands." The third method is by "organized campaigns," that is, by trained armies.

Morgenthau goes on to explain that "in all parts of this incentive to murder and assassination there are indications that a German hand has exercised an editorial supervision." Only those infidels "who rule over us" are to be slain. The Germans and Austrians, in short, are excluded. (*Ambassador Morgenthau's Story* [Ann Arbor, MI: Gomidas Institute, 2000; orig. 1918], pp. 107–11) As Zur Mühlen implies, the plan for an Islamic Jihad against Germany's enemies did not come close to meeting the expectations of its advocates.

(See Gottfried Hagen, *Die Türkei im ersten Weltkrieg* [Frankfurt a.M./ Bern/ New York/ Paris: Peter Lang, 1990], pp. 3–8, 26–44; Peter Heine, "Al-Ğihād: eine deutsche Propagandazeitung im 1. Weltkrieg," *Die Welt des Islams* [1980], 20: 197–99; id., "C. Snouk Hurgronje versus C.H. Becker. Ein Beitrag zur Geschichte der angewandten Orientalistik," ibid. [1984], 23/24: 378–87; Peter Hopkins, *On Secret Service East of Constantinople. The Plan to Bring Down the British Empire* [London: John Murray, 1994], pp. 54 ff.; Herbert Landolin Müller, *Islam, ğihād (Heiliger Krieg) und Deutsches Reich* [Frankfurt a.M./ Bern/ New York/ Paris: Peter Lang, 1991], pp. 172–213; Ulrich Trumpeter, *Germany and the Ottoman Empire 1914–1918* [Princeton: Princeton University Press, 1968], pp. 117–21; and the text of the Proclamation and the fatwās justifying it, transl. by G. Lewis, "The Ottoman Proclamation of Jihād in 1914," *Islamic Quarterly* [1975], 19: 157–63).

63 Baron Dummreicher

André von Dumreicher was indeed a Württemberger, as Zur Mühlen noted. In 1899, on being honoured by the government of Württemberg for distinguished service abroad, he was described in the citation as "Major in the Egyptian Camel Corps, André von Dumreicher of Stuttgart." Earlier members of his family had grown cotton and owned cotton mills in Egypt, and Napoleon, it is said, stayed at their house in Alexandria during the Egyptian campaign. He himself served for many years in Egypt, with ever widening responsibilities, as head of the Camel Corps section of the Egyptian Coastguard Administration. "In 1900," he recounts, "I took over the five newly built coastguard  stations between Alexandria and Soloun, at the border with Tripoli, and in 1905 I also took over command of the Camel Corps of the Suez Canal district and was appointed Director of the 'Desert Directorate,' which embraced the Libyan, Arabian, and Nubian deserts, as well as the Sinai peninsula, with a complement of 500 camels."

His chief responsibilities, in his own words, were "to prevent the smuggling of hashish and salt," the Egyptian government having imposed a salt monopoly, of which, as it happens, Dumreicher did not approve, "to establish and maintain order in the desert areas bordering the Nile valley, and to prevent the illegal landing of pilgrims on the coast of the Red Sea and along the Suez Canal, chiefly on account of the danger of cholera." He also took over the selection and purchase of camels for the Corps, after he succeeded in persuading the authorities that he was a better judge of the animals than the Veterinary Department. In addition, he supervised various building projects, including the construction of a new harbor for the sponge-fishing fleet and a new mosque in Mersa Matruh.

Dumreicher was a good friend of the all-powerful British Consul-General in Cairo, Sir Eldon Gorst (1861–1911), to whose niece he was married. On the outbreak of war between Great Britain and Germany in 1914 he was protected by Kitchener, the newly appointed Secretary of the Army, but on Kitchener's death in June 1916, he was interned in England. In 1931, two years after the appearance of Zur Mühlen's memoir, von Dumreicher published *Fahrten, Pfadfinder und Beduinen in den Wüsten Ägyptens* (Munich: Drei Masken Verlag), which appeared simultaneously in English as *Trackers and Smugglers in the Deserts of Egypt* (London: Methuen; New York: Dial Press).

This engaging and well-written book confirms Zur Mühlen's brief description of the Camel Corps commander. He understands and admires the Bedouins among whom he lives and he also demonstrates great respect and affection for the 20 or so officers who served under him, both Egyptian and European, as well as for his men, many of whom came from the Sudan. His narrative is full of delightful anecdotes — signs of an independent temperament that was likely to appeal to Zur Mühlen. One of them in particular must surely have greatly pleased her if she heard him tell it:

> Among the colonists ["mostly small hawkers and shopkeepers," Dumreicher had explained, "anxious to trade with the fishermen and Bedouins, but also some unfortunate derelicts driven here, to Mersa Matruh, by starvation"], I was particularly impressed by a young Frenchman named E. because of his modesty

and polite manners. He kept completely to himself, and I was not particularly curious about his earlier life. He traded in a small way with the Bedouins, was interested in cultivating barley, and made unfired bricks from a mixture of clay, mud, marl, and sand. With these he was able to build a better kind of hut.

After a few months the chief of police in Alexandria sent me a telegram inquiring whether I had a dangerous French anarchist named E. at Matruh. He had been recognized there by the Khedive's French chauffeur. I replied that E. was my best colonist; whether he was an anarchist or not was not my concern; he was certainly no danger to anybody. Yes, I was told, but the French consulate wants him extradited from Egypt, because, besides being an anarchist, he is a deserter. I sent for E. and asked him if he was an anarchist. "Oui, Monsieur," he replied. I asked him why. "Well, he had seen so much undeserved misery among the workers in France. He had also left France when he was about to be called up for army service because he considered it morally wrong, in case there should be a war, to have to shoot at one's fellow men. He had come to Mersa Matruh in the hope that the Egyptian government would be less brutal than the French one." That last was in fact the case, for I had advanced him money out of my Colonist Fund to help him build his little house. I promised him that I would protect him and that I would give him secret warning if he was about to be extradited so that he could go into hiding for a while. Thanks to my intervening with the various authorities, he was given permission to stay on in Matruh after he had promised me that he would not make anarchist propaganda. Whereupon he simply expressed his honest regret that a decent man like myself was not an anarchist and he made a sincere effort to convert me. He gave me the anarchist pamphlets he had smuggled into the country and, according to the terms of our agreement, could no longer distribute, and asked me to read them. E. had certainly never fabricated a bomb. But in putting together the various kinds of earth and soil to make his bricks, he had demonstrated that he was a professional. So I appointed him my architect for the construction of the many buildings the Coast Guard had to put up and later I was able to get him a good job with a big company in Cairo. Then he asked me for a letter of recommendation to the head of the municipality of Alexandria. I wrote in the letter: "E. is an anarchist but he is the only man of my acquaintance about whom I know for certain that he is more honourable than I." With this recommendation he also got a good job working for the municipality. When E. maintained that I was the more honourable of the two of us, I asked him if he would tell a lie if that was necessary to save his life. He replied emphatically that he hoped not. I then said that he was in that case the more honourable of the two of us, because I would be willing to lie twice in order to save my life." (Translated from the German text, p. 16)

Dumreicher also published a small book in French (Colonel de Dumreicher Bey, *Le Tourisme dans les déserts d'Égypte* [Alexandria: La Cité du Livre; Paris: Larose, 1931]) on "developing tourism, encouraging agriculture as well as the raising of sheep and camels, and promoting geological and archaeological research in the Egyptian deserts." The little volume also includes an extremely sympathetic account of "La Mentalité des nomades" (pp. 79–85) and, at the end, translations into French of highly favorable reviews of the author's *Trackers and Smugglers* in the British Press (*The Daily News and Chronicle*, *The Spectator*, and *Near East*). The review in the first of these closes on a note very similar to that sounded in Zur

Mühlen's memoir: "He loved his work, his men, and the solitary desert life." (p. 146)

(Sources: André von Dumreicher, *Fahrten, Pfadfinder und Beduinen in den Wüsten Ägyptens* [Munich: Drei Masken Verlag, 1931]; id., *Le Tourisme dans les déserts d'Égypte* [Alexandria: La Cité du Livre; Paris: Larose, 1931]; Archie Hunter, *Power and Passion in Egypt: A Life of Sir Eldon Gorst 1861–1911* [London: I.B. Tauris, 2007]; https://www2.landesarchiv-bw.de/ofs21/olf/struktur.php?bestand=4026&klassi=&anzeigeKlassi=002.001.001; Durham University has several photographs of Dumreicher from the years 1905 and 1906 in its George Gillett Hunter Photographic collection).

64 Count K.

Carl, Count zu Khevenhüller-Metsch, Austrian Consul in Beirut from 1898 to 1908, came from a family of diplomats. Rudolf zu Khevenhüller-Metsch (1844–1910), for instance, had been consul-general in Sofia (1879–1881), envoy to Belgrade (1881–1886) and Brussels (1888–1902), and finally, after the death of Foreign Minister Gustav Kálnoky, with whom he did not get on, Austrian ambassador in Paris (1903–1910). In general, while a posting to Beirut was assuredly anything but a great prize, the Levant was not unimportant to Austria at the time. Efforts were being made to promote trade with the region and Austria also had an interest in protecting the local Christians. One historian, citing a passage from one of Khevenhüller-Mertsch's reports to the Foreign Ministry in Vienna, has described the records of the Austrian consuls in Beirut as a rich and lively source for the history of Lebanon. (Arthur C. von Breycha-Vauthier, *Österreich in der Levante* [Vienna and Munich: Herold Verlag, 1972], p. 33)

65 Governor of Lebanon

Known as Muzzafar Pasha, the Governor of Lebanon from 1902 until his death in 1907, was born (circa 1840) Ladislas Czajkovski, the son of a Polish count.

His father, who had been active in the Polish independence movement against Russia, had fled to Constantinople after the failure of the 1830 uprising, entered the service of the Sultan, acquired the rank of general, converted to Islam, and adopted the name of Sadik. He also renamed his two sons: Adam became Enver and Ladislas became Muzzafar, though they remained Roman Catholics. Sadik Pasha fought in the Crimean War (1856) on the Ottoman side. Adam (Enver) returned to Poland and had a career there as a military officer. After graduating from the prestigious *Ecole militaire de Saint-Cyr* in 1863 Muzzafar entered the cavalry corps of the Ottoman army. In 1867 he became a military aide to Sultan Abdul Aziz and accompanied him on his European tour of 1870. He fought in the 1877 war against Russia, became an aide to Abdul Hamid II, and served as a member of the military reforms and military inspection committees. Simultaneously, he was appointed commander of the Imperial Stable, a position which required the sultan's confidence. In 1902 his name came up as a surprise candidate for the governorship of Mount Lebanon. Though his rivals, high officials in the Ottoman Foreign Ministry, were much better known in diplomatic circles, the failure of the parties concerned to agree on any other person than Muzzafar, determined the final choice, and in the autumn of 1902 he was appointed governor of Mount Lebanon for a term of five years with the rank of *mushir* (field marshal). His own sons held posts in the Ottoman Foreign Ministry.

(Source: Engin Akarli, *The Long Peace: Ottoman Lebanon 1861–1920* [Berkeley and Los Angeles: University of California Press, 1993] pp. 64–71, 197–98 *et passim*; John P. Spagnolo, *France & Ottoman Lebanon 1861–1914* [London: Ithaca Press, 1977; St. Antony's Middle East Monographs, 7], pp. 222–28).

66   Stenka Razin

Stepan Timofeyevich Razin (c. 1630–1671), a popular Russian folk hero, was the son of a Don Cossack leader. He led a following of poor newcomers to the Don region, mostly peasants escaping from serfdom, on a number of successful pillaging expeditions in the lower Volga region and on the shores of the Caspian Sea. These expeditions were extremely successful — Russian and Persian caravans were plundered, Persian commercial settlements were devastated, a Persian fleet was defeated, and Razin's warriors won riches and glory. As he passed through the lower Volga cities of Astrakhan and Tsaritsyn, hundreds of townsmen, fugitive peasants, and even regular soldiers flocked to his standard. Having raised an army of seven to ten thousand, he announced a new campaign in 1670, aimed at settling scores with the boyars and officials of Tsar Alexei I, the "traitors and oppressors of the poor." The towns of Saratov and Samara opened their gates to him, and Russian peasants and indigenous peoples rose up in revolt by the tens of thousands throughout the lower and middle Volga region. The rebels' intention was to march on Moscow. They were defeated, however, when they besieged the town of Simbirsk. Stenka Razin fled to the Don region, but he was betrayed soon after by another Cossack leader, captured, delivered to Moscow in an iron cage, and executed on June 6, 1671.

In the legend referred to by Zur Mühlen, Stenka Razin, taunted by his followers with having become soft and weak for love of a woman, tosses his new Persian princess bride into the Volga, exclaiming that "mother Volga" has never before received such a beautiful gift. For the popular song in which the legend is preserved, see https://www.youtube.com/watch?v=rXc4AXAm7l0&list=RDrXc4AXAm7l0&t=3

67   Freiherr v. d. G.

The initials refer almost certainly to Wilhelm Leopold Colmar, Freiherr (Baron) von der Goltz (1843–1916), also known as Goltz-Pasha [seated], a high-ranking German army officer, a historian and theorist of war (his books were more widely read by French, British, and American military leaders between 1870

3. Notes on Persons and Events Mentioned in the Memoir 235

and the First World War than Clausewitz), and one of the most important players in the consolidation of German-Turkish relations in the critical decades leading up to the First World War. He had been seconded to Constantinople in 1883 as head of a German military mission requested by the Sultan for the purpose of reorganizing the Ottoman army after its defeat in the Russo-Turkish War of 1877–78. Goltz spent twelve years in Turkey and appears to have carried out his mission with some success, for in the Greco-Turkish war of 1897 the Turkish army advanced to the gates of Athens and was halted only when Czar Nicolas II threatened to attack the Ottomans from eastern Anatolia unless the campaign was stopped. In return for his services Goltz was given the title of Pasha and in 1895 just before his return to Germany, the rank of *Mushir* (field-marshal) in the Ottoman army. He was in Turkey again several times between 1909 and 1913 before being sent back to Constantinople, as special adviser to the Sultan, soon after Turkey entered World War I on the side of the Central Powers. His power and influence in Turkish affairs led to disgruntlement on the part of some Turks, as Zur Mühlen suggests.

The difficulty is that Goltz was never German Ambassador (*Botschafter*) in Constantinople, though that is how "Freiherr v. d. G." is identified by Zur Mühlen. The Ambassador in Constantinople from 1897 until 1912 was Adolf, Freiherr Marschall von Bieberstein (1842–1912) and he was succeeded, from 1912 until 1916, by Hans, Freiherr von Wangenheim (1859–1915). In addition, the chief periods of Goltz's residence in Turkey (1883–1896, 1909–1913, 1914–1916) do not coincide with the time of Zur Mühlen's stay in Constantinople (1906, though no date is given in the text). It is, of course, possible that he was there on a shorter visit at the time, but I have not been able to verify this. It may therefore be that she is in fact referring to the Ambassador, Marschall von Bieberstein, but, writing almost a quarter of a century later and remembering Goltz's reputation as a powerful force in Turkish affairs, has misnamed him Goltz. Alternatively, she is indeed referring to Goltz but, because of the major role he played in German-Ottoman relations, mistakenly remembers him as the Ambassador.

Both men, as it happens, were fervent German nationalists. Marschall had taken a strongly imperialist position in general European politics. After the ill-conceived Jameson raid on the Transvaal Republic, he was responsible, according to Kaiser Wilhelm II himself, for drafting the telegram in which the Kaiser congratulated President Kruger and assured him that a free republic of the Transvaal was a major German interest. Writing much later, after he had been forced to abdicate in the aftermath of Germany's defeat in World War I, and eager to prove that he "never had warlike ambitions," the Kaiser claimed that, despite his strong sympathy with the Boers, he was "much worried at the violent excitement" which the raid had provoked in Germany and which had "also seized upon the higher classes of society." In the tense situation, "the influence of such an energetic and eloquent personage as Herr von Marschall" — at the time "one of the secretaries of State" — and the willingness of Prince Hohenlohe, the Chancellor, to go along with him did Germany "an ill turn in this matter and damaged me seriously both in England and at home." Knowing "how ignorant Freiherr Marschall and the Foreign Office were of English national psychology," he had "sought to make clear the consequences such a step would have among the English." However, "Marschall was not to be dissuaded," and as the Chancellor then remarked that "I, as a constitutional ruler, must not stand out against the national consciousness and against my constitutional advisers," he yielded. Marschall also advocated a strong naval policy for Germany — another position that was sure to be read as provocative by the British. It might have been easy enough for Zur Mühlen to confuse Goltz and Marschall.

(Sources: *Neue deutsche Biographie*, vol. 6, pp. 629–32; Ex-Kaiser William II, *My Memoirs: 1878–1918* [London, New York, Toronto and Melbourne: Cassell, 1922], pp. 79–81).

68   Young Turks

The Young Turks — so called on the model of earlier radical literary and political reform movements in France and Germany (*Jeune France* and *Junges Deutschland*) — were a coalition of various groups (Turkish nationalists, ethnic pluralists, Western-oriented secularists) agitating for reform in the Ottoman Empire in the late nineteenth and early twentieth centuries. They demanded re-establishment of the constitutional monarchy set up under the short-lived 1876 constitution. The movement grew out of secret societies of progressive university students and military cadets that had been driven underground, along with all other forms of political dissent, after the 1876 constitution was annulled by Sultan Abdul Hamid II in 1878. In 1902 a first congress of Ottoman advocates of reform was held in Paris, a second five years later in 1907. In 1908 the Young Turk Revolution successfully reversed the suspension of the constitution and reinstituted a parliament, thus initiating the so-called Second Constitutional Era in the Ottoman Empire. In power, the Young Turks were keen nationalists, eager to exploit German interest in Turkey for their own ends but resistant to German efforts to turn Turkey into a client state.

69   Count Szechenyi

Edmund Georg Stephan Karl, Count Széchényi, born in 1839 into a large noble Hungarian family, is described in the *Gothaisches Gräfliches Taschenbuch* for 1900 (p. 819) as *General-Chef des kaiserl. Ottomanischen Pompierskorps* (Commander-in Chief of the Imperial Ottoman Fire Brigade) and as Adjutant-General of His Majesty the Sultan. Many members of his family had served in the Austro-Hungarian diplomatic corps. It is not clear how he came to occupy the position he held in Constantinople. The recently refurbished Fire Brigade Museum in present-day Istanbul bears his name.

70 Paul Weitz

By the time the Great War broke out and Germany began exploiting the influence it had built up in Turkey to make trouble for Britain, France, and Russia (see "Jihad"), Paul Weitz had represented the respected *Frankfurter Zeitung* in Turkey for thirty years, according to Henry Morgenthau, the American ambassador in Constantinople. This is not quite accurate, but close enough. Born in 1862, Weitz was first employed in the retail trade but soon gave it up for journalism. He found work in his native Regensburg, then in Vienna; then, on the outbreak of the Serbo — Bulgarian War in 1885, he went under his own steam to Belgrade and was hired as a correspondent by the London *Daily News* and the *Vossische Zeitung*. As of 1887, he was employed by the relatively liberal *Frankfurter Zeitung*, becoming the paper's permanent correspondent in Belgrade two years later. His reports were often subject to censorship by the Serbian authorities and on one occasion he was expelled from the country. In 1896, he was appointed the *FZ*'s correspondent in Constantinople. But in Morgenthau's view, he was "more than a journalist. He had the most intimate personal knowledge of Turkish affairs, and he was the confidant and adviser of the German Embassy. His duties there were actually semi-diplomatic. Weitz had really been one of the most successful agencies in the German penetration of Turkey; it was common talk that he knew every important man in the Turkish Empire, the best way to approach him, and his price." "There was not a hidden recess to which he could not gain admittance." (*Ambassador Morgenthau's Story*, p. 179, p. 20) "A particularly influential outpost of Pan-Germany," as Morgenthau described him, "he was constantly at Wangenheim's elbow, prompting, advising, informing." (p. 20) (Wangenheim was the German Ambassador to the Porte from 1912 to 1915.) Although Wangenheim constantly looked to Weitz for information, "he did not always take his advice." Thus in the important matter of the Armenian massacres Wangenheim took the view — which was also that of the Foreign Ministry in Berlin as a whole — that Germany should stand by its ally Turkey. Weitz, in contrast, was convinced that his country's refusal to intervene was doing it irreparable damage and he "was constantly pressing his view on Wangenheim, but he made little progress." On the contrary, he told Morgenthau, when he urged his view on Wangenheim, the latter "threw me twice out of the room." (pp. 246–247) As it turned out Weitz was not far off the mark. German complicity in what has come to be known as the "Armenian genocide" was soon quite well documented and was exposed and condemned by German scholars themselves, notably by Hans Niemeyer, a Professor of Law at the University of Kiel, who was part of the defence team in the 1921 trial in Berlin of a young Armenian accused of having assassinated Talât, the former Turkish Interior Minister generally considered the architect of the genocide.

Weitz was also well informed about Zionist efforts to settle Jews in Palestine — to which the Imperial German government was not always ill-disposed. In an article in the *Frankfurter Zeitung* he explained why Turkish officialdom was in two minds about the settlement of the Jews and in the end tried to halt it. Though the Ottomans appreciated the economic improvement brought about by Jewish settlement, he explained, they could not tolerate the erosion of their power that followed from the Jews' insistence on holding on to whatever nationality they already had and thus giving more and more authority in the areas of settlement to the foreign consuls responsible for their protection. This process "went so far," Weitz wrote, "that the Sublime Porte ceased sometimes to be master in its own country." Nevertheless, Weitz and his newspaper supported Zionism "in view of the very promising commercial prospects" for Germany and recommended trying to reach an agreement with the Turks by emphasizing "the good relations between Ottoman Jewry and the Porte."

Weitz, in sum, at the time Zur Mühlen encountered him, was a figure to be reckoned with in the complex politics of the Near and Middle East.

(Sources: Henry Morgenthau, *Ambassador Morgenthau's Story* [Ann Arbor: Gomidas Institute, 2000; originally published 1918], pp. 20, 179, 246–47; *Geschichte der Frankfurter Zeitung* [Frankfurt am Main: Verlag der Frankfurter Zeitung, 1911], pp. 639, 640, 884; Isaiah Friedman, *Germany, Turkey, Zionism* [New Brunswick and London: Transaction, 1998; orig. Oxford: Oxford University Press, 1977] pp. 49, 256–59, 330–35; Vahakn N. Dadrian, *The History of the Armenian Genocide* [New York and Oxford: Berghahn Books, 1995], pp. 248–300).

71   Herr Gutmann

Eugen Gutmann (1840–1925) was one of the founders, in 1872, of the Dresdner Bank. By 1906, when Zur Mühlen ran into "Herr Gutmann" in Therapia (Tarabya), the summer resort about seven miles north of Constantinople, the Bank, which had moved its headquarters to Berlin in 1884, had already taken over many other banks in Germany, had branches all over the country, and had opened offices in several foreign capitals. It is highly likely that the Dresdner Bank had contributed significantly to German commercial penetration of Turkey. In 1906, an affiliate, the *Deutsche Orientbank*, was founded. Zur Mühlen's "Herr Gutmann" was doubtless there to oversee its operations in Turkey.

In 1906, however, Eugen Gutmann was 66. A rather large portrait of him painted the following year by Max Liebermann (presently in the Berlin *Stadtmuseum*), shows a solid member of the cultivated German upper bourgeoisie, in a relaxed but imposing, almost Bismarckian pose. If this portrait bears any likeness to the subject, no one looking at Eugen Gutmann could have been surprised, as Zur Mühlen was, that "so young a man should know something about banking." It is therefore almost certain that the Herr Gutmann in question was Eugen Gutmann's son Herbert (1879–1942), who was only a little older than Zur Mühlen herself, but who had already served, at age 24, as Vice-President of the London branch of the *Dresdner Bank* and who was a partner with his father in the founding of the *Deutsche Orientbank* in 1906.

Zur Mühlen might conceivably have met him again, many years after the publication of her memoir, in London, where both he and she sought refuge from the National Socialists. Accused of responsibility for the *Dresdner Bank*'s great losses in the financial crisis at the end of the 1920s, Herbert Gutmann was forced to resign from the board in 1931. In 1934 he was arrested by the S.S. — the family was Jewish — but succeeded in emigrating to England in 1936 on payment of a very large emigration tax. In 1939 his house, the Herbertshof, with a valuable collection of artworks, was seized, and in 1940 all his and his wife's assets in Germany were confiscated. He died in 1942 in London, nine years before Zur Mühlen herself. The present-day Dresdner Bank runs a program for promoting the study of banking history to which it has given the name of Eugen Gutmann. There is no mention on the bank's website of Herbert Gutmann or his fate.

72 The Loreley and its commander

The *Loreley* was a yacht serving as a German station ship in Constantinople. For years the small, rather elegant *stationnaire S.M.S. Loreley* — she was 225 and a half feet long and 27 and a half feet wide — was the only ship of the Imperial German Navy permanently deployed in the Mediterranean. Built on the Clyde in 1884, she had been purchased from her first owner by the German Navy in 1896 to replace an older *Loreley* and was used chiefly for ceremonial functions.

The commander who sought Zur Mühlen's hand in marriage but did not please her at all might possibly have been Hans Humann (1878–1933). The son of the engineer and archaeologist Carl Humann, who discovered the Pergamon altar while building roads in Anatolia, Hans Humann was born in Smyrna and spent the first twelve years of his life in Turkey. A highly successful German naval officer, he was appointed naval attaché in Constantinople in 1913. On account of the long periods of time he spent in Turkey, his attachment to the country, his complete command of the Turkish language, and his exceptionally close friendship with the Turkish War Minister, Enver Pasha, with whom as an infant he had shared a wet-nurse, he was sometimes considered more Turkish than the Turks. As he was at the same time a particular protégé of the nationalist and Pan-Germanist Minister of the Navy, Admiral von Tirpitz, he was in an excellent position to serve as mediator between the Germans and the Turks. One observer noted that he "became the unofficial German envoy. [...] He had direct access to the Kaiser's entourage over the head of any ambassador. It was an outstanding position of extraordinary influence." Though he is said to have been appointed commander of the *Loreley* only in 1913, he could conceivably have been on assignment in 1906 and have met Zur Mühlen. Certainly what we know of him (and of her) would make her dislike of him seem almost inevitable. A crucial player in German-Turkish diplomatic and military negotiations and in Turkey's entering the War on the side of Germany in late 1914, he supported and justified Turkish action against Armenians. "Armenians and Turks cannot live together in this country," he reportedly told American Ambassador Henry Morgenthau. "One of these races has to go. And I don't blame the Turks for what they are doing to the Armenians. I think that they are entirely justified. The weaker nation must succumb." To a report that the Armenians are being "more or less exterminated," he is said to have responded, "This is harsh, but useful." Count Wolff-Metternich who replaced von Wangenheim as German ambassador to Turkey and was far less disposed than his predecessor to find excuses for the massacres, described Humann as an "arch scoundrel."

Humann's activities in the 1920s appear to confirm Zur Mühlen's description of him, at the time she wrote her memoir (1929), as "today one of the leading lights of the German nationalists." He is said to have participated in the unsuccessful 1920 Kapp-Putsch (a rightwing attempt to topple the Weimar Republic) and he was subsequently befriended by Hugo Stinnes, the influential rightwing industrialist. Stinnes set him up as one of the editors of the widely read *Deutsche Allgemeine Zeitung*, in the pages of which he advocated a return to the monarchy and justified the Armenian massacres. Another of his friends at that time was Franz von Papen. In his eulogy at Humann's graveside in October 1933, von Papen, then vice-chancellor in Hitler's government, praised him as a fighter for "the new Germany that we are today in the process of building."

(Sources: http://de.wikipedia.org/wiki/Hans_Humann; Vahakn N. Dadrian, *The History of the Armenian Genocide*, 6th ed. revised [New York and Oxford: Berghahn Books, 2003], pp. 271–73); Ernst Jäckh, *The Rising Crescent. Turkey Yesterday, Today, and Tomorrow* [New York: Farrar and Rinehart, 1944], pp. 117–120; the Jäckh papers, correspondence between Ernst Jäckh and Hans Humann, Princeton University Library, microfilms 11747).

73   Saharet

Saharet (real name: Clarissa Campbell) was a celebrated dancer from Melbourne or nearby Ballarat in Australia who took New York by storm in 1897. Innovative and expressive female dancers were much in vogue at the time. Along with another dancer, who was also a sensation at the turn of the century — Chicago-born Lois Fuller — Saharet was as well known and as fêted in Europe as in the United States. Both were the subjects  of portraits by prominent German artists — Fuller by Thomas Theodor Heine, Saharet by Franz von Stuck and Franz Lenbach. The best remembered of the dancers of this time is, of course, San Francisco-born Isadora Duncan, who spent her entire career in Europe.

74   Dannecker

A native of the South German state of Württemberg and friend of the poet Friedrich Schiller, Johann Heinrich Dannecker (1758–1841) was one of a great generation of German neo-classical sculptors that also includes Gottfried von Schadow and Christian Friedich Tieck. Though these artists are less well known in the English-speaking world than their Italian contemporary Antonio Canova, Dannecker's *Ariadne mit dem Panther* (in the Liebighaus, Frankfurt) was perhaps — along with Schadow's sculpture of the two Prussian princesses

(Berlin, Alte Nationalgalerie) — the most popular sculpture in Germany in the nineteenth century. It is not obvious why *Ariadne* is described as "fat," unless in comparison with Zur Mühlen herself, who, by her own account, was judged too thin. From her point of view, many people appeared *"fett"* or *"rund"* — terms that are used frequently in her portraits of others.

75 Niederwald monument

The Niederwald monument at Rüdesheim am Rhein, to designs by the sculptor Johannes Schilling and the architect Karl Weisbach, was built to commemorate the founding of the German Empire in the aftermath of Prussia's victory over France in the war of 1870–1871. The foundation stone was laid by the King of Prussia, as the newly proclaimed Kaiser Wilhelm I, on September 16, 1871. The central figure of Germania in the massive and busy composition holds the recovered crown of the Empire in one hand and the Imperial sword in the other. It is not surprising that Victor de Crenneville thought it ugly. It is. In addition, its message can hardly have appealed to an Austrian diplomat whose father had been a Field Commander at the time of the Austro-Prussian War of 1866 and had been honoured for his many services to the Habsburg Emperor. Austria's defeat in that war effectively established the Prussian King, rather than the Austrian Emperor, in the role of leader of the movement to reunite the German peoples, a role confirmed by the Prussian victory over France and celebrated by the Niederwald Monument.

76 Nous l'avons eu, votre Rhin allemand

A provocative poem indeed to recite at the Niederwald Monument! Victor de Crenneville was lucky that, unlike the Austrian aristocrat, the patriotic German tourists gathered there did not, apparently, know French. The poem he recited was by the French Romantic poet Alfred de Musset (1810–1857). Musset had been the librarian of the French Ministry of the Interior under the July Monarchy. The Minister at the time was the conservative politician and historian Adolphe Thiers, who, in 1840, after he had become Prime Minister, provoked a political and diplomatic crisis by reviving France's claim that the Rhine was the country's "natural" frontier on the east and that it therefore had a right to the territory west of the river. To the Germans, to whom "Father Rhine" was indissociable from the very being of Germany, this was an outrage and gave rise to many popular anti-French songs and poems, chief among them Nikolaus Becker's "Rheinlied" and Max Schneckenburger's "Die Wacht am Rhein." Becker's poem opens on the lines (repeated at the beginning of the third, fifth, and final stanzas):

> Sie sollen ihn nicht haben,
> Den freien deutschen Rhein.
> (They shall not have it,/ The free German Rhine)

Musset's poem was an answer to those lines, with its repetition at the beginning of the first four stanzas of the riposte: "We have had it, your German Rhine." It evokes past French victories over Germany under the *Ancien Régime* and under Napoleon. In the second stanza, the Rhine even seems (ultimate insult) to take on the character of a woman whom the French have "had."

> LE RHIN ALLEMAND
> Réponse à la chanson de Becker
>
> Nous l'avons eu, votre Rhin allemand,
> Il a tenu dans notre verre.
> Un couplet qu'on s'en va chantant
> Efface-t-il la trace altière
> Du pied de nos chevaux marqué dans votre sang?
>
> Nous l'avons eu, votre Rhin allemand.
> Son sein porte une plaie ouverte,
> Du jour où Condé triomphant
> A déchiré sa robe verte.
> Où le père a passé passera bien l'enfant.
>
> Nous l'avons eu, votre Rhin allemand.
> Que faisaient vos vertus germaines,
> Quand notre César tout puissant
> De son ombre couvrait vos plaines?
> Où donc est-il tombé ce dernier ossement?
>
> Nous l'avons eu, votre Rhin allemand.
> Si vous oubliez votre histoire,
> Vos jeunes filles, sûrement,
> Ont mieux gardé notre mémoire;
> Elles nous ont versé votre petit vin blanc.
>
> S'il est à vous, votre Rhin allemand,
> Lavez-y donc votre livrée;
> Mais parlez-en moins fièrement.
> Combien, au jour de la curée,
> Etiez-vous de corbeaux contre l'aigle expirant?
>
> Qu'il coule en paix, votre Rhin allemand;
> Que vos cathédrales gothiques
> S'y reflètent modestement;
> Mais craignez que vos airs bachiques
> Ne réveillent les morts de leur repos sanglant.

77 Merano

Until the end of the First World War Merano ("Meran" in German) was part of the Austrian province of Tyrol and for a time the capital of the Tyrol.

78 Herr von Pribam

The name Pribam (sometimes written Pribram) appears to be that of a family or of several families from Bohemia. As is well known, Jews often took the name of the cities they came from (Frankfurt or Frankfurter, Hamburg or Hamburger, Wiener, etc.) and Pribram is a mining town about 50 miles south-west of Prague. It may well be, therefore, that most Pribams or Pribrams were Jewish or of Jewish origin. A number of them achieved some eminence — there are several doctors, a chemist, a biochemist, a well-known neurosurgeon and psychologist, a famous economist who worked for the Austrian government from 1909 until 1921, and a noted historian, Alfred Francis Pribram (1859–1942), who after a successful career at the University of Vienna, where he rose through the ranks from Privatdozent to Professor in the years 1887–1913, emigrated to England after the *Anschluß* and continued his career at the London School of Economics. Of the individuals I have been able to locate, however, only two could have been referred to around 1906–1907 as "*old* Herr von Pribam" or conceivably been the tutor of Victor, Count Crenneville. (Alfred Francis Pribram, for instance, was twelve years younger than the Count). These are Alfred Pribram (1841–1912), an eminent doctor and professor of medicine, mostly in Prague, and his brother Richard, a noted professor of chemistry, one time Dean and Rector of the University of Czernowitz (the capital of the Austrian duchy of Bukowina) who had been given the honorary title of *Hofrat* (court counsellor) in 1905, taught at the University of Vienna as of 1906, and was exactly the same age as Zur Mühlen's father. It is possible that Richard Pribram retired to Merano and he did have one son — Bruno Oskar, born in 1887, hence about 19 at the time described, a student of chemistry in Vienna, later a surgeon and university professor — but if Richard Pribram wrote his memoirs they do not appear to have been published and there is no evidence that he had the literary interests Zur Mühlen attributes to him or that he "filled a rather high post in some ministry." The identity of "old Herr von Pribam" thus remains, regrettably, a mystery.

79 A young Balt

This was Viktor von zur Mühlen (1879–1950).

Zur Mühlen's future husband was born in Estonia, where a German Junker landowning class still dominated but had come under increasing pressure both from above, with the Russians favoring the substitution of Russian for German as the language of administration and encouraging the Orthodox Church at the expense of the German Lutheran Church, and from below, with the native Estonians increasingly restive and resentful of both Germans and Russians.

Viktor von zur Mühlen's father, Leo von zur Mühlen, had abandoned the study of medicine in order to take over the management of his parents' estate. He proved to be a good manager but was known as a domestic tyrant, strict with his wife and children and particularly harsh toward house servants and peasant labourers. A son and one of his brothers even tried to persuade him to leave the estate during the First World War, when there was a good deal of local peasant unrest, since his very presence, they thought, was enough to cause trouble. Leo von zur Mühlen's upbringing of his five sons and two daughters must have left a mark on their character, for the marriages of all seven ended in divorce, an unusual pattern in the strictly observant Lutheran community to which they belonged. Even Leo and his wife separated after the end of the First World War.

Viktor in particular appears to have taken after his father. His career was typical of the sons of the local German landowners. He attended the German Gymnasium, completed his military service with the Russian army as a cavalry reserve officer, got his training in estate management from his father on his property at Woiseck, and in 1908, the year of his marriage, bought the nearby estate of Eigstfer from his father. That is where he brought his young Viennese bride. He appears to have been strong-willed, resolute and authoritarian. During the First World War, for instance, disgusted by what he saw as the incompetence and corruption of the Russian administration, he noted in his diary: "Everthing is rotten. The best thing in such times is absolute monarchy." Before that, during the 1905 Revolution, when bands of Estonian and Russian revolutionaries were wandering through the woods, attacking and setting fire to landowners' houses, Viktor von zur Mühlen had responded by organizing an armed militia in the area in which his estate was situated. According to his wife at least, his interests were largely confined to farming, horses, dogs, and the hunt. He had no feeling, she claims, for literature or art and there were only two books in the entire house when she arrived — "the Bible and a pornographic novel."

One might well wonder what could have appealed to Zur Mühlen in such a man. To begin with, he seems to have been very good-looking. It is also likely that at the age of twenty-seven, he was not without charm and was not yet as gruff and domineering as his father. In addition, the family, of which Zur Mühlen paints a bleak portrait in her memoir, had (and continues to have) highly talented and even artistically gifted members. Zur Mühlen does make an exception in her memoir for "Uncle Max," her father-in-law's brother, who had given up his share of the estate in order to devote himself to his scientific interests and of whom she writes lovingly. She must also have known of an artist in the family, Rudolph von zur Mühlen (1845–1913), who drew and painted landscapes, seascapes, and scenes from the nearby city of Dorpat. She can hardly not have known of Raimund von zur Mühlen (1854–1931), who was generally regarded as the greatest singer of his day, particularly of Lieder, and who gave recitals all over Europe — including Vienna. Though he too had grown up on his family's estate near Fellin in Estonia and, typically, suffered from his father's domineering ways, he had, with the support of his mother and elder brother, run away to Berlin at the age of nineteen in order to pursue his love of music. He had studied with Stockhausen and Clara Schumann, who sometimes accompanied him in his recitals. According to the writer of his obituary in the British journal *Music and Letters*:

> The first 'Lieder-Abend' given by Mühlen in Vienna was quite an event in musical circles. He started his programme with 'Die Allmacht '; suffering agonies of mind at the failure he thought he must be when, at the end of the song, not a single person applauded. But his apprehension at those moments of silence was quite unfounded, for presently the whole audience rose as one man to give him an ovation, all the more impressive after that silent tribute of appreciation and recognition

His singing of Brahms Lieder roused the composer to enthusiasm. This is how the same author describes the occasion:

> Brahms turned to Mühlen and said: 'Can you sing, and what will you sing?' Mühlen answered: 'One of your own songs, "Botschaft."' (This is one of the composer's most difficult songs.) Brahms looked surprised, and smiled; but went to the piano. Neither singer nor pianist had any music, and Brahms was still more surprised as one Lied after another revealed Mühlen's unique gift as interpreter; in the end he put his arms around him, and said: 'At last, at last I have found my singer.'

Raimund's debut recital took place in 1878, he gave his first London recital in 1883, but deliberately ended his concert career soon after the death of his mother in 1904. In 1907 he emigrated to England and began a busy and much appreciated career there as a teacher, which ended only with his own death in 1931. In 1904 and then again in 1905, however, he had returned to the family estate in Estonia to run summer courses. It is hard to imagine that there was no talk in the family about this extraordinarily successful member.

It is not impossible that when Hermynia met Viktor von zur Mühlen, her view of him was affected in some measure by what she — in all likelihood — knew about his musical relative. He, on his side, cannot at that time have been as devoid of imagination or as narrow-minded as he appears in the memoir. Otherwise, it is hard to conceive why he, on his side, was attracted to her. Her rank alone was not likely to impress the German Junker class he came from in Estonia, and her religion was no recommendation either. It should also be remembered that Zur Mühlen wrote her memoir twenty-two years after meeting Viktor, and sixteen years after the two had separated and she had left, for health reasons, for Davos, Switzerland. She may well, in writing it, have sought, at some level, to make her decision not to go back to him seem justifiable and in a way inevitable.

(Sources: Gladys Newberry, *Music & Letters*, 13.2 [Apr., 1932], pp. 215–17; http://www.ostdeutsche-biographie.de/muehra04.htm; Manfred Altner, *Hermynia Zur Mühlen, Eine Biographie* [Bern: Peter Lang, 1997], pp. 42–47).

80 "Punishment expedition"

The czarist regime responded to every protest action in the cities or in the countryside, especially at the time of the 1905 Russian Revolution and in the years following, with a "punishment expedition" against the workers or peasants. These occurred everywhere and frequently.

(Source: Ernest O.F. Ames, *The Revolution in the Baltic Provinces of Russia* [London: Independent Labour Party, 1907], pp. vi, 66; William E. Walling, *Russia's Message: The True World Import of the Revolution* [New York: Doubleday, Page, 1908], pp. 243, 247).

81 Uriadnik

Russian term for a village policeman. Note that Russian, not Estonian or German, is the language of officialdom.

82 Maximilian Harden

Maximilian Harden (1861–1927), born Felix Ernst Witkowski, the son of a Jewish merchant in Berlin, had a reputation as a fearless, muckraking journalist, largely because of his public exposure, in *Die Zukunft*, the weekly newspaper he founded and edited, of a homosexual group of close advisers and members of the inner circle of Kaiser Wilhelm II, chief among them Prince Philipp zu Eulenberg and Count Kuno von Moltke, who, Harden claimed, exercised a nefarious influence on the Kaiser. Harden had been an admirer and strong supporter of Bismarck, whom Wilhelm had forced to resign in 1890. Eulenberg and his friends, in contrast, in Harden's view, had introduced weakness and vacillation into German foreign policy, and were responsible in particular for the Moroccan crisis of 1906 and for a resolution of it that he considered humiliating and unfavorable to Germany. Many other prominent, high-placed advisers and military men were involved in the Eulenberg scandal, which led to a series of libel cases and which assumed something of the dimensions in Germany of the Dreyfus affair in France. To many — Zur Mühlen seems to have been among them — Harden was a hero for having dared to challenge those close to the seat of power. Harden and *Die Zukunft* did follow an independent line that was often critical of official policy. The paper was also open to innovation in the arts and published informed and favorable articles on modern writers and dramatists. Harden, however, frequently shifted position; the one constant appears to have been his nationalism. An article, translated into English and published in the *New York Times* on December 6, 1914, for instance, justifies Germany's position at the time of the outbreak of war in the name of a high-minded vision of Germany's world mission and of war as a glorious and legitimate means of expressing and fulfilling it. Nevertheless, Harden did support the signing of the peace treaty in 1918 and for that, no doubt, as well as for the damage done to the monarchy by his articles of 1906, an attempt was made on his life on July 3, 1922 — within days of the assassination of Walther Rathenau (another German-Jewish nationalist who had rallied to the Republic in 1918) — by members of one of the rightwing *Freikorps* (ex-servicemen's militias). Harden was seriously injured, retired from journalism, and in 1923 moved to Switzerland, where a few years later he died.

83 Browning

This refers, of course, to a pistol designed by the American firearms designer John Moses Browning. It was manufactured in Europe by companies in Belgium and Sweden. As of 1899, Browning pistols were in use not only in various armies and police forces, including the Imperial Russian police, but in the civilian population also.

84 Memoirs of a Singer

"Le plus fameux livre érotique allemand," according to the modern French poet Guillaume Apollinaire, was originally published in 1862 as *Aus den Memoiren einer Sängerin* (Altona: Verlagsbureau), with a second volume following in 1870. The work is a classic of erotic literature and has been frequently republished, both in the original German and in English and French translations — most recently in English in 1965, in French in 1970 and in German in 1995. It is usually attributed to Wilhelmine Schröder-Devrient (1804–1860), "la célèbre cantatrice qui [...] enthousiasma le public de son temps," in the words, once again, of Apollinaire, who provides a list of 67 roles she sang in operas by — among others — Glück, Mozart, Beethoven, Grétry, Weber (who chose her for the role of Agathe in *Der Freischütz*), Cherubini, Spontini, Rossini, Bellini, Donizetti, Auber, Halévy, and Wagner. She created the roles of Adriano in Wagner's *Rienzi*, Senta in *Der fliegende Holländer* and Venus in *Tannhäuser*. She also won great acclaim as a singer of Lieder, as well as some notoriety for what Apollinaire describes as her "vie et carrière très agitées" and the "caractère violent" which "la portait aux extrêmes." The authorship of the work characterized by Apollinaire as "the only feminine autobiography comparable with Rousseau's *Confessions* or the celebrated *Memoirs* of Casanova" is, however, much disputed. In two Introductions he wrote for French translations of the work around 1913 Apollinaire goes over the evidence, discusses the views of German scholars, one of whom argues that the first part is indeed the work of Schröder-Devrient, while the second is an imitation of de Sade, and offers his own assessment.

(Sources: http://de.wikipedia.org/wiki/Wilhelmine_Schröder-Devrient; Guillaume Apollinaire, *Oeuvres en prose complètes* [Paris: Gallimard, 1977], 3 vols., vol. 3, ed. Pierre Caizergues and Michel Décaudin, pp. 839–44, 1306–07).

85 Dorpat

Dorpat is the German name of a city in south-eastern Estonia now known by its Estonian name, Tartu. Though smaller than the capital Reval (now Tallinn), it was for long considered the cultural capital of Estonia, with the region's oldest University, founded in 1632 on the model of Uppsala in Sweden. In the early twentieth century, when Zur Mühlen visited it, it may have had a population of about 40,000. As in the rest of Estonia, which from 1729 until 1920 was a province of the Russian Empire, the German-speaking aristocracy was the ruling class, but in Dorpat it was the Baltic German bourgeoisie, the *literati* — as Zur Mühlen calls them, following local practice — that dominated culture, education, and local politics. Both the City Hall and the University buildings were designed by German architects and many, if not most of the students at the University were of German heritage, as was over 90% of the faculty. By the late nineteenth century, however, Estonian nationalists were trying to make Estonian culture a presence in the city (an Estonian national theater opened its doors in 1870), while, from above, the Russian administration officially restored the city's Russian name, Yuryev, in 1893 (so it appears, for instance, in the *Geografiya rossiskoy Imperii* of P. Dvornikov and S. Sokolov, published in Moscow in 1912) and attempted to russify the University, by imposing Russian as the language of instruction. Zur Mühlen still refers to "Dorpat" not only for the sake of her German readers in 1929, but because that is what the city was naturally called in the only milieu she knew in Estonia. The bookstore she found there was obviously accustomed to a German-speaking clientele.

86 Marseillaise

The following observation from an as yet unpublished paper by the historian Patrik von zur Mühlen, the great-nephew of Zur Mühlen's husband, is pertinent here. Drawing attention to the literary character of Zur Mühlen's memoir, that is, to the fact that her text is not a simple mirror image of reality but a creative reconfiguring of it, Von zur Mühlen writes: "Hermynia mentions that her husband had thrown out one of the servants for whistling the *Marseillaise*, whereupon she had sat down ostentatiously at the piano and played the song as loudly as she could. What she does not mention is that the *Marseillaise*, the song of the French Revolution, was strictly forbidden in the Russian Empire and that any playing or singing of it could result in deportation to Siberia. As the use of police informers was no less widespread in czarist Russia than later under the Soviets, Hermynia's action had in fact put both the servant and her husband Viktor, who as proprietor of the estate exercised certain police functions, in the greatest danger. It is unlikely that Hermynia did not know this [at the time of writing up the episode], for Viktor must have explained his action to her after the event at least."

87 Uncle Max

"Max von zur Mühlen (1850–1918), 'Uncle Max,' was my great-grandfather. He was interested in science and gave up the large estate of Woiseck in favor of his younger brother Leo, Hermynia's father-in-law. He let himself be bought out of his inheritance and lived as a private scholar. He gave up the idea of an academic career, the czarist regime having instituted instruction in Russian, instead of

German, at Dorpat. His special field of study was ichtyology, and as a scientist he undertook research chiefly on the relation of water characteristics, climate, and other factors and on their impact on the populations of different species of fish — a very modern area of research. On 24 December, 1918 he was shot by Bolsheviks in the garden of his home."

[Translated by the editor from an e-mail kindly sent to him by Patrik von zur Mühlen, 7 September, 2009. "Max von zur Mühlen (1850–1918), 'Onkel Max,' war mein Urgroßvater. Er war naturwissenschaftlich interessiert und verzichtete auf das große Gut Woiseck zugunsten seines jüngeren Bruders Leo, des Schwiegervaters von Hermynia. Er ließ sich sein Erbe auszahlen und lebte als privater Wissenschaftler. Eine akademische Karriere verweigerte er, da das Zarenregime 1888 in Dorpat die russische Unterrichtssprache (anstelle der deutschen) eingeführt hatte. Sein Fachgebiet war die Ichtyologie, die Fischkunde, und als Wissenschaftler untersuchte er vor allem den Zusammenhang von Wasserqualität, Klima und anderen Faktoren und ihren Einfluss auf die Populationen verschiedener Fischarten, eigentlich eine sehr moderne Forschung. Er wurde am 24. Dezember 1918 von Bolschewiki im Garten seines Hauses erschossen."].

88   Tchinovnik

The Russian term for any government official or bureaucrat.

89   Sombart

At the time Zur Mühlen is writing about, the economist and sociologist Werner Sombart (1863–1941) was seen as radically leftwing. Engels described him as the only German academic who understood Marx and he identified himself as a "convinced Marxist." As a result of this reputation, he did not find it easy to get good academic positions. Despite his prolific output, when he was at last offered a chair in 1906, it was at the Berlin *Handelshochschule* or School of Commerce. He was finally appointed to a chair at the Friedrich-Wilhelms-Universität in Berlin in 1917. Even in some of his early books, however (e.g. *Die Juden und das Wirtschaftsleben*, 1911; *Händler und Helden*, 1915), there are clear signs of his later turn, under the Weimar republic, to German nationalism. Though there was some ambivalence in his relation to National Socialism, there were many elements in his thinking that were entirely compatible with it (as in his *Deutscher Sozialismus* of 1934, for instance) and he continued to teach in Berlin until he died in 1941.

The books that Hermynia is likely to have been interested in while she was living on her husband's estate at Eigstfer are: *Sozialismus und soziale Bewegung* (first ed. 1896, followed by many further editions and many translations), and *Der moderne Kapitalismus* (1902).

90 Coppée

François Coppée (1842–1908) was a minor but prolific French poet, dramatist, and author of short stories. His work was popular, sentimental, easy to read, and superficial. His facile poetic style (*Intimités*, 1867; *Les Humbles*, 1872; *Contes en vers*, 1881; *Paroles sincères*, 1890) was parodied by Rimbaud. One of his poems was, however, set to music by a great composer, Henri Duparc, who mostly set work by Baudelaire and Théophile Gautier. Coppée also wrote patriotic stories and poetry and was on the side of the anti-Dreyfusards at the time of the *Affaire*. *La bonne Souffrance* (1898) tells the story, in prose, of his return to the Roman Catholic Church. The dash before the word "indecent" indicates Zur Mühlen's surprise and amusement that a writer she must have considered not exactly challenging could be so judged. Perhaps anything in French was assumed to be indecent in the *milieu* she is describing.

91 Stratz

The reference is to Rudolf Stratz (1864–1935), one of the most prolific producers of popular novels in Germany in the period from about 1890 until his death in the mid-1930s. Strongly nationalist and rightwing in tone, many of his novels revolve around army officers. He also wrote a few plays and during the First World War turned out patriotic books and articles. Here are some of the works that might have been read in the reading circle described by Zur Mühlen (i.e. between 1908 and 1913 approximately): *Unter den Linden, Berliner Novellen* (1893); *Arme Thea* (1896); *Der weiße Tod* (1897); *Die letzte Wahl* (1899); *Alt-Heidelberg, Du Feine: Roman einer Studentin* (1902); *Der Stern von Angora* (1903); *Gib mir die Hand* (1904); *Herzblut* (1908); *Für Dich* (1908); *Montblanc* (1912). All of these novels, like the many that followed, went through numerous editions and most were translated into other languages — French, English, Dutch, Finnish. Even as it was being published in serial form, one of Stratz's novels, *Schloß Vogelöd* was made into a film (English title: *The Haunted Castle*), by the great filmmaker Murnau in 1921.

92 Rudolf Herzog

Before success made it possible for him to earn a living by his writing alone, Rudolf Herzog (1869–1943) was briefly editor of the *Hamburger Neueste Nachrichten*, then *feuilleton* editor of the *Berliner Neueste Nachrichten*. A producer of popular literature like Stratz, perhaps even more prolific, he turned out novels, short stories, and plays at a dizzying pace, as well as occasional volumes of verse, and at least one popular history (*Preußens Geschichte*, 1913). Like those of Stratz, his novels went through numerous editions (24 editions of *Die Wiskottens*, for instance, between 1905 and 1951) and some were translated into other languages. Politically, he was also, like Stratz, a rightwing nationalist. "In one of his novels, *Die Kameraden* (1922), the aristocratic hero collects bitter ex-officers on his landholdings and prepares a leadership group for the Free

Corps... In another novel Herzog glorifies the Krupp family (*Die Stoltenkamps und ihre Frauen*, 1917) and in yet another he praises an entrepreneurial family who support Hindenburg and Ludendorff unquestioningly during the war and the reaction after it (*Die Buben der Frau Optenberg*, 1920)." (Lynda King) In 1932 he published an article strongly supportive of Hitler in the *Völkische Beobachter*. Among the novels that the circle might have read in the years between 1908 and 1913 are *Frau Kunst* (1893), *Zum weißen Schwan* (1897), *Der Graf von Gleichen: Ein Gegenwartsroman* (1901), *Die vom Niederrhein* (1903), *Das Lebenslied* (1904), *Die Wiskottens* (1905), *Abenteuerer* (1907), *Hanseaten* (1910), and *Die Burgkinder* (1911). Two volumes of poems might also have made an appearance in the circle: *Aus aller frauen landen: lieder eines unstäten* (1895) and *Aus dem Märchenbuch der Liebe* (1896).

(Sources: https://de.wikipedia.org/wiki/Rudolf_Herzog; Lynda King, *Best-Sellers by Design* [Detroit: Wayne State University Press, 1988], pp. 57, 216).

93 Gerhart Hauptmann

Hauptmann (1862–1946), the son of an innkeeper and the grandson of Silesian weavers, revolutionized German theatre with the performance of his first play *Vor Sonnenaufgang* at the avant-garde *Freie Bühne* in Berlin in 1889. The artistic inspiration of the *Freie Bühne* — established as a theatre club in order to circumvent the Prussian censor — was the naturalist *Théâtre Libre* founded by Antoine in Paris in 1887. Hauptmann's play brought naturalism and overt, realistic treatment of social problems to the German stage. (For comparison, Ibsen's *A Doll's House* was first played in 1879, *Ghosts* in 1881, *An Enemy of the People* in 1882). His next important play, *Die Weber* (1892), a dramatization of an 1844 uprising of Silesian weavers against their exploiter, in the heyday of the putting-out system, was one of the first dramas in which a collective hero replaced the usual individual hero. "Like the canvases of Millet and the heroic figures of Meunier, *The Weavers* represent the epic of the age-long misery of labour, a profoundly stirring picture," according to the celebrated anarchist and radical Emma Goldman (*The Social Significance of the Modern Drama* [Boston, 1914]). Hauptmann continued to write naturalist plays, but he also experimented with symbolism and fantasy, as in *Hanneles Himmelfahrt* (1893), which, not without some sentimentality, portrayed a poor, abused working-class child's dying fantasies of redemption. Stanislavsky directed the production of this work in Moscow. *Die versunkene Glocke* (1897) was an enactment of the inner conflict in the life of an artist between the artistic aspiration that isolates him from his immediate human community, and the instinctive human solidarity that unites him with it. It combines naturalism and symbolism. Hauptmann continued to write plays (about 35 in all) into the 1930s, along with novels and novellas. He was awarded the Nobel Prize for literature in 1912, probably the year in which the "'intellectual' woman, who was said to have had an affair...

with the revolutionary tutor of her son, dared to contribute" his works to the reading circle attended by Zur Mühlen.

Hauptmann remained in Germany throughout the Nazi regime. Though the Third Reich refused to allow him to receive the Schiller Prize, for which he was repeatedly recommended, nothing was done to prevent a complete seventeen-volume edition of his works from appearing in 1942. Both Hauptmann himself and the regime seem to have been content for him to be regarded as the grand old man of German letters.

94   Myedvyed

The *Myedvyed* — "*Myedvyed*" is Russian for "Bear," the animal representation of Russia — was an expensive restaurant opened on 1 October 1878 by a Belgian entrepreneur named Hiegel. It was located on 27 Bolshaya Konyushennaya Street, close to Nevski Prospekt, the great central avenue of the former Russian capital, in the building of the Demoute Hotel, which had been founded by a French immigrant in the 1760s and where Pushkin stayed in 1811 on his first visit to St. Petersburg and then again many times between 1827 and 1831. Other literary figures who stayed at the Demoute include the dramatist Griboyedov, the Polish national poet Adam Mickiewicz, and the great Russian liberal writers Turgenev and Alexander Herzen. In the entrance hall of the Myedvyed restaurant in the hotel, there was a large stuffed bear carrying a tray in its front paws. The restaurant itself had two very large dining rooms (with 100 and 150 tables) and 29 private dining rooms; there was a staff of 200, and an orchestra of 24 musicians. One of the dinners held there — in honour of the great actress M.G. Savina (1854–1915) had over 1,000 guests. Another dinner honoured the popular actress Vera Komissarzhevskaya (1864–1910), the co-founder, with Meyerhold, of a new company promoting symbolist theater; yet another, in 1902, marked the fifth anniversary of the great art nouveau journal *Teatr i iskusstvo* (Theatre and Art); and, in 1908, a celebration was held to honour A.S. Suvorin (1834–1912), the conservative editor of the newspaper *Novoye vremya* and the publisher of Chekhov. The *Myedvyed*, in short, was one of the largest and most distinguished venues in the Russian capital. Its character and size highlight the extraordinary humiliation imposed on the young woman in the episode recounted by Zur Mühlen.

(Sources: http://www.encspb.ru/en/article.php?kod=2804025933; Ю. Л. Алянский, *Увеселительные заведения старого Петербурга* [St. Petersburg: Avrora, 2003], pp. 212–213; В. Ковалевский, *Душа деянием жива* [St. Petersburg: Posokh, 1999] pp. 82–86) .

95   Krasnoye syelo

Krasnoye syelo is a town south-west of St. Petersburg to which many residents of the former Russian capital resorted in the summer. It was founded around

1714 when Peter the Great had a mill for linen (later paper) manufacture established on the site.

96   Peterhof

Sometimes called the "Russian Versailles," Peterhof is on the south shore of the Gulf of Finland, close to St. Petersburg. It is a vast ensemble of palaces and gardens, the first of which, Peter the Great's relatively modest *Monplaisir*, dates from the early eighteenth century and was based on sketches made by Peter himself. The plans were then expanded and a grander palace was built a little further inland. After Peter, the Empresses Elizabeth and Catherine the Great made further additions to Peterhof's architecture, fountains, and gardens, though Catherine subsequently moved the court to the no less imposing Tsarskoe syelo, south of St. Petersburg.

97   Duma

In response to the unrest caused by the 1904–1905 Russo-Japanese War and the wave of uprisings, strikes and mutinies referred to as the 1905 Revolution, Czar Nicolas II announced the convocation of a *Duma*, or State Parliament, in August 1905. At first it was conceived as a purely advisory organ, but later in the year the Czar agreed to endow the Duma with legislative and oversight powers, and to provide for broad participation in it. The Duma, it seemed, was to be the lower house of a Russian parliament, the State Council of Imperial Russia the upper house. Nine months later, however, in May 1906, the Czar issued the "Fundamental Laws," which stated that ministers could not be appointed by the Duma and were not responsible to it. Before it had even come into existence, therefore, the Duma was deprived of real executive power. Moreover, the Czar had the right to dismiss it and call new elections whenever he wished. The elections for the First Duma (April - June 1906) returned a significant bloc of moderate socialists and liberals who demanded further reforms. Within ten weeks it was dissolved. The Second Duma (February–June 1907) did not last much longer. The Social Democrats and Social Revolutionaries elected a large number of deputies. This resulted in major conflicts both within the Duma between the Left and the Right and with the Czar. On June 1, Prime Minister Pyotr Stolypin accused the Social Democrats of conspiring with members of the armed forces to prepare an uprising and demanded that the Duma exclude 55 Social Democratic deputies and strip 16 of them of parliamentary immunity. When this ultimatum was rejected by the Duma, it was dissolved by order of the Czar (the so-called Coup of June 7). Using emergency powers, Prime Minister Stolypin changed the electoral law and gave greater electoral weight to the votes of landowners and owners of city properties. This ensured that the Third Duma (1907–1912) would be dominated by gentry, landowners and businessmen. It was soon nicknamed "The Duma of the Lords and Lackeys."

98 Novoye vremya

Novoye vremya (*New Age*) was a newspaper published in St. Petersburg from 1868 to 1917. Until 1869 it came out five times a week; thereafter it was a daily and from 1881 on there were morning and evening editions. In 1891 a weekly illustrated supplement was added.

It began life as a liberal publication. In 1872, for instance, it published an editorial welcoming the appearance in Russian of the first volume of Karl Marx's *Kapital*, but after it was taken over by A.S. Suvorin in 1876, it acquired a reputation as a servile supporter of the government. Still, it was one of Russia's most widely read newspapers, with a circulation of 60,000, and it published important writers, most famously Anton Chekhov, until he broke with Suvorin in the late 1890s. It was generally looked down on by the liberal intelligentsia of the early twentieth century and despised by the Bolsheviks. Immediately after the October Revolution, on November 8, 1917 (October 26 Old Style), Lenin shut it down.

99 Berchtold

Leopold, Count Berchtold (1863–1942), an aristocrat with large estates in Hungary and Moravia, had entered the diplomatic corps in 1893, following what Zur Mühlen describes as the classic career path of aristocrats in the former Austro-Hungarian Empire. He spent time at the embassies in London and Paris before being appointed Ambassador to Russia in 1906 and Foreign Minister in 1912. According to two recent historians of the Habsburg Monarchy, he was "hesitant and indecisive by nature" and fearful of any change in the status quo. "His views on the internal affairs of Austria were — typically for a conservative supporter of the dual monarchy system — simple, sober, and thoroughly pessimistic. He was intelligent, industrious, and charming, without being in the least domineering or ambitious. He had withdrawn from his post in St. Petersburg twice in order to have time for his private life and accepted Franz Joseph's nomination as Foreign Minister only out of a feeling of duty to the Emperor. He was truly glad to be relieved of the burden of office in 1915." (Adam Wandruszka and Peter Urbanitsch, *Die Habsburgmonarchie 1848–1918*, vol. VI/1 [Vienna: Verlag der Österreichischen Akademie der Wissenschaften, 1989] pp. 323, 386)

Berchtold did, however, take a number of steps that may well have contributed to the outbreak of war in 1914. After the assassination of Archduke Ferdinand by Serbian-backed nationalists in then Austrian-ruled Bosnia, it was Berchtold who, arguing that Russia would not come to Serbia's aid, persuaded an apparently reluctant Franz Joseph to issue an unacceptable ultimatum to Serbia, and it was Berchtold who, as Foreign Minister, disregarded Serbia's largely compliant reply and persuaded the Emperor to declare war.

100 General Keller

This is Count Fyodor Arturovich Keller (1857–1918), who, not long after Zur Mühlen met him, was placed in command of the Tenth Cavalry Division and the Third Cavalry Corps of the Imperial Russian Army in the First World War. From the intimate correspondence (written in English) between Czar Nicholas II ("Nicky") and his wife, the Empress Alexandra ("Alix" or sometimes "Wify"), a granddaughter of Queen Victoria), in which his name comes up frequently, it is clear that "our brave Keller" was devoted to the Romanoffs and enjoyed the trust and affection of the royal couple. In one letter (17.6.1916) the Empress reports to her husband that she has received a telegram from Keller in which he tells her that he has been wounded twice, once in each leg, but hopes "soon to return to the ranks for further service to Your Imperial Majesty." She adds that she has heard from others "how the soldiers adore him & when he goes to the wounded, how each tries to sit up to see him better. He rides, followed by an immense banner with the image of the Saviour, & 40 cossacks, of wh. each has 4 St. George's crosses, otherwise they don't guard him — they say it is an imposing & emotioning picture. How glad I am for him — he always yearned for this great chance to prove to you his intense love, loyalty & gratitude." After Nicholas's forced abdication in the wake of the March Revolution of 1917, Keller refused to serve the Russian Provisional Government and subsequently saw action as a commander in the Western-supported, anti-Bolshevik Northwestern Army.

At the beginning of the War, in 1914, Zur Mühlen's "blond Russian giant" is said to have "participated in anti-Ukrainian pogroms in Galicia." These were directed against the considerable Ukrainian population in Austrian-ruled Galicia — a hotbed of Ukrainian nationalism invaded by Russia in the early months of the War — and reflected the decision of the czarist administration to go back on the concessions it had made intermittently on matters such as the use of the Ukrainian language and to stamp out the Ukrainian autonomy movement once for all. Keller's anti-Ukrainian zeal, however, did not prevent him from accepting appointment as commander of the army of Pavlo Skaropadski the Ukrainian "Hetman" or leader, who had come to power in April 1918 in a coup organized by a combination of wealthy landowners, the generals of the German and Austrian armies that had occupied Ukraine after the signing of the Peace Treaty of Brest-Litovsk, and anti-Bolshevik Russian officers. Skaropadski's regime was itself toppled, however, after only a few months. A revolt in Eastern Ukraine by elements loyal to the pre-coup government, under the leadership of Symon Petliura, defeated Skaropadski's army. Keller was killed in the course of the fighting.

(Sources: *The Complete Wartime Correspondence of Tsar Nicholas II and the Empress Alexandra, April 1914 - March 1917*, ed. Joseph T. Fuhrmann [Westport, CT: The Greenwood Press, 1999], pp. 23, 24–25, 48, 65, 195, 196, 412, 424, 429,

484, 501, 502, 507, 515, 519, 523; Michael Hrushevsky, *A History of Ukraine*, ed. O.J. Frederikson [New Haven: Yale University Press, 1941]; Serhii Mazlakh and Vasyl' Shakhrai, *On the Current Situation in the Ukraine*, ed. Peter J. Potichnyj, Introduction by Michael M. Luther [Ann Arbor: University of Michigan Press, 1970; orig. Ukrainian 1919, republished New York, 1967]; Anna Procyk, *Russian Nationalism and Ukraine* [Edmonton and Toronto: Canadian Institute of Ukrainian Studies Press, 1995]).

101 Sport im Bild

Barnes gave this title only in English translation (as *Ilustrated Sports*), which makes it difficult to identify. The magazine's German name (as given by Zur Mühlen in *Ende und Anfang*) was *Sport im Bild*. A weekly, *Sport im Bild* was launched in Berlin in 1899 in response to a growing interest in sports and games in Germany, acquired by Rudolf Mosse, the Jewish publisher of the *Berliner Tageblatt* newspaper in 1904, and shut down by the Nazis, because of its Jewish ownership in 1934. Erich Maria Remarque, the author of *All Quiet on the Western Front* (written in 1927 but not published until 1929) got a start as a professional writer when he was hired as a reporter and assistant editor of the weekly around the very time that Zur Mühlen was working on her memoir. His novel *Station am Horizont* (*Station on the Horizon*, not published separately until 1998), was serialized in *Sport im Bild* in 1927.

102 Die Woche

One of the first illustrated magazines in German. It was launched in 1899 by the Berlin publisher August Scherl, at a time of intense competition among the three main Berlin newspaper and magazine publishers — Ullstein, Mosse, and Scherl — in response to the Ullsteins' 1894 purchase, redesign, and mass marketing of the *Berliner Illustrierte Zeitung*. Like the latter, *Die Woche* was generously illustrated and aimed at a mass market. A family magazine, it offered general interest articles and photographs, news of the fine arts and literature, and reports on woman's fashions and household matters, along with serialized novels and the odd poem.

103 Semi-Gotha

The *Almanach de Gotha*, first published in 1763, was and still is the recognized directory of the European nobility. The thrust of the *Semi-Gotha* or *Weimarer Historisch-genealogisches Taschenbuch des gesamten Adels judäischen Ursprunges* [Historical-Genealogical Directory of all noble families of Judaic origin] (Weimar: Kyffhäuser-Verlag, 1912) was overtly anti-Semitic — to expose the extent of the penetration of the European aristocracy by a racially alien element, the Jews. Zur Mühlen uses it with characteristic irony to lay claim to a Jewish ancestor.

104 Saint Ignatius Loyola

It was quite widely believed at one time that the parents of the founder of the Jesuit order were Marranos — Spanish Sephardic Jews who had been forced to convert to Christianity under threat of expulsion but continued to practice Judaism secretly. This idea was still being promoted in early 2009 in anti-Semitic websites, such as http://www.encspb.ru/en/article.php?kod=2804025933 or http://zioncrimefactory.wordpress.com (accessed 27/4/2010).

Even in 1912, before she met her longtime partner, the Jewish writer and translator Stefan Isidore Klein, whom she finally married in 1939, Zur Mühlen was obviously amused and not displeased to learn that one of her ancestors might be Jewish. It is also worth noting that in some of the *völkisch* (racist and nationalist) circles Zur Mühlen already detested, Jews and Jesuits, were lumped together as dangerous, rootless schemers in the service of foreign, un-German powers — i.e. the Rothschilds or the Pope.

105 Whistler's book *On the Gentle Art of Making Enemies*

The full title of the book by the painter James McNeill Whistler, as published in 1890 by William Heinemann in London and John W. Lovell in New York, continues: *As pleasingly exemplified in many instances wherein the serious ones of this earth, carefully exasperated, have been prettily spurred on to unseemliness and indiscretion while overcome by an undue sense of right.*

Zur Mühlen's father clearly knew his daughter well and felt confident — rightly — that she would take his teasing her about her tendency to high-minded indignation in good part. Whistler's entertaining book consists of material relative to the famous libel suit he brought against Ruskin in 1877, as well as of numerous other more or less witty and malicious attacks on the artist in the press, chiefly by art critics, followed by the artist's more or less witty and malicious responses in the form of letters or public lectures. The publishing history of this collection of jabs and counter-jabs contributed to its notoriety. Whistler had entrusted an American journalist in London by the name of Sheridan Ford with the task of collecting and arranging the material. He then decided to publish it and copyright it himself. Ford, who claimed that Whistler had given him publication rights, made repeated attempts, in London, New York, Antwerp, and Paris, to bring the book out, but in each case publication was stopped in the nick of time, so that in the end it was Whistler himself who oversaw and benefitted from the publication. This publication saga was itself well publicised in Britain, America, and Continental Europe.

(Source: E.R. and J. Pennell, *The Life of James McNeill Whistler* [London: William Heinemann; Philadelphia: J.B. Lippincott Company, 1908]).

106 Attempt on the life of the king of Italy

Assassination attempts had been made by anarchists against Umberto I of Italy — who was hated by the Left — in 1878 and again in 1900. The second of these was successful. Zur Mühlen is referring to yet another attempt that had just been made, on 14 March 1912, on the life of a reigning Italian monarch, Vittorio Emmanuele III. The king was not killed in the attack, but he was injured.

107 Livland

The territory known as Livland — a traditional, but by Zur Mühlen's time no longer current political designation — embraced part of present-day Latvia and the southern part of present-day Estonia, in which von zur Mühlen's estate was situated.

108 Stepniak

Sergei Michailovitch Stepniak (a.k.a. Kravchinski, 1851–1895), son of an army doctor, had a brief military career, reaching the rank of second lieutenant in the artillery by the age of 20. In 1871, moved by the misery of the Russian peasantry, he resigned his commission and joined the *Narodniki*, well-intentioned Russians of the upper classes, who aimed to bring socialist ideas to the peasants. His activities resulted in his arrest in 1874, but he was released shortly afterwards and went to the Balkans to take part in the Bosnian uprising against the Ottomans. He also participated around this time in the insurrection that the Italian anarchist Enrico Malatesta had incited in the province of Benevento, south of Rome. In 1878, back in Russia, he was involved in the assassination, on the streets of St. Petersburg, of the head of the Russian secret police and had to flee Russia, eventually settling in England where he set up the *Friends of Russian Freedom* and its print organ, the *Russian Free Press*. Always close in his political position to anarchists like Bakunin and Kropotkin, he gradually abandoned his earlier support for terrorist acts as an effective instrument of political change. His first book, *La Russia sotterranea: profili e bozzetti rivoluzionari dal vero* (Milan, 1882) was written in Italian and published in English translation as *Underground Russia: Revolutionary Profiles and Sketches from Life* (1888). Other works written in exile include (in English) *The Career of a Nihilist: A Novel* (1885), *Russia under the Czars* (1885), and *The Russian Peasantry* (1888). Zur Mühlen could have found three of these works in German translation in Herr Krüger's bookshop: *Das Unterirdische Russland* (Bern, 1884), *Der russische Bauer* (Stuttgart, 1893), and *Die Laufbahn eines Nihilisten* (Magdeburg, 1894).

Stepniak was killed by a train at a level crossing near his home in Bedford Park, London, in 1895.

109 Kropotkin

Pyotr Alekseyevitch Kropotkin (1842–1921), sometimes referred to as "the Anarchist Prince," though he renounced his title of Prince at a young age, was born into a noble family which owned large estates and many serfs. He was admitted to the elite *pazhski korpus* — a combined military school and court institution reserved for 150 boys of high nobility. After a brief career in the army in the course of which he led a number of well regarded geographical survey expeditions, he became more and more interested  in the workers' movement and in 1872, on a visit to Switzerland, joined the International Workingmen's Association (IWA) which had been founded in London in 1864 in order to unite a variety of leftwing and trades union associations under a common umbrella. He went back to Russia with a large quantity of prohibited socialist pamphlets, which he proceeded to rewrite in Russian in terms intelligible to the uneducated. For his pains, he was arrested and imprisoned in the notorious Peter and Paul fortress, from which, however, he escaped in 1876. Returning to Switzerland, he established ties to the Jura Federation, a federalist and anarchist section of the IWA that had been expelled from that organization in 1872 but was still strong among the watchmaker artisans of French-speaking Switzerland. Its emphasis on "egalitarian relations... and independence of thought and expression" was closer to Kropotkin's own ideals than the IWA's increasing emphasis on discipline and central planning. In 1881, after the assassination of Czar Alexander II — which Kropotkin justified on the grounds that an explosion is more effective than a vote in inciting the workers to revolution — he was expelled from Switzerland. He settled for a time in France but was arrested there in 1883 on account of his membership of the IWA. Released in 1886, he moved to England, living in various suburbs of London and associating with English-speaking socialists like the writer and artist William Morris and the playwright George Bernard Shaw. He returned to Russia after the February 1917 Revolution but did not welcome the October Revolution. "This buries the revolution," he said. The Bolsheviks, in his view, had shown how the revolution was *not* to be made, i.e. by authoritarian rather than libertarian methods. Kropotkin's influence in Germany was considerable, especially in the climate of disillusionment at the end of the First World War, when not only the working class and soldiers returning from the front but well-meaning people from all classes espoused pacifism and socialism but rejected what they saw as the authoritarianism of the nascent Communist Party. Many of Kropotkin's books were republished in multiple editions in those years.

In Herr Krüger's bookshop in 1912, Zur Mühlen might have found the following works by Prince Kropotkin in German translation:

Revolutionäre Regierungen (Berlin, 1893; Anarchistische Bibliothek, 1); *Die historiche Rolle des Staates* (Berlin, 1896, transl. from the French, *L'Etat, son rôle historique*); *Memoiren eines russischen Revolutionärs* (Stuttgart, 1900, 1906, 1912); *Landwirtschaft, Industrie und Handwerk, oder Die Vereinigung von Industrie und Landwirtschaft, geistiger und körperlicher Arbeit,* translated by Gustav Landauer (Berlin, 1904); *Gegenseitige Hilfe in der Tier- und Menschenwelt* (Leipzig, 1904, 1908, 1910); *Der Wohlstand für alle — Die Eroberung des Brotes* (Berlin, 1906, transl. from the French, *La Conquête du pain*, 1892); *Die Schreckenherrschaft in Russland* (Stuttgart, 1909); *Die große französische Revolution 1789–1793* (Leipzig, 1909, translated by Gustav Landauer). It is obvious why Herr Krüger, the bookseller, had to keep those books hidden away under lock and key.

110 Kennan

The reference is to George Kennan (1845–1924). Though his fame has been eclipsed by that of his great-nephew of the same name (the late United States ambassador to the Soviet Union and world-renowned diplomat George Frost Kennan), the earlier Kennan also had a considerable influence on Western views of Russia. Growing up in Norwalk, Ohio, he was drawn like many in his generation to the West, in his case, to Alaska, which Russia was in the process (1867) of selling to the United States, and from where he crossed over into Siberia. He chronicled his experience of the Russian East and North in his *Tent Life in Siberia and adventures among the Koraks and other tribes in Kamchatka and Northern Asia* (New York: G.P. Putnam, 1870; London: Sampson Low, 1871). On his return from Siberia he pursued a career as a journalist, working as an Associated Press reporter in Washington, D.C. and writing for the *New York Herald*, the *New York Times*, and magazines such as *Century, The Outlook, The Nation,* and *Forum*. In 1885, he went back to Siberia in the company of an artist friend from Boston, George Frost, having been commissioned by *Century* magazine to travel around and write up whatever he could find out about the penal settlements in Siberia, the revolutionaries who had been exiled and imprisoned there, their treatment, and, in general, Russian government policy with regard to political dissidents. The product of Kennan's investigations appeared in 1891, in two hefty volumes, profusely illustrated by Frost, of over 400 and over 500 pages respectively, as *Siberia and the Exile System*. Published simultaneously in New York by the Century Company and in London by J.R. Osgood, McIlvaine, this work was immediately translated into French and German and was cited by Tolstoi himself — whom Kennan twice interviewed. An excerpt from it, an article that had appeared in *Century*, no. 34, had already appeared in Russian in Geneva (a gathering place of Russian exiles and socialists) as *Tyuryemnaya zhizn Russkikh Revolyutsionyerov* [The Prison Life of Russian Revolutionaries] in 1889.

Siberia and the Exile System is an extraordinarily well written, lively, engaging, and fair book. Kennan relates in the Preface that when he set out he "believed that the Russian government and the exile system had been greatly misrepresented by such writers as Stépniak and Prince Kropótkin" and that he had said as much in a talk to the American Geographical Society in New York in 1882. "I also believed," he adds, "that the nihilists, terrorists, and political malcontents generally, who had so long kept Russia in a state of alarm and apprehension, were unreasonable and wrong-headed fanatics. [...] In short all my prepossessions were favorable to the Russian government and unfavorable to the Russian revolutionists." In fact, it was because those views of his were known, he explains, that he was able to travel in Siberia and was given access to places that would otherwise have been closed to unauthorized individuals. By the end of the second volume, however, Kennan had been thoroughly persuaded that "most of the Russian terrorists were nothing more, at first, than moderate liberals, or, at worst, peaceful socialistic propagandists, and [that] they were gradually transformed into revolutionists, and then into terrorists, by injustice, cruelty, illegality and contemptuous disregard by the Government of all their rights and feelings" (vol. 2, p. 455). As a consequence of the publication of his book, Kennan was banished from Russia in 1891 and when he tried to return in 1901, was ordered out of the country. In 1917 he was among a group of Americans who publicly welcomed the February Revolution of 1917 and the end of the czarist regime. The speeches at the meeting the group held were published immediately by the Carnegie Endowment for International Peace in 1917 as *Greetings to the New Russia: addresses at a meeting held at the Hudson Theater, New York, April 23, 1917 under the auspices of the National Institute of Arts and Letters, Washington, D.C.*

Kennan's writings on Siberia were widely available in German translation. Individual chapters from *Siberia and the Exile System* even seem to have come out in German before the book appeared in English. (Along with seven appendices, there are 30 chapters in all in the book, some of which had appeared in the form of magazine articles in *Century*.) An indication of the author's enormous success in Germany is given by the fact that two major popular series — Philipp Reclams *Universalbibliothek* in Leipzig and Meyers *Volksbücher*, also based in Leipzig, both offered his writings in several cheap paperback volumes. The large number of German public libraries holding copies — often multiple copies — of Kennan's books and the frequent new editions put out by each publisher are a further sign of unusually wide dissemination. In addition, a number of different translators and a number of different publishers had a hand in the production and distribution of Kennan's work in Germany. (The copyright situation seems quite murky.) Moreover, each publishing house chose its own title for its translation of *Siberia and the Exile System*. While Herr Krüger might not have had to conceal the translation of *Tentlife in Siberia* (*Zeltleben in Siberien und Abenteuer unter den Korjäken und anderen Stämmen im Kamchatka und*

Nordasien [Leipzig: Reclams Universalbibliothek, nos. 2795–97; also Meyers Volksbücher, nos. 1192–96; and Berlin: Cronbach, 1890]), he was certainly well advised, in Russian-ruled Estonia, to keep the other titles out of sight. Had they been discovered, he would almost certainly have had first-hand experience of Siberia himself.

He might well have had any or all of the following in his secret underground store:

Sibirien, nach dem im Century Magazine erschienenen Aufsätzen, transl. Georg Gästner (Halle a.d.S.: Hendel, 1890; Bibliothek der Gesamtliteratur des In- und Auslandes).

Sibirien, transl. E Kirchner (Berlin: Cronbach, 1890 [7th ed.],). Some editions have a subtitle: *Briefe aus einem Todtenhause* [Letters from a House of the Dead].

Sibirien und das Verbannungssystem, transl. Ottmar Dittrich (Leipzig and Vienna: Bibliographisches Institut, 1891). This was the version adopted for the Meyers Volksbücher series, nos. 886–93, circa 1899. It also appeared with the Bibliographisches Institut of Leipzig under a slightly different title: *Russisches Gefängnisleben* (1891).

Sibirien, transl. David Haek (Leipzig: Reclams Universalbibliothek, vol. 1, 1890 [nos. 2741–42]; vol. 2, 1890 [nos. 2775–76]; vol. 3, 1891 [no. 2883])

Aus Sibirien und Rußland: Neue Beiträge zur Kenntnis des Gefängnis- und Verbannungswesens, transl. Leopold Kutscher (Klagenfurt: Kleinmayr, 1892).

111 Rütten and Loening's series called "Society"

The series entitled "Die Gesellschaft" [Society] was launched by the distinguished Frankfurt publisher Rütten & Loening in 1906 with the philosopher Martin Buber as general editor. By the time it closed in 1912, it consisted of forty volumes, each by a leading scholar in the field in question. The first volume, on the proletariat, was the work of Werner Sombart (*Das Proletariat*, 1906). Subsequent volumes dealt with religion (*Die Religion*, 1906, by Georg Simmel), world trade (*Der Weltverkehr*, by Albrecht Wirth, 1906), language (*Die Sprache*, 1907, by the prolific novelist, playwright, essayist, and linguist Fritz Mauthner), revolution (*Die Revolution*, 1907, by the leftwing anarchist Gustav Landauer), parliament (*Das Parlament*, 1907, by Hellmuth von Gerlach), colonies (*Die Kolonie*, by Paul Rohrbach, 1907), the state (*Der Staat*, 1908, by Franz Oppenheimer), the church (*Die Kirche*, 1909, by Arthur Bonus), customs (*Die Sitte*, 1909 by Ferdinand Tönnies), the women's movement (*Die Frauenbewegung*, by Ellen Key, 1909), eroticism (*Die Erotik*, 1910, by Nietzsche's friend, Lou Andreas-Salomé), technology (*Die Technik*, by Julius Goldstein, 1912). The series also included monographs on the social and human impact of more mundane, everday, material phenomena, such as the department store, sport, crafts, the stock-exchange, and the newspaper. Not all the contributors would have been considered dangerous by the czarist authorities but a number assuredly would: e.g. Sombart, Landauer, Key.

112 Bebel

A wood-turner by trade, August Bebel (1840–1913) collaborated with Wilhelm Liebknecht in founding the political party that ultimately became the Social-Democratic Party of Germany (Sozialdemokratische Partei Deutschlands or SPD). He led the Party and represented it in the Reichstag for many years. His antimilitarism and his social program earned him the enmity of Bismarck and in 1872, he and Liebknecht — the only members of the North German parliament not to vote credits for the war with France and later, in 1871, outspoken defenders of the Paris Commune — were charged with treason and sentenced to two years' imprisonment. The effect of this was to solidify Bebel's popularity and leadership of the Social Democrats — he was sometimes referred to as "der Arbeiterkaiser" ["the emperor of the workers"] — and ensure that he would be reelected to the Reichstag. By 1912 the Social Democrats, embodied by Bebel, had become the largest political party in Germany. A pragmatic Marxist — he had a small factory of his own and justified his participation in an economic system he rejected on the grounds that it gave him the independence he needed to pursue his political goals — he constantly tried to mediate between the left and the right wings of the SPD. Had he lived, it is highly likely that he would again have been one of the few who refused to vote credits for the 1914 war. Bebel was the author of a number of books — on the German Peasant War, on the French "Utopian Socialist" Charles Fourier, on French culture from the 16th to the 18th century — but the work that is likely to have been in Herr Krüger's underground collection is the popular *Die Frau und der Sozialismus*. First published in 1879, this work was explicitly banned under the Anti-Socialist law in Germany (in effect from 1878 to 1890). Nevertheless it circulated widely, went through numerous editions and was translated into many languages, including English (*Woman under Socialism*, 1904, translated from the 33rd German edition).

113 Island of Moon

"Insel Moon" in Zur Mühlen's German original. "Muhu" or "Muhumaa" in Estonian. Situated at the northern end of the entrance to the Gulf of Riga, it is one of many Estonian islands in the Baltic Sea.

114 Poor Konrad

"Poor Konrad" (*"Der arme Konrad"*) was a term used, partly in contempt, to describe the poor, downtrodden peasant of the late Middle Ages. The "Poor Konrad Revolt" — a precursor of the German Peasant Revolt ten years later — broke out in 1514 in Beutelsbach, Württemberg, in protest against new taxes imposed by the ruling Duke Ulrich, which fell most heavily on the poor. The leader of the revolt, Peter Gaiss, presented himself as "Poor Konrad" i.e. as representing all the peasants. The revolt was crushed and its leaders beheaded.

115 Stolypin

Pyotr Stolypin (1862–1911), the son of a large Russian landowner, joined the Ministry of State Domains on graduating from St. Petersburg University in 1885. In 1902 he was appointed governor of Grodno province and the following year of Saratov province. Thanks to his ruthless and effective suppression of peasant unrest there in 1905, he gained the reputation of being the only governor who, in a period of widespread revolt, had been able to keep a firm grip on his province. His success against the revolutionaries in Saratov led in 1906 to his appointment as Minister of the Interior, then, a few months later, Prime Minister. In this latter capacity, Stolypin introduced reforms aimed at giving peasants greater opportunity to acquire land. The plan was to create a stable group of prosperous farmers or kulaks with an investment in the established order, who would form a natural conservative political force. At the same time there was no let-up in his policy of ruthless suppression of revolutionaries. A new court system was instituted that made it easier to arrest and convict them. Between 1906 and 1909 so many suspects — over 3,000 — were convicted by these special courts and executed that the hangman's noose came to be known in Russia as "Stolypin's necktie." In politics he was responsible for the emasculation of the Duma. (see under 'Duma') He got Nicholas II to dissolve the first Duma in 1906, and introduced changes designed to make the second Duma more pliant. After dissolving the second Duma also, in June 1907, he changed the voting system in such a way that the nobility and the wealthy were favored and the Duma was made into little more than an instrument for legitimizing government action. In September 1911, despite a police warning of an assassination plot, Stolypin went to Kiev, and on September 14, while attending a performance in the Kiev Opera House, and in the presence of the Czar and his family, he was shot, once in the arm and once in the chest, by an individual who was both a revolutionary and an agent of the Okhrana or secret police. He died four days later.

116 Citizen of an "enemy" country

By her marriage to Viktor von zur Mühlen, who, though of German heritage, was Russian by nationality (Estonia being still at the time a province of the Russian Empire), Zur Mühlen had herself become Russian, and therefore a citizen of a country that, in the First World War, was an "enemy" of her native Austria-Hungary.

117 The Gotha

The *Almanach de Gotha*, first published in 1763, was and still is the recognized directory of the European nobility. The following description is from a no longer available official web-page. (For a similar, longer version, see http://www.almanachdegotha.org/id266.html):

The Gotha Book entered the language in its own right with the phrase 'the entire Gotha was there.' Historically it has charted the ruling royal and princely houses of Europe; coming to an end only with the Soviet occupation of the former Saxon Duchies of Saxe-Coburg-Gotha in 1945.

The Almanach de Gotha made its debut in Saxe-Coburg in 1763, the Court which, during the 1760's under Duke Friedrich III and later under Duke Ernest II, attracted the likes of Voltaire and which in the mid 1800's produced Prince Albert as consort for Queen Victoria. The Gotha's own familiar crown was stamped on the cover of what was to become the ultimate power register of the ruling classes. As the publisher was not to be moved by government decrees or bribes to include or exclude and refused to compromise the integrity of the volume, those not listed in its pages found their ambitions thwarted, and Pretenders' claims were left in ruins.

Napoleon's reaction was typical. On 20 October 1807 the Emperor wrote to his Foreign Minister, de Champagny: 'Monsieur de Champagny, this year's Almanach de Gotha is badly done. I protest. There should be more of the French Nobility I have created and less of the German Princes who are no longer sovereign. Furthermore, the Imperial Family of Bonaparte should appear before all other royal dynasties, and let it be clear that we and not the Bourbons are the House of France. Summon the Minister of the Interior of Gotha at once so that I personally may order these changes'.

Unmoved, the Almanach de Gotha simply produced two editions the following year, the first the extremely rare "Edition for France — at His Imperial Majesty's Request" and the other "The Gotha — Correct in All Detail." Historically the Gotha was the determining instrument when it came to matters of protocol. Not only were orders of precedence easily checked, but marriages between parties not listed in the same Gotha section were often considered unequal at some courts, participants thereby loosing dynastic privileges and sometimes title and rank. The term morganatic applied to such marriages; it derived from the High German morgangeba, a gift by a groom to his bride on the morning following their wedding. It indicated that this was the full and only entitlement that the wife could expect from her new husband. Morganatic marriages were often called 'left hand marriages' due to the fact that inequality in rank required the groom to use his left hand instead of the right during the wedding ceremony.

118 Moissi

Alexander Moissi (1879–1935), born in Albania, grew up in Vienna where his career as one of the most acclaimed European stage actors of his time began. He then moved to Berlin as a protégé of the great director Max Reinhardt. In 1911, he accompanied Reinhardt's troupe to Russia, where his interpretation of the role of Oedipus won high praise from the influential Marxist critic and future Soviet "Commissar of Enlightenment," Anatoly Lunacharsky.

In her autobiography, Elisabeth Bergner, an internationally celebrated actress of the time, writes of him with affection and with the greatest respect not only for his extraordinary artistic talent but for his qualities as a human being. "Aside from his crazy chasing after women," she recalls, "he was one of the finest, kindest, most modest and most lovable people I ever met in the world of stage and screen. And never, not once in the many years we knew each other, from our first meeting in Zurich until much later in Vienna and Berlin, did I ever hear him say a bad word about others. That is something very rare indeed in theatre and film circles." (*Bewundert viel und viel gescholten... Elisabeth Bergners unordentliche Erinnerungen* [Munich: Bertelsmann, 1978], p. 34) Though his repertoire encompassed the entire range of European drama from the ancients to Strindberg, Chekhov, and Pirandello, Moissi's most famous role was as Fedya (Fyodor Protasov) in Tolstoi's *The Living Corpse* (*Zhivoy Trup*, also sometimes referred to in English as *Redemption*), first produced after the author's death at the Moscow Art Theatre, under Stanislavsky's direction, in 1911. He performed this role, in which Zur Mühlen saw him in Davos in 1917, 1400 times all over Europe, as well as in North and South America. By reporting that news of the Revolution in Russia distracted the Davos audience from a performance by an artist such as Moissi in his most famous role, Zur Mühlen obviously intended to emphasize its enormous impact.

119 K.P.D.

In the old Imperial Austria the initials K.P.D. signified *Kaiserliche Palast-Dame* — from the French *Dame du palais* — i.e. lady-in-waiting to the Empress. The reference to Marie Louise is to Archduchess Marie-Louise, daughter of the Austrian Emperor Franz I, who was married to Napoleon in 1810, at the age of eighteen, thus becoming Empress of the French. After the fall of Napoleon in 1814, she returned to Vienna along with her son, the King of Rome, but by the terms of the Treaty of Fontainebleau (1814) she retained her title of Empress.

By 1929, when Hermynia Zur Mühlen wrote her memoir, the initials K.P.D. signified *Kommunistische Partei Deutschlands* — German Communist Party. Zur Mühlen was a member of the Party throughout the 1920s. She resigned in the early 1930s, around the time of the first Stalinist purges and the banishment of Trotsky.

120 Leonid Andreyev

Leonid Andreyev (1871–1919) won an international reputation with *The Red Laugh* (1904), a ferocious indictment of war inspired by the Russo-Japanese War of 1904–1905. It was immediately translated into English and published by Unwin in London in 1905. Republished in the United States in 1915 it was hailed in the *New York Times* (4 July 1915) as probably "the most vivid piece of war realism in any language." Andreyev's other writings — in particular his short stories and plays — were widely translated and continue to be republished to this day. Gorki, who discovered him, was one of his great admirers. Both Stanislavsky and Meyerhold, the two giants of twentieth-century Russian theatre, directed plays by him in Moscow and St. Petersburg respectively. Though Andreyev was not as supportive of the Russian Revolution as Gorki — he wrote several critical pieces from his exile in Finland — he was treated as a major Russian writer even in the old Soviet Union. New editions and translations of his works continue to appear in many languages and there is a very substantial body of critical writing about him, again in many languages. One of his plays, *He Who Gets Slapped* (1915), was made into a Hollywood movie in 1924.

121 Andreas Latzko

Born and educated in Hungary, Andreas Latzko (1876–1943) wrote first in Hungarian but soon switched to German. In 1901 a short play by him was put on in Berlin. When World War I broke out he was in the East (Egypt, India, Ceylon, Java) preparing to write books and articles on what he had observed there. As a reserve officer in the Imperial army, he returned to Europe and was posted to the then border area between the Austro-Hungarian Empire and the Kingdom of Italy. He almost immediately fell ill with malaria and then suffered severe shell-shock during one of the many inconclusive engagements between the Italians and the Austro-Hungarians along the Isonzo river in 1916. After a few months in an army hospital he was sent to the Swiss health resort of Davos to recuperate. Here, where Zur Mühlen and her partner Stefan Klein, who had also been raised in Hungary, could well have met him, he wrote the stories that make up his *Menschen im Krieg* [*Men in War*], published anonymously by the Rascher-Verlag in Zurich in 1917 and in English, French, and Dutch translation the following year. The book was soon translated into a dozen more languages, including even Yiddish and Esperanto, and became an enormous worldwide success. Reviewing it in *Die Fackel* shortly after its publication the acerbic Viennese critic Karl Kraus hailed it as one of the most powerful documents about the Great War and about humanity in general, while the *New York Times* described it as "a bitter attack on the by-products of the Teutonic military idea." In 1918 Latzko published another series of anti-war stories, *Friedensgericht* [*The Judgement of Peace*], in which he described the lives of German soldiers on the Western Front. This was also widely translated. In 1920, he contributed a paper on "Women in War" to the International Socialist Women's Conference in Bern. During his stay in Switzerland, Latzko became friendly with Stefan Zweig and Romain Rolland, to whom — "my compatriot in the love of man" — *Friedensgericht* was dedicated. At the end of the War, Latzko moved to Munich, the capital of the short-lived *Räterepublik* or Soviet Republic of Bavaria. When it collapsed he returned to Austria and settled in Salzburg, where he worked as a journalist. In 1931 he moved to Amsterdam (his papers and correspondence are still preserved at the University of Amsterdam), but like many other Jewish writers soon had to seek refuge in the United States. He died, impoverished, in New York, in 1943. Latzko wrote a number of books in the 1930s but none had the success or the impact of the first two, which continue to be republished to this day.

122 Leonhard Frank

Leonhard Frank (1882–1961) began a productive literary career with short stories in the avant-garde journal *Pan*. He gained acclaim in 1914 with his first novel *Die Räuberbande* [English translation, *The Robber Band*, 1928) which won the Fontane Prize. The following year, however, he created a scandal when, as a socialist and confirmed pacifist, he was outraged by a Social Democratic journalist's loudly proclaiming in a Berlin café that the sinking of the British passenger liner *Lusitania* (with the loss of 1198 lives) by a German U-boat was "the most heroic feat in human history" and slapped him in the face. As a result, he had to go into exile in Switzerland (1915–1918), where he finished *Die Ursache* [*The Cause of the Crime*], a novel critical of the death penalty, and also wrote a series of pacifist short-stories, published together under the title *Der Mensch ist gut* [*Man is Good*] in 1917 and then republished by the Rascher Verlag in Zurich in 1918. The book, translated into many languages, was a huge success, and led to Frank's being awarded the Kleist Prize by Heinrich Mann in November 1918. Just before that, it had been given a reading in her Berlin home, before some 300 guests, by the celebrated actress Tilla Durieux (Käte Kollwitz was in the audience and describes the episode in her diaries), after which the assembled guests had to be held back from marching to the Potsdamer Platz to protest against the war.

Like Latzko, Frank was drawn to Munich on the establishment of the *Räterepublik* there under Kurt Eisner and Gustav Landauer and was wounded in the fighting that accompanied its brutal suppression. He returned to Berlin, where he continued to enjoy success as a prolific novelist (*Der Bürger* [1924; Engl tr. 1930], *Im Letzten Wagen* [1925; Engl. transl. 1934], *Carl und Anna* [1927; Engl. transl. 1929], *Absturtz* [1929], *Brüder und Schwester* [1929]), playwright, and finally screen-writer. He wrote the screen-play for the film *Der Mörder Dimitri Karamasoff* [*Dmitri Karamazov Murderer*], based on the Dostoievski character and worked with the Russian-born director Victor Trivas on *Niemandsland* [*No Man's Land*], an anti-war film that was savagely attacked by nationalists and National Socialists and was soon banned by the German government under pressure from those groups.

When the Nazis seized power in 1933, Frank left Germany first for Zurich, then London, and finally Paris. His books were burned in Germany and his German citizenship was taken away. On the outbreak of war in 1939, he was interned by the French authorities, as were all German exiles, but he managed to escape and made his way to Marseilles where he lived in constant danger and deprivation until, with the help of the Emergency Rescue Committee, founded in New York by — among others — Thomas and Erika Mann, he was able to cross the Pyrenees into Spain and reach Portugal from where he set sail for the U.S.

Frank found work as a screenwriter for Warner Brothers in Hollywood but did not have a successful career in the U.S. Moreover, as he was considered a "violently pacifist" communist, he was continually under observation by the FBI and the immigration authorities. He returned to Germany after the war and resumed his literary career, but with much less success than before the war. Though he received many honours in recognition of his work and his stand against National Socialism (the Silver Medal of the City of Würzburg, where he was born in 1952; the Culture Prize of the City of Nürnberg in 1953; the National Prize of the German Democratic Republic in 1955; the Service Medal of the German Federal Republic; an honorary degree from the Humboldt University in East Berlin in 1957; and, from the Soviet Union, the Tolstoi Medal in 1960) and a street was named after him in the city of Leipzig for having been a "bourgeois democratic antifascist writer," he continued to be the object of FBI surveillance, even in Germany, while in the Federal Republic he was regarded with some reserve because of his close contacts with and frequent trips to East Germany, his constant re-examination of the Nazi era, and his obstinate pointing to the successful careers, in the Federal Republic, of former National Socialists.

123 Henri Barbusse

In the decade before the Great War, Henri Barbusse (1873–1935) made a modest name for himself in Paris literary circles as a writer of poetry and the author of the novel *L'Enfer* (1908), which tells of what a young man in a Paris boarding-house observes when he spies on his neighbours through a hole in his bedroom wall. On the outbreak of war in 1914, though aged 41, a pacifist, and in poor health, he enlisted in the French army but by 1917 had been invalided out of active service. In the preceding year he published *Le Feu*, a vivid account of the horrendous carnage of the war and at the same time a moving portrait of the men who endured it. The book created a sensation, won the Prix Goncourt, and was immediately translated into English (*Under Fire*, 1917) and then into many other languages (Chinese, Czech, Dutch, German, Japanese, Russian, Turkish, Yiddish to name a few). After the war, Barbusse visited Moscow, married a Russian woman and joined the Communist Party. Thanks to the huge success of *Le Feu*, the earlier *L'Enfer* was now translated into English (*The Inferno*, 1918) and other languages, as were the politically inspired novels and other writings he now began to produce: *Nous autres* (1918; *We Others*, 1918), *Clarté* (1919; *Light*, 1919), *Les Enchaînements* (1924; *Chains*, 1925), *Les Judas de Jésus* (1927; *Jesus*, 1927), *Faits divers* (1928; *Thus and Thus*, 1928). He also turned out many purely political tracts calling for the overthrow of capitalism and an end to imperialist wars. The birth of Soviet Russia, he declared, in words that would have resonated with Zur Mühlen in those same years, was "the greatest and most beautiful phenomenon in world history." However, unlike Zur Mühlen who left the Communist Party after Trotsky was expelled from the Soviet Union and the harsh rule of Stalin began (though she never renounced her socialism), Barbusse became an apologist for Stalin and just before his death, wrote an admiring biography of the Soviet leader.

124 Rudolf Jeremias Kreutz

Rudolf Jeremias Kreutz, originally Kříž (1876–1949), graduated from the military academy in Vienna and served as an officer in the Imperial army and in the Imperial War Ministry. Even at this stage in his life, however, he was publishing witty satirical sketches and verses (*Vom grinsenden Leben* [*Of the Smirking Life*], 1911; *Aus dem Affenkasten der Welt* [*From the Monkey-Box of the World*], 1914; both illustrated by the talented Viennese caricaturist Fritz Schönpflug). His reputation as a writer was such that on the appearance of his anonymously published novel, *Quo vadis Austria?* (1913), which pilloried the corruption and inefficiency of the Austrian military, he himself was asked to respond to it with a counter-novel. The outbreak of the First World War relieved him of this task, though it later served as the topic of a satire (1929) and a comedy (1932), *Der befohlene k. und k. Roman* (*The Commissioned Royal and Imperial Novel*). In November 1914, Kreutz was wounded and taken prisoner by the Russians. During his captivity in Siberia, he became a convinced pacifist. Two novels, *Die große Phrase* (1919 [*Big Talk*]), and *Die einsame Flamme* (1920 [*The Solitary Flame*]), reflect his new anti-war stance. Both seem to have been published first (1918) in Danish and Swedish translation. Rascher Verlag in Zurich then put out the German text of *Die große Phrase*, a scathing indictment of the Austrian high command's conduct of the war on the eastern front, in 1919. An English translation (from the Swedish) also appeared in 1919, under a different title, *Captain Zillner*, https://archive.org/details/captainzillnerhu00kreurich

Back in Austria and in retirement from the army, Kreutz used his literary talent to spread his ideas for a new society in a world at peace (*Der neue Mensch* [1920; *The New Man*], *Die Krise des Pazifismus, des Antisemitismus, der Ironie*, 1931). He also expressed himself in poetry (*Gesänge der Erde* [1933; *Songs of the Earth*]). In 1933, at a general meeting of the P.E.N. Club, he put forward a resolution, signed by 25 writers, condemning the inhumanity of the National Socialist regime in Germany. His books were banned in Germany as a result. After the *Anschluß* in 1938, he was banned from publishing in Austria too and in 1944 was imprisoned for several months. He resumed his literary career after the War with the publication of a volume of poems, two volumes of short stories and, posthumously, *Ich war ein Österreicher*, an anti-Nazi, Austrian nationalist novel written during the War years.

125 *Arbeiter-Zeitung*

Launched in 1889 by veteran Austrian Social Democrat Victor Adler as a socialist workers' newspaper, it was banned after the February 1934 disturbances in Vienna (see below). Publication resumed in 1945, when it served as the organ of the Austrian Socialist Party.

126 Schiller Marmorek

Schiller Marmorek, who was Jewish, was the art critic of the journal *Kleine Blätter* and one of the editors of the *Arbeiter-Zeitung*. He translated Clémenceau's *Au Pied du Sinai* (1898) into German as *Jüdische Gestalten* (1924) and George Soulié de Morant's French translations of Chinese tales as *Der chinesische Dekameron* (1925). He fled Austria for Czechoslovakia after the 3-day Austrian revolution of February 1934 (see note below) and finally made his way to the U.S.

(Source: Herbert Exenberger, "'Bis uns als Vaterland geschenkt der Staub, der unter den Schuhn uns hängt': Sozialistische Schriftsteller im Exil," in Johann Holzner, Sigurd Scheichl, Wolgang Wiesenmüller, eds., *Eine schwierige Heimkehr. Österreichische Literatur im Exil, 198–1945* [Innsbrücker Beiträge zur Kulturwissenschaft, Germanistische Reihe, vol. 40, 1991], pp. 171, 174, 177, 178).

127 Julius Braunthal

As a prominent socialist activist and member of the outlawed Social Democratic militia, the "Republikanischer Schutzbund," Braunthal (b. 1891), who, like Marmorek, was Jewish, was among those arrested in February 1934, but he managed to reach Belgium shortly afterwards and in 1938 moved to England, where he lived until his death in 1972, and where he had an active political and literary career. His papers, preserved at the Internationaal Instituut voor Sociale Geschiedenis in Amsterdam, contain exchanges of letters with Karl Kautsky, Thomas Mann, Karl Mannheim, Karl Popper, and a host of liberal or leftwing British figures, including H.N. Brailsford, Fenner Brockway, G.D.H. Cole, Michael Foot, G.L. Gooch, Kingsley Martin, Raymond Postgate, and R.H. Tawney. From 1941 until 1948 he was the editor of *International Socialist Forum*. In Austria he had published *Die Arbeiterräte in Deutschösterreich* (1919), *Die europäische Krise und der Sozialismus* (1920), *Die kranke Welt* (1922), *Vom Kommunismus zum Imperialismus. Bilder aus dem bolschewistischen Georgien* (1922), and he had been one of the editors of the *Arbeiter-Zeitung*. In England, where many of his books were published by the left-leaning Victor Gollancz, his *Need Germany Survive?* (1943) carried an introduction by Harold Laski; *In Search of the Millennium* (1945) had an introduction by H.N. Brailsford; *The Paradox of Nationalism: An Epilogue to the Nuremberg Trials* (1946) had an introduction by Leonard Woolf; and *The Tragedy of Austria* (1948) was introduced by Michael Foot. The first volume of a 3-volume *History of the International* appeared in 1966. Braunthal was an editor of *Die Zeitung*, a daily, later a weekly, which was published in London from 1941 until 1945 and to which Zur Mühlen contributed a number of *feuilletons*.

128 February 1934

For four days, from 12 to 15 February 1934, civil war raged in several parts of Austria. The rightwing Austrian government, under Chancellor Engelbert

Dolfuss, had shut down the Parliament in March 1933, was governing by decree, and aimed to transform the Austrian Republic into a corporate state on the model of Mussolini's Italy. While the Social Democratic left was paralysed by the leadership's extreme caution and unwillingness to support calls for action from the left wing of the Party and from some grassroots workers' groups, the *Heimwehr*, an extreme rightwing paramilitary organization, had carried out acts of violence against Social Democrats and members of the *Schutzbund* or Social Democratic defense league, but the perpetrators had been released without punishment by the courts. Angry calls for mass protest and industrial action were resisted by the leaders of the Social Democratic Party. Following an attack by the *Heimwehr* on Social Democratic Party premises in Linz, however, and house searches and arrests of Party members, protest turned violent. The working class districts of Vienna and some other Austrian cities rose up. But the Social Democratic Party leadership failed to guide and organize the revolt, a call for a general strike was not answered, and significant segments of the working class stood back from the fray. The combined forces of the police and the military succeeded in putting down the uprising. The leaders of the Social Democratic Party were arrested and imprisoned or fled the country. Chancellor Dollfuss, who planned to maintain Austrian independence from Nazi Germany and to associate his country rather with Mussolini's Italy, was himself assassinated by Nazi agents five months later.

For excellent accounts of the failed February revolution, see G.E.R. Gedy, *Betrayal in Central Europe. Austria and Czechoslovakia: The Fallen Bastions* (New York: Harper Brothers, 1939); Otto Leichter, *Glanz und Elend der Ersten Republik. Wie es zum österreichischen Bürgerkrieg kam* (Vienna: Europa Verlag, 1964); and the moving, highly personal, day by day account of Ernst Fischer in his *Erinnerungen und Reflexionen* (Reibeck bei Hamburg: Rohwolt, 1969).

129 Gsur Verlag

The Gsur Verlag, which published Zur Mühlen's novel, was a courageous player in Austrian resistance to National Socialism. Established in January 1930, it got its name from one of its two founders, Gusti Gsur, a Viennese businesswoman. She withdrew only a few months later, leaving the firm entirely in the hands of its co-founder, the sociologist, historian, and future Vice-Mayor of Vienna, Ernst Karl Winter.

During a first phase (1930–1933), the books published by Gsur Verlag reflected Winter's strongly Catholic and conservative politics, which went hand in hand with a deep and enduring commitment to the idea of Austria as a distinct nation and culture and not simply a branch of a larger German *Volk* (as the Nazis claimed), and increasingly, in face of the growing power and influence of National Socialism in Germany, to the idea that Austria had a special mission to stand up for the traditional values Germans had once shared with other European nations. As early as the Spring of 1932, before Hitler had become Chancellor and when there was as yet no broad-based campaign against National Socialism, the Gsur Verlag brought out two volumes by the Franciscan Father Zyrill Fischer — *Die Hakenkreuzler* [Followers of the Swastika] and *Die Nazisozis*, an extract from that work. In Winter's own words, these two publications "marked the first attempt in Austria to combat National Socialism from a Catholic point of view and were accepted for publication for that very reason by the Gsur Verlag, the goals of which are not, in the first instance, commercial, but intellectual and spiritual." (*Wiener Politische Blätter*, 1, no. 4 [3 December, 1933], p. 242; on Fischer and his work, see Martin Kugler, *Die frühe Diagnose des Nationalsozialismus: Christlich motivierter Widerstand in der österreichischen Publizistik* [Frankfurt a. M.: Peter Lang, 1995]). In November 1932 the Gsur press published another book, *Der Nazispiegel*, in the same anti-Nazi vein (in fact it was so close to its predecessors that there was some question of plagiarism) by an author (Alfred Missong) writing under the pseudonym of Thomas Murner, the celebrated early sixteenth-century Catholic satirist and formidable critic of Luther. In April of the following year, Winter began publication through the Gsur Verlag of a bi-monthly periodical, *Wiener Politische Blätter*, the very first number of which was immediately banned in Germany, where the National Socialists were now in power.

In 1935 the Gsur Verlag announced a new series of publications. Winter explained the policy guiding it in an article in his *Wiener Politische Blätter* (3, no. 5, 13 October 1935): "In the spirit of the orientation of our... publications to date, we shall publish literary, political, and scholarly works in three areas. In area A we shall follow the *social line* begun by the book *Arbeiterschaft und Staat* [by Winter himself]*... In area B we shall continue the *Austrian line* hitherto represented by four books in the series 'Austrian Religion and Culture' and by the study of Rudolph IV [also by Winter himself]. Area C will continue the *anti-National Socialist line* established by the writings of Thomas Murner."

---

*   The term *Arbeiterschaft*, as distinct from *Arbeiterklasse*, in the title of this collection of articles and other documents, which appeared in 1934, was in itself programmatic in that it marked a rejection of the Marxist view of society as historically divided into conflicting classes and proposed instead a view of the workers as an essential element of an organic *Standesgesellschaft* — a society made up of different component parts, each of which, being necessary to the wellbeing of the whole, deserves equitable and just treatment by the state. This was also the view of society held by the rightwing Austrian Chancellor Engelbert Dolfuss, who appointed Winter Vice-Mayor of Vienna after the uprising of February 1934 and to whose memory (after his assassination by Nazi agents in July 1934) Winter dedicated the second volume (1936) of his social, historical and political study *Rudolph IV von Österreich* (the first volume had appeared in 1934), except that Winter was more generously and sincerely concerned with the welfare of the workers than most advocates of the *Standesgesellschaft*, including Dolfuss.

Within 15 months eight such anti-Nazi works appeared, of which the first was a witty satire of the "Blood and Soil" theme dear to the Nazis — this was *Müller. Chronik einer deutschen Sippe* (1935) by Walter Mehring, a well-known writer of satirical prose and verse and of songs for the Berlin cabarets, who, like Zur Mühlen, had fled Germany for Austria in 1933 — and the second was Zur Mühlen's *Unsere Töchter die Nazinen*. The German ambassador to Austria, Franz von Papen, communicated his extreme displeasure at both publications in the form of protests to the Austrian Chancellor's office. About Mehring's book he declared: "In this novel, with its general anti-National Socialist tenor and special aim of ridiculing the meaning of blood and soil in the life of the people, the author has produced a concoction that can only be described as downright pornographic and that demeans and insults German culture in the most outrageous manner." There followed a diplomatically couched demand that the book be banned and all copies confiscated as quickly as possible. While the Austrian side appears not to have acted on this demand, it found a way to respond positively, without appearing to have simply yielded to pressure from a foreign state, to a similar demand made a day or two later that Zur Mühlen's book be banned. (See below, the essay "Remembering Hermynia Zur Mühlen: A Tribute," note 34) These setbacks did not prevent the Gsur Verlag from continuing to publish books in area C — among them *Die Judenfrage in Deutschland* (1936) by Peter Drucker, who after leaving Germany in 1933 for England, then the U.S., became a well known writer, in English, on issues of management and social policy, holding positions at Bennington College (1942–49), New York University (where he was professor of management, 1950–71) and the Management School (now named after him) of the Claremont Graduate University in California (1971 until his death in 2005).

With the banning of an important Beiheft of the *Wiener Politische Blätter*, written by Winter himself, the Gsur Verlag reached the end of its short road. Winter had been appointed third vice-mayor of Vienna by the Dolfuss administration in 1934 after the suppression of the February uprising, in the hope that he would be able to win support for the regime in the working class, whose interests he had always defended. Soon afterwards, Dolfuss's commitment to Austrian independence from Germany resulted in his assassination by Nazi agents. Winter, who remained deeply opposed to German designs on Austria (as well as to National Socialism and anti-Semitism), finally came to believe that only a revival of the monarchy under Otto Habsburg could save Austria. Hence the Beiheft, entitled *Monarchie und Arbeiterschaft*, which appeared on October 1, 1936. By the end of the month it had been banned by a police order as "dangerous to public peace, order, and security," and all further publication of the *Politische Blätter* was also forbidden. An additional consequence was that Winter had to step down as vice-mayor of Vienna. These developments were greeted with joy not only in the German embassy but among Austrian Nazis and their sympathizers, the regular targets of Winter's criticisms. According to the official organ of the Austrian extreme Right, the *Heimatschützer*, Winter's *Monarchie und Arbeiterschaft* "contains Popular Front slogans and constitutes a threat to the state." This, it was explained, "is consistent with the author's position that he 'feels humanly close to Dr. Bauer' [Otto Bauer, the leader of the Social Democratic Party, with whom Winter did in fact enjoy a cordial relationship]. Dr. Winter praises Bolshevism in this publication."

In view of the ban on further publication of the *Politische Blätter*, Winter ceded his official authorization to operate a publishing house to the Austrian Catholic League. Gsur & Co. survived for a while as a name, but after Winter's departure from Vienna for Zurich at the time of the *Anschluß* in 1938 the firm was officially dissolved.

The career of the scholar, writer and politician who, as founder and head of the Gsur Company, agreed to publish Zur Mühlen's book has been admirably summarized by Franz Richard Reiter in his Foreword to *E.K. Winter. Ein Katholik zwischen Österreichs Fronten 1933–1938* by K.H. Heinz, Winter's chief editor at the Gsur Verlag:

> Winter's main *goal* was always the same: to defend Austria against absorption by Germany. and the National Socialist threat to liquidate it. His leading *idea* was also always the same: to bring about a reconciliation of workers, state, and church.
>
> The *means* proposed by Winter varied according to circumstances, however. At the beginning of his energetic political activity there are the letters to President Miklas, whom he urges and expects to defend the parliamentary constitution. When his hopes in this respect are dashed, he encourages Otto Bauer to combat any move to outlaw the Social Democrats — and thus weaken the front against Hitler Germany — with armed resistance. When the Social Democratic Party is banned on February 12, 1934, however, Winter accepts from his student society brother and onetime regimental comrade Dollfuss — with whom, as in other cases, despite sharp disagreements, he maintained a long established friendship — the charge of winning the support of the workers for the new state. As third Vice-Mayor of Vienna, Winter is now the representative of the established political order. At the same time, he also takes an oppositional stance towards it — about which he always expresses himself openly. "Aktion Winter," then "Österreichische Arbeiteraktion" [Austrian Workers' Action], is the name the Vice-Mayor gives to his efforts to promote an understanding between left and right. After little more than a year *Die Aktion*, a weekly paper he has been putting out, is banned. With the conclusion of the 1936 agreement between Austria and Germany, Winter finally recognizes that it will be impossible to win the support of the workers for the current Austrian state. In Dr. Otto Habsburg† he comes to see someone "without any baggage" who might be capable of uniting all Austrians in a single popular front. It is this last way out for Austria in his view that he expounds in the Beiheft to the *Wiener Politische Blätter*. The booklet, entitled *Monarchie und Arbeiterschaft* is banned, just as *Die*

---

†   Otto Habsburg was the Crown Prince, the son of Karl, the last Emperor of Austria. As ranks and titles of nobility were abolished under the constitution of the Austrian Republic, the "von" was dropped from his name.

Aktion and some previous numbers of the *Politische Blätter* had been. But this time Winter himself becomes the object of direct action. On October 24, 1936 he is dismissed from his post of Vice-Mayor and the *Wiener Politische Blätter* are banned permanently. Just before Hitler's occupation of Austria, Winter makes one last attempt to persuade Schuschnigg [Dolfuss's successor as President] that Austrians must take up arms to prevent the liquidation of their country. To no avail.

Winter flees to the United States to escape the National Socialists. It is 1955 before he returns to Austria. Despite his scholarly qualifications he does not obtain a professorship in his native land. On February 12, 1959, Ernst Karl Winter was quietly buried.

– Karl Hans Heinz, *E.K. Winter: ein Katholik zwischen Österreichs Fronten 1933–38* (Vienna: Böhlau, 1984), Vorwort, pp. 11–13.

Winter's difficult, perhaps untenable position — between his deep Christian faith, with its rejection of violence, and his commitment to redressing the wrongs suffered by the working class and to defending Austria's independence against Germany — is reflected in the novel *Barabbas. Erzählung aus der Zeit Christi* by Andreas Hemberger, published by the Gsur Verlag in 1936 (Dutch translation, Rotterdam, 1938; English translation, revised by Emery Bekessy, New York, 1946; Danish translation, 1948). The central conflict of the novel is between Barabbas, the power-hungry but popular robber, murderer, and advocate of violence as the only means of liberating Israel from Roman oppression and bringing about a just social and economic order, and Christ's teaching of love and forgiveness.

Though Winter taught sociology and political philosophy at the New School in New York City during his years of exile, his application for a post at the University of Graz at the end of the War was unsuccessful. The courageous publisher of *Unsere Töchter die Nazinen*, who finally made the decision to return to his native land, thus appears to have experienced the same fate in post-War Austria as the novel's author, who chose to die in exile: indifference, at best.

130 Hlinka

Andrej Hlinka (1864–1938), a Catholic priest, was the leader of the Slovak People's Party, which sought autonomy for Slovakia, in the 1920s and 30s. He was considered a national hero in the fascist puppet republic of Slovakia during World War II. The *Hlinka Guard* was the Party's militia (1938–45).

131 Hacha

Emil Hácha (1872–1945), a Czech lawyer, became the third President of Czechoslovakia, taking office in 1938 after the forced resgination of Beneš. He was the first and only State President of the Protectorate of Bohemia and Moravia.

132 Tuka

Vojtech Tuka (1880–1946), a constitutional lawyer, challenged the unity of the Czech state and led the Slovak People's Party's radical wing, which demanded complete independence for Slovakia. Imprisoned on a charge of espionage in 1928, he was released in 1938, became Prime Minister and Foreign Minister of the puppet Slovak Republic (1940–45), and in that capacity energetically pursued a policy of persecution and deportation of Slovak Jews.

133 *Deutsche Allgemeine Zeitung*

It might seem odd that carrying a copy of the *Deutsche Allgemeine Zeitung* could be intended as a sign that the bearer was not a Nazi. Since its founding in 1861, the paper had consistently pursued a conservative line and been close to the centres of power. Refounded near the end of the First World War, ostensibly to give the collapsing regime a more democratic profile, it was acquired soon afterwards (1920) by the extreme right-wing industrialist Hugo Stinnes and in 1922 was briefly banned for having supported the Kapp-Putsch, a right-wing attempt to overthrow the Weimar Republic. Throughout the 1920s and 1930s the paper continued to represent the views of the extreme right. In 1933, however, it was almost banned again because of an article that had enraged Hitler. The Sinnes family appointed a new editor, Karl Silex, who appears to have thought that hewing to a conservative pro-government line would ensure a modicum of independence for the paper. In fact, the slightest deviation from the official Nazi Party line resulted in run-ins with the Propaganda Ministry and several issues of the paper were banned. Carrying the *Deutsche Allgemeine Zeitung* could thus be construed as an assertion of independence, however restrained and timid.

134 Marianka

Marianka in *Came the Stranger* is a simple, hardworking, devoutly and sincerely (Catholic) Christian peasant woman who follows the moral precepts of the Gospels without question and without fear.

4. *Feuilletons* and Fairy Tales: A Sampling

by Hermynia Zur Mühlen
(Translated by Lionel Gossman)

Editor's Note

The following short stories and newspaper *feuilletons*, all translated by the editor, have been selected from among the hundreds published by Zur Mühlen because of the light they throw on her inspiration and motivation as a writer. Their themes and topics pervade her entire *oeuvre*: the injustice, violence, and cruelty of modern capitalist societies; the miserable lives of the poor and downtrodden; the way a patriarchal culture prevents women of all classes from developing into full human beings; and, not least, the tensions within her own utopian aspirations. On the one hand, for example, the conviction that it is a human responsibility, and especially a responsibility of the artist, to confront an ugly and unjust world and rouse others to confront and combat it, so that a better world may come into being; on the other, nostalgia for the beauty, peace, and harmony of the *hortus conclusus*, the protected childhood paradise that Zur Mühlen herself once knew in her grandmother's villa in the little lakeside resort town of Gmunden. On the one hand, the writer's moral responsibility to create a literature of combat, a *littérature engagée* ("We Have to Tell Them"); on the other, the temptation of estheticism, of excluding ugliness from one's writing in order to create a manageable and esthetically satisfying imaginary world ("Painted on Ivory"). In her *feuilletons* as well as in her novels, Zur Mühlen suggests that withdrawal from the world of conflict and violence is not only immoral, but may result, for the artist, in an impoverishment of her art, and that, in addition, an individual who has shut herself off from the everyday world of passions and desires or who has been protected from it, is rendered defenceless against the world ("Death of a Shadow" — recognizably contemporary with the novel *Unsere Töchter die Nazinen*). One of the *feuilletons* seems to suggest, however, that any career as a writer requires sacrifice. To the degree that sympathizing and identifying with others is the condition of her ability to create fictional characters, the writer may find that her own life has been diminished as well as enriched by her capacity for empathizing and living vicariously ("A Secondary Happiness").

Like everything Zur Mühlen wrote, these short pieces are rooted in her own experience and that of her time. Thus, for instance, the three samples from the collection entitled *Der rote Heiland*, which was published soon after the First World War (the little dramatic scene that gave the collection its title, together with "Confession," and "High Treason"), reflect the widespread pacifism, the revulsion against war, and the demand for radical social change in Germany in the years following the country's disastrous defeat. "Miss Brington" and "The Señora," both published in 1941, reflect the experience of exile. The former evokes the characteristically drab, run-down English boarding-house with which many exiles, who were accustomed to a very different kind of life, became unhappily all too familiar after fleeing Hitler's Germany and Austria. At the same time, Zur Mühlen manages to transform the watchful, frugal, hard-working, and worn-out landlady, Miss Brington, who is always on the brink of falling from respectability into poverty, into a universal figure of emotional and physical deprivation and loneliness. "The Señora" dramatizes the dilemma faced by refugees, particularly those who happen to be writers in a language other than that of their country of asylum. Should they adapt to their new environment and risk losing the anger and indignation, the passionate opposition to tyranny that is the core of their identity, the most precious possession left to them? Or should they nurture their hatred and risk losing their humanity?

To the *feuilletons* have been added two samples of the "socialist" fairy tales for which Zur Mühlen achieved a degree of international renown — one ("The Spectacles") in a new translation by the editor, and one ("The Sparrow") in Ida Dailes' translation (considerably revised by the editor) for a collection of four of Zur Mühlen's tales published by The Daily Worker Publishing Company under the title *Fairy Tales for Workers' Children* (Chicago, 1925). A short essay by the editor on the fairy tale and its use for propaganda purposes has been included among the supplementary on-line materials.

Lionel Gossman, November 2010

The Red Redeemer

(A church. The candles on the altar have been lit. Above the altar there is a large black wooden cross. In front of it, on the steps, a man in rags, barefoot, with a worn, tormented expression. He is leaning on one arm, which rests on the altar.)

The priest (in his vestments, enters through the open church door, followed by two altar-boys in surplices. He marches up to the altar, suddenly stops in his tracks, and stares at the man in rags): A man in front of the altar. Unconsecrated hands touching the most holy. Sacrilege! Away with you! Away with you!

The man in rags: This is my house.

The taller altar-boy (shyly pulls at the priest's vestments): Reverend Father, the cross…

The priest (quickly turns to look at the cross and cries out): Gone! Where is the Redeemer?

The smaller altar-boy: On the altar, don't you see?

The man in rags: Blessed are they who are pure in heart, for they shall behold the Lord.

The priest (glares at the man in rags and seems gradually to recognize him. He is horrified.): What? What is going on here? The Redeemer belongs on the cross.

The man in rags: And if he got down from it and came among the living? Don't you yourself teach that your God is not dead? Now you can see that he is alive.

The priest (confused): The Redeemer's place is on the cross… The faithful will be coming to Mass… If they find the cross empty… and the

Redeemer here, alive, like a man…. (Shouting) Get back on the cross. We need a God that is dead.

The man in rags: Yes, a God that neither sees nor hears, a lifeless piece of wood.

The priest (desperate): Such disorder! You get up off the cross like a man getting out of bed. You sow confusion in people's minds… This conduct does not become our Redeemer…

The man in rags: Aren't all of you celebrating my Resurrection today? So you know that I am alive.

The priest: That's what we teach the ignorant, the people.

The man in rags: Why?

The priest: They yield to our wishes better when they believe in you.

The man in rags (astonished): I don't understand.

The priest: They are afraid of angering you if they oppose us.

The man in rags: That is not what I taught.

The priest: Your teaching is a distorting mirror. Everyone finds a distorted image of himself in it.

The man in rags. The lesson of my life is something quite different.

The priest: Your life? Do we know that you ever lived?

The man in rags: So you teach something you yourself don't believe in?

The priest: Who believes in fairy tales today?

The man in rags: What do you call a fairy tale?

The priest: The Resurrection.

The man in rags: You are all blind! I rose from the dead a hundred times before your eyes and yet you didn't see it?

The priest (correcting him sternly like a schoolmaster): You appear not to know the legend that was spun around your name. You arose from the dead only once. In Jerusalem.

The man in rags: No, a hundred times, in everyone in whom love was stronger than death. I lived in every rebel languishing in prison in his chains. I was crucified in everyone who was hanged on your gallows.

The priest: Blasphemy!

The man in rags: Can God himself be guilty of blasphemy?

The priest: Your divinity is questionable. You yourself described yourself as the son of man.

The man in rags: There is only one God: the man who loves.

The priest: You speak of love. Did your rebels love the victims they killed?

The man in rags: In pure hands, killing can be good.

The priest (outraged): Criminal! Murderer! Communist!

The man in rags: Are you going to call the police?

The priest: Why am I talking to you? You don't exist. You never really existed.

The man in rags: For you and your like, I don't.

The priest: No one may arise from the dead. That is not permitted by law. A dead man must stay dead. Get back on the cross!

The man in rags: Doesn't the Church teach that with the commission of every sin the Redeemer is crucified anew?

The smaller altar-boy (eagerly): Yes, that is what I learned in Sunday school.

The man in rags (suddenly fearsome): You all crucify me every day, every hour. Wherever someone suffers because of you, wherever a child cries because it is hungry, wherever someone sick dies in misery, wherever someone is worn out by daily drudgery, I am crucified.

The priest: You are a dead, lifeless piece of wood. You cannot see.

The man in rags: Your guilt is so enormous that dead matter acquires eyes to see it and a mouth to scream in protest against it.

The smaller altar-boy (begins to cry): I'm scared.

The man in rags (gently): You need not be scared. (He kneels down next to the boy). Look, now I am smaller than you, and that is as it should be, for you, little Man, little God, are the future.

The priest (shrieks): Blasphemy!

The man in rags (rises): It is all of you who blaspheme against God. Every act of yours, every gesture is blasphemy. The potbelly that waltzes past the hungry, the silk dress that rustles past the half-naked, that is blasphemy. The factory that reaches to the heavens and devours its workers is blasphemy. The foul-smelling hovels where the poor are housed, that is blasphemy. The brothel, where love is put up for sale, that is blasphemy. The battlefield where human beings die like dogs so that you all can line your pockets, that is blasphemy. You yourselves, your very being, your persisting, that is blasphemy.

The priest (mockingly): You won't ever be able to rid the world of us.

The man in rags: You think not? Perhaps you aren't aware that I have already come down from every cross you all have nailed me to. Perhaps you don't know that I have risen from every grave you all buried me in.

The priest (bewildered and unsettled): You speak like a madman. Who are you?

The man in rags: I am the Resurrection and the Life in Humanity.

The priest (dully, as if he had lost his wits): What is the Resurrection and the Life?

The man in rags (in a strong, clear voice): The revolution!

The priest (shrieks): Revolution... Help... Police... (To the altar-boys): Run! Call the police! I always suspected that if Jesus did really exist he had to have been insane. Normal people don't get themselves crucified.

The man in rags: No, they look around for ministerial positions.

The priest (in despair): Nothing is sacred for this individual. Now he is maligning the government! That is more dangerous than blaspheming against God, for God doesn't have servants with rubber truncheons and machine-guns that he can call into action. Get a move on, boys, run. Get the police. (The two altar boys rush off. The church bells begin to ring.)

The priest: The faithful will be here in a moment. The empty cross above the altar... All this disorder... If the Bishop hears of it... Why did all this have to happen in my parish?... (Pleading) Get back on the cross and I will be your servant for the rest of my life.

The man in rags: How often have you said that same thing to the people?

The priest (at a loss): The people, the people! What does the people matter to me?

The man in rags: I am the people, the people that you all have crucified. I am the people that was killed and that has arisen from the dead. Woe unto you. (Two policemen rush into the church,)

The priest (panting): Here... This is the man... Blasphemy... Incitement to class hatred... A Communist...

One of the policemen: That's enough.

The other policeman: Wait. (To the man in rags) Do you have identity papers? Who are you?

The man in rags (rises to his full height) I am the red Redeemer who has come to pass judgment.

The first policeman: There you have it. A Red. (The two policemen take hold of the man in rags and drag him out of the church)

The priest (confused): A bad dream… a terrifying nightmare. Didn't someone come and say that the story we tell about Christ is true, that God is alive?

(The organ begins to play. The choir is heard singing lustily: Christ is arisen. Halleluja! Halleluja!)

Der rote Heiland (Leipzig-Plagwitz: Verlag Die Wölfe, 1924), pp. 49–52.

Confession

Dear Doctor:

When you left my cell an hour ago, you were extremely irritated and told me angrily that no one would be able to make any sense of what I had been saying; that my violent outbursts were making things even more difficult for you; and that in light of my behaviour it had become impossible for you to build a case for my defence. You are quite right. Although I did try very hard to explain the matter to you, I could not find the right words, and it was impossible for me, without flying into a rage, to say the one thing that holds the key to the whole situation. If that thing were to cross my lips, I felt, a dam would burst somewhere inside me: despair, hatred, fury, and an uncontrollable desire for revenge would surge like storm waves over my brain and completely overwhelm any rational thought. Maybe I can present my case better in writing.

I am accused of murder, of the murder of an honourable citizen of our town — and a good friend.

I know how people see me. They think I am a bloodthirsty monster still greedy for blood after three years at the front and ready to commit murder to get it.

Three years at the front, doctor — do you know what that means? It means three years of misery, horror, despair — and blood! Three years of living in mortal fear, three years of committing murder! This can change a man. And yet when I came home after having been lucky enough to get shot in the leg and invalided out, I immediately took up my old life again, went to the office, worked, and lived contentedly with my wife — as though nothing had happened.

From time to time, at night, in my dreams, I heard the thunder of artillery fire and the groans of the wounded, but those phantoms vanished with the dawn and everything was normal again.

Until one summer evening, when the horror that seemed to have been forgotten opened its hellish maw and belched its stinking, diabolical breath in my face.

I was sitting with my wife at dinner. The last rays of the setting sun were streaming through the red curtains of the dining-room. Suddenly my wife cried out: "Look at your hand. It looks as though it was covered with blood!" I glanced down at my hand and all at once felt cold shivers run down my spine. When had I seen this before? Yes, it was during a bayonet attack, I remembered. I also remembered my horror and disgust as I tried to wipe off the sticky gore. My wife laughed and placed her hand on mine for a moment. How white that hand was, how pure and unsullied. But mine?

From then on I had the feeling that my hand could never be washed clean again. The sickening smell of blood hovered around me day and night. Grisly images would spring up before my eyes. There was now a hole in the curtain that had come down between me and the things I had experienced.

Perhaps I could have borne all this. Perhaps I would have sunk back again into my blissful mindlessness. But I noticed something else: *All the people around me had clean hands*. In the office I would stop in the middle of writing as I observed my fellow-employees' hands gliding white and spotless over white paper. I no longer saw people's faces or bodies, I saw only hands.

Gradually a hatred of those with white hands began to stir in my heart. Repressed and concealed, it grew more and more fierce. I had had to commit murder, I had had to besmirch myself with the blood of my fellow-man; while they had stayed home, innocent and good, with their clean hands.

In order not to have to see those accursed white hands, I withdrew from all human company. My lovely wife became abhorrent to me. I was overcome by disgust whenever she touched me.

The man I murdered had been my friend. He tried to shake me out of my depression, he made every conceivable effort to distract me. There were times when I was touched by his goodness and kindness, times when I felt aching compassion and fervent love for all human beings, when I wanted to help them and liberate them. But no sooner did my glance fall on their hands than hatred boiled up in me again and poisoned my soul.

This situation may have lasted for about three months. Finally, I reached a point at which I no longer saw human beings, only spotless white hands fluttering derisively before my eyes and pointing accusingly at my guilty, bloodstained fingers.

A new thought had wormed its way into my brain: that the world will not be redeemed until all human beings have had their hands dipped in guilt and blood, until there is nobody who can go about bearing the mark of innocence. Everybody must be driven into guilt and smut so as to be made aware of his or her wickedness and led to do penance for it. Anyone who refuses must be eliminated.

One evening my friend came to visit me and would not be put out by the surliness with which I received him. He chatted animatedly about all kinds of things, including attacks on him by his enemies in the newspaper. Suddenly he uttered the fateful words. Laughing, he raised his hand and said: "Their attacks don't bother me in the least. My hands are clean!"

In that moment all the horror I had experienced raced through my brain, I saw the chaos of combat, heard the screams of the wounded, the death rattles of the dying, I saw on both sides a huge mass of innocent murderers rushing into battle, goaded on by whips wielded by clean, white hands.

You know the rest; there was a revolver in my desk drawer. But now you will understand a detail that puzzled the police; namely that the victim's hands were smeared all over with blood.

I have confessed to the murder and I am ready to pay with my life for my crime — not, however, for the crime that the court will condemn me for, but for the killing of my brothers at the front. I was a murderer long before I used my revolver against my friend.

One more request, dear Doctor. If the death sentence is carried out on me, please see to it that my hands are not washed. I do not want to appear before my eternal Judge with the mark of inexpiable guilt — white hands.

With the deepest respect, Doctor,

I am,

Yours truly,

Karl David.

Der rote Heiland (Leipzig-Plagwitz: Verlag Die Wölfe, 1924), pp. 71–74.

High Treason

The uniform hung loose on his long, skinny body. He walked with his shoulders hunched, like some one carrying an enormous load and he shuffled about in his heavy army-issue boots. Everyone made fun of him, mocked his slow speech, the strong Jewish accent with which he spoke Russian, the awkward movements of his perfectly beautiful hands. Impatient officers would yell "Durak" (dumbell, fool) at him more than at anyone else and the name stuck to him. Soon no one knew his real name. In the entire regiment he was known only as "Durak."

And yet he was well-liked. If you did not feel well or were homesick, you coud go to "Durak" and get consolation. If you were hungry, you could be sure that "Durak" would share his skimpy ration with you. And rumour had it that you could die more easily, even joyfully, if "Durak" sat at your bedside and held your hand.

The officers considered him a halfwit. Yet he obeyed orders willingly, if clumsily, and he was touchingly eager to oblige. Once, however, there had been a painful incident. The lieutenant, a good-natured young fellow, ordered "Durak" to do night duty in the sick bay, and "Durak" went there as commanded. He cast a glance at the long row of sighing, groaning bodies and quietly asked the doctor:

"Nikolai Ivanovitch, would you kindly tell me if these men can be made well again?"

The plump doctor laughed.

"Hopefully they can. You must just take good care of them."

"And when they are well again, what will happen to them?"

"What will happen to them? Why, they'll be ready to be put to work again."

"What for?"

"What for? Why, for the war, you idiot!"

"I take care of them and make them better, so that they can kill and be killed themselves?"

"Quite so," the doctor said, somewhat perplexed.

Suddenly, in mounting rage, "Durak" tore off his white overall and threw it at the doctor's feet.

"I won't cure murderers!" he screamed in a shrill, breaking voice, "I won't cure sacrificial animals for the false god Baal." And he rushed from the room.

Some time later, his regiment came under fire. A major offensive was ordered for the next morning. The soldiers slunk around despondently. In the general melancholy no one noticed "Durak"'s somber fury. At eight in the evening a solemn religious service was held. In his gleaming robes the Orthodox priest came out of his tent and took up a position on an elevated spot, surrounded by the soldiers. After the prayers he began a speech. He spoke of God's goodness and the loyalty each soldier owed to the top war commanders. He spoke of the army's courage. "You are marching forth to destroy the enemies of God and Man," he said unctuously. "The battle that lies before you is pleasing to God, and…"

He was interrupted by a piercing cry of "No." "Durak" was pushing his way through the motionless crowd, a riding whip in his raised hand. He threw himself like a madman on the priest and a whistling sound filled the air as the whip tore through it.

"You lie, Priest. You blaspheme against God. You turn a place of prayer and spiritual healing into a den of murderers." He had pushed the priest down and taken his place, His voice rent the darkness.

"I kept silent because I was afraid, because I knew what would happen to me if I spoke out. But now I have to speak. Hear me, brothers. The battle that lies before us is the work of the devil. We are murderers. We march out with intent to murder. To murder other men. Men like ourselves. And we blaspheme against God when we pray to Him — from Whom we received the command 'Thou shalt not kill' — and ask Him to help us murder other human beings. They lie to us when they tell us that the others are our enemies. There are no enemies, only other human beings, children of God, brothers and sisters. March out tomorrow morning, brothers, and when you see the others, throw down your weapons, stretch out your arms to them, and call out "Peace be with you."

Led by the lieutenant, several soldiers had pushed their way through the confused crowd of men. "Durak" was set upon and overpowered from behind. Half smothered, his voice still rang out through the hall. "Do not kill! Love one another!"

This time it was not possible to excuse his behaviour on the grounds that he was mentally confused. Certainly the man was crazy, but on the eve of battle he had called on the soldiers to mutiny. For that there was no pardon. When he was informed that he would be shot within the half-hour, he smiled like someone hearing something old and familiar and spoke the following strange, incomprehensible words:

"The Third Day is still a long way off. But in the far distance I can already see it dawning."

***

A short time later a soldier called the lieutenant from his tent. "Sir, come and see the dead man!"

"Why? What's up?" The lieutenant looked in astonishment at the man's pale, distraught face.

"It's… a miracle… I don't dare to tell you. We pulled off his boots. For it would be a shame to let them go into the ground with him…"

"And?"

"Come and see for yourself, Sir."

The lieutenant followed the soldier. "Durak" lay stretched out on the ground, his feet bare and his arms spread out. A bullet had hit him on the left side and opened up a gaping wound. With a flashlight, the lieutenant bent over the dead man, then drew back in terror. "Durak"'s hands and feet bore bloody stigmata as if they had been pierced through by something sharp.

In the darkness a few soldiers fell on their knees and prayed.

Der rote Heiland (Leipzig-Plagwitz: Verlag Die Wölfe, 1924), pp. 67–70.

Death of a Shade

"Have you heard," I was asked by an acquaintance, "that Perdita W. shot herself?"

I nodded. "I've been expecting it for months."

"You were expecting it? I don't understand. She was so, so…"

He looked for the right word. Revealingly, it did not come to him.

"The truth is that she was not so…," I replied. "And that's why she shot herself."

"You don't seem very upset." My acquaintance was rather indignant. "I had always thought you and she were close friends."

"That's exactly why. I know she had no other option. It was the only possible thing she could do."

He looked at me uncomprehendingly.

"Let me explain. The Perdita you knew was not the real Perdita. The woman who was passionate about politics and ran to all the public meetings of her Party was not the same woman as the one who reached for a revolver the day before yesterday… Outwardly she had no reason to commit suicide. She was financially secure, she was in good health and, for a person of forty-three, she looked very good, which even today is still one of the most important things in life for a woman. And yet, there was simply no other way out for her."

"I really don't understand you."

"We were school friends and I often spent the holidays with Perdita's parents so as not to have to stay on at the convent. Perdita's parents had a large villa in a health resort, a short way out of the little town itself. It was surrounded by a wonderful, beautifully tended garden. I can still remember the large beds of roses in front of the house. The garden was set back from the road, and the life Perdita's parents led was set back a little from real life. I have never since come across anything quite so harmonious. No voice was ever raised in that house. The servants came and went without a sound. No door was ever slammed shut. On Sundays no one in the family ever left the garden. 'There are so many people on the road on a Sunday,' Perdita's father used to say.

"Perdita was an only child. Though she was not spoiled, everything revolved around her, and for her there was really nothing in this world except the two quiet, distinguished people she called Papa and Mami. Don't imagine that Perdita's parents were boring or uncultured. Her very name reveals her father's love of Shakespeare. During the holidays, when it was raining, the old gentleman — he had married late in life and when I got to know him, his hair was already grey — would read to us from the works of classical German literature or, from time to time, from those of other writers — Stifter, Dickens, Bulwer Lytton. Those were lovely quiet hours that we spent in the large library. We sat up very straight in the high mahogany chairs — for 'ladies do not sprawl on furniture.' I sometimes had the feeling that the raindrops fell more gently here, around this house, than anywhere else.

"Later, when we were grown up, we drifted apart, as often happens. Once Perdita wrote me about a rather vague love affair, of which nothing came, because Papa and Mami found the young man 'loud and vulgar.' Perdita appears not to have taken the matter very much to heart. She was happy enough with Papa and Mami. Being separated from them would have caused her much grief.

"The years passed. The World War broke out, then came the Revolution. From time to time I paid a visit to Perdita and her parents. Here, nothing had changed. The same stillness, the same harmony: three people who loved each other and had shut themselves off from the world. No, that is not quite right: three people who had absolutely no idea that there is another world than theirs.

"Five years ago Papa and Mami died, the one soon after the other. It turned out that Perdita still possessed a considerable fortune — not large enough, however, for her to hold on to the spacious villa and the numerous servants needed to maintain it. She sold the villa and moved into town. Here, in her pretty house, she lived as she had lived at home. Quiet, refined people came in the afternoon for tea or in the evening for dinner. She had kept on the cook, who had been with her parents for twenty years, and the food was always excellent. But Perdita did not feel right. She always went around a little lost. She missed Mami's love and Papa's kindly authority. At thirty-eight, she faced life like an eighteen-year old.

"She had brought much of the old furniture with her as well as an enlarged photograph of the villa, showing, in front of the house, next to the large bed of roses, Papa, Mami, and Perdita at the age of ten.

"I liked visiting her. The quiet did me good, even though I found it unnatural in our present day and age.

"Then came the great experience that completely altered Perdita's life and finally drove her into the arms of death. An acquaintance took her 'for fun,' wanting to see how she would react to something of that kind, to a political gathering. At first Perdita felt uncomfortable, because of the large numbers of people, the countless loud voices. She could not quite understand the speech but when it was followed by wild applause and shouts of 'Heil' from all present, she suddenly noticed that she too had raised her voice in loud, unconstrained yelling, as she had never done before in her entire life. For forty years, she had conducted herself quietly and with dignity, but now suddenly she could shout, scream, clap, stamp her feet. The primitive and the elemental broke loose in her and she experienced something she had never experienced before: an overwhelming feeling of being one with the screaming, yelling mass. Beside her stood an elderly little man with fanatical blue eyes: he gave Perdita a benevolent look and whispered: 'Yes, indeed. The Führer gave a great speech.'

"The Führer, the Leader, that was just the word Perdita needed to hear. She had found the authority that she substituted for Papa's, she had found the man who gave orders and who had to be obeyed without one's ever having to think for oneself.

"I met Perdita a few weeks after this political gathering. She had already joined the Party. I hardly recognized her. She seemed a good few years younger, she moved freely and gracefully, her eyes had a sparkle in them, she was a different person. In an earlier time, when people were still romantic, young girls in love looked like that. And the comparison is apt: Perdita was in love with the Party. Perdita gave the

Party all the overflowing love she had stored up within herself for years. She could speak of nothing else. She could think of nothing else.

"As you know, I am on the opposite side politically and it came to an argument between us. 'You have no notion of what is at stake here,' I said to her. 'Do you have any idea what your program is?' 'Program?' She stared at me. 'When we come to power, everything will be right again.'

"Despite my irritation with her, I felt that for Perdita what really counted was the 'we' and not the 'power.' She had been lonely for so long, and now she belonged to a great Party which took the place for her of everything she had lost or had never possessed. 'Read your pamphlets,' I said impatiently. 'I'd like to know what you think of their tone.' She smiled. 'I will do that.'

"As I said, we parted at odds with each other and for a long time I did not see Perdita again.

"Then one day I ran into her in the street. She had become quite white and went about just as lost and alone as before her 'conversion.' She greeted me shyly, as if she feared I might not return her greeting. That sent an arrow through my heart. 'May I stop by and pay you a visit?' I asked. Her mouth formed into a smile, which truly was not one. 'Yes, do. I would like that very much.'

"The house had not changed a bit: the elegant Empire style chair still stood in front of the tiny, un-practical ladies' writing desk, the same silk cushions still lay on the Empire chaise longue, albeit somewhat faded and worn, and the enlarged photograph of Perdita's parents' house still hung on the wall, above the chaise longue. But it had faded; it was almost impossible now to discern the individual figures on it.

"Conversation was somewhat strained at first. It wasn't until Perdita made us tea in the old silver teapot I had known as a child at her parents' house that we began to unbend. 'Are you still in the Party?' I asked her. 'No.' Her soft voice sounded even softer than usual. 'I couldn't take it. All the noise, the shouting and bawling, and the newspapers. They shout too, just like the people. I had to have quiet about me again.' 'Have you found it?' Her pale face became sad. 'No. There is no quiet any more. Even when I don't actually hear the shouting, it rings in my ears. The whole world is shouting…'

"A car passed in the street, honking its horn; Perdita twitched nervously. 'On Sundays,' she said, half dreaming, 'we never left the garden, because of the crowds of people. I don't go out on Sundays now either, but the noise comes right through my windows… I can't get away from it.' I felt sorry for her. 'You live too much on your own. You have to spend some time with friends, as you used to do.' She smiled. 'I don't live altogether on my own,' she said. 'You see, when I can't stand this whole world any more, I gaze on the picture of our villa and I can feel the deep peace and the quiet happiness of those times. You remember, don't you? — my bedroom was here, and here, under it, was the verandah and the main drawing-room, and over there you can see the window of the library where Papa used so often to read to us. But' — here her voice became filled with sadness — 'the picture is fading. The house looks a bit like a house of ghosts now. The figures of Papa and Mami are almost impossible to make out. Only mine is still really there. When it too fades…'

"She fell silent, and something in the expression of her face frightened me. 'Don't be childish, Perdita. The picture is old and the photographer used matt paper. Matt paper doesn't hold the image well.' She again smiled. 'Matt paper that doesn't hold the image well. A down-to-earth explanation. You're probably right. But we are like the photograph. We have turned out matt too. We couldn't tolerate the real sun, real life, and we faded as soon as we came into contact with them.' She looked over at the picture: 'I'm curious to know how long I will still be recognizable in it.'

"My visit to Perdita took place on a cool day in February. I had planned to go back and see her again soon, but something always came up — work, sickness, something. In May — it was an especially hot, sunny May — I drove off to the country for a month. I came back a week ago and resolved to visit Perdita the following day.

"On that next day, I received a registered letter. When I opened it, the photograph of Perdita's parents' house fell out. Undoubtedly the maid had forgotten to close the shutters on one of the hot days, for shadowy outlines were all you could now make out in the photograph. The three figures had totally vanished. I am a down-to earth person, a realist, but a cold shiver ran down my spine as I looked at that picture: I knew what it meant.

"Perdita saw herself fading away and vanishing from this life; she watched herself growing more and more shadowy and unreal with each passing day… On that same day I was informed that she had shot herself the night before."

"It really was the photographer's fault," my acquaintance suggested. "If only he had used glossy paper…"

"He couldn't use glossy paper if he was to get the right tone for this house and these people. He was a good photographer with genuine artistic sensitivity. You really shouldn't blame him."

I took the picture from the writing desk and showed it to my acquaintance.

"You can still make out the bed of roses," he said.

"Yes, but that's all. Everything else has vanished, as if it had never been. And when I look at that picture, I wonder whether Perdita W.'s world was ever real, whether everything in it was not a shadow, everything — except for the roses."

"Tod eines Schattens," *Der Wiener Tag*, 8 December 1932, reprinted in *Fahrt ins Licht. Sechsundsechzig Stationen. Erzählungen* (Vienna: Verlag Ludwig Nath, 1936; reprint Klagenfurt: Sisyphus Verlag, 1999), pp. 167–173.

A Secondary Happiness

Christine was fourteen years old when the World War broke out — a quiet, well brought up, shy girl with long brown braids and large, grey, somewhat startled eyes.

"She won't be as pretty as her mother," people said in the little provincial town where her father was the Mayor. "But there is something very sweet about her, and she is so touchingly unselfish."

Christine owed her selflessness to her upbringing by her mother. From earliest childhood, it had been impressed on her that she herself was completely unimportant, whereas everybody else was enormously important. One should not think about oneself but only take a keen interest in the lives of others.

Little Christine was constantly being asked the same question: Aren't you pleased that Mama can go to the beach? Aren't you thrilled that your dear Papa has received a decoration? Isn't it wonderful that your friend has won first prize in school?

At first Christine would dutifully answer yes. She would never have dared to contradict her attractive, strong-willed mother. Then gradually this automatic yes turned into a yes that expressed conviction. She had no pleasures of her own, but as she was nonetheless eager, being young, for a little happiness, she participated in the pleasures of others the way a smoker, whose doctor has ordered him to give up smoking, sits beside cigar and cigarette-puffing strangers so as to get a whiff, at least, of the smoke. She took pleasure in her girlfriends' new clothes. She herself wore her mother's cast-offs which were altered to fit her, for Madam Mayor needed the family money for her own purposes. She took pleasure in the good marks of her school friends. That she too had all A's in her report card was simply a matter of course; she had her dear parents, who had done so much for her, to thank for it. And as she grew older, she took pleasure in the engagements and marriages of the other girls and then, later, in the babies and the *maternal joy* of her former school friends. Everything came to her second hand, as her clothes had done. She knew no happiness of her own, only a secondary happiness; no joy, only the joy she got from the joy of others; no pain, only the pain she felt at the pain of others. And when the thought did strike her that she too could have a personal life, she was alarmed by it and rejected it brusquely, feeling that she had committed a sin. To everyone in her small circle she was "dear, good Christine," to whom one came when one was in trouble or had some overflowing happiness that one simply had to tell someone about.

She lived many lives; the life of her best friend Myra, that of her parents, that of her brother and his young wife. She fell in love along with others and lay awake at night thinking of the tender words some male friend had whispered to some female friend, she experienced the feelings of the bride standing at the altar, she watched, full of joy, as the *young couple* set off on their honeymoon. She was a bride, a wife, a mother, and a widow through others. But at no time, not for a single hour was she ever Christine, a person, a pretty girl with a right to her own experiences and her own happiness.

She grew older, yet she looked younger than all the others. She walked dreamily through the narrow streets of the little town — no, not she herself, but Myra or Trudy or Sylvia. Her father died, her mother re-married and Christine took pleasure in her mother's new happiness, in the proximity of which she was given the privilege of living. Later she took pleasure in a little step-sister and as the latter learned to speak and to walk, she took pleasure in the pleasure this gave the little one. Without ever having had a life of her own, Christine was happy. Was so, until happiness of her own approached in the shape of the new pharmacist. The tender words addressed to her, the kisses that seemed almost brutal to her and a lot less blissful than those her friends had told her about, filled her with alarm. Her mother, to whom Christine had begun to be burdensome, insisted that her daughter marry the pharmacist. Christine, who as a bridesmaid, smiling happily, had so often accompanied her friends to the altar, wept bitterly as she herself stood in the church in her bridal veil. Everything was so alien and yet so close, so unbearably close. The honeymoon trip to Venice was a nightmare. She had the feeling that she was a shade forced into becoming a living human being. She remembered her friends and the happy times when she had followed them, in her thoughts, on their honeymoon trips. She remembered the daydreams in which she had imagined for herself the happiness of the young couple. How different that had been. Her own happiness strutted around prosaically in his slippers in the evening, drank rather more beer than he could hold, snored loudly next to her in bed, woke up unexpectedly in the middle of the night and pulled her into his arms. In vain Christine told herself: He is a good man, he loves me, I have to be happy. She had grown too used to a secondary happiness to be able to bear her own. Little by little she was assailed by tormenting doubts: Had it been the same with the others too? Had they been lying to me when they said: It was heavenly.

She had been thrilled by the picture postcards of Italian cities that she had received from her girlfriends. Now that she could view the churches and palaces with her own eyes, she saw only lifeless stone; the sea struck her as a desolate watery waste; and she became homesick for the little grey town where she had lived for thirty years. But she was also fearful of returning to a home of her own. She who had so willingly helped others set up house, felt only exhaustion and a leaden sadness when she thought of furniture of her own, a household of her own — and of the life, the life of her own, that she would now have to lead as Frau Grunder. She will no longer be "dear, good Christine," she will no longer be the person people come to so that she can take part in their joy or their sorrow; she will no longer be absorbed completely in the lives of others and thus escape from her own. The thought of all this was unbearable, and with each passing day it grew still more unbearable, until one evening, when the pharmacist was asleep, she packed her little travel bag and took the next train to Florence.

From here she wrote to her husband, asking for a divorce. The pharmacist would not agree to it. He could not understand what Christine had against him and he was fond of her.

But Christine knew that if she wanted to go on living, she had to get free, at all costs. With the help of an impoverished young Italian, who was ready to do anything for a little money, she set up an adulterous affair that was no more real than all of Christine's earlier life.

The marriage was dissolved. For a month the little town had a topic of conversation that mostly began with "Who would have thought it of that well brought up girl? That's the way it is, that's the way it is. Still waters run deep."

Christine, who had been left a small inheritance by her father, did not return to her home town. She settled down in a different part of the country. Within a few months people here also spoke of "dear, good Christine," and came to her to tell her of their joys and sorrows.

After a year Christine had almost completely forgotten the dreadful episode of her marriage. She went on living the lives of others and once more enjoyed the secondary happiness that is without a dark side.

She was happy again.

"Nebenglück," *Neues Wiener Tagblatt,* 28 November 1933, p. 2ff.

The Señora

From time to time, some old, long forgotten image suddenly emerges, unsolicited and for no apparent reason, from the picture gallery of a memory stretching back over many, many years, and springs to life. A ray of sunlight shines on it, colours we thought were faded revive, and the subject of the image — a person or a landscape — pushes its way into the forefront of our mind, obscuring everything else.

That is what is happening to me these days with the Señora. The frame of the image is springtime in Switzerland, blossoming fruit-trees, the blue waters of a lake, and a large, bright hall. In the hall, always in the same corner, a slight, gaunt woman, whose thin tapered fingers work on netting, day in, day out, restlessly, almost without a moment's pause.

No one could have told how old the Señora was. Her dark, shining eyes suggested a woman of twenty; the hard, embittered lines around the mouth a woman of sixty. Her husband, plump and bald, seemed to be a man in his fifties. As girls in South American countries were usually married to older men at the time, the Señora could well have been about thirty.

To the children playing in the hotel garden the two of them were romantic figures: refugees! In one of the many revolutions, the party of Señor Geraldo had been overthrown and his enemies in that unhappy land on the other side of the ocean were able to wield their power with unspeakable harshness and cruelty. That had happened five years before. And for five years the Señora and her husband had been living in Switzerland and waiting. Waiting for the day when they could return to their liberated homeland and when that homeland would once again live and breathe freely.

Señor Geraldo had settled down in Weggis. The Señora, in contrast, seemed to have no idea where she was living. Her dark eyes looked right through the people who passed by her and though she spoke English and French fluently, if anyone spoke to her, she understood not a word of what was said.

Señor Geraldo would probably have been happy to mix more with the other residents of the hotel; he would have enjoyed a game of cards from time to time, and he would have very much liked to make an occasional trip to the casino in Lucerne. But his wife would not let him leave her side. He had to sit with her and read to her from the many newspapers piled up on the table before him. The Señora had no interest in European politics. What did Europe matter to her? She could think only of her enslaved homeland, of the terrible things that were happening there. She did not notice the scent of the purple lilac blossoms; her nostrils were filled with the choking smell of homes set on fire; their leaping flames drew a red curtain between her and the blue, spring sky.

The Señor read to her, reported on the South American republic through lead articles and items of daily news. Now and again the Señora would smile, pull the knots of her netting tighter as if she wanted to draw the noose tighter around someone's neck, and ask the Señor to read a particular paragraph again.

Every disaster, every epidemic reported in the newspapers made her happy. She would pull her knots tighter, say "muerto," and smile. Every now and then she would point with her gleaming netting needle at an obituary notice and repeat it out loud. At such moments her face became beautiful, transfigured, like that of a blessed spirit that has seen the heavens.

She would put her netting aside, reach for a little diary, and write in, under the appropriate date, the name of the deceased enemy. She would laugh on days when she was able to write in more than one name and would show the little green leatherbound book to her husband: "Muerto, muerto, muerto."

For the Señora there was no more beautiful word in the whole wonderful language of her native land. One enemy had died. Or his son — a youngster who, if he had grown to manhood, would also have tortured their homeland and reduced it to slavery — had been killed in a serious riding accident. Now he could no longer do that. He lay stiff and dead. Muerto, muerto, muerto. And she smiled when she read the obituaries of the enemies' wives: they would bear no more children for the hated regime. Muerta, muerta, muerta. A house had collapsed, burying thirty workers under the rubble — renegades who had cheered as the enemy made his grand entry. Now they would cheer no more; now their dead mouths, which had betrayed the homeland, were stopped up with dust and plaster. Muerto, muerto, muerto. A ship had gone down; from its stern the new flag of the old homeland had fluttered. The Señora tapped the table impatiently with her needle. She could not wait to hear how many had perished in the disaster. The captain — good; and the first officer — good; and twenty sailors — only twenty sailors? And the second officer had been saved along with the rest of the crew? The Señora wrinkled her brow: "Poor show," she muttered to her husband. "What was God thinking of, allowing all of those to be saved?"

She reached for her netting again and pulled the knots tighter and tighter, as though she was tying a noose around the neck of one of those who had been saved and drawing it ever tighter.

"Yes," Señor Geraldo said to an acquaintance one day. "She has been like that for five years now. At night she gets up, turns on the light, and re-reads the old newspapers from the first to the last page. She is afraid that I may not have reported all the deaths to her. And then she comes back to bed and whispers the names of the dead to herself. No she doesn't need sleep. One or two hours are enough for her. At the crack of dawn, she wakes up and shakes me to awaken me also. She asks how long it will be before the newspaper comes. Every day she again believes that the front page will carry the news of the fall of the regime. And in the meantime, she contents herself with deaths and catastrophes; she collects them and reads them out to herself from her diary. As if to pray. Then she knots her netting. I have no idea how many pieces of netting she has stored in her trunks or how large they are. Yes, in her trunks. In the five years we have been here she has never unpacked her trunks. "What for?" she would ask. "Tomorrow or the day after tomorrow we could be going home. And it would be a shame to have to waste time packing."

In a frame of springtime in Switzerland, blossoming fruit-trees, the blue waters of a lake, and a large, bright hall, I see before me the long forgotten image of the dark-eyed woman whose fingers work restlessly on her netting and on whose thin pale lips a smile forms from time to time as she whispers to herself "Muerto, muerto, muerto!"

"Die Senora," *Die Zeitung* (London), 1 April 1941; *Zeitspiegel* (London), 8 June 1946; *Arbeiter-Zeitung* (Vienna), 18 February 1949.

Miss Brington

Every evening, when the residents of the boarding house, with unshakable optimism, tried to turn on the radio, the landlady appeared and, with a deep sigh, said: "Do give the machine a rest."

Miss Brington — no one knew her by her first name; she was one of those people from whom one gets the impression that in their entire lives no one ever called them by their first name, let alone by a friendly nickname — Miss Brington had raised the art of sighing to a level perhaps never attained by any other human being. Her scale of sighs embraced not just eight tones, but twenty-four at least. It began with an exhalation that wafted through the dining room like a gentle spring breeze whenever one of the residents asked for more bread, increased in volume and intensity with each new request, until, if someone reached for the knob on the radio, it became so strong, deep, and sustained that you were reminded of autumn gales blowing through the moonlit ruins of old castles on eerie nights.

Miss Brington was not unfriendly and she was not friendly. You could almost say that she simply was not. Something swept out the rooms and dusted, something cooked the meals in the kitchen no one was permitted to enter, something laid the table and cleared it afterwards, something served the food, something worked in the little house from morning to night — you could see hands, feet going up and down the stairs, a brown dress, and a yellow sweater — and the name of this something was Miss Brington. But what might lie hidden behind the expressionless face, whether Miss Brington had any idea of what went on around her, whether she could feel happy or angry, whether she liked people or hated them — *that* there was no way of knowing.

She seemed possessed by a single idea: the idea of rest. If the water heater broke down — which happened often — she would write on a slip of paper not, as other people would: "Do not turn on the water heater," but "Please give the water heater a rest." Even the broom, which she grudgingly let people borrow, sometimes had a notice stuck to it: "Please give the broom a rest." And one Monday morning, after the residents had had more visitors than usual on the preceding Sunday, a slip of paper was found tied to the door knocker with a little piece of blue ribbon: "The door knocker needs a bit of rest."

Once and once only Miss Brington made a comment about the political situation. She stood in the garden and looked up into the bright sky in which gleaming barrage balloons floated like giant silver fish, uttered one of her middle-range sighs, and declared: "They ought to bring the barrage balloons in. After all, they have to get a bit of rest."

You were tempted at first to laugh at this endlessly repeated, hackneyed expression. But you soon came to see that it was the hole in the curtain behind which was concealed the inapprehensible, toiling, sighing something that was known publicly as Miss Brington. Through the hole you could glimpse the scene of a life which in fact had never been a proper life.

Thanks to a faded photograph marked with a date that hung in the dining room, you knew that Miss Brington's father had died when she was ten years old and that at that point she already owned the little house. A little house of one's own — the dream and pride of every family on King's Row. A little house that widow and daughter had to hold on to if they were not to slide down into the lower ranks of society where people have no home of their own and have to live in rented rooms.

Perhaps little Miss Brington learned to utter some of her lighter sighs when, instead of playing with her school friends, she had to stay home and help her working mother. Perhaps coming home from school as it was already getting dark and having to deliver the sewing her mother took in (the later the better; the neighbours don't have to know we need to earn money this way), perhaps that is what first gave her the idea that it would be nice to sit still and rest a while. Perhaps it was when she was scrubbing the outside steps that she first began to feel it would be good to give the wash-rag and the broom a rest, so that even they could enjoy a little peace and quiet after what, for a child, had been an over-full day.

And so life must have gone on. Times did not get easier. The mother aged quickly and the daughter was left with all the work. At first she rented out one room, then two, then three. But at least they still owned the house and, as night began to fall, could go into their own little garden and breathe in the fresh air. And that was worth all the sacrifices.

Doubtless the two women never spoke to each other. What was there to say? They worked away side by side and each of them longed for night to come and with it, finally, rest and sleep. Possibly, for a while, night time was also a time when the young Miss Brington allowed her imagination to wander: other girls go dancing, gossip and laugh with each other, people fall in love with them and marry them… But, of course, other girls are not so constantly tired and do not carry the weight of a whole house on their shoulders. Perhaps there were nights when the young Miss Brington hated the house that deprived her of rest and happiness, but if so, it was likely to be an impotent hatred, the kind of hatred people feel for an invincible, all-powerful tyrant. And her stone tyrant made ever more demands on her. Her tyrant was often sick and in need of a great deal of care and attention. The roof needed to be repaired; the gutters had started to leak. All that cost money, lots of money. The rooms became shabby; the old furniture needed a rest too, and if it did not get it, became sullen and difficult, let its legs and arms break, and in anger spewed horsehair and kapok out of its cushions. And so it caused more work.

The war came. Miss Brington hardly noticed it. She had no relatives or friends to worry about. She only had her old mother, who was becoming meaner by the day, and the ageing, ever more demanding house.

She had become almost completely unaccustomed to speaking. As her mother was now stone deaf, it was pointless talking to her, and her lodgers appeared strange and incomprehensible to Miss Brington — noisy people who always wanted something and were never at rest, not even on a Sunday. It was better to communicate with them through sighs and little slips of paper. It was around this time that Miss Brington developed sighing into an art; around this time too, perhaps, that for the first time in many years a feeling was aroused in her: a feeling of compassion for things that are used every day, often enough every hour, and that — who knows? — were perhaps as weary as she. She was unhappy when someone forced the broom, which had already put in a morning's work, to sweep again in the afternoon. She was firmly convinced that the water heater had given up out of weariness and would return dutifully to work if it were granted just a few days' rest. As for the radio, it had to be protected from the heedless residents who kept wanting to turn it on.

She herself could not ask for protection, she herself could not give up working; but she could stretch out a helping hand to dumb, helpless things, and this capacity gave her something she had never had before: self-awareness and confidence. She — who in her entire life, had never had enough money, who in her entire life had never been able to exercise her will on anything — had the power to grant rest to someone or something; she had the power to give the most precious gift she could imagine.

And so she lived on, a something that worked and sighed and, if only from time to time, quite rarely, smiled to herself when she thought of the day that house and garden, people and things would disappear and she would wake up in a more beautiful world and discover that an angel had tied a broad blue ribbon around her, to which was attached a slip of paper that said: "Please give Miss Brington a bit of rest. She has worked enough."

"Miß Brington," *Die Zeitung*, London, 10 November 1941, p. 3; *Zeitspiegel*, London, No. 23/24, 8 June 1946, p. 6; *Arbeiter-Zeitung*, Vienna, No. 176, 30 July 1949, p. 5.

Translator's note

This little story obviously reflects the author's many years of familiarity with boarding houses. At the time of its publication it must have been especially meaningful to the readers of *Die Zeitung* — largely middle-class German and Austrian refugees in England, many of whom had had to settle in such boarding houses. In England, as is well known, the boarding house is a peculiarly drab and depressing institution.

At the same time, Zur Mühlen was clearly able to identify with the downtrodden, narrow-minded, deprived landlady. She too knew what it was to have to toil ceaselessly and she too transcended her own miseries to some extent by seeking to lighten the burdens born by others and placing her hopes in a better world to come.

We Have to Tell Them

By June the little girl was beginning to count the days until the vacation. At eight years of age, she had made the discovery that all days are not equally long. Toward the end of the holidays, they rush by like crazy, faster than horses, faster than cars — but just before the holidays they creep along like snails or like the old man who stood outside the Church on Sundays begging, and to whom the little girl was permitted to give a few pennies. The little girl spoke to her father about this curious discovery of hers and found it hard to believe him when he told her that all the days are of equal length and that it is only fear or longing that makes one hour stretch out to two, sometimes even three or, in contrast, makes the same hour shrink to half an hour or even just a quarter of an hour. She did understand about longing, however. Had she not been longing for months now for the day when she would be told: "Tomorrow we are leaving for Wognin." Wognin was the family estate in Slovakia, but it might just as well have been called "Heaven" or "Paradise." Perhaps it wasn't so much the old castle and the property itself that she loved — though the paddock was every bit as beautiful as the Garden of Eden could have been. It was the little village itself, with its brightly painted houses, its little shops, and its weekly market. That was even more marvellous, alluring, and exciting. And this year everything was especially wonderful, for poor nanny had gone off to see her sick mother, and the little girl, who was now ten, was allowed to go into the village by herself and play with the village children.

Early one bright, sunny day she set out, neat and clean, in a white dress, beaming with joyful anticipation. But as she turned into the little street by the brook, she heard terrible screams. She ran in the direction the noise was coming from. Half an hour later, she was heading home, beaten up, panting, crying, red-faced, her white dress torn and dirty.

Her parents were still sitting at the breakfast table when she burst on to the veranda.

"What you look like!" her mother said sternly. "Go and get changed immediately."

Her father, however, glanced at her little face and said, "Sit down, Nina. Tell us what happened."

Still panting and sobbing, Nina struggled to get her breath back, and finally let out a string of unconnected words: "Jan and Hanus and Svata and miller Nedbal's big son…"

"Yes?" her father asked gently. "What about them?"

"You've got to give them a hiding, father. Right away. Let's go. You've got to give them a good hiding."

"Why so?"

The little girl blew her nose. Her voice trembled. But it was with anger now.

"Do you know what they did? All four of them, such big boys, and Nedbar's son is already a grown-up, all four of them jumped on little Heini — you know who I mean, father, Heini Neuwirth — and beat him up, four against one, and Heini is still so small, and then they threw stones at him and screamed *Zid* (Jew) at him…"

Nina's mother wrinkled her forehead. "I keep telling you, Nina, you should not be playing with the brats from the village. That's what happens. Just look at your dress…"

"Brutes," her father said crossly. Then: "And what did you do, Nina?" he asked in a tense voice.

"I hit Jan a good clip round the ears," said Nina. "He is the smallest of them. Then I yelled at them and threatened them. And they all ran away. They're cowards into the bargain, the brutes."

"Don't use such common expressions, Nina," her mother interjected reprovingly.

"But even father said… And anyway they *are* brutes. Four against one. All the stronger ones against one weak one. Come on, father. Let's go and give them a good hiding."

"We can't do that, Nina."

"But someone has to do something. There was no one on the street at the time. No one saw what those wicked boys did. Father…"

"Look, Nina, I can't do anything about this," said her father, and if it had not been so unthinkable, Nina might have thought he was embarrassed.

She reflected for a moment. "Someone has to do something."

Her mother chimed in. "Don't get mixed up in things that are none of your business. And now go and change."

"Look, Nina, such things happen," her father said soothingly. "People don't know…"

"They don't know?" The bright summer's day that had so suddenly become dark and sad for Nina grew light again.

"Well, then, if they don't know about it, then they're not so bad. But we have to tell them."

Her father looked at her with a worried expression. "You have your work cut out for you, child."

"Go and change," her mother repeated.

Nina nodded and went, but she had no intention of changing. Beaten up and dirty, she ran back into the village in her torn dress. She would tell everybody what happened and everybody would be outraged and angry and the bad boys would be punished. If such things happened only because people did not know about them, it wouldn't be difficult to set matters right. Someone just had to tell them. And she would do it.

Her first stop was at the priest's. Nina didn't care for the young reverend who had come to the village after the good old priest died. He looked stern and mean. But he is a big man and everyone listens to him. The priest himself opened the door. Nina didn't even wait for him to ask her in. Still standing in the corridor, she recounted to him what had happened. "Reverend Father," she concluded, "you have to ex-com-muni-cate these boys!" And she thought of the Emperor Henry at Canossa, the subject of her last religious instruction period before the vacation. The priest wrinkled his forehead. "These things happen," he said testily. "There's no need to make such a fuss about a little Jew-boy."

Nina stared at him. Cold shivers suddenly ran down her back.

"You… you know that such things… You really know?"

"Naturally. There's absolutely no reason for you to get so worked up." Nina noticed that the priest no longer used the familiar "du" form with her, as he had in the past. He was speaking to her now as he would to an adult who had displeased him. Her little face turned pale and hard. "You have always known that such things happen — among us, in our village?"

"I am busy right now. I have no time," the priest replied.

"No time! But that is like… like the people who passed by until the Good Samaritan came along."

The priest's face became red with anger.

"I will report you to your father," he said and pushed Nina out the door.

She walked on slowly. She felt as though someone had struck her a blow on the head. He knows about it, our priest knows about it, and he doesn't do anything!

She clenched her little hands into fists. He is a wicked man. He will go to hell. Or at least be sent to purgatory for a thousand years. And when he dies, I will not pray for his soul.

Somewhat consoled by those thoughts, she went to the next house to tell the people what had happened. She went from one house where she knew the people to another. She pleaded, then she got angry, then desperate. She, who had always loved everyone, began to hate the people in the village. Everybody knew, it seemed, and no one did anything.

The sun stood high in the heavens. The air shimmered from the heat. Nina dragged herself along, her weary feet sending up little clouds of fine dust. Now she had stopped at the home of everyone she knew. So many houses, she thought, so many people, and they all know, and no one does anything, no one. What kind of a world is this? Father was wrong about people not knowing. But father himself won't do anything.

She struggled slowly, very slowly homewards. They will still be sitting at their breakfast as though nothing has happened, she thought, utterly bewildered. And all mother could speak of was my dress. I don't want to go home.

All of a sudden, everything appeared strange to her. And then she had an insight. It was so terrible that she sank down on the edge of a ditch, as though she had been struck by a blow, and held her head in her hands. If that's the way it is everywhere, all over the world, if injustice happens everywhere and everyone knows and no one does anything… no one…

The sun shone brightly, spreading its warmth over the land; the sky was clear and blue; all around there was beauty and peace. At the edge of a ditch a little girl sat and stared into a black, impenetrable night of horror. Tears streamed down her cheeks as, full of despair and apprehension, she kept repeating amid sobs: "They all know about it, they all know about it."

"Man muß es ihnen sagen," *Arbeiter-Zeitung,* Vienna, 12 December 1948, p. 5.
For comment on this story, see Gossman,"The Red Countess: Four Stories,"
Common Knowledge, 15 (2009), pp. 82–91.

Painted on Ivory

October had turned the leaves yellow and red. In the afternoon sun their colours glowed brightly. The approaching evening had sent a gentle wind ahead as its messenger. Yellow and red leaves were swept into the pond where they sailed for a while over the grey water, like tiny boats, until they sank.

Jane Austen stood by the pond and observed the little performance. How often she had done that in the seven years since 1809 when the three of them, the widow and her orphaned daughters — Jane, her two years older sister Cassandra, and their mother — had moved from Bath to the country at Chawton House.

Strange that she was affected for the first time, today, by the melancholy of autumn. Until now autumn had been only a time of transition to Chawton's cosy winter warmth, which in its turn held out the promise of spring. Today, however, she felt a leave-taking in the air and she shivered slightly. But only for a moment. Impatiently she threw back her head with its dark curls and straightened her tall slim body. A smile formed on her small mouth and danced in her hazel eyes as she chided herself for having yielded to *sentimentality*. For there was nothing she hated so much as exaggerated feelings. She had not tolerated them in any of the heroines of her novels. All the young females in her books were complete mistresses of their hearts.

As she often did, she thought of these figures as if they were living creatures. Among them were several of whom she was fonder than of friends and relatives — Cassandra, the cleverest and best of sisters, excepted. Above all, Elizabeth in *Pride and Prejudice*. She had never been able to forgive anyone for not loving Elizabeth. Perhaps because there was a good deal of herself in Elizabeth — the keen eye for human weaknesses, the energy, the wit. She remembered exactly how she had written the book as a twenty-one year old in her first, beloved home, Steventon Rectory, where her father had been rector. It had come out three years ago in 1813; anonymously, of course, as a *Novel by a Lady*.

Could there have been a finer pseudonym for her? Were not the "lady" and the "gentleman" her ideal — people with good manners, a solid education and culture, like her father, and a select social circle. That circle might be a trifle narrow perhaps, but it was harmonious. Only the ridiculous traits of a few arrogant aristocrats and the naïve snobbery of a small number of social climbers heightened its colour somewhat. How well she knew those people. She had spent her entire life among them. Was it not natural that they figured in all her books?

Now the *Big House* on the hillside [Chawton House — L.G.] was turning red in the light of the setting sun. Even the lower lying church was touched by its wine-dark rays. On the other side of the valley the small, thickly wooded hill could be seen fading into the darkness, and the breeze had become cooler.

Jane strode through the carefully tended garden into the house. She entered the large living-room, where her mother and Cassandra were already waiting for her. Jane loved this room, she loved the walled-up window that had once looked out on to the public road and was now transformed into a bookcase. Perhaps, she reflected — and her own thought startled her — perhaps in my books too I always walled up the window opening on to the road. The road means the larger world out there with its noise, its loud pleasures, its unconcealed tragedies. It means people and more people, people who are different from me, people passionate about politics — and I have always hated politics. It means the tragic condition of poverty in the big cities, about which I know nothing and want to know nothing — though I have never neglected our own worthy, well brought up poor. There was one time when the road reached right into our lives. That was years ago when my cousin Elizabeth's husband was guillotined in France. But that was so far away and so much less real than my books or than a malicious smile espied in company, or a clever turn of phrase, or a gesture revealing a person's whole character. Yes, even tragedy once came quite close — that was in 1805 — through my brother Frank who was serving in the Navy.

In one of his letters he described Nelson's death at Trafalgar which he had witnessed personally. How much better it is to fill up the window that looks out on to the road with books and to see out only through the other window on to the garden, on to lawns and trees and on to the high wood fence that cuts us off from others, on to the hedge of hornbeam with its delicate leaves...

She gave her sister a smile and walked over to her writing desk. From the drawer she pulled out some small loose sheets of paper, so small they could easily be hidden if company came, sat down, and began to write. She loved working quietly in the large, handsome room, she loved to look up and see Cassandra's gentle gaze turned on her, and the still sturdy figure of their mother, who on days when she had spent the morning working in the garden, often dozed off on the sofa in the twilight hour. These two people, along with her brothers and their children, and her work, made up her world.

But her books too meant something different to her than to most women writers. She smiled as she thought of Fanny Burney, who was so ambitious and set such store by the judgment of others, and of that dreadful Madame de Stael whose heroines revealed their feelings so shamelessly and seemed to know of nothing but love — not a tender love respectful of the boundaries that preserve a certain distance between people, but a wild, vulgar, at times ridiculous passion. In London once, when the secret of the "Lady" who had written *Pride and Prejudice* was no longer a secret, an attempt had been made to bring her together with Madame de Stael. But she had explained that she could not accept an invitation to a house where she was to be welcomed, not as Jane Austen, but as the author of *Pride and Prejudice*. Besides, Madame de Stael had said that Miss Austen's books were "commonplace."

She began to write, quickly, as was her manner. Her energetic yet fine handwriting filled one loose sheet of paper after another, until darkness forced her to stop.

Cassandra, who sensed all the moods of her sister, did not hurry to light the lamps. She knew that Jane continued to spin out her stories in the semi-darkness and that she was not to be disturbed by a single spoken word.

Today, however, Jane's thoughts were not about the new novel *Persuasion*, on which she had been working for months. Something or other was leading her to reflect on her own life. What was it exactly? Normally, for her, the past was truly past, and she was not especially interested in her own person. Impatiently she straightened the little cap she wore. (Years ago — far too soon, according to their mother — she and Cassandra had decided to cover their curls with the headgear of elderly women.) She hated every kind of obscurity, in words as in feelings. In her books too every word had to be the *mot juste*, the only right one. She loved words, and she loved an orderly, clear, rather sober style, a style that — so it seemed to her — best reflected life, at least the life of her caste. Now she was tormented by the question why, today, as she stood at the pond, she had for the first time felt the sadness of autumn, why, as she thought about her books, she had suddenly felt a desire to defend them — not in the eyes of others, but in her own. She wrinkled her forehead and reflected strenuously. Everything was caused by something and until that something had been identified, one was obliged to wander around in a fog and could not find one's way into the bright, somewhat cold, somewhat harsh light of day that, for her, was the only proper light. Why?... Her sister, only a shadowy outline in the darkness, looked over toward her, and all at once she knew what the something was. This morning, in the bedroom they shared, while Cassandra was combing her hair, she had seen, for the first time, a white strand in the dark locks, and had thought, slightly shocked: Cassy is getting old; we are both getting old. Afterwards she had laughed at her own silliness: old at forty and forty-two! How much time do we still have, how much time do I still have to write my beloved books?

Now this thought occurred to her again and she smiled at her own silly sentimentality. I have written only five novels so far! Like a child, she enumerated them on the fingers of her left hand: *Sense and Sensibility, Pride and Prejudice, Mansfield Park, Emma, Northanger Abbey*. The smile on her finely shaped features grew broader. Dear, good Mrs. Radcliffe had forgiven her the parody of her famous book *The Mysteries of Udolpho* and had even laughed at it herself. It had been too tempting to make a fool of those popular horror stories with their dark dungeons, spirits, murders, cruel villains and supernaturally virtuous heroes and heroines. Real life was something altogether different, something quiet and peaceful. Even death was not too frightening when one had faith in an afterlife.

The index finger of Jane Austen's right hand still rested on the palm of her left hand. Suddenly she felt how skinny it was. She raised her hand and held it in front of her face, but it was too dark to make anything out and now she grasped one hand with the other a little more vigorously, a little more impatiently than was her wont. Yes, her hand is skinny, and her round face has become long and narrow. That she could see in the mirror. She always feels tired now and rather often she is visited by pains that she hides from her mother and Cassandra…

Time — to write more books… Who knows how much time has been granted to us? It occurred to her that Cassandra, to whom she read each new chapter aloud, had said: "I don't know what it is, Jane, but this book is different. There are none of your dear little malicious comments and gestures. Your heroine, Anne Elliot, strikes me as the most interesting of your female characters, she is gentler, more sensitive…" "Please, Cassy," she had interrupted her sister. "I beg you, don't tell me that Anne is sentimental." "No, but somehow, I'm not sure how, she is more connected to life out there than your other heroines." "I don't understand you. Elizabeth and Elinor and Emma also fall in love, are loved, and get married. Isn't that what happens to everyone?" Cassandra had not answered and had left the room almost in anger. Now as Jane stared at the loose sheets of paper lying in front of her, she admitted that her sister had been right. But she had been right too, for it was the first time that she had allowed feeling to have the leading role in one of her books. Perhaps the world did not consist only of country gentry, middle-class landowners, vicars, and their daughters. Perhaps, after all, there was something else, something that had remained foreign to her.

"Cassy," she called out in the darkness, "do you know what my books are? Little ivory pieces, two inches high, painted with such a thin brush that all my work, in the end, has only a quite slight effect."

"Jane," Cassy cried out in shock. "What has got into you? What are you thinking of?"

"I don't know myself. Perhaps it is better to paint large pictures. Pictures that encompass everything. But I wasn't capable of that. I could only portray the world I knew. Perhaps I was wrong not to want to get to know the other world."

"I don't know what you mean, Jane," Cassandra said uncomprehendingly.

Jane Austen laughed, softly, gently, as a lady should laugh.

"Forget about it, Cassy. It was just a thought. I've already chased it away. Light the lamps. As you well know, darkness confuses people and makes them sentimental. Do light the lamps please, quickly."

"Auf Elfenbein gemalt," *Die Zeit* (Vienna), 16, 15 December 1948, p. 24ff/

Translator's note

Zur Mühlen's interest in and knowledge of Jane Austen were unusual in the German-speaking world. Until fairly recently, Austen's work was virtually unread and untranslated in Germany. Even academic studies of it by German scholars of English literature were extremely rare.[1] Zur Mühlen may have been introduced to Austen by her Anglo-Irish grandmother, Isabella Louisa Blacker, or she may have discovered her during her years of exile in England. For obvious reasons, she must have been intrigued by Austen's status as a woman writer whose class and gender identity was in conflict with her literary ambition and by the way she chose to resolve that conflict. But she may also have felt that she shared with Austen a peculiarly feminine way of attending to speech, gesture, and other characteristics of class and individual personality, as well as to the complexity of human relations in general. In addition, her fictional portrait of Jane Austen provided an opportunity for reflecting on the role and responsibility of the writer. Her late eighteenth and early nineteenth-century English predecessor is presented as having deliberately chosen to restrict herself, for the sake of her art, to the portrayal of the world she knew well and never left — in marked contrast to Zur Mühlen's own decision to break out of her world in order to address a wide and varied audience on the pressing political and social issues of her time. What is an author's obligation? Should she write finely observed, literary pieces on domestic themes, as Zur Mühlen with her novel *Der Riesenrad* had demonstrated she was quite capable of doing, or should she look out on to "the street, with its noise, its loud pleasures

---

[1] See Annika Bautz, "The Reception of Jane Austen in Germany," in *The Reception of Jane Austen in Europe,* ed. Anthony Mandal and Brian Southam (London and New York: Continuum, 2007), pp. 93–116. Zur Mühlen's *feuilleton* is not mentioned in this otherwise well-documented article.

and its unconcealed tragedies" — which to Zur Mühlen had meant writing about pressing social and political problems, in particular the dangers of National Socialism — and get her readers to do likewise? Zur Mühlen's choice was never in doubt. But she was not unaware of the sacrifices, literary as well as pecuniary, that her choice entailed. Finally, despite her political commitment, Zur Mühlen, who had struggled with ill health for most of her life, was acutely conscious of the fragility of existence and, in general, of the transitoriness of everything. In this *feuilleton* she projects that consciousness, not implausibly, on to her heroine. Apparently her knowledge of Austen's biography extended to the illness of which Austen began to be aware when she was about forty, not long after she had begun work on *Persuasion*, and which carried her off less than two years later. In Zur Mühlen's autobiographical memoir, *Ende und Anfang*, written and published in 1929, when she was in her mid-forties, there is a short passage that is quite similar in tone to the tone set at the very opening of the *feuilleton*. It evokes the feeling of melancholy that overcame the future writer as she watched darkness gathering over the small town of Gmunden in Austria, where, in the company of her beloved grandmother, she spent her happiest childhood years:

> I loved our mountain, the pride of the little town, rising up on the opposite shore of the lake. On fine summer evenings the whole mass of stone turned pink, like the finest marble, and then, when it was already dusk all around, the Traunstein (as our mountain was called) shone forth out of the shadows like an undying flame. Gradually, however, it paled and turned cold and dead, and everything lost life and became suddenly old and joyless. At that moment, without knowing why, I felt a deep sadness. A day was dead, a day of childhood was irrevocably gone.

The fact that this little *feuilleton* was published in *Die Zeit*, a short-lived (1948–1950), leftwing fortnightly devoted to literature and art, on the occasion of her own 65th birthday is an indication of how keen and personal Zur Mühlen's interest in Austen was. (My thanks to Debora Vietor-Engländer for informing me about this now little-known journal.)

The Sparrow

Quarrel and disagreement ruled in the Sparrow family. Mother Sparrow squatted in her nest all day and Father Sparrow swore and grumbled and found fault with everything. The family that had once been so happy was completely changed. And for all this misery the youngest Sparrow was to blame. One evening at supper he had declared briefly and boldly, "I am not going to school any more. I am not putting up any more with all the insults I receive. I am tired of our whole life here. I want to go out into the world." He stuck up his bill cheekily and gave his parents a defiant look.

Mother Sparrow was so shocked that all her feathers stood up. She stared helplessly at her ill-mannered son, and all she could do was to say weakly, "Peep, peep." But Father Sparrow opened his beak so wide in horror that the long worm he had been about to eat fell out of it and slithered away as fast as it could. This made Father Sparrow even angrier. Now, on top of everything else, his supper had got away. Father Sparrow was a man of action. This time too, as in the past, he bent down and beat his son in the face with his sharp beak.

Sparrow screamed more defiantly than ever, "I won't stay here any longer. I've had enough. I'm going out into the world."

Then Mother Sparrow found her voice again and said tearfully, "You wicked child! Is that how you thank your parents for the love they have given you! Have we not brought you up well and provided you with everything? You are the first sparrow in our village to attend Professor Swallow's school and learn how to build artistic nests. You move in the best circles. You mix with the Swallows, the Starlings, and the Yellow-bills. And this is how you repay us!"

"I don't care a straw about the best circles," Sparrow replied rudely. And he opened his beak and whistled defiantly, "Tweet, tweet!"

"No other sparrow is studying for such a respectable profession," piped Mother Sparrow despairingly.

Then Young Sparrow began to make such a rumpus that the whole nest shook. "A respectable profession, yes, truly a beautiful profession. Building nests for others to live in. Slaving in the heat of the sun, carrying straws from all over, weaving them together, making sure that everything is just perfect — only to have the fine ladies and gentlemen move in and throw me a little worm for my wages, barely big enough for a decent meal. Fine people, indeed! The Swallows, always dressed up in their frock-coats; the Yellow-bills showing off all their gold. And the arrogance and scorn they treat us with! A common labourer, they call me contemptuously. I have had enough of it. I am as good as they are, and maybe better."

Mother Sparrow shrank back in horror, but Father Sparrow puffed himself up until he nearly burst and thundered, "Be silent, you rogue, you little scoundrel. You talk like a Communist. You forget that I am Chairman of the Sparrow Village Council. My son may not rebel against the established order."

"Yes," groaned Mother Sparrow, "and what if the neighbours were to hear you! How dreadful!" Young Sparrow laughed shamelessly, seated himself on the edge of the nest and whistled a revolutionary song.

Father Sparrow rose hastily and muttered in an undertone to his wife, "See to that young fool and get him to behave. I have to go now. There is a meeting of the Choral Society." He flew away without one look at his naughty son.

Mother Sparrow sighed deeply and asked in a plaintive voice, "Now what is it you really want?"

Young Sparrow came closer, nestled against his mother and said with a sweet smile, "I want to go away, little Mother, far away. To foreign lands where it is always summer."

"But Son of my Heart, you know that even the stupid children of humans are taught in their schools that the sparrow is not a migratory bird."

"What is that to me? I can't stand it here any longer. I am tired of always seeing the same things: the old church steeple in the distance, the farm-house and the dung-hill right here in front of our noses. No, I want to go away, far away."

At that he spread out his wings and pushed himself head first out of the nest into space. It seemed very dangerous, but his wings carried him safely through the air.

Still, Young Sparrow was by no means as joyous and light-hearted as he seemed. His parents' words had raised all sorts of doubts in his mind. "Mother was really right," he said to himself. "The sparrow is not a migratory bird. No one has ever heard of a sparrow flying across the great ocean and going to distant lands. But why," he asked himself, with defiant courage, "shouldn't I be the first one to do this? Some one always has to be the first. If my venture succeeds I will have proved to the entire sparrow people that they don't have to freeze and starve in the wintertime, but can move to warm countries and live well there. To be sure, the ocean…" Young Sparrow became disheartened. He remembered what his teacher, Swallow the master builder, had once told him about the great, wild stretch of boundless water with its angry, foaming waves that you had to fly over day after day. If the strength of your wings failed, you plunged down and were lost. You were swallowed up by the waves.

Beset by these thoughts, Young Sparrow almost wanted to give up the idea. He felt completed deflated and began to tremble. Then suddenly he thought how many wretched sparrows had died of hunger and cold in past hard winters.

"No, no," he said to himself. I mustn't be so cowardly. This is not just about me. It's about all my brother sparrows, about all the future generations of Sparrows who will be around when I am long dead. If I can help them to a happier life, it will be worth every effort and every sacrifice."

And brave Young Sparrow resolved to strike out the very next day.

He spent that night in his parents' nest, huddled close to his mother, and wept a little in secret, because it was hard for him to leave her. Father Sparrow got home late and quite drunk from the Choral Society meeting, threw himself with such force on his bed that it creaked noisily, and immediately fell asleep.

The grey-white sky began to turn rosy. Morning came flying in on the wings of the wind and brought light to the world. Young Sparrow awoke, looked for the last time at his sleeping parents, and flew away. He knew which direction to fly in, for he remembered the stories that the swallows had told. Now he flew exactly that way.

The sun climbed higher into the heavens, it became hotter and hotter, and poor Sparrow could scarcely breathe. His wings were so sore that he could hardly lift them. Still, he flew on. He had resolved not to rest until the shades of night fell on the earth.

Never had Young Sparrow lived through such a long day. In vain his bright little eyes explored the heavens; the great golden sphere of the sun shone brightly and would not go down.

"I was a fool," thought Sparrow. "At this moment I might be sitting comfortably at home in our nest, or bathing in the big puddle by the cherry-tree. Oh, how pleasant it would be to bathe. Even the ocean would not be too big for me right now."

Still, he did not lose heart but flew steadily on. True, he was now flying very slowly. Every beat of his wings caused him terrible pain. He began to hate the sun, the merciless red sphere that would not go down. To give himself courage he made up a little song, sang it very softly, and flapped his weary wings in time to its rhythm.

> My cause is the cause of my brothers,
> My strength must save them all;
> If I fail, I do wrong to the others,
> And their chains will never fall.

At last, at long last, great black shadows fell upon the earth. A refreshing breeze came flying in, coolly fanning Sparrow, who was very weary, and bearing him gently along on its mighty wings.

As the sun went down behind a blue hill, Sparrow alighted, utterly exhausted, on a large meadow. He lay panting in the tall grass. The soft chirping of the crickets lulled him to sleep; his eyes closed.

Rough, loud voices, human voices, awakened him. He peeked out through the tall blades of grass and saw two ragged, dust-covered men seated under a knotty old nut-tree. One of them was pulling his torn boots off and, looking woefully at his blistered feet, said: "I can't go on any more. I have to rest for a day."

"Just another half hour," the other man said comfortingly. "Just to the next railroad station. There we will hide in a freight car and ride until morning. Then it will not be far to the sea."

"All right, then," the first man mumbled grumpily. "But I can't go a step further than that today." Slowly he pulled his boots on again.

Young Sparrow had listened attentively to their words. "So humans get tired too," he thought, "and then they ride. I don't know what that means, but I know that you don't tire yourself out that way. If humans ride, why shouldn't sparrows ride too?" He decided to follow the two men and not to let them out of his sight. As they left soon after, he flew after them.

They arrived at a house. On the ground in front of it stretched two gleaming ribbons. Now night had really come. Everything was hidden in darkness. Only the stars shone faintly in the sky. Sparrow stayed near the two men and waited.

Suddenly something dreadful happened. Through the darkness a gigantic black beast came rattling along, its red eyes shining so brightly that you could see them from a great distance. It puffed and panted, and the earth shook under it. As it came near, it let out a frightful shriek. Then suddenly it stopped. Clouds of smoke poured from its long black nose.

Sparrow was astonished that neither of the two men, nor the other humans who were there seemed to be afraid of the monster. On the contrary, they ran up to it and disappeared into its maw. Then Sparrow noticed that the monster pulled a large number of little black houses behind it. He saw the two men sneak into one of those houses and flew on to the roof of the same house. Scarcely had he settled down when the monster again began to puff and pant and started to move.

Poor Sparrow thought he would die of fright. The monster rattled along at such speed that the little bird could neither hear nor see. At home he had often flown with the wind for the fun of it and had enjoyed the swift motion. But this was altogether different. A fearful wind storm beat on him and tried to blow him off the roof. He made himself as small as he could, clung on tightly, trembling all over, and was convinced that his last hour had come. If humans call this rest, they surely are strange creatures. It is true that, though he could see over all the roofs, he could not see a single human on any of them. Perhaps it is not so terrible where the people are, as it is here. He was a clever Sparrow and when the monster stopped again to catch its breath, he flew down from the roof of the house and had a look at it from the front. The door was not quite closed. Sparrow squeezed through the crack, and entered a dark room piled high with crates. He squatted on one of them and waited to see what would happen.

The monster began to run again. Sparrow laughed with joy; he had found the right thing to do. He sat there at rest and the monster had to slave to carry him along. So this is what humans call "riding." Evidently, humans were not as stupid as he thought.

The countless feet of the monster pounded over the earth singing a rattling, rumbling, monotonous song. To Sparrow the words seemed to be: "Into the distance! Into the distance!" For a while he listened to the song, then he fell asleep.

He must have slept for a long time. When he awoke, the sun was high in the sky and its rays came through the narrow open crack in the door into the dark room. Sparrow saw his two acquaintances crouching on the floor, hidden between two tall crates. They seemed to be in good humour, chatting with one another and laughing.

"We have travelled a good part of our way without trouble," said the older one. "Now we only have to walk one more day and ride another night. Then we will have reached the ocean."

"How long will we have to swim?"

"About five days."

Terror seized Sparrow. For five days he would have to swim over the endless waters. For five long days he would not be able to rest if he was not to sink under the waves. How would he be able to hold out? He began to reflect anxiously. Could humans swim for so long in the water? He had seen boys bathing in the village pond, but they would come out of the water in a short time and none of them ever remained in it all day long. Perhaps there were also tamed monsters that carried humans over the water. Again he decided not to leave the two humans' side and to do everything they did.

When the two men jumped unnoticed off the freight car at a busy railroad station, Sparrow followed them. He flew very close to them. He felt that they were his friends and that as long as he stayed with them nothing would happen to him.

All day long the men walked, through fields and meadows, through little villages with funny pointed church steeples. The younger of the two men limped. He could only walk slowly. This pleased Sparrow, for it meant that he did not have to hurry but could fly along at a comfortable speed. When the men stopped, Sparrow followed their example, using the time to look for food, as the long journey had made him unusually hungry. He also chatted with a few foreign birds, all of whom advised him not to continue his dangerous journey. The migratory birds he spoke to looked him over scornfully. "Do you think you can do the same as high class people like us?" they said with a sneer. "Travelling, seeing the world, spending the winter in warm climates — that is not for common people."

An old blackbird minister, black-frocked and solemn, delivered a sermon to him from a high branch. "We must obey God's commandments. God has ordained that sparrows must spend the winter in the north."

"If your God has ordained that our entire people is to be destroyed by cold and hunger and that only the upper classes, the Capitalists, like the Swallows and the Starlings, can escape the harsh winter, I don't want to know anything about him!" cried Sparrow, and his feathers bristled up in anger.

The old blackbird minister primped his shining feathers with his bill and muttered something unintelligible. But Sparrow was sad. "How cruel we birds are to one another," he thought to himself. "I am trying to do something that will be helpful to all, and I am just laughed at. Can't anybody understand me?"

"Yes, I can, I can!" called a sweet voice from a great height, and a young lark shot down, swift as lightning, and alighted by the side of the despondent Sparrow. "I understand you. Everybody jeers at me too because I don't fly close to the earth as they do, but always try to soar higher and higher into the blue heavens. Do not be downcast, dear brother, you will reach your goal."

The young lark flew close to Sparrow, looked at him and said: "Fly a little for me, brother, so that I can see how strong your wings are."

Sparrow flew up, hovering over the lark. As he returned, she gave him a sad look and said earnestly: "Your wings cannot carry you over the great ocean, my poor friend. But you must not give up on that account. You must do as humans do. They cannot fly at all, and yet they travel all over the world. They have invented a kind of house that swims over the water. They call it a ship. You must find a ship…"

Sparrow did not wait to hear the rest. The two men had left unnoticed while the Lark was speaking and now Sparrow saw them in the distance like two dark spots. Frightened, he cried out: "My two humans have left me," and he flew after them as fast as he could.

When it grew dark the men once again sneaked into a freight train. Sparrow followed them and slept all night while the black monster again carried him over hills and mountains, past lakes and streams.

When dawn broke, the two men crept out of the train and Sparrow flew after them. They walked for a little while and then Sparrow saw an immense body of water that stretched before him. This blue-grey expanse of water extended infinitely outwards, far beyond the range of his vision, while terrifying high, wild, white-capped waves beat the shore.

So this was the ocean! Never had Sparrow felt so small and helpless as at the sight of this dreadful water. What was he in comparison? A poor helpless little bird, a tiny, anonymous something. From his little breast he heaved deep sighs, and tears rolled down from his bright little eyes. "If I were only safe at home, in our snug little nest," he moaned. "If only I could creep under Mother's wings as I used to do when I was small."

The waves roared eerily, threateningly; the white foam flew upwards. But the two men walked unconcerned along the damp, sandy beach. They seemed to have no fear at all of the raging sea as it lashed the shore. With beating heart, Sparrow followed them. And then he saw an astonishing sight. In a great bay strange things were tossing about. They looked partly like houses, with tiny windows and tall chimneys, from which came a stream of heavy grey smoke, and partly like a forest in which bare trees without branches seemed to grow. Although these trees bore neither fruit nor leaves, Sparrow was delighted to see them. They seemed familiar. He began to feel at home. But how strange it was that these houses with the tall trees on them were on water and were being tossed up and down by the waves. Suddenly Sparrow remembered the words of the lark. "Humans call these houses that swim on the water 'ships.'" So these were ships! On one of these tossing, swimming houses he would travel to warm lands.

But which should he choose?

It occurred to him that at home it was the largest trees that were best able to withstand the wind. Probably the same was true of ships, and so he must choose the largest.

His two friends walked towards a small ship. Sparrow piped "Farewell! Farewell!" several times, but they did not hear him.

Sparrow flew on to an immense ship from whose chimneys great clouds of grey smoke were streaming, and hid himself high up at the top of one of the leafless trees.

What noise and activity there was below. Countless humans ran hither and thither, calling and shouting to one another; something rattled, something clattered, the great chimneys let out a loud shriek. A bridge that connected the ship with the land flew up into the air, then fell down with a bang into the ship. The ship started on its journey. Slowly, gravely, it cut through the water bubbling up on either side. The large house with the leafless trees, the little bird's new home, swam away from the land.

All the noise and the hurrying and scurrying had left Sparrow in a state of great confusion. But another terrible fright was in store for him. Suddenly a young fellow climbed up his tree. Sparrow was convinced that he had come to capture him. But the fellow did not seem to notice him and after a while climbed back down. As it grew dark, the ship became quiet and only the sound of the waves could be heard. Sparrow flew down from his tree and sat down on the ground, where he soon fell asleep.

When he awoke in the morning, he thought he would die of fright. The land had disappeared. Wherever he looked, he saw only water. Great grey waves rolled sluggishly against the ship, causing it to sway slightly, as a gentle wind shakes the nests in the trees. Not a tree, not a shrub, not a flower was to be seen anywhere. The ship swam all alone on the boundless ocean.

Poor Sparrow felt quite lonely and abandoned. "If I could just find another bird, any bird," he sighed. "Even if it were a haughty swallow or a strict blackbird. I could at least speak with someone who knows my world and speaks my language." Once again, all his courage deserted him and he began to weep bitterly.

"Who are you?" suddenly asked a thin, piping voice, and when Sparrow looked up he beheld a little mouse standing before him and staring at him with large round eyes.

Sparrow was happy, for he was acquainted with mice at home. He bent down and politely answered the mouse's questions.

"You are a brave sparrow," she said, after she had heard his story. "I bid you welcome to my ship."

"To your ship?" exclaimed Sparrow. "I thought the ship belonged to the humans."

"That is what the humans think too," the mouse replied sharply. "But don't you know that humans always think everything belongs to them?"

"That is true. The farmer at home also thought that the cherry-tree was his, and yet it is quite obvious that the cherry-tree was made for us sparrows."

While they were conversing, a very old mouse came over and began to speak." Not all humans believe that everything belongs to them," she said in a schoolmistressly tone. "There are also humans who do not possess anything. You can see that on this ship. On the upper decks people live in large, beautifully appointed, airy rooms, and eat all day long. My mouth waters when I smell the rich dishes that are set before them."

"But down below people are so crowded together that they can hardly find a space to lie down in at night, and many have nothing to eat on the whole journey but the dry bread that they brought along with them. That idiotic expression, 'my ship,' that too you learned from humans," she said, scolding the little mouse."You know that among us everything is shared in common. Don't let me hear such words from you again."

"Forgive me, grandmother," the young mouse begged.

"You are a stranger here," said the grandmother mouse to Sparrow. "We will try to help you to survive the long journey. I advise you not to fly to the rich people. They will play with you for a day or two, and then forget you. The rich believe that everything in the world is there to serve and please them. To be sure, you will only find a few breadcrumbs among the poor on the lower decks, but these humans will be kind to you, because they know what it is like to be a poor creature who has nothing."

Sparrow followed the advice of the wise grandmother mouse and soon realized that she had spoken truthfully. The small children were delighted with him and they saved breadcrumbs for him from the few that were provided for their own little mouths. And as they were children, they understood Sparrow's language and chatted with him. In this way, Sparrow heard many very sad stories. The children told of need and misery, they told how hard their parents had to work and how, even so, there was often nothing to eat in the house. Our good-hearted Sparrow felt very sad when he heard about this. "There must also be a beautiful land for humans, where conditions are good and they do not have to be cold and go hungry," he said to his little friends.

"Perhaps," said a pale little girl. "But we have not yet found the way to it."

"When I am big," declared a dark-haired little boy, "I will go away in search of that land. And when I find it, I will lead all poor, deprived humans to it."

The two mice also visited Sparrow often. They always came towards evening, when everything was quiet.

And so quite a long time passed, until one day Sparrow saw land in the distance, with houses and trees, and knew that he had now reached his goal.

The grey ocean had become quite blue and gleamed in the sunshine. It was very hot, and grandmother mouse said that this was the land where there is no winter.

When the ship docked, Sparrow tenderly took leave of his friends and flew ashore to inspect his new home.

All the humans had brown faces and wore strange clothes. The faces of the women were covered, so that only their large black eyes could be seen. He also saw funny animals that walked on four long legs and had a great hump on their backs. Even the trees were different from those at home. Some had long pointed leaves and sweet, brown fruit that tasted delicious to Sparrow. There was plenty to eat. Here no sparrow would have to suffer hunger, and snow and cold were unknown.

"Is this not also the right country for poor humans?" Sparrow wondered. But then he saw that in this sunny land too there were rich and poor, that a few went richly clothed, while others wore rags, that a few lazy folk rode in handsome carriages, while others groaned under heavy burdens. And he thought, "It is much easier to find a sparrow paradise than a land where all humans live well." This pained him, because on his journey he had come to like humans. "But how strange this is," he thought in amazement. "Humans can tame wild monsters so that they will carry them all over, they know how to build houses that swim on the water, and yet they are poor and destitute and let a few greedy scoundrels take everything away from them."

Now that he had reached the warm country, Sparrow rested from his dangerous and wearisome journey, flew about lazily, and spent each night in a different tree.

One day he came to a beautiful stream and flew along its course. He came to a very great plain. At first he thought he had reached the ocean again, but then he saw that it was covered with fine yellow sand. In the distance he saw something rising out of the sand that looked like a monstrous animal. Out of curiosity he flew closer to it and realized that it was a gigantic creature with the head of a human and two huge paws. It was made of grey-brown stone and was partly covered with sand.

The ugly animal lay quite still and grinned evilly. Sparrow bowed anxiously: would the beast try to eat him in the end? But no, it graciously acknowledged his greeting and said: "I have been lying here for thousands of years, yet I have never seen a bird like you. Who are you? What are you doing here?"

Sparrow told his story and the great beast listened patiently. Then the little bird asked humbly: "Will you now tell me who you are? We have no animals like you at home."

The great beast laughed and replied: "Humans call me the Sphinx. I am so old that I have lost count of my age. I have seen everything, know everything."

"In my country the owls also say that," was Sparrow's pert response.

The Sphinx looked at him angrily. "The owl is a conceited braggart!" it exclaimed testily.

Sparrow was alarmed. "Forgive me!" he stammered. "I did not wish to offend you. "You also look much older than the owl."

"Indeed I am. I count my years only by the thousands."

"How much you must have seen!" cried Sparrow.

The Sphinx opened her gigantic mouth in such a huge yawn that the sand flew about her as though a whirlwind had hit it.

"For millennia," she said, "I have always observed the same thing. I see humans who live amid riches and pleasures and who force their starving slaves to drudge. At first the slaves were driven with great whips which the overseer used to beat them with when they became tired from the heat of the sun. Often these slaves were kept at work with chains on their feet, so that they could not run away. Later the whips disappeared, and the masters boasted of their kindness, saying, "In these enlightened times, no man is a slave.' But secretly they concealed an invisible whip, hunger, and this drove the people to slavery as surely as the terrible whip the overseers had used previously. I see humans pass here, rich strangers who visit this country out of curiosity, and I see poor Arabs, who work as muleteers, running alongside the mules of the rich, or dragging heavy stones, and barely keeping alive with a few dates and a little corn, just like their ancestors of thousands of years ago."

The Sphinx fell silent and gazed gloomily out into the desert. Finally, she spoke again: "Thousands of years ago, there were gorgeously dressed, bejewelled priests here, who strutted around under the same canopy, next to the rich. They tricked and deceived the people, threatening them with the anger of the gods if they did not suffer their lot patiently. Today, these priests are dressed in black, but they still lie and still stand by the rich, although they worship a god who was a poor carpenter. It has always been the same, for thousands of years." And the Sphinx yawned once more.

"Can you also see into the future, wise Beast?" Sparrow asked shyly.

The Sphinx nodded her enormous head.

"Yes, I can do that too. Listen to my words, little bird. A day will come when all the slaves will rise up in a dreadful struggle against their oppressors. After a long and bloody struggle, they will be victorious, and then a new world will come into being, a world in which everything belongs in common to all, and all humans are free. Even today the earth is trembling in joyful expectation. In the quiet of the night I can feel it quivering. But now you must leave me. For thousands of years I have not spoken to any being. I will speak again only when the day of freedom dawns. Then my voice will join in the jubilation of the liberated peoples."

Sparrow flew out of the desert where he could find nothing to eat, returned to the green stream, and spent many glorious days there.

One day, as he was sitting on a stone by the banks of the stream, he heard familiar voices above him. "Tweet! Tweet!" he heard.

He looked up and saw three swallows who flew slowly down towards him and landed by his side.

"Are you here already?" Sparrow asked in surprise.

"We are, we are indeed," twittered the swallows. "At home rough winds are already blowing and there is frost in the meadows at night. Winter is coming."

How frightened Sparrow was when he heard that. Here in this beautiful land, where he had plenty of fat worms and warm sunshine, he had forgotten about his sparrow brothers. And in the meantime, death-bringing winter had come. He must hurry home to teach them how to get to the sunny land. Would he reach them in time? How selfish he had been; if many poor sparrows were freezing and starving at home, it was his fault.

Even as he was thinking these thoughts, he spread his little wings and flew towards the ocean.

In the harbour many silvery-white seagulls were flying about, crying with shrill voices, "A storm is coming! A storm is coming!"

"Which ship is heading north?" Sparrow asked hurriedly.

"None," one seagull answered. But this was not true. She was a mean bird and wanted to frighten Sparrow.

But he believed her. "Then I must fly over the ocean," he thought. "I must do it, for whether my brother sparrows live or die depends on me. I cannot leave them in the lurch."

Sadly, he looked back on the wonderland once more. Then he flew out over the great ocean.

Wild waves dashed up, the storm howled, and a fine rain fell. Within a few hours, Sparrow was so tired that he could no longer fly high. The huge waves wet his feathers, they became heavy with water and dragged him down, deeper and deeper. A monstrous wave reached out for him with its white arms and Sparrow fell into the ocean and was swallowed by the waves.

Because of that, sparrows must still freeze and starve every winter, for there has not been another courageous sparrow to show them the way to the land of the sun.

But did Sparrow endure so much suffering in vain, and die in vain?

No, for the little dark-haired boy on the ship had paid special attention to the story Sparrow had told him and had listened carefully to what Sparrow wanted to do for his sparrow brothers. And this the little boy wanted to do for his fellow-humans. He grew up, and wherever oppressed workers struggled against their oppressors, he was their leader. But the tale of the dark-haired boy, of his life and his death, is another story and does not belong here.

Der Spatz. Ein Märchen (Berlin: Verein Internationaler Verlags-Anstalten, 1922).
Illustrations by Karl Holtz.

The Spectacles

Once upon a time there was a big, rich country, where quiet and order always reigned. Although in this country too there were rich and poor and the poor were exploited by the rich, not a word of complaint was ever heard, let alone grumbling or threats. The King sat on his golden throne, fat, well-fed, and satisfied; the well-off citizens lived in their fine houses, fat, well-fed, and satisfied; and the poor toiled patiently twelve hours a day in the factories and in the fields. If they did not get paid enough and went hungry, they seemed not to notice it.

Here is how this came about. Many hundreds of years before, a wicked magician, who was a friend of the King's, had lived in this country. This magician had the power to see into the future and he foresaw that the poor would not let themselves be treated like animals for ever, that they would one day demand their rights, and that the grand lifestyle of the kings and the well-off citizens would then become a thing of the past. He wanted to keep this from happening. All his life long, the magician sat in his workshop, cutting glass into little round discs, which he tinted with various colours and made into spectacles. Then he told the king that he and his successors should see to it that each newborn child was immediately fitted with a pair of the spectacles. These were never, on pain of death, to be taken off.

Countless pairs of spectacles, carefully placed on fine pine shavings, were laid out in a vast warehouse. A descendant of the magician was in charge of them. He was immediately informed when a child had come into the world; whereupon he selected the appropriate spectacles for it, and either fitted them himself on the child's tiny nose or had one of his underlings do it.

The Spectacles

The spectacles were of very different kinds. The most complicated were those made for the children of the poor. The old magician had worked on them for almost fifty years, until he finally got them the way he wanted. The lenses were ground in such a way that, when they looked through them, the poor saw their brothers and sisters as very small, helpless, and inferior creatures, but when they looked at the well-off citizens and especially at the King, they saw them through the spectacles as mighty, almost divine beings who were entitled to everything good in the world, whose power no one could resist, and who had the right to make all others into their servants. Finding the right tint for the lenses had also required the old magician to rack his brains for many a day. For the tint had to make the wearer of the spectacles see the wretched hovel he lived in as altogether cosy, comfortable, and agreeable; on the other hand, when he passed by the mansions and gardens of the well-off or the palaces and parks of the King, he was not to see how splendid and grand they were, since he would otherwise ultimately become dissatisfied.

The magician had an easier time producing the spectacles intended for the well-off citizens. Here he had only to mix a little gold or silver with the glass so that, wherever they looked, they would always see only gold and silver, never real living human beings. Moreover, the magician ground the lenses in such a way that the well-off saw the workers as machines made exclusively for their use and benefit.

Making the King's spectacles was the easiest job of all for the magician. They did not even have to be ground. They had only to be dipped once in the blood of the cruellest man who had ever lived and twice in the blood of the dumbest man who had ever lived. When he looked through them the King immediately saw all the things that kings customarily see, in exactly the way that it is suitable for a king to see them.

There were, in addition, a small number of large, rose-coloured spectacles, which were used only very rarely. In the three centuries since the death of the old magician, his descendants had needed to fit them on only three people. These spectacles were intended for a few remarkable individuals who, though fitted with the usual spectacles, still beheld something of how things really are.

For example, there had once been a young poet, a court poet, who lived grandly amid the pleasures of the royal court and enjoyed the admiration and respect of all the better-off citizens. He wrote fine poems in praise of the King and the wisdom of his government and agreeable lyrics for the citizens, extolling their virtues. This young poet could well have been thought to be the happiest man in the world, and in truth he too looked out on it quite cheerfully through his silver-tinted glasses. The citizens were disturbed, it is true, despite their respect for him, by the fact that he did not wish to become majestically fat like them, but as he was, after all, a poet, they forgave him.

But one day it happened that the poet wandered by accident into the section of town where the poor people lived. It was a beautiful summer's day and the sun's rays were so warm that the silver on one of the lenses of his spectacles melted. And so with one eye the poet saw how things really were, and what he saw so shook and scared him that he could not help crying out. He saw tired, toiling men; haggard, sickly women; starving, emaciated children. Except for him, he thought, no one had seen this, and he had to inform everyone. He ran to the better-off citizens, buried his head in his hands and, in tears, told them of the horrors he had seen. They laughed, figuring that he had gone off his head because of the hot weather. Then he looked up and with his one eye saw the reality. "Thieves! Murderers!" he screamed at the citizens, and ran to the King, hoping to get help from him. But when he found the King and saw him sitting on the throne, he had to shout: "You wicked, cruel fool! What right do you have to sit here on the throne?!"

The poet was put in chains, taken away, and would certainly have been executed, had not the magician, who was in charge of the spectacles, put in a good word for him and explained to the King how the mishap had occurred. And so the ranting, raging poet was dragged before the magician, who placed a pair of rose-coloured spectacles on his nose and said: "Your old spectacles had become faulty, my friend, and that is why you thought you saw such terrible things. Go back on to the street now, look around you, and you will see how mistaken you were."

The poet did as he was asked, and now, seen through the rose-coloured spectacles, everything once again appeared good and beautiful to him. Poverty seemed to him something sublime and holy. "Work dignifies and ennobles," he thought. "How fortunate are those who can be ennobled twelve hours a day." In the well-off citizens, he rediscovered his virtuous friends, and when he came before the King, he was dazzled by his splendour and fell on his knees in veneration.

After this incident the entire country once again enjoyed many, many years of quiet and order.

But when the young poet had become an old poet and lay on his deathbed, he pushed the spectacles away from his dying eyes, and in that split second thought he once again saw what he had seen on that summer's day many years before. By his bedside sat a young girl who had spared no pains to take good care of him. The poet reached for her hand and stammered: "The spectacles! Take off the spectacles. Look!" Thereupon he died.

The girl went home to her family pensive and confused. She had not properly understood the dying man's words, for the spectacles affected not only vision but the brain. Yet they stuck in her memory and from time to time she wondered what the world might look like if it was looked at without spectacles.

Soon after, she was married to a shoemaker and when their first child, a sturdy boy, entered the world and she saw his large, shining eyes, she remembered the poet's words and, troubled and perplexed, thought it a shame to conceal those beautiful eyes behind an ugly pair of spectacles. Still, things followed their usual course, the magician came, fitted the spectacles on little Fritz's tiny nose, and so everything was in order.

But something strange happened: little Fritz could not abide the spectacles and kept trying to take them off, so that his parents had to be in constant fear that one day he might succeed in doing so, run out on to the street without spectacles, be caught by the forces of order and, in accordance with the law of the land, be put to death. All their pleas and threats were of no avail, however; as soon as Fritz was alone he would tear and pull at the hated spectacles which had been ingeniously tied to the back of his head.

When the boy was almost fully grown, he finally succeeded from time to time in pulling the spectacles off. And then his startled eyes beheld frightful things: misery, deprivation, and impotent helplessness on the one hand; wealth, high living, splendour, and injustice on the other. But he always caught only a glimpse of this, for on each occasion his mother or sister would soon come running after him, scolding and pleading, weeping and threatening, until they got the spectacles put back on him again.

The little he had been able to get a glimpse of was enough, however, to cause great sadness and also arouse great anger in the boy's heart. He constantly tried to figure out how the world might be rid of the injustice he had perceived. Finally he became convinced that the spectacles were chiefly to blame for it all. If his friends and playmates could only look out on the world without spectacles, they too would recognize the injustice that had been done to them and would also see that they were in no way as weak and helpless as the spectacles had deceived them into thinking they were.

So one day, when his father was away in the workshop and his mother and sister were busy in the kitchen, Fritz tore the spectacles off, stamped on them, and smashed them to smithereens.

He was at first stunned, as if by a blow to the head, by what his seeing eyes now beheld. But then a fire blazed up in his heart that almost consumed him and he swore not to rest or relax until his comrades had also removed their spectacles and recovered their true sight.

But first and foremost it was essential to conceal what he had done from the well-off citizens and the King. Fritz tied a black cloth over his eyes and explained that the light hurt them. The citizens were satisfied with this explanation for they figured that it is even harder to see through a black cloth than through spectacles.

When the darkness of night provided its cover and protection, Fritz slipped out and went to his comrades. He recounted to them all that he had seen, and urged them to throw away their spectacles.

At first they laughed at him, but when he succeeded in talking a number of them into taking off their spectacles for a few short minutes, those who had done so took his side. With time their numbers kept growing, until finally three quarters of the workers had become "anti-spectacles" people.

One day, armed and ready for anything, the "anti-spectacles" people marched out toward the houses of the well-off citizens and the King's palace, pushed their way into the houses, tore the spectacles off the citizens and the King, and demanded their rights. The King was so terrified that he rushed onto the street, began to run, and ran and ran until he came to a country where everyone still wore spectacles and peace and order reigned. At first the well-off citizens prepared to defend themselves, but as they no longer wore spectacles, they could not fail to recognize the might of the "anti-spectacles" people and to acknowledge that they themselves were pathetically dumb scoundrels. Grumbling and with rage in their hearts, they acceded to the demands of the "anti-spectacles" people.

The latter now truly made order in the land: everyone who worked received sufficient pay, anyone who was too lazy to work received nothing. Arrangements were made to take care of the children, the sick, and the elderly, and no one possessed more than he was entitled to.

The country in which the events in this story took place lies in the East, where the sun rises. Perhaps the light is brighter there and so people have learned to see more quickly than in other lands. Yet we all know how fast light travels; it will travel to other lands too and people there will also smash their spectacles. For once they have learned to truly see, they will also act. In those lands that are still in darkness every individual must help by tearing off his own spectacles, informing his comrades of what he has seen, and recruiting people to the "anti-spectacles" party, until their number is so great that they can become the masters of a happy and free world.

"Die Brillen" in *Es war einmal... und es wird sein. Märchen.* Umschlag, Initialen und Bilder zeichnete Heinrich Vogeler (Berlin: Verlag der Jugendinternationale, 1930), pp. 27–31. [First published in *Ali der Teppichweber.* Mit Zeichnungen von John Heartfield (Berlin: Malik-Verlag, 1923), pp. 34–38.]

5. Our Daughters the Nazi Girls. A Synopsis in English

Prepared by Lionel Gossman

The conditions in which *Our Daughters the Nazi Girls* (*Unsere Töchter die Nazinen*) was written, published, and subsequently banned, are briefly described in the essay "Remembering Hermynia Zur Mühlen" which follows this chapter.

Zur Mühlen and her life's partner Stefan Klein both gave their own accounts of the novel's genesis and subsequent fate. Here is Klein's as it appeared in the *Österreichisches Tagebuch* soon after Zur Mühlen's death:

> When we returned on April 1, 1933 to Vienna, her native city and mine, Hermynia was deeply shaken by all the things she had witnessed and experienced in the Third Reich, and as she observed the general lack of concern among the Austrians, she became truly obsessed with the desire to tell them what was really going on in the 'fraternal' German land and what Austria, which she still thought of as her beloved homeland, should expect. The only way she could do this was by writing. But 'in the shadow of the Third Reich,' some 'democratic' editors — men who, in their snobbery, would otherwise have been flattered by a visit from a countess — refused even to receive 'the damned Red.' Even a truly dear and decent features-page editor told her that he could do absolutely nothing with the sort of thing she had written and that she should bring him humorous sketches that would make readers 'split their sides laughing' (his very words). When we got back to our rented room in the Alserstrasse, Hermynia, in despair, flew into a rage. In the three weeks that followed, she did not write a single humorous sketch. Instead, she

completed at one go the novel *Unsere Töchter, die Nazinen*, which was published by the Gsur Press of Dr. Karl Winter, a leftwing Catholic former vice-mayor of Vienna and a critic of the Dolfuss dictatorship,[1] only to be banned two weeks later at the behest of Hitler's ambassador to Austria, Franz von Papen.[2]

In a supplementary chapter written in 1950 for a post-war republication of *The End and the Beginning* (*Ende und Anfang*), Zur Mühlen had already given her version of the circumstances in which she wrote her novel and of the difficulties she experienced as she tried to get it published:

---

1 Klein's brief characterisation of Winter needs to be nuanced. See "Notes on Persons and Events mentioned in the Memoir" under "Gsur Verlag", p. 272, and the essay "Remembering Hermynia Zur Mühlen: A Tribute," note 33.

2 Klein's testimony is quoted in Manfred Altner, *Hermynia Zur Mühlen*, pp. 140–41. The text of the German Embassy protest (dated 17 December 1935) is reproduced in facsimile on http://www.literaturepochen.at/exil/multimedia/image/hzm2.jpg Roughly translated, it reads: "The German Embassy has the honour to inform the Foreign Affairs section of the Chancellor's office that among the anti-National Socialist writings published by the Gsur Publishing Company a book has recently appeared, the overall content of which is full of derogatory and defamatory comments about the National Socialist movement in the Reich. Worse still, there are seriously offensive remarks about the Führer and Reichskanzler Adolf Hitler and members of the government of the Reich in innumerable places, and also insulting statements about the German Ambassador von Papen. The book is *Unsere Töchter die Nazinen*, listed as a novel, by Hermynia Zur Mühlen. The aforementioned directly offensive comments appear on pp. 20, 32, 47, 50, 80, 125/26, 138, and 155. For example, p. 20: 'The swindler, the charlatan, the guy who can only open his mouth and yell and who is in the pay of heavy industry, Hitler'; p. 32: 'What this Party (the NSDAP) is made up of — the leader, the members, the fellow-travellers — is scum.'" The Austrian government official's comments on the note (marked "Urgent") read as follows: "The novel that appeared with Gsur Verlag, Vienna, contains a series of severe personal attacks and insults directed against Reichskanzler Hitler, as well as Goering and Goebbels. There are also some remarks about Herr von Papen on p. 103. Apart from its hostile attitude to National Socialism, the novel is marked by a strong Marxist, indeed Communist orientation (pp. 112, 127, etc.), along with comments indicating a free-thinking, anti-religious position. All 'good' characters in the novel are for the most part members of Communist organizations, some are Social Democrats. The Soviet Union is the object only of friendly comment. One of the leading characters in the novel, an old Countess, is converted to Communism and indeed to active terrorism at the end. It almost seems as though a clear line of social revolutionary propaganda is being pursued beneath the mask of hostility to National Socialism." The recommendation is that the book be immediately banned and all copies confiscated, "less on account of the offences to Hitler, [which would be punishable] in virtue of the law protecting the honour and respect due to foreign heads of state, than on account of the virtually unconcealed marxist-communist propaganda in it (see, for instance, pp. 112, 123, etc.)." See http://www.literaturepochen.at/exil/multimedia/image under "hzm1" through "hzm5" for relevant documents.

I immediately got it into my head that the people here had to be warned. We had to write the truth about National Socialism, we had to write it day and night, we had to write it when it was convenient for us to write and when it was not convenient for us. Somehow we had to get the indifferent to open their eyes to the frightful truth — and to the terrible danger threatening Austria. But in this enterprise I was not very successful. Only very few newspapers — among them the *Arbeiter-Zeitung* — agreed from time to time to publish an anti-Nazi short story. Most wanted humorous stories. When one features-pages editor explained that he did not want anti-Nazi things and that I should bring him entertaining little sketches that would make readers split their sides laughing, I flew into such a rage, that I went home, sat down at my desk, and in three weeks wrote my anti-Nazi novel *Unsere Töchter die Nazinen*. It took a good deal longer than three weeks to find a publisher for it. This novel had a strange fate: every publisher who was given a copy to consider, declared he was willing to publish it — on condition that certain passages were altered or eliminated, Every one of them was bothered by something different. But I was unwilling to make the required changes, since I believed they would result in a false representation of the way things truly were. Then I took the novel to Schiller Marmorek, the Socialist, who, with his genuine friendship and infinite willingness to come to the assistance of others, was helping greatly to make our lives easier. (In my first youthful enthusiasm for socialism, I had imagined all socialists were like him.) I shall always think of him with love and gratitude.[3] He read the novel and recommended it to Julius Braunthal. Braunthal did not let himself be put out by certain esthetic shortcomings, from which, from his point of view, the book unavoidably suffered, and he agreed to publish it. Naturally, I was delighted — but he wrote at the end of January 1934. Then February came,[4] and the manuscript disappeared without a trace. After the assassination of Dolfuss, the book was finally put out by the publishing house of Gsur, without any changes, only to be banned two weeks later at the behest of Von Papen. Proceedings were instituted against me, the

---

3   On Schiller Marmorek, see "Notes on Persons and Events Mentioned in the Memoir," p. 271.
4   In February 1934, weapons searches by the extreme rightwing Dollfuss regime among members of the already outlawed "Republican Defence League" [*Republikanischer Schutzbund*] and the arrest of many well known Social Democrats led to calls for nationwide resistance to the government. A limited civil war broke out (February 12–15), with some of the fiercest fighting in the districts in Vienna where the celebrated workers' apartments built by the leftwing municipality were situated. The resistance was put down by the police and the military; the Social Democrats were outlawed; and their leaders were imprisoned or fled abroad. On Braunthal (b. 1891), who, like Marmorek, was Jewish, see "Notes on Persons and Events Mentioned in the Memoir," p. 271.

sole effect of which was that from that time on I received a monthly visit from a detective, who inquired in a friendly manner how I was getting along, said: "You haven't got up to anything, have you?", politely kissed my hand, and left. The good man must have been very well informed, moreover, for about a month before the *Anschluss* he advised us to move to Czechoslovakia where the climate, he said, might well be healthier for us. Even after the Liberation the unfortunate little book still could not find a publisher. Although the spirit of National Socialism is by no means dead, publishers once again prefer humorous novels.[5]

Finally, Klein gave an even fuller account of the episode in a letter to Wilhelm Sternfeld, dated 18.4.1951:

When we came back to Vienna in April 1933, my wife tried to place anti-Nazi pieces warning people in all possible newspapers. People laughed at her and made fun of her warnings, just as they did later in Slovakia. ('Such things can't happen here!'). When the *feuilleton* editor of an otherwise uncompromisingly anti-Nazi paper told her he wanted not horror stories from her but humorous sketches that would make readers split their sides laughing, she flew into a rage, came home, and wrote the novel *Unsere Töchter die Nazinen* in the space of three weeks... The Allert de Lange firm (Amsterdam) [an important publisher of "exile" German literature — L.G.] said it was willing to publish the novel if my wife would present the workers in a less "positive" light. My wife refused. The Malik-Verlag (Wieland Herzfelde), then located in Prague, was ready to print the novel if a female character in it, a Communist who becomes a Nazi, were recast as a Social Democrat who becomes a Nazi. My wife again refused. The Oprecht firm in Zurich [another major publisher of exile literature — L.G.] declared it would publish the novel if my wife — a penniless writer — would guarantee the translation fees of 800 Swiss francs. That was impossible for financial reasons. The editor-in-chief of the Social Democratic *Kleines Blatt*, Julius Braunthal, accepted the novel and planned to bring it out in a large, popular edition at a low price... Then came February. The novel could not be published. The manuscript vanished from the printing press of the *Arbeiter-Zeitung*. After the assassination of Dolfuss, it was published by the left-wing Catholic Gsur Press of Dr. Ernst Karl Winter, but, within two weeks, at von Papen's behest, all copies were confiscated and proceedings

---

5   Final chapter of the serialized republication of *Ende und Anfang* in the socialist woman's magazine *Die Frau* October 6, 1949–April 20, 1950, reprinted in *Nebenglück: Ausgewählte Erzählungen und Feuilletons aus dem Exil von Hermynia Zur Mühlen*, ed. Deborah J. Vietor-Engländer, Eckart Früh and Ursula Seeber (Bern: Peter Lang, 2002), pp. 243–55 also pp. 167-68 of the present volume.

instituted against my wife. However, as she had voluntarily renounced all royalties from the book, even though she was in financial straits, in order that the book might be sold at a very low price, "idealist motives" were acknowledged... and the proceedings were dropped. (But the book was still banned and all copies were destroyed.)[6]

Unsere Töchter die Nazinen — the term "Nazine" was an invention of Zur Mühlen's and has a satirical ring to it — did in fact make its way into print two years before its short-lived publication in 1936 by the Gsur Verlag in Vienna. It appeared in instalments in the Social Democratic Saarbrücken newspaper *Deutsche Freiheit*[7] between June and August 1934 — a few months before the referendum of January 13, 1935, in which the Saar voted overwhelmingly to rejoin the German Reich.[8] It thus formed part of the campaign to persuade the Saarlanders to reject reincorporation in the Reich. It was also published that same year (1934) in a Norwegian translation, as *De tok vare dotre* [*They Took Our Daughters*], by the Tiden Norsk Forlag in Oslo, a new press founded by the Norwegian Labour Party. (Tiden Norsk was the only publishing house shut down by the Germans during the occupation of Norway.)

***

---

6   Quoted by Beate Frakele, "'Ich als Österreicherin...' Hermynia Zur Mühlen [1883–1951]," in Johann Holzner et al., eds., *Eine schwierige Heimkehr. Österreichische Literatur im Exil, 1938–1945* [Innsbruck: Institut für Germanistik, 1991], pp. 378–79).

7   The editor-in-chief of *Deutsche Freiheit* was the Socialist Wilhelm Sollmann. A member of the National Assembly in Weimar in 1919, Sollmann was elected to the German Parliament in 1920, served on its foreign affairs committee, and was the founder and director of the Social Democratic Press Service. He sat on the executive board of the SPD and was one of the first Socialists to be beaten up, imprisoned, and tortured by the Nazis in 1933, but managed to escape to Luxemburg and then to the Saar, against the French occupation of which, ironically, he had demonstrated in the early 1920s. After the referendum of 1935, he fled to England and from there to the United States. He taught international affairs at Haverford, Swarthmore, and Reed Colleges and became an American citizen. Sollmann died in the U.S. in 1951.

8   "I believed that even at very worst, a bit more than 50 percent of the Saarlanders would vote for the status quo, that is for anti-Fascism," the Austrian writer Manès Sperber wrote. "The fact that in this free election 98 percent had hurried to the polls made us even more hopeful. This made the results even more terrible; they were shattering. [...] We had not been defeated but [...] pulverized: 90.3 percent wanted to 'come home to the Reich' immediately, and only 8.8 percent had voted against it. In that region of miners and industrial workers, the Catholics, Socialists and Communists had not even been able to induce 10 percent of the electorate to oppose solidarity with Nazi Germany." (*Until my Eyes are Closed with Shards*, transl. Harry Zohn [New York and London: Holmes & Meier, 1994], pp. 61–62)

As a deliberately political and polemical work, *Unsere Töchter die Nazinen* does not have the nuanced historical and psychological richness characteristic of Zur Mühlen's major works of narrative fiction, such as *Das Riesenrad* (1932; Engl. transl. *The Wheel of Life*, 1933), *Reise durch ein Leben* (1933; *A Life's Journey*, 1935), and *Ewiges Schattenspiel* (serialized in the Bern newspaper *Der Bund*, 1938–39; *We Poor Shadows*, 1943) or even of lighter works that Deborah Vietor-Engländer, one of the Austrian writer's few champions, has described — somewhat unjustly in my view — as "potboilers," such as *Nora hat eine famose Idee* (1933; *Guests in the House*, 1947) or the quite witty and ingenious *Vierzehn Nothelfer* (serialized in the Vienna *Arbeiter-Zeitung*, 1933).[9] It does not move the reader and provoke a wide range of reflections, as those other works do. Instead, it is narrowly focused on exposing an immediate political situation and on provoking a practical response to it. One might say that it is related to the author's other works as a political cartoon is related to an oil painting.

Its structure is unusually tight, clearly outlined, and symmetrical for a work by Zur Mühlen. It consists of six interlocking parts, each of which is a first person narrative. The narrators are three women, three mothers of three daughters in a small town on the shores of Lake Constance in Southern Germany, representing three major social classes — Kati Gruber, a working class widow and staunch Social Democrat like her late husband Anton; Countess Agnes, the widowed descendant of an old aristocratic family, who has withdrawn, after a lonely childhood and an unhappy marriage, to a villa by the lakeside where she spends her days in a world of her own; and Frau Doktor Feldhüter, the socially ambitious middle-class wife of a scheming, equally ambitious doctor, who has a club foot, like Goebbels, and whose practice lags far behind that of the long-established and caring local Jewish doctor.

Each of the women has two narratives — an earlier narrative (just prior to the elections of March 1933, which gave the Nazi Party a majority of seats in the Reichstag), and a somewhat later narrative (shortly after the elections). These are arranged symmetrically in the

---

9   Deborah Vietor-Engländer, "Hermynia Zur Mühlen's Fight Against the 'Enemy Within: Prejudice, Injustice, Cowardice and Intolerance'," in *Keine Klage über England? Deutsche und Österreichische Exilerfahrung in Großbritannien 1933–1945*, ed. Charmian Brinson et al. (Munich: Iudicium, 1998), pp. 74–87.

following sequence: Kati Gruber (first narrative), Countess Agnes (first narrative), Frau Doktor Feldhüter (first narrative), Frau Doktor Feldhüter (second narrative), Countess Agnes (second narrative), Kati Gruber (second narrative). The novel thus turns full circle, opening and closing on the testimony of the Social Democratic working-class woman. The testimony of the ambitious and opportunistic middle-class Frau Doktor Feldhüter occupies the centre, where it stands in striking contrast to the accounts of the other two women.

While Zur Mühlen is often ironical in her writing, here, in the testimony attributed to the Doctor's wife, she exhibits a remarkable talent for sustained and vigorous satire. The distance between the narratorial voice of the novel and the voice of the character as narrator of her testimony is minimal in the first and last two testimonies; in the case of the two central testimonies by the scheming but unintelligent Frau Doktor, in contrast, the narrator of the novel maintains maximum distance from the voice of the narrating character. This stylistic feature unites the Frau Doktor's two testimonies, which are otherwise given a formal distinction intended to reflect the fact that the electoral triumph of the National Socialists, which occurred between the first and the second, significantly affected their content and tone. Whereas — appropriately in view of her social class and her self-described impulse to express her feelings openly — both Kati Gruber's testimonies are represented as spoken and both Countess Agnes's testimonies — appropriately in view of her social class and reclusive life — are represented as written into a personal diary, Frau Doktor Feldhüter's two testimonies are delivered differently. The first — before the elections confirm the Nazi hold on power — is said to be "whispered" ("Frau Doktor Feldhüter erzählt flüsternd"). This corresponds both to the opportunistic Feldhüter's insistence that his wife keep her mouth shut prudently in public until the political situation has become absolutely clear and to the Frau Doktor's feeling that she counts for nothing, either in society or in her own family, where she is respected neither by her husband nor by her daughter. Her thoughts and her feelings of frustration, rage, and resentment must be concealed not only from the public but from her family and may only be "whispered" to herself. The second testimony — after the Nazis are securely entrenched in power, the super-cautious Feldhüter has publicly declared his family's support for the movement, and the Frau

Doktor has finally realized her dream of being respected as "somebody" in the small town — is represented, in contrast, as told "out loud."

There are already signs in the first testimony of the Frau Doktor's capacity for rewriting her own history and of her quite extraordinary Sartrean bad faith. For instance, by the time Hitler has been appointed Chancellor, she has reinterpreted her previously avowed attraction, when she was still an unmarried hospital nurse, to a handsome, young, and, above all, very well-to-do Jewish patient, and her eagerness to marry him (the marriage was frustrated by the opposition of the young man's parents to their son's marrying a non-Jew) as a — fortunately unsuccessful — attempt by a filthy Jew to sully a pure German maiden. Likewise a fleeting night of love with a handsome young Austrian — her unique, barely confessed infidelity as Feldhüter's wife — is recalled at a later point in the narrative as a cunning attack on her Protestant virtue by a Jesuitical Catholic foreigner, while the young man's lack of interest in pursuing the relationship is explained as the consequence of the awe inspired in him by German womanhood. In the second testimony, however, not only does the Frau Doktor appear as a changed person, sure of herself and increasingly aggressive, but the feelings, situations, and events recounted in the narrative that she "whispered" are totally reconfigured. The hatred, contempt, and physical repulsion she feels for her physically impaired, mean-spirited, ever calculating, and affectless husband and admits to in the "whispered" narrative is suppressed in the second narrative and replaced by expressions of admiration, love, and devotion The abortion Dr. Feldhüter performed when his flirtatious daughter, who is chiefly interested in having a good time, had "ein Malheur" vanishes from memory in the second narrative as the Doctor and his wife loudly champion the breeding duty of healthy Aryan German women and condemn the selfishness of those who avoid this obligation. Upper-class and aristocratic ladies, whose recognition had been craved — vainly — in the "whispered" testimony, are loudly suspected in the second narrative of having Jewish ancestors. With the electoral victory of the National Socialists, in sum, the Frau Doktor's covert narrative of repressed envy, resentment, rage, and frustrated ambition explodes into a triumphant, exemplary narrative which is not only adopted by the speaker herself but offered for public consumption in the new German Reich. The ugly reality of envy, resentment, and rage underlying the heroic "Aryan" façade of National Socialism is thus exposed through the Frau Doktor's double narrative of the life of the Feldhüters and in particular of her own relation to her husband, her daughter Lieselotte, and other members of the community.

Zur Mühlen also uses the successive testimonies adroitly to advance the narrative gradually through time. Each one reflects a slightly later stage in the historical evolution toward total Nazi dominance of the life of the little town; each one bears witness to the lawlessness and organized violence that increasingly characterize everyday life. At the same time, there is sufficient overlap to allow for anticipations in one narrative of what will be developed more fully in the succeeding one as well as for contrasting versions of the same events by different narrators.

The tour de force of *Unsere Töchter die Nazinen* is to have located the complex issue of the rise of National Socialism not only in the social history of the time — war, revolution, inflation, economic depression, unemployment — but in the personal life experiences and family relationships of the characters, which are, in turn, seen as influenced by social class and class ethos. The focus of the novel might be said to be, in short, on the way family relations both affect and are dramatically affected by politics.

***

The opening narrative by Kati Gruber provides the basic historical background for the novel — and at the same time the elements of a general historical explanation of the rise of National Socialism. While in service as a maid with Countess Agnes, we learn, Kati met and married Anton, a good-looking working man with a steady job as a typesetter. The marriage is soon blessed with a child. Kati might have died giving birth to her daughter, however, had not the Countess called in her own doctor, the compassionate Jewish Dr. Bär, who often treated the poor of the little town without charge and who, it turns out later, is a Social Democrat like Anton. Kati, who is not well-read and does not know much about politics, greatly admires her husband, a model of the serious, self-educated, and well-informed member of the working class. She shares his Social Democratic political convictions, partly because she trusts his judgment and partly because her common sense and her instinct, as a woman and a mother, tell her what he has learned by reading and reflection. Like all Social Democrats, Anton believes in a new and better world in the future, after a time of struggle and hardship. The War comes, however, and with it the first significant setback to Social Democratic hopes. Anton had long foreseen that the ruling class would instigate a war, Kati recounts, but he had been convinced that in every country the workers would refuse to serve. Normally strong and in full control of himself, he wept when the Social Democrats in the Reichstag voted the necessary credits for the Kaiser's war and when workers' organizations everywhere went along with the policies of their national governments. Women might have been expected to be opposed to the war, Kati reflects, but in fact many women, no less swayed by nationalist fervour than their menfolk, enthusiastically supported it. Anton, in contrast, predicted that it would be a bloody and ugly affair. And so it was. Many local boys who had been fired by patriotic zeal never came home from the front, many others returned maimed and incapable of supporting themselves or their families. For those behind the lines, the problem was the ever worsening shortage of food. Kati's daughter Toni began to look like a starving stray cat. Once again Countess Agnes helped her former servant out as much as she could, but her resources were stretched as she was trying to help others too. Her own daughter Claudia, nineteen years old by then, was nothing but skin and bone. Only the ten-year-old daughter of Dr. Feldhüter had fat, rosy cheeks, Kati reports. That, she explains, was because, with Dr. Bär serving at the front, Feldhüter, who, like Goebbels, had been exempted from military service because of his club foot, was temporarily the only doctor in town.

Anton is one of the lucky ones who return from the war unharmed. But once again he is disappointed. The war is over, Germany has become a republic, and the Social Democrats are in power. But they do little to bring about the far-reaching social changes they advocate. As a result, there is a splintering of the left into rival groups — Communists, Independent Socialists, and Social Democrats. Anton is concerned that in its eagerness to establish its credentials as a responsible defender of the new constitution, the Social Democratic government has adopted harsh policies toward its rivals on the Left, while pursuing a more accommodating and lenient policy toward its opponents on the right — even though the irreconcilable hostility of the latter was clearly demonstrated by the failed Kapp putsch. On the material side, the war reparations are a heavy burden on the defeated country and the uncontrolled hyperinflation of 1922 makes life extraordinarily hard for working people. Kati finds some solace in Toni's growing up to be a fine young woman, tall and reflective like her father, and like him, an avid reader and stalwart socialist. She and her father march in the May Day parades, proudly bearing the red flag. Toni's boyfriend at this time is a young Communist and Toni is soon touting the merits of Soviet Russia and comparing it favourably with Germany. Anton worries about his daughter: he fears that she is in for a hard time because of her idealism and her unwillingness to recognize that the road to socialism will be accompanied by many setbacks and disappointments, which it will take patience, determination, and shrewdness to overcome. Kati, for her part, notices with some misgivings that Toni has inherited her father's undemonstrativeness and laconicity, his way of keeping his thoughts and feelings to himself.

Meantime there is a new development in the little town. The National Socialists are gaining ground, making new recruits, parading noisily through the streets, claiming they are the only party that is both socialist and German, fostering enmity between Christians and Jews, and announcing their intention to get rid of the Marxists along with the Jews, since both groups, according to them, are behind Germany's misery. When Kati calls a young Nazi recruit — the errand-boy from the local dairy-farm, whom she has known since he was a child — an utter idiot for being taken in by the Nazi propaganda about "internationalist," un-German Jews and Marxists, she finds a large swastika painted on her door the next day.

After Anton falls sick and dies, Kati takes in washing and mending clothes to make up for the loss of his wages. Toni's Communist boyfriend Seppel wants to help out but Toni rejects his offers and Kati notices that the two are no longer on as good terms as they once were. Meanwhile the depression has hit the little town and there is rising unemployment. Of the many who are let go at the factory where Toni is employed, most of the white-collar workers and a fair sprinkling of blue-collar workers join the Nazi Party. Street fights between Nazis and Social Democrats and between Nazis and Communists erupt more and more frequently. On January 3, 1931, the factory is closed altogether and Toni too is out of a job. She looks desperately for work, but in vain. Kati finds employment as a cleaning woman for a couple of middle class families and with the income from that and Toni's unemployment benefits, she says, the two of them could have scraped by. But Toni is restless and frustrated, like a caged animal. She spends her time studying the books in Anton's little collection and she and Seppel quarrel more and more frequently and heatedly. She also begins to quarrel with Kati too, as well as with her long-time friends from the Social Democratic movement. "I did not hold it against her," Kati explains. "I knew that idleness and anxiety about the future were eating away at her." (p. 19)[10]

As the 1932 elections for Reichspräsident approach, Kati is surprised that "our Party" (i.e. the Social Democrats) has pledged its support to Hindenburg. "After all, the old man is still a Junker and isn't a proper President for a workers' party." Still, she reflects, he had held to his oath to defend the constitution. "He may not be very smart, he may not sympathize with the workers, but he is an honourable, decent man and he will keep his word." (p. 19) Seppel tries to persuade them both to vote for the Communist candidate, Ernst Thälmann. Kati sticks loyally to the Social Democratic party recommendation. Toni's unexpected and vehement reaction, however, hits Kati like a thunderbolt and opens the central scene of her first narrative.

"Your Thälmann has to dance to Moscow's tune," Toni objects. "I wouldn't dream of giving him my vote." Seppel gets angry. He can understand that Kati, a loyal Social Democrat for so long, will follow the party line and vote for "the old man," but Toni? Toni responds that she has no intention of voting for the old man. "I have to tell you something," she adds. "This international socialism doesn't mean a thing to us Germans. We've seen how much help we got from the International. What we need is German socialism, a socialism that is right for *our* country." Seppel stares at her: "What do you mean by that?" Toni looks at her mother, then at Seppel. "I don't know yet," she replies, somewhat embarrassed. "But when I vote it will be for a leader of the workers." "So you mean Teddy [Thälmann] after all," Seppel cries. "Silly girl, why didn't you say so right away?" But Toni answers: "There is someone else." For a moment, Kati does not understand.

---

10 Page references are to Hermynia Zur Mühlen, *Unsere Töchter die Nazinen* (Vienna: Gsur Verlag, n.d. [1936]).

But Seppel immediately grasps who is meant: "That swindler, that charlatan? Have you lost your mind? A lowdown bum who can only shout and scream and is in the pay of the big industrialists — Hitler?" Kati feels a weakness in her knees. That cannot be what her Toni means, what Anton's child means. Seeing how pale Kati has become, Seppel sits down beside her and tries to comfort her. "She is just having us on, comrade," he says. "She's far too smart to do anything like that." But after a moment's silence Toni gives her response in a tormented and sad tone of voice: "I have so much time to think about things now, Seppel," she says. "And I've realized that none of the promises of 1918 have been fulfilled. Our Chancellor is a man of the Centre and the Party [the Social Democrats] lets him get away with everything he wants, every single emergency decree, everything. The Communists yell, but do nothing. The others [the National Socialists] have a program that is right for Germany. No, don't say anything yet. I'm not completely sure yet where I stand. But I have a sense that the real revolutionary energy is now with them. And that's what it's all about. All the parties have disappointed us. We have to give the National Socialists a chance to show what they can do. They'll help the German worker, they'll get rid of the greedy capitalists, and they'll nationalize the big industrial companies. They'll release us from the peace treaties and our country will become strong again, a strong workers' state." (p. 20) Kati is flabbergasted. "My God, Toni, where did you get all this?" Toni answers in her quiet, serious way ("as though trying to excuse herself," Kati thinks): "I have so much time on my hands, so many vacant hours. And I know that if things go on the way they are, I will never find work again. But I want to work. I've read the National Socialist newspapers, I've spoken with National Socialists, and just recently I went to a meeting and heard the Führer speak." Seppel strikes the table with his fist. "The Führer! The Führer! If you already speak like that, you're a lost cause. You... you Nazi Girl!"[11] Whereupon he picks up his cap and runs out of the room without a good-bye. (pp. 20–21)

Kati now questions her daughter. "You can't be serious, Toni? You can't, I won't let you do that." "Let me be, mother," Toni replies. "We all have to work this out for ourselves." Suddenly Kati is overcome by rage: "You are not going to any more Nazi meetings, do you hear. You

---

11   The German reads "Du... du Nazine!"

will have nothing more to do with that mob." But Toni has her answer ready. "Many years ago the Social Democrats were also called a 'mob,' mother. I read that in father's books. Besides, I'm not a child any more. No one tells me what to do and what not to do." Kati resorts to pleas and what few arguments she can muster, but Toni is unmoved. "Don't torture me, mother, please. It's no use... Do you think it was easy for me to break with everything I've believed in for so long? Look, I'm a working class girl. I have to be on the side of those who side with us. Not with a Herr von Hindenburg and not with a man who takes his orders from a foreign country and from the Jews, but with an honest German worker and with a party that is being persecuted just because it *is* revolutionary." (p. 22)

After this exchange, Kati and Toni grow more and more estranged. Toni keeps reading Anton's old books, but also the new books and pamphlets being put out by the Nazis. Kati does not know how her daughter voted in the April 1932 runoff elections for President and does not dare to ask. [Hitler had placed second behind Hindenburg in March but as Hindenburg had not won a clear majority the constitution required a runoff election. — L.G.] Meanwhile the situation in the little town is going from bad to worse. The Nazis are attracting more and more supporters, especially after the lifting of the ban on uniforms. There are more and more threats and attacks against Jews and Socialists. Two workers are killed; the culprits never found. One evening after dinner, Toni puts on her coat and goes out. Kati knows she is going to a big Nazi rally. "If only Anton were still alive" she thinks, "our Toni would not be where she is today. He would have explained everything to her and she would not have let herself be taken in by stupid slogans. I know my Toni. I know she acts only out of conviction. But she is just not as smart as her father was. Still, she is smarter than me, and so she doesn't listen to me." (pp. 25–26) At this point, Kati hears shouting and bawling from the street: "Heil Hitler!" "Deutschland ewache!" [Germany awake!]. "Juda verrecke!" [Death to the Jews!] Then comes the Horst Wessel song "and then another with the line 'Wenn das Judenblut vom Messer spritzt!'" [When under the knife spurts the blood of Jews] She thinks of Dr. Bär, who lives in the same street and must also have heard it. What must he feel, she wonders, after spending his life taking care of the sick in the little town and never sending a bill to the poor?

Suddenly the door opens and Toni enters wearing a swastika badge. She greets Kati with a "Good evening, mother," then hangs up her wet coat. Kati cannot respond. Words stick in her throat. She looks at the Swastika sign and her thoughts course wildly through her brain. Toni nods. "Yes, mother," she says, "it's our only salvation, even if you don't believe it. When the Führer comes to power, there will be jobs for everybody." Kati is overcome by rage: "I was never so angry in my whole life. I berated my child as though she were the lowest of the low. I spoke the coarsest and harshest words. I wanted to give her a thrashing. Finally I screamed. 'Get out of this house and don't come back, you swastika trollop, you are a curse on me.'" Toni does not answer. "She has a way of keeping silent that reminds me of Anton," Kati explains. "She just stood there, then turned and went for her coat, bending down first to wipe up the little pool of water that had dripped from it. 'I'll just wipe this up, mother, then I'll go,'" she says. Suddenly Kati feels a sharp pain shooting through her heart. "What am I doing? Driving out my child, our child, my Anton's daughter? Yes, she is Anton's daughter. But she is also a swastika type, she has become our enemy. She has betrayed us. Still, she is our child. Who else should try to have patience with her, if not me?" At that point, though Toni never cries, Kati sees two tears running down her daughter's cheeks. She relents. "Stay," she says, "stay, I spoke in anger." Toni looks at her, her eyes still full of tears. "I don't want to leave you, mother," she says. "But you need to think this over. I'm in the National Socialist Party now. I'll often act in ways you can't understand. But, believe me, as soon as the Führer comes to power, everything will be all right, and you too will see where the workers really belong." (p. 26) "She spoke so earnestly, so from the heart, my Toni," Kati notes, "that I knew no words could get her to change her mind... Maybe later on she will see that she has been bamboozled by liars and cheats. But I'm not the one who can get her to see it." She simply tells Toni to go to bed. Toni "came over to me and wanted to kiss me — which normally she does only on my birthday. Even as a child she was never demonstrative." But as Toni bends down to kiss her — for she is a head taller — Kati sees the swastika sign again and turns her head away, "as though I wanted to look at the clock to see the time." Toni, however, is not fooled and quietly sighs. Suddenly Kati reflects that Anton's photograph is hung over Toni's bed and she has the feeling that he will see the swastika and be upset. She tells Toni to wait a moment while she goes into the room and stealthily removes the photograph. "My Anton should not be in the same room with a swastika," she thinks. (p. 27) Nevertheless, "from that day on I never again had a swastika painted on my door; for I had one right here in my own home." (pp. 27–29)

A few days later she has a momentary pleasure. The "old man" [Hindenburg] seemed to want to keep his oath to preserve the constitution — albeit not much of it remained — for he had refused to accept Hitler as Chancellor. But the Nazis only laughed. They demanded nothing less than total power, they jeered, and they would get it. By now it had become dangerous to show the Social Democratic three arrows sign in the street.[12] Kati shows it all the same, partly out of fidelity to the party but also a little, as she says, "because nothing mattered much to me any more and I wouldn't have cared if I had got beaten up by our enemies." (p. 29) The only thing that now worried her was that Toni might get hurt by "one of our people" when she was marching in one of the frequent Nazi processions. Toni, she knew, had the same worry about her, for she kept trying to keep her from going out and wanted to pick up and deliver the washing she did for people. But that was not possible, Kati, explains. All her clients were opposed to the Nazis and would have refused to do business with a girl wearing a swastika. In any case, the danger was not so great in daytime for the Nazis preferred to beat up people at night, when they could easily slip away, and were satisfied with verbal abuse at other times. Though mother and daughter, while still living under one roof, now communicated little, Kati could not refrain, on one occasion, from bringing up the way the Nazis fall upon defenceless people: "Don't you see what a bunch of cowards they are. They attack people who can't defend themselves and they do all their shooting and stabbing in the dark. And this is the crowd you belong to!" (p. 30) Kati can spot that Toni is upset. "The daughter of my Anton could not justify such actions; and she did not try. She said

---

12 A circle with three arrows shooting downward through it to the left was the symbol adopted by the Social Democrats in opposition to the Nazi swastika and the Communist hammer and sickle.

nothing and looked depressed."[13] Kati wonders what will happen when Toni's eyes are finally opened to the truth about the Nazis.

At the same time she derives some consolation from the fact that Toni acts out of conviction, not opportunism — unlike most of those who join the Nazi Party, according to Kati. For of the large numbers who were now flocking to the Nazis, "most were doing so because they expected to get something out of it" or because, if they were young, they could strut around and be important in their Nazi uniforms, or if they were workers, because they were desperate after having been out of work for so long and because the Nazis promised them jobs.

Still, her unhappiness weighs on Kati and she goes to the villa by the lake to unburden herself to her old employer Countess Agnes, who has always been kind to her. After Kati tells her story, the Countess is silent for a moment. "Then her face turned deep red. 'Your Toni, with that rabble?' she said. Whereupon her face grew even redder and she looked apologetically at me. 'You know what I mean by that rabble, don't you, Kati? I don't mean the workers. Everyone in that party is rabble — the leaders, the members, the fellow-travellers.' Heaven knows the woman was speaking what was in my own heart, but somehow it bothered me that she had thrown my Toni to the rabble, so to speak, and so I said maliciously: 'There are quite a few aristocrats in it.' The old woman laughed. I think she knew why I had made the comment. They are the worst rabble of all,' she said. 'The very worst. For they have no excuse.'"

At this point the Countess's still unmarried, thirty-year old daughter Claudia, whose sullenness and resentfulness had given her mother so much to worry about over the years, came into the room. Kati was surprised and pleased to see how well the once plain, discontented young woman now looked. "How good Claudia looks," she says. "She seems ten years younger." The old woman laughs joyfully. "Yes, I'm so pleased about it. She no longer avoids people. She runs into town every day. And everything interests her. She reads the papers, she listens to the radio. I think she is normal again at long last." (pp. 32–33)

---

13   Outrage at attacks on the weak and defenceless is a recurrent motif of Zur Mühlen's writing — both in longer works like *Reise durch ein Leben* and *Ein Jahr im Schatten* and in short *feuilletons* like "Man muß es ihnen sagen." It can doubtless be traced to the stories of chivalrous knights that she read with her grandmother as a child. As often happens, an old aristocratic virtue is reinterpreted by Zur Mühlen as universally human.

For their part, Kati and Toni continue to live together. When Kati's rheumatism flares up, Toni helps out by taking over the housework as well as the washing Kati takes in to earn a few pennies. Kati has only to pick it up and deliver it. Toni does the rest. But they cannot communicate with each other. By Christmas, because of rheumatism in her hands, Kati has not been able to finish a sweater she was knitting for Toni. She has dusted off a little Christmas tree and lit the candles on it — "not because I am religious, but because we always used to do it for Toni when she was little" — and she is upset that without the sweater she now has no Christmas present to put under the tree. When a package arrives for Toni, Kati is relieved. It can go under the tree. Toni tries to reassure her that she doesn't mind if there isn't anything under the tree. But Kati insists, gets hold of the package, and opens it. Toni snatches it out of her hands, but it is too late. Kati has seen that it is a copy of Hitler's *Mein Kampf*. The evening on which she had hoped she would be able to forget her worries for a while and which was to have been like old times is spoiled. Toni senses what she is thinking. "I told you not to open the package, mother," she says. "I felt as if I had received a blow to the head," Kati relates. "I wasn't angry. Just sad and confused. I had only one thought. 'Just don't put it in Father's bookcase, Toni, just not in Father's bookcase.' Toni only nodded and then we sat for a long time in silence by the side of the tree, with its burning candles — mother and child, and yet two strangers who can no longer understand one another. The candles began to sputter. As each one went out, I had the feeling that my Anton had died again and taken my Toni with him."

On the first of January, Kati pays a New Year's call on Countess Agnes, as she does every year. The maid opens the door and looks pleased and relieved to see her. "'Good that you have come, Frau Gruber,' she says. 'I'm at my wits' end. The dear old lady' — Marie the maid, a young thing of nineteen, finds it beneath her dignity to refer to the Countess by her title," Kati explains; "Countess Agnes knows Marie calls her 'the dear old lady' and laughs about it — 'the dear old lady has been sitting there all morning crying. She won't tell me what is wrong. I'm worried that she might be falling ill on me.'" Kati runs into the living room and finds "the Countess huddled near the fireplace weeping so much that her body is shaking. 'What happened?' Kati asks. The old woman looks up, her face contorted, as if she were in acute pain and stretches out her hand. 'I came to wish you a Happy New Year,' Kati says. 'Make your wish that I should die soon, Kati,'" the old woman answers. "That's the best thing you can wish for me." Kati is surprised that the Countess has reverted to the familiar "du" form of address which she used when Kati was a young girl in service with her but has not used since. The old woman tries in vain to control her tears. Kati thinks that perhaps she has lost all her money "since that happens quite often these days, and then what would she do, since she has never had to work and Claudia has no experience of working either." She asks if that is what is wrong. The old lady shakes her head. "If that were all it is, Kati," she answers. Kati feels truly sorry for her, though she also thinks inwardly that people who have money don't understand how important it is. Even Countess Agnes, who is so completely unpretentious, has no idea what it means to be really penniless. "That would be a serious blow, I know," the old lady says at last. "I'm old and can't work. But at least, there would be no disgrace. And I wouldn't have to wonder whether I might not be partly to blame." To all Kati's efforts to find out what the problem is, she responds only that it is "the worst thing, the very worst thing that could have happened, the most terrible disgrace that could have befallen me." For over an hour, Kati tries to get her to tell her what is wrong. To no avail. "I can't Kati, I can't, I'm too ashamed," is the only reply she can elicit. "Maybe tomorrow. I just can't talk today, I can't." The Countess clasps Kati's hand tightly in hers and suddenly bursts out: "We were always decent people, always. When I think of my father and my grandfather and their womenfolk, I have absolutely no reason to be ashamed. My grandfather served time in Spielberg prison because he fought for freedom." Then she begins to cry again, uncontrollably and desperately. Finally she says: "This is not a good start to the new year for you, Kati. Go home. You can't do anything for me. Come back tomorrow. Maybe I'll be able to tell you what it is then." (pp. 36–37)

Kati did not have to wonder what the old woman's problem was for long. On her way home along the lakeside promenade, she sees Claudia walking ahead of her, briskly, like a young girl. A local lawyer's son who has become a Nazi comes toward her and Claudia raises her arm. "Heil Hitler!" she says "in a loud voice audible to everybody around." He responds in kind, and the two of them go off together. Kati feels her legs weakening under her. "I thought of Countess Agnes and of what she had said about aristocrats who join the Nazis — that they are the very worst kind of rabble. And now the old woman has to go through it herself with her Claudia — she who is so proud that her grandfather fought for freedom. My Anton fought for freedom too — and now our Toni… Toni and Claudia, our children, our daughters, the Nazi girls. Such was our New Year's Day." (p. 37)

***

Countess Agnes's narrative describes a much more fraught mother-daughter relationship than that of the working class Kati and Toni Gruber. The very first lines hint at the reclusive nature of the old Countess and her estrangement from her child. "I always used to hide from my daughter Claudia when I wanted to write in my diary. There is something ridiculous about it after all — an old woman writing down her thoughts and feelings like a teenager. And Claudia's scornful laughter always hurt me. She never understood that a lonely person has to share her thoughts, feelings, and anxieties with someone, even if that someone is only a blank piece of paper." (p. 38) Further reflections fill in the picture of the Countess — a lonely childhood as a sickly little girl, set apart from her boisterous and healthy brothers and sisters, always being warned that she has to be careful not to overexert herself, always being forbidden to go riding, play tennis or join the others on trips. "I was always 'poor Agnes,' too frail to hold up." Yet she also hints at a tough fibre in her frail body. Strange," she reflects, "that of all of us I am the only survivor. Both my brothers fell in the war and my sister died ten years ago." We learn how, from an early age, she sought refuge from the humiliating and unpleasant reality of her life in books and that these offered her another world in which she felt more at home and happier than she ever did in the real world:

> This cowardly fear of reality has pursued me all my life. I shut my eyes when I should have opened them; I stopped up my ears so as not to hear the discordant sounds of life. I did so as a child, as a growing girl, and as a grown woman. And now that I am sixty-six years old, reality is suddenly staring me in the face, horrifying and threatening — an enemy I can't deal with, an enemy that comes in and out of my house and shouts and screams so loudly in the street that the racket comes all the way through the garden into my quiet living room. I am old and I tremble before this enemy.

> But no, I won't paint myself worse than I am. A life that has never been besmirched, a long line of honourable ancestors, pride, aristocratic distinction, are these not weapons too? And did I not use these very weapons as a young woman to hold out in an unhappy marriage. Neither my parents nor my relatives nor any of my acquaintances ever knew how unhappy my marriage was. I always appeared content, always had a smile on my lips, and when my husband stayed away for months at a time, I always had an explanation to give for his absence. (pp. 38–39)

These reflections provide Countess Agnes with an opportunity to unburden herself to her diary (and tell the reader of the novel) about her unhappy marriage and to explain why her relations with her daughter Claudia were always distant and difficult.

> To tell the truth, it was hard for me at first. I could not and would not believe that the handsome young officer, six years my junior — I was thirty at the time — had married me for money. I loved him, and when I became his wife I thought I was about to begin the life of bliss I had read so much about in the books of the Romantics. But after six months, I had to acknowledge that I bored my husband to death. All the quiet pleasures that made me happy — books, beautiful landscapes, paintings — meant nothing to him. Horses, gambling, and women — other women, women bursting with life — that was all he was interested in.
>   When our daughter was born, he insisted that we name her Claudia. I knew very well that he was then in love with a beautiful Roman woman by the name of Claudia, and that his love had not gone unrequited. That name and that memory created a wall between me and my child. Long after Ferdinand had forgotten his Roman Claudia [....], I still thought of that woman who had dealt me the first blow in my marriage whenever I spoke my daughter's name.
>   Perhaps Claudia felt this instinctively. Who knows what children experience? In any case, she was not the same with me as other children are with their mothers and I often secretly envied my sweet Kati who got on so well with her little girl. But that came later, after we gave up our house in Munich and bought the villa on Lake Constance.
>   At first Ferdinand was against this move. But I was strongly drawn to this place — perhaps because Annette von Droste-Hülshoff lived, suffered, and wrote her books nearby. She too had been unhappy, sickly, and frail, but what power is expressed in her work! (pp. 39–40)

Unfortunately, Countess Agnes reflects, "I was not creative like her. I could do nothing, nothing. I was a woman who had failed to hold on to her husband, and a mother who did not know how to make contact with her own child." (p. 40)

With the years the distance between mother and daughter only increased. "There was a restlessness in the grown girl that was completely foreign to me," the Countess notes. "As though she was looking for something she could not find." She had become quite good-looking,

> but there was an off-putting coldness about her. I had no idea what lay hidden behind this coldness. I only noticed that she had neither friends of her own sex nor any of the innocent little flirtatious relations with boys that girls of her age usually have. For a time, when she was about twenty, she became very religious. Her room was filled with pictures of saints and she spent hours at church. She fasted like a Carmelite nun. But this seemed not to satisfy her in the end. [...] One day all the pictures were gone from her room and she stopped going to Church. She wouldn't even visit her father's grave. For me she had nothing but scorn and contempt. [...] And she made no secret of it. She laughed at my books, mocked my love of the flowers in the garden and made a fool of me for my pathetic efforts to be of help to others. She laughed at my passion for reading, though she read quite a bit herself at this time. Once I took a look at her bookcase and I was horrified. I had no idea that such books existed — ugly, vulgar books that were about nothing but sex. Not serious or scientific treatments of the subject, but revoltingly frivolous and cynical trash. But the worst was yet to come. These books must have worked like a poison on Claudia, for one day the young gardener who worked for me asked if he could have a word with me. (p. 40)

It turns out that Fritz, the gardener, whose skill and personal good nature the Countess has come to value, wants to hand in his notice. The Countess refuses to accept it. Believing he is reacting to disagreements they have had over the garden, she offers to allow him to cut down a large pine tree, even though she is attached to it, since he insists it is necessary to do so. She makes other concessions on the management of the garden. But Fritz only becomes more and more embarrassed. "For God's sake, please try to understand me, Countess Agnes," he blurts out finally. "It's way too difficult for me to have to tell you this, but my wife has noticed it and has become jealous. Countess Claudia will not leave me in peace. [...] The other day, in the early morning, she came into the garden in her night gown and asked me whether she wasn't attractive and whether I mightn't…" (p. 40)

5. Our Daughters the Nazi Girls. A Synopsis in English

The Countess finally has to understand. Fritz looks away in order not to embarrass her but, overcome by shame, she becomes unsteady on her feet. The young man puts his arm around her and leads her back into the house. She begs him not to stop working for her and promises to deal with the situation. Fritz leaves and she sits motionless. "I am an old woman," she thinks. "A very old woman. I don't understand the young people. I don't understand Claudia. I am certainly to blame. How old is Claudia now? Thirty. I was thirty too before I got married, but then I was always so sickly and frail, whereas Claudia is a healthy girl… Maybe… Still, to throw yourself at a man, a married man into the bargain." At this point Claudia comes into the garden. "What's the matter," she asks. "You are so pale." "If I could only find the right words," the Countess reflects, "if I could only get Claudia to feel that I understand her, perhaps everything could still be right between us." "Fritz has spoken to me," "she says. "He…" She notices that Claudia does not blush and is not ashamed: "She only gave a wicked laugh. 'Is he scared of me, the chicken? And you mother, of course you are morally outraged. But it is all your fault, you know. I have to hang around here, in this godforsaken hole, where one never meets anyone and hasn't a chance in China. What kind of life is that for a young person? Young, did I say?' She laughed, a cold, cutting laugh. 'Young? I turned thirty last month. What have I got out of my youth? Just take a look at me? Can any man find me attractive? But you wouldn't understand any of this.'" Countess Agnes's desperate response that she wants so much to understand her child falls on deaf ears. "You, you're not a real woman, and you never were," Claudia replies. "That's why poor father couldn't stand to live with you. That's why he needed other women." The Countess is stunned. She always thought Claudia knew nothing of her father's affairs with other women. "He was a real man, that's what," Claudia continues mercilessly. "A man like that is what I need. All the young men you used once to invite over — yes, I know you were trying to find a husband for me — what kind of men were they? They were all the kind of men that would have suited you — bookworms, poets, people you could at best carry on a sentimental correspondence with, like your beloved Annette with her Levin Schüking. But I want a real, strong man, not someone refined and sensitive. I am not a half-woman like you… Do you know how it feels on these summer nights, when the air is filled with the scent of jasmine and the nightingales sing in the garden. No, you don't. You only find it poetic. But I don't want poetry; I want life, real life." (pp. 44–45)

The Countess senses that if she fails to come up with the right response, Claudia will be lost to her for ever. "Would you like to travel, dearest?" she suggests. "We could spend the winter on the Riviera." Secretly, she almost hopes that Claudia will say no, because she loves the quiet winters in the little lakeside town, the mists that roll in off the lake, the snow-covered garden paths, the leafless tree branches standing out delicately against the sky as in a Japanese drawing, the long evenings by the fireside plunged in a book that opens up another, free, beautiful, secret, yet familiar world. She did not have to worry. Claudia is scathing: "The Riviera? What would I do there? Compete with the cocottes? Or move in the same circles as here, among quiet, refined people of the kind you like, shadows, ghosts from another age that vanished long ago. No, mother, it's too late for that."(p 45) Thereupon she turns on her heels and leaves the room. "I remained sitting there," the Countess notes in her diary, "with a leaden weight pressing on my heart and frightful feelings of guilt in my head. I hated myself because I had never understood Claudia and I hated my dead husband from whom she had inherited everything that I could not understand in her." (pp. 45–46)

Countess Agnes now remembers Claudia's attempt at suicide and the months she spent in a psychiatric institution. On her return home, she recalls, it was not Claudia herself she feared, but the unidentified thing living inside her and driving her, the thing she, her mother, was incapable of understanding.[14] This thing had now returned, she

---

14 The simmering of unruly, irrational energies in women, in whom natural impulses have been unnaturally repressed by culture and convention and who have never been permitted to confront and deal with their own emotions, is a theme that recurs in much of Zur Mühlen's writing. It informs, for instance, two striking short stories in the collection *Fahrt ins Licht* (Vienna: Ludwig Nath, 1936, rprt. Klagenfurt: Sisyphus Verlag, 1998). In "Kultur" (pp. 148–53) Edith, the wife of the psychiatrist Sir Percy Langton, is known for the impeccable taste with which she creates her surroundings and her own social persona. Sir Percy, however, tells how he once deliberately removed his wife from an environment, in which the shutting up of their bodies in "corsets, tight-fitting clothes, and long dresses" was emblematic of the general condition of women, and took her to Africa in order to shake her out of the "harmonious monotony" of her existence. The explosion of passion that occurred in the new environment taught Edith to revise her understanding of human nature and, in particular, to come to a better understanding of her own nature. "Tod eines

reflects, and destroyed the peaceful world she had created for herself by retreating into her garden and her books. The reality she had feared and tried to shut out of her life had invaded her house and it was impossible to ignore it any longer. Anticipating later developments in her narrative, Countess Agnes associates the frightening demonic force that she cannot understand in her daughter with developments in the street and the political arena, from which she had also always held back. This allows Zur Mühlen to develop one of the few passages of explicit political rhetoric in the novel. In politics too, Countess Agnes reflects, an ugly reality had intruded into her world and was destroying the modest hopes for peace and a more just social order that, as an aristocrat with a conscience and a descendant of brave men who had sided in their time with the forces of emancipation, she had hoped would follow the end of the World War in 1918. A new Germany was indeed emerging now, but it was neither "the cultivated, perhaps no longer viable Germany of the poets, nor the decent, realistic Germany of the immediate post-War years. A fraudulent, barbarous mass had begun to take control of the street." She remembers the beautiful autumn day when the results of the elections of 1930 were announced and she could not understand how "liars, cheats, and murderers" had won so many votes. "What is the use of all our culture when such people can come to power, led on by a dodger, a crazy megalomaniac, a charlatan without a conscience?"[15] Dr Bär, the Jewish doctor who was her regular physician had been on a house call and had tried to calm her down. "It's the unemployment, the economic crisis," he had said. But she did not accept this explanation. These rowdies were no revolutionaries, she had insisted, their motivation was only envy and deceit. Some members of her own class supported the National Socialists, she admitted to herself, with a feeling

---

Schattens" (pp. 167–72; here pp. 294–99) has a less happy outcome. Perdita W. has been brought up in a highly civilized and controlled environment. Her adoring and cultured parents allow nothing vulgar or dissonant to enter the refined world they have created and share with their child. After their death, Perdita loses her bearings and is easy prey to the wild enthusiasms of National Socialism. When she realizes the utter vulgarity of what she has succumbed to, she is totally disoriented and kills herself.

15 These were obviously fighting words in 1934 when Zur Mühlen's novel appeared. They were also the words to which the German ambassador, von Papen, objected in his diplomatic note to the Austrian authorities, on the grounds that they were insulting to the leader of a neighbouring power.

of shame. "They did so not out of conviction, not even out of foolishness or ignorance, but because they hoped this would enable them to protect their own fortunes. They seemed to me — and still do — more vulgar and more despicable than the murderers and criminals in the S.A. For there was no way for them not to have seen the truth. And if there is one unforgivable sin, it is to know the truth and reject it." To Countess Agnes, unpolitical as she says she is, no aristocrat worthy of his or her class could possibly support the National Socialists. Aristocrats have a special obligation to humanity. "I thought of the bad days of serfdom. How many men and women suffered so that a single class of people might have the opportunity to develop culturally, what a debt this class owes to mankind, and how is it repaying it now? I am an unpolitical woman and I am not very worldly-wise, but I would have liked to be the head of state of our country so as to take the most energetic action possible against this party. As for the members of my own class, I would gladly have sent them to the guillotine. But such betrayers of humanity, who were perfectly aware of what they were doing, would not even have been able to die with dignity." (pp. 47–48)

The year 1932, the Countess continues, looked at first as though it would be a better year for her. Claudia suddenly became more cheerful; there was colour in her cheeks and a sparkle in her eyes. She even behaved in a more friendly manner toward her mother. The two women no longer sat together at mealtimes in oppressive silence. Claudia went out a lot and had started reading again — not the horrible pornographic books of the past, which had now disappeared from her library, but all kinds of pamphlets. To the Countess's inquiry as to what these were about, Claudia replied offhandedly, but in a friendly way, that they would be of no interest to her and that she would not understand them anyway. During the wonderful spring and summer of 1932, the Countess spent entire days in the garden, reading. Sometimes Claudia would come and sit by her. "Your Romantics, as usual," she once said teasingly, with a smile. "I think you haven't a clue, mother, what century we are living in. What counts today is strength, toughness." "There is also a quiet kind of strength, dear, and in my view it is more unshakable than the noisy variety," the Countess countered. But Claudia, paying no attention, went on enthusiastically: "Strength, mother, and the power to win people over, the power to mean everything to them. That's what counts.

A name that fires up whoever hears it." As she said that "her cheeks glowed; she looked beautiful; and her blue eyes shone mysteriously." Countess Agnes recalls that once, many years before, being in love had given her too a glow that had transformed the rather plain girl she was in reality. She wonders what had magically transformed the expression on Claudia's face, but does not dare to ask, for "a single thoughtless word might disturb our good relationship." She cannot help imagining, however, that Claudia might be in love and be loved in return. She lets herself hope that "perhaps everything will still work out for her." (p. 49)

Once again, however, she notes in her diary, she had only allowed herself to flee reality. "In the long run, however, reality cannot be banished. In vain we wrap ourselves in the rose-coloured dream clouds of other times and other places; in vain we shut our eyes and stop up our ears to keep out the harsh sounds that destroy all harmony. One day the clouds break, one day something forces us to open our eyes, and the shrill scream of reality shatters everything." (p. 50) What awakened the Countess and shattered her dreamworld was no loud scream, however, but a low moaning that she heard in her room one October evening and that seemed to come from beyond the garden wall. It turns out to be Fritz, the gardener, who, it transpires, is a Communist, and who has been shot in the leg by a Nazi gang.

Countess Agnes interrupts her narrative at this point to provide the background of this event. She tells of the increasing political prominence of Hitler; of the possibility — in March and April 1932 — that he might be elected President of Germany, "which would be laughable if it were not so shameful" (p. 50); of her own support of Hindenburg, which, like Kati Gruber's, was unenthusiastic, motivated only by a residual trust that he would at least respect the constitution; and of her failure even to consider the third (Communist) candidate, since — perhaps wrongly, she reflects — she knew nothing about the Communist Party and, in any case, disliked every form of dictatorship. She notes that she is herself surprised that she is constantly writing in her diary now about politics, whereas in the past she had always written about books, about quiet walks, about beautiful landscapes. "At first my dislike of the National Socialists had been a matter of esthetics," she observes, "the repugnance with which a cultivated person reacts to barbarism, the repugnance of a quiet, peace-loving person when she is confronted by noisy ranting and raving. I still remember the first time I saw a picture of their *Führer*. He was in the midst of a rant and his mouth was wide open. Instinctively I felt, at the time, that whoever rants so much must have something to hide. The truth expresses itself quietly because it is the truth. As for their constant refrain of '*Deutschland erwache*' [Germany, awaken], Germany *had* awakened after the terrible war; it *had* opened its eyes and it had seen that great things can be achieved only in peace. The Germany of this new party was not my Germany; it was not the earnestly struggling, hard working land that in my mind resembled a good man who has made a serious blunder and tries as hard as he can to repair the damage and change his ways. That was my Germany, the Germany I knew and loved, a noble Germany that behaved chivalrously to its enemies." (p. 51) The thought of chivalrousness sends the diary-writer back to the attack on Fritz, the gardener.

After she finds Fritz lying on the ground beyond the garden gate, unable to move because of the bullet wound in his leg, Countess Agnes runs back to the house to fetch Claudia and the maid. Together the three of them manage to get the young man into the house. The maid calls Dr. Bär who comes over immediately. To Fritz's repeated statements that he was set upon by ten men, Claudia responds in disbelief and anger, repeatedly claiming that it is not so, that it cannot be true. Countess Agnes is so busy tending to Fritz and so pleased by her daughter's outrage at the "unchivalrousness" of an attack by ten men against a single one that she does not pay attention at the time to Claudia's retort to Fritz: "That's what you all say," or to the meaning of the "you" in that remark. Instead, she and Dr. Bär commiserate on the increasingly dangerous situation in Germany. The good doctor tries, without much success or conviction, to reassure his aristocratic friend that "perhaps" the country won't get to the point where "these people" actually come to power. But Countess Agnes notices that he seems to have grown years older in a few weeks and gives the impression of a man who has seen an abyss opening before him.

The next weeks are spent in growing agitation and horror as Countess Agnes reads the newspapers and listens to the radio, mostly alone, for Claudia is now very often out. She cannot understand why all decent people do not overcome their differences and unite in opposing the monstrous thing that threatens them all; she cannot understand what magic the Nazis use to entice so many people into their ranks — "people like my dear Kati's daughter, that good and clever Toni." (p. 55) She can understand why certain lower middle-class people are drawn to them — employees or struggling small shopkeepers who have had to cringe and cower all their lives. The Nazis make them feel they are somebody. But the workers and so many people who struggled for culture and human rights even under the old Kaiser, how can one explain the attraction National Socialism has for them? The question turns out to affect the Countess more directly than she had realized. One day Claudia develops a fever and her mother says she will call Dr. Bär. Claudia tells her she should not. "Why not, dearest. Just to put my mind at rest." "Well, not Dr. Bär" Claudia answers. "If you really must, call Dr. Feldhüter." Countess Agnes is surprised: "But why? He has never treated you before." "Because I do not want to be treated by a Jewish doctor [...] The Jews have brought ruin to our country. It will not develop to its full greatness until we have driven them all out." The Countess cannot believe her ears. "How can you say such things," she cries. "Isn't Dr. Bär one of our best friends? Haven't the Jews helped to make Germany into a country admired everywhere for its culture? Where did you learn this kind of talk?" Claudia tries to avoid an argument. She does not feel well, she protests, she is too weak to discuss the matter. But Countess Agnes "felt no sympathy for her. I think I did not realize at that moment that I was speaking to my own child," she writes in her diary. "The individual lying before me was a stranger. The thought ran through my mind: What is this person doing here in my house? 'We *have* to discuss it, Claudia,'" she retorts, barely recognizing the harsh, unforgiving tone of her own voice. In the ensuing conversation, she learns that her daughter has become a Nazi. She is beside herself. The aristocrat in her is outraged. "It was impossible, it couldn't be, my daughter and that scum." Hard words follow and she leaves the room. Neither mother nor daughter has the courage to pursue the matter. Countess Agnes then relents somewhat. Perhaps it was because of the fever, she thinks. When Claudia gets over it, they will both laugh at the whole episode. It is impossible that her Claudia "who was so haughty and who set such store by good manners and chivalrousness" should have become a Nazi. She remembers her as a little girl of six responding with pride and joy to the stories of her honourable and brave ancestors, especially the one about her great-grandfather who had been imprisoned for his independent stand. Her husband had wanted a son, the Countess recalls, but she had felt that a girl can carry on family traditions of honour, courage, and principle, just as well as a boy. (pp. 56–58)

Her tactic is to keep out of Claudia's way. She does not go to her room. For days, the two women hardly see one another. On the rare occasions when they do run into one another, they exchange politenesses like two strangers. On New Year's Eve, Claudia announces that she is going out. "Won't you catch cold again?" "No, I'll wear the fur." "Do you have to go out? It's New Year's Eve. Are you going to leave me here all alone?" "I have to go." Claudia turns to the maid and tells her that a man will call for her and that he should be brought into the living room. She then looks challengingly at her mother. "Don't you want to know who the man is that will be calling for me?" Countess Agnes does not respond. "My friend," Claudia says. "My Party comrade. He is with the S.A." The Countess feels she has been slapped in the face. At one time, she reflects, the term "my friend" would have shocked her, old-fashioned as she was, but by now she might have been pleased for Claudia, had her daughter not added that the "friend" was her Party comrade and was with the S.A. "Something stirred in me," she writes,

> something stronger than all acquired good manners, stronger than all our culture. "So that's what it's all about?" I asked scornfully. "Because that's the only way you can get a man. […] I'd rather you had gone on the street. I can live with a whore in my house but not with what you have become." "I should go then, and not come back?" Claudia asked quietly. Something in her tone of voice reminded me of the child that I had loved in my way — no doubt it wasn't the right way. Did I really want to send that child away? What trouble would she get into without a home to come back to? "You can stay here," I said. "But I don't want to see you. I don't want to sit at the same table with you. You are a stranger to me, no, an enemy." Claudia paled. "If only you would try to understand, mother." "I understand only too well. Put your coat on and go now. I won't have your friend, your Party comrade, in my house." (p. 59)

Claudia goes to the door slowly, "as if she were waiting for me to call her back." But I could not, Countess Agnes writes, and thought of Kati who had acted differently with her child. "Perhaps she was wiser than I; but I could not call her back." (p. 59)

Countess Agnes is now alone with her anger. She was prone to outbursts of anger as a child, she remembers, but became gentler and calmer during the difficult years of her marriage and then, later, age brought further calm. Now she is overwhelmed by anger and shame, far greater shame even than she had felt when Claudia had tried to seduce Fritz.

> I hated Claudia, but not only Claudia, I hated myself because I had brought her into the world, I hated my body and my womanhood, I hated the hour when I had been impregnated with her and I hated the hour when I gave birth to her. I felt as though I was sinking into filth and slime and could never be clean again. I had tried to live a decent, honourable life, causing pain to no one and bearing my own with dignity. But what was the value of such a life now that Claudia had gone over to those who, to me, were the very essence of scum and vulgarity. Where in me did the evil that had come to light in Claudia lie hidden? (p. 60)

She felt ashamed in front of the maid, who almost certainly knew about Claudia's activities. She wished the maid, a decent upstanding girl, were her daughter instead of Claudia. She remembered how Claudia had nearly died of scarlet fever when she was ten years old and how she had been saved only thanks to Dr. Bär who had come three times a day to see her. "If she had only died at that time... I shuddered: is it possible for a mother to think such thoughts. But I am not only a mother. I am also a human being, a thinking, feeling human being terrified by something unfathomable." (p. 60) The night passes for Countess Agnes in nightmarish imaginings. This is how the men and women of the Middle Ages must have felt, she reflects, when a devastating plague, the cause of which they could not understand, overwhelmed the land. At times she wanted to rush out into the street crying "Save yourselves, save us all, while there is still time." But she could not move. "My legs were like lead and what I saw was a fearful Dance of Death." In the morning — it is New Year's Day — the maid brings her hot tea and forces her to drink some. Her kindness moves the Countess to tears. Then Kati calls on her. "She wanted to know why I was crying so. But I could not tell her. I could not bring myself to. She will find out soon enough." For the next few days she keeps to her room so as not to run into Claudia. Kati visits her, Dr. Bär visits her. They are worried about her, she can see that, but they seem like ghosts. Endless days and endless nights pass, full of anguish and anxiety. From time to time she hears Claudia's footsteps. "It is as though she was treading on my heart. I knew where she was going." (p. 62) For almost a month she does not see Claudia. "It was strange, this living under the same roof, without exchanging a word, without any contact. Like two dead people in a family tomb. I wondered if Claudia felt this too. If she sometimes had a longing to see me. There was no way for me to know. What did I know of my own child?" (p. 62)

On January 30th 1933 the Countess finally enters the living room in order to listen to the news on the radio. Claudia had the same idea, for as the Countess enters the room, Claudia is switching on the radio. The two of them sit, one on either side of the radio, two people who had become strangers to each other and each of whom hoped to hear something different. The music stops and the announcer's voice is heard. A tremor goes through Claudia's body as the news is broadcast. Hitler has been appointed Chancellor of Germany. "Hitler is Chancellor and I see opposite me a face glowing with happiness and I hear a voice say 'Now everything will go well. You'll see, mother.' Whose face was it? Whose voice? Who was this person who was exulting over the ruin of our country? The face, the voice came closer. 'Mother, you're not going to pass out?' Everything had gone black, but who was this stranger? 'Don't touch me,' I said. 'Don't touch me.' The blurry figure stood for a moment, then disappeared. A few moments later, I heard footsteps in the garden. Claudia was going out to celebrate victory." (p. 63) The Countess returns to her room, thinking that this is now the end for her and all who think and feel as she does. "But for the others it was the beginning. About an hour later, the street was ringing with their hateful songs and cries of 'Heil.'… And I thought, Claudia is there with them… I no longer wept. I stopped trembling. I stared into the dark night and saw the wounded champion [of freedom] lying on the ground. Will he be able to rise again?" (p. 64)

On that despairing note, the Countess concludes her first diary entry.

***

The third testimony now opens — that of Frau Doktor Feldhüter "whispering to herself." The tone is set immediately in the first few paragraphs:

5. Our Daughters the Nazi Girls. A Synopsis in English

I would like to know if there are other women in our town who have as many worries and vexations as I have? The maid handed in her notice today — she is the fourth in three months. And she has absolutely nothing to complain about. I work my fingers to the bone keeping the house in order. [...] Yes, it would really be good if my husband had a better practice and we could afford two maids.

To tell the truth, when I married Arthur I had a very different idea of how things were going to be. I was a pretty girl and at that time a nurse had opportunities to make a good match. I would have much preferred to marry into industry. I still remember young Kurt Frankfurter, the son of super-rich parents. I took care of him after his appendectomy. He was a good-looking, likable, generous young fellow and he would have married me if his parents had not objected to his marrying a Christian. These Jews are so intolerant. It was not easy for me to accept that I was not about to become the wealthy Frau Frankfurter. And the other nurses, the dears, made merry over my misfortune. Women are so mean. I was so disappointed, that I consented to marry Arthur, who was then working in the hospital. It certainly wasn't an easy decision — a cripple, with a club foot, crabbed, always grumpy, and, as I could easily tell, being a nurse, a bad doctor as well. Still, he seemed to have prospects. He wanted to settle down in the little town by Lake Constance because at that time there was only one other doctor there — a Jewish doctor, quite well on in years. One thing I have to admit about Arthur: he looks intelligent. Whether he really is I have not been able to tell in all the years of our marriage. In general, I would have to say that I do not really know him. At times, when I was still not long married to him, I would ask myself, somewhat anxiously, what there is behind the mean mask of his face. I know only one thing for sure: that he is ambitious. In fact, I had counted on that ambition when I became his wife. And yet the nurses and the patients in the hospital did not call him "Dr. Wait-and-See" for nothing. He was always for "waiting and seeing" and that has been a real handicap to us, both financially and socially. I remember the time just before war was declared. We were all up in arms against the enemy powers and enthusiastically supporting our fatherland. I wept when I heard the national anthem played. And my little Lieslotte sang "Deutschland über alles" so touchingly in her bright child's voice. Only Arthur refused to reveal where he stood. "Wait and see," he would say. "It may not come to a war and then we'll be considered warmongers."

Then, when it did come to war, he was as patriotic a German as any, I have to grant him that. Except that he wouldn't buy any war bonds. But he made speeches, excellent speeches, about our invincible army and about Germany's mission in the world. In 1916 he began to hold back again. I could not understand him. It made a bad impression — just at the point when I was finally succeeding in gaining entry into the local officers' wives' circles. It was my hope that by war's end our position in the town would finally be secure; that old Dr. Bär's patients would come over to us; and that I would play the role in our town that the local doctor's wife has a right to play. Even that arrogant old woman, that Countess Agnes who lives in her lakeside villa and has always kept me politely at a distance, will have to invite me over, I thought. I could already see us moving out of our rented apartment into our own house, I could see our mixing in the best society, Arthur's becoming rich, and Lieselott's making a better match than her poor mother did. I complained to Arthur that he was spoiling all this for us with his behaviour. He cast a strange look at me out of his small, sunken eyes.

"Wait and see," he said. "No rushing into anything."

In the summer of 1918 he suddenly began to express pacifist views and to lament the sacrifice of so many young lives on both sides of the conflict — though I knew perfectly well that he had no interest in anyone on the planet except himself. (pp. 65–67)

Then comes the collapse. The Frau Doktor is deeply distressed and weeps profusely at the news that "our poor Kaiser has had to flee to Holland." But soon enough she realizes that the officers' families and many of the better class of people in town have a less generous view of the Kaiser's flight than she and so she too begins to see the matter differently. The repression of the Spartacists by the Social Democratic government leads her to take a more favourable view of the new republican regime. "It wasn't easy to look up to a former saddler as the head of state, but he seemed like a decent man, and after all, one has to adapt to changing circumstances." She now pleads with Arthur to join the Social Democratic Party as the party in power. But his response is, as usual, "Wait and see. I'm not joining any party. I am for peace. That's enough." (p. 67) In the same breath he forbids his wife — "in the intolerably bossy tone that I hate in him," as she reports — to join any party. "Don't make any ill-considered move, Martha. I will not stand for my wife joining a party and inevitably involving me too." "Whenever he spoke to me in that vein," the Frau Doktor "whispers," "I had to get a good grip on myself so as not to scream in his face: 'You cripple, you dwarf' (I am nearly a head taller than he is), 'how dare you speak to me in that tone of voice?' And I would be overcome by the utter physical disgust I feel in his presence and would remember my fear, during my pregnancy, that my child would also come into the world as a cripple." Fortunately, Lieselotte did not. She is a strong, healthy girl. (pp. 67–68)

At this point we are given a glimpse of Lieselotte's character. There was a moment, the Frau Doktor recalls, when her daughter wanted to marry a poor engineer. For once Arthur and she were of one mind — in their opposition to this marriage. Lieselotte yielded, but warned them angrily that she proposed thenceforth to live her life as freely as she chose, and wanted no comments or interference from them. The Frau Doktor was incensed. "How can you speak in that tone to your parents?" But Arthur only replied icily: "So long as your behaviour doesn't damage my practice, you can entertain yourself in whatever way you please. Appearances must be kept up, however, you understand?" Lieselotte did precisely as she said she would and when on one occasion "she got into some trouble," Arthur took care of the problem. "Well, why else does one have a doctor for a father...?" the Frau Doktor comments. "After that, Lieselotte was more careful." (p. 68) In fact, Lieselotte despises her father's ambitious scheming and annoys her mother by mocking her small-town social ambitions and hypocrisies. In contrast to Claudia and Toni, she is interested only in having a good time. As a result, while she is incapable of any generous action, she is also unmoved by grand phrases and heroic posturing and, unlike her mother, does not lie to herself. To the despair of the Frau Doktor, Lieselotte will not pretend to be other than what she is: a self-centred young woman who is out for a good time. Her refusal to participate in the hypocrisies of her parents — even later in the narrative, after her parents have become leading Nazis — is Lieselotte's form of revolt against them, but the simple egoism that is the source of her revolt — also sets its limitations. Even though, in contrast to Claudia and Toni, she is not deluded by ideology and propaganda, Lieselotte is never remotely tempted to openly question them, much less to offer any form of resistance or to seek and support an alternative. She has no ideals of any kind, but is totally focused on her own self. On the contrary, as soon as it suits her to do so, she follows her father into the Party. In her own way, she is an opportunist like her parents — in the cold, calculating style of her father rather than the deliberately self-deluding style of her mother.

In the little town, things are not going too well for Feldhüter. His patients are leaving him. Only those who for one reason or another don't want to go to a Jewish doctor have stuck with him. It is his own fault, the Frau Doktor observes impatiently. "If you aren't a good doctor, you should at least show some interest in your patients." She also notes that he conceals his hatred of his rival, the elderly Dr. Bär, beneath a mask of admiration and courtesy. Dr. Bär, she remembers, helped them out during the worst of the inflationary period, and though they still owe him money, he never asks for it. "Well, my God, he had plenty," she thinks, "and these Jews always want to maintain good collegial relations." (p. 69)

As the political climate shifts, the Frau Doktor comes to acknowledge that her husband was right about not joining the Social Democrats. She begins to have some success in cultivating the officers' families she considers the leading families of the town, and is eager to enhance her standing with them by joining the political party they support — if only she knew which of the conservative parties that was. Was it the *Deutsche Volkspartei*, or the *Zentrum*, or the *Deutschnationale Volkspartei*, she wonders. As this milieu is also strongly Protestant (hence probably not *Zentrum*, she guesses), the Frau Doktor takes care to assure the officers' wives of her own and her family's strong commitment to the Evangelical Church, expresses her distrust of Catholics, and, conveniently forgetting an early relationship that she would have liked to see blossom into a marriage, confides to them her conviction that "mixed marriages are extremely dangerous" and that she could "never in her life have married a member of another faith." (p. 65) Arthur allows her to join the monarchist *Luisenbund*,[16] to which most of the officers' wives belong, but insists that he not be involved, evoking his usual wisdom: "Wait and see." Lieselotte, for her part, refuses to join: "What is there for me among all those old wives?" she objects. To her mother's response that there are also young women in the association, she has an easy answer: "Yes, but what sort of young women! I know the routine: you sit around endlessly drinking bad coffee, knitting or doing embroidery, lamenting the collapse of the monarchy, and composing congratulatory telegrams to send to the Kaiser and his wife. Thanks very much. I don't belong in that crowd." (p. 72) She raises her eyebrows in a gesture that irritates the

---

16   A women's group founded in 1923 and named for the revered Queen Louise of Prussia in Napoleonic times. The group supported the Nazis at the time of the *Machtergreifung*, but like other monarchist groups was disbanded in 1934.

Frau Doktor intensely because it reminds her of her husband. "You and your good society, mother!" she goes on. "First you ran after Countess Agnes and wanted me to become friends with her daughter, that old maid. And when that didn't work out, you got on your middle-class high horse and started running down the aristocracy. Later, after the revolution, you changed your tune again. Now it ran: 'Lieselotte, don't be so stuck up, speak to that dear, sweet Toni. Everything has changed; we have to see that we get into the best social democratic circles.' But you had no luck with the best social democratic circles either. And now you are on to me with your *Luisenbund*. Let me tell you something. I don't give a damn what party anybody belongs to. I want to have a good time, that's all. I'm not here to help you get into 'good society.'" She concludes with a comment that could well also have reminded the Frau Doktor of her husband: "Anyway, no one knows how things are going to work out. I have no intention of taking a position." (p. 73)

In her *Luisenbund* circle, the Frau Doktor does her best to explain Feldhüter's unwillingness to declare himself politically on the same side as the officer's families by invoking his noble professional conviction that, however much he may sympathize with a particular political position, as a doctor he must remain neutral publicly and see in others only the sick or suffering human being. (p. 72) Lieselotte for her part, she explains, so admires her father, that she follows his example in everything and feels that a doctor's daughter must stand above all parties. The Frau Doktor is not at all pleased, however, that she is constantly being placed in a difficult situation by her husband and her daughter: "It is really hard for me to maintain our social position with a husband and a daughter like mine." (p. 74) Finally, in face of their constant mockery of her, she gives up communicating honestly with them both. She feels oppressed by being unable to express her real feelings to anyone.

> I can't really say out loud what I truly feel. My whole life has become a kind of whispering, a fruitless conversation with myself. Watching every word and gesture, hiding one's true feelings, making sure to tell everyone what he or she wants to hear, what kind of life is that? How I would love to belong to the crowd that is in power and be able to shout out my opinions as I wish. The terrible thing is that you never know who will ultimately be in power. Now, there's this new party, under Hitler. I don't care much for him because he is an Austrian and a Catholic, but at least he lets the Jews have it. [...] Sometimes I wonder whether we

shouldn't join this new party [...] rather than the Deutschnationalists. If only I were sure that the new party isn't serious about socialism. (p. 75)

Besides, Lieselotte is not altogether wrong about the Luisenbund. It *is* boring. She has been a loyal monarchist all her life, the Frau Doktor reflects, "but do we have to talk all the time about Doorn!" And "the old goats" — the term she now uses to refer to the two leading members of the circle, a Major's wife and a baroness Hellsdorf (whose son will later become engaged to marry Lieselotte) — "never let me get in a word." Because they once visited the Kaiser in Doorn they never stop talking about how graciously they were received. Everyone else, she observes resentfully, is made to feel small and insignificant. (p. 76)

Feldhüter is somewhat less resistant to his wife's new political enthusiasm for the National Socialists. He reassures her that the National Socialist leaders are unlikely to build a socialist system. "That is only to get the workers to go along with them," he explains. But when the Frau Doktor asks whether they shouldn't encourage Lieselotte to join the party, since its leader is now the new Chancellor, and cites the example of Claudia, who has been a member for a month already, Arthur again says no. "A lot of hysterical women have joined," he replies. Lieselotte should not join — not at least for now. "First we have to wait and see the results of the elections." (p. 75) The Frau Doktor is beside herself: "Wait and see, Doctor Wait-and-See. God, how I hated him at that moment. Wait and see. He wouldn't even have married me, the hideous clubfoot, if I hadn't talked him into believing I was pregnant." (pp. 75–76)

The Reichstag fire provokes a violent outburst in the Frau Doktor, a family row, and an unexpected reconciliation with her husband. She is more and more drawn to the National Socialists as they talk of closing down the department stores — where ordinary Germans, she notes, are sold shoddy goods at high prices, like the summer dress, bought only the year before, that became unwearable after the first wash — and getting rid of the Jews and the Communists. When she reads of the Reichstag fire in the newspaper, she immediately announces to Lieselotte that it was the work of the Communists. Lieselotte, however, only yawns and observes that it was an ugly building anyway. The Frau Doktor is enraged: "Our Reichstag, the embodiment of Germany!" "We have to destroy them, root and branch," she declares. "Who?" Lieselotte asks in a bored tone. "The Communists naturally." "Is that what the old wives in the *Luisenbund* say?" Lieselotte asks, yawning again. Feldhüter himself now chimes in. Raising his eyebrows in the way that infuriates the Frau Doktor, he gives her a harsh look and tells her to stay out of politics. "Politics are men's business. Why don't you see to it instead that the soup isn't burned again today. I don't know any woman who talks so much about how well she runs her house and puts such terrible food on the table." (p. 77) She was used to Feldhüter's meannesses, the Frau Doktor relates, and usually bore them in silence. This time, however, what with the burning of the Reichstag and the new maid's handing in her notice, she could no longer contain herself.

> I gave vent to all the bitterness in my heart: the Reichstag fire, the summer dress that shrank in the wash, the maids who are becoming more insolent and demanding by the day, Arthur's lack of success, the affection Dr. Bär is held in, the inner loneliness to which I am condemned, the way I am treated by the ladies in the *Luisenbund*, as if a former nurse were of no account, a nobody, the worry Lieselotte causes me, and the price of butter that keeps going up, the vicious Russians who got the German Communists to set fire to the Reichstag, the kitchen stove that needs to be repaired, Arthur's meanness to me, Lieselotte's lack of respect, the two genuine Meissen cups that the maid broke yesterday, and our poor Kaiser... it all poured out of me... Lieselotte was staring at me, Arthur smiled mockingly. I myself could hear that my voice was becoming ever louder and more shrill. Suddenly Arthur banged on the table with his fist. "Will you shut up!... The window is wide open. Anyone who happens to be passing by can hear every word you say. Can't you learn to wait and see? Do you have to blurt out all your opinions right away? Do you want to spoil everything for me?" Lieselotte got up from the table. "Nice family breakfast," she drawled. "Really heart-warming. Thank God I am not married." (p. 78)

Then the unexpected happens. Feldhüter looks at his wife, leans forward, and places his hand on hers. "Just be patient for a little longer, Martha," he says. "Then maybe you will get everything you have wanted for so long: the house, the second maid. Then maybe the ladies in the *Luisenbund* will learn to be humble. Then maybe, as my wife, you will play the role in our town that you have always wanted to play." The Frau Doktor looks at him in astonishment. "Had he lost his mind?" He notices her reaction and smiles: "Only, for now, no rushing into anything. Not a careless word. When one has two irons in the fire,

Martha, one has to watch both of them. Today is February 27th. Can you not wait until the end of March? Then we will know." (p. 79)

The weeks go by. Finally it is election day. Feldhüter disappears in the early morning. Unable to ask him how she should vote, the Frau Doktor simply does not vote. With her customary indifference, Lieselotte also does not vote. As the radio is out of order, the Frau Doktor decides to wait up until her husband returns to hear the results of the election. The hours pass. It is late at night. Lieselotte wants to go to bed, but the Frau Doktor is too anxious and worked up and will not allow her to. Lieselotte stretches out on the sofa with a novel and falls asleep. Finally at one in the morning Feldhüter appears. "His sallow complexion had become red with excitement," the Frau Doktor relates.

> He slammed the living-room door shut. "We won!" he shouted at me. I looked at him in puzzlement. "We won" — what can it mean when Arthur says "we"? And then I noticed a large swastika in his buttonhole and I knew who "we" meant. Lieselotte had awakened and she was also staring at the badge. She had never seen her father wearing one. "Since when have you been a Nazi, father?" she asked in a sleepy voice. "Talk respectfully when you speak of the mightiest party in the land," he commanded her, " — of the party you are also a member of." "I am a member of?" "Yes, you. I signed you up months ago." "But I don't want to be a member. All that marching and shouting is a bore. What does it have to do with me?" (p. 83)

Feldhüter goes up to her. At first the Frau Doktor thought he was about to strike her. Instead he says:

> "I've been in the National Socialist Party for months. But I explained to the district commander that, as a doctor, I couldn't declare myself openly a member. Now, however… Now everything is different. And you will do as I say, Lieselotte." She shrugged. "Well, all right then…. So long as I don't have to sleep with proletarians." Arthur laughed. I don't know why, but a cold shiver runs down my spine when Arthur laughs. "That won't be necessary. It wouldn't hurt, but if you insist on the more distinguished types, some SS man will surely turn up. You're still a good-looking girl." Lieselotte now laughed too, like an echo of her father. I was of course completely forgotten. Neither of them had a thought for me.

It turns out, however, that there is something for the Frau Doktor too. "Now you will get your house," Feldhüter tells her. "What would you say to Dr. Bär's house?" The Frau Doktor feels her heart pounding in her breast. "I had never felt so German, so German through and through," she relates. "Yes, everything was working out as it should, The Jew yields his place to the German whom he has held down for so long. The German woman takes over where once the Jewess was mistress. I almost felt love for my husband. He is after all a good and clever man. Smarter than I am. Now let the Major's wife dare to call Dr. Bär! Now let Countess Agnes dare go past me on the street with only a curt greeting! Now, I looked at Arthur, now we are the masters. And woe to them who stand in our way." (pp. 84–85)

As cries and songs of jubilation resound through the street, Feldhüter goes to the window, throws it open, takes Lieselotte by the arm and stands with her looking out at the scene below. The marching men come to a halt and shout up: "Sieg heil! Germany awake!" Feldhüter and his daughter respond with the Nazi salute and the cry of "Heil Hitler!" Not to be left out, the Frau Doktor hurries over to the window, places herself beside her husband and daughter, raises her hand too in the Nazi salute and echoes their shouts of "Heil Hitler." That evening, as the couple gets ready for bed, the Frau Doktor's heart is so full, she feels she has to kneel in prayer and thank God for all He has done for them. Feldhüter asks her what is keeping her from coming to bed. "I am praying, Arthur," she replies. He shrugs and by the light of the night lamp she catches a glimpse of a mocking smile on his pallid face. (p. 85)

***

The Frau Doktor's second testimony, which follows immediately on the first, is no longer one of whispered frustration and resentment but an outspoken expression of triumph and satisfaction. The opening sentences again set the tone.

> My beloved husband, my good, clever Arthur, how right he was with his "Wait and see." Only the individual who submits patiently and humbly to God's will receives his reward here on earth. I never asked anything of life. It was always enough for me to have a good husband, an obedient daughter, and a modest home which I looked after lovingly and joyfully. I was never one of those who demand a lot from life and for that reason, now that everything has turned out so splendidly for us, I am entitled to rejoice with a good conscience. (p. 86)

She goes on to tell how her "dear husband" and her "good Lieselotte" accompanied her to Church where they heard an edifying sermon about the world mission of the "deutsche Christen"[17] and the duties of the German "Frau und Mutter" [wife and mother]. She notices how at Church the Frau Major waved to her eagerly from afar and tried, albeit without success, to get her mother, the haughty old Frau General, to follow suit. She admires the SA and SS men in their handsome uniforms.

> I felt real love for those brave lads who for years were persecuted, treacherously attacked, and murdered, and who now stand before us as conquerors. I also thought of the boycott of Jewish businesses the week before and how the SA marched up and down in front of the department store (where, by the way, I had bought another summer dress a week earlier, the prices being so low that it would have been a sin not to take advantage of them). The owner, chicken-hearted as all the Jews have now become, had had the window shutters rolled down. One delivery boy was late, however, and tried to slip out of the building without being noticed. But our fearless SA men caught him and gave him a proper beating. It was fun to watch. (p. 87)

The reader is given a hint of what is to come in the later testimonies of Countess Agnes and Kati Gruber when the Frau Doktor tells how she recognized "that crazy Claudia" in the crowd, standing "pale as death and as if turned to stone." The "awful Toni, whom I never could abide" was standing next to her, holding her tightly by the arm. At one point it looked as if Claudia was about to dash forward, but Toni pulled her back. "These aristocratic women are frightful," the Frau Doktor comments. "Degenerate and neurotic. They can't even stand to see a harmless scrap. In general, that Claudia ought not to be in the Party. They say she had something going with a Jewish doctor in the psychiatric clinic she was once sent to. I took good care to see that that information got spread

---

17 There had been agitation in German Protestant circles since the end of the nineteenth century for the freeing of German Christianity from its alien, "oriental" origin in Judaism. In his *Foundations of the Nineteenth Century* (1899), Houston Stewart Chamberlain had argued that Christ was not a Jew but an Aryan. In May, 1932, with National Socialism going from strength to strength, a group calling itself the "deutsche Christen" (German Christians) was formed within the German Protestant Church. It excluded baptised Jews, endorsed the "Aryan paragraph," and generally pursued a racist and anti-Semitic agenda. It soon dominated many of the local *Landkirchen* and won a third of the vote in the Prussian church elections of November 1932.

around. We don't need women who are so shameless that they let men of an alien race… I simply can't understand how an Aryan woman doesn't feel utter disgust when a man of an alien race touches her. It would never have occurred to me, when I was young, to even glance at a Jew. I still remember how hard it was for me when I had to take care of one in the hospital." During the church service she reflects how she "had to laugh with delight, like a child, when the airplanes flew overhead and dropped white leaflets calling on the population to observe the boycott" and how wonderful it had been, even though there were only three Jewish businesses in the little town. "In Berlin and the other big cities it must have been grand." She also begins to "wonder" whether the elderly, aristocratic Frau General, who has always studiously avoided greeting her and who had expressed skepticism at one of the *Luisenbund* gatherings about the responsibility of the Communists for the Reichstag fire, might not have Jews among her ancestors. All in all,

> it is wonderful to feel oneself one with the entire Volk and with all classes of the people. One Germany, united against the enemy within and against the enemy without. And for this we have to thank our great Führer. His picture hangs in our living room and I never tire of gazing on his noble, thoughtful features. A man of the people, no Kaiser and no prince, just a simple human being who raised himself up. That is the strength of the German people — that it always recognizes true greatness even when it appears in the humblest guise. I never really could understand the circle around the major's wife with its glorification of the Kaiser. I was always a good republican — though not, for sure, at the time of the old republic that has now collapsed. For I found the Social Democrats as repulsive as the Jews. (pp. 88)

The Frau Doktor notes with satisfaction that her husband's waiting-room is now always full, people having "finally realized who the better doctor is," whereas "only a few proletarians" with workers' insurance "and that stupid Countess Agnes still go to Dr. Bär." (p. 89) And there is "something fishy about her. Everybody knows about the fine morals of aristocratic women. Their menfolk are unable to satisfy them, and so there is always a Jewish tutor around. Not hard to imagine the outcome. I always thought that that Countess Agnes didn't look like a true German woman. That's why for years I refused to have anything to do with her, even though she kept trying to become friends with me." (p. 89)

Given Feldhüter's position in the town now, it is unacceptable, according to the Frau Doktor, that he should have only a miserable five-room apartment. For herself, she declares, she doesn't care, but she has to think of Arthur and Lieselotte. She types up an anonymous letter warning Doctor Bär that he is in danger and sends it to him in several different mailings. Others in the town do the same. But nothing happens. Then some lively lads throw stones at Dr. Bär's windows and smash them. A little later stories begin circulating about concentration camps. "I was thrilled. Our revolution isn't carried out barbarously, like the Russian one. We don't murder people. We place even our enemies in secure places and give them the chance to correct their ways. No other nation would be capable of such a thing." (p. 90) Still, Dr. Bär does not try to leave as so many other Jews have.

> The stubborn old man just wouldn't let himself be helped and his equally stubborn workers' insurance patients still went to him, even though SA men were stationed outside his office warning people politely that he is a Jew and that Germans should have themselves cared for by an Aryan doctor. [...] On the very day of the boycott a boatswain, a Communist, even had the nerve to go to Dr. Bär to get help with an infected finger. But the fellow got the same treatment as the delivery man for the Jewish department store. The fact that things turned out badly wasn't the SA men's fault. How were these poor young fellows to know that the boatswain had come back from the war with a heart condition and couldn't tolerate even a little thrashing. Naturally, they were all shocked when he suddenly lay on the ground, stiff and still as a stone, and never regained consciousness. They carried him back into Dr. Bär's house and some communist provocateur placed a note on his chest that read: "Dr. Bär, this is what happens to the patients you treat." (p. 91)

But after all, "he would most likely have died of a heart attack anyway, even without the couple of blows he took. God has marked the appointed end for each one of us and the boatswain's last hour had struck. Perhaps if my Arthur had gotten to him, he might have lived a little longer. For Dr. Bär is now in his seventies and such an old man sometimes doesn't quite know what he is doing."

The Frau Doktor's house problem is finally resolved when Dr. Bär and his wife commit suicide. Feldhüter at first only tells his wife that they will be moving into Dr. Bär's house in a week. The Frau Doctor thinks at first that Bär has finally given in and decided to emigrate.

Then suddenly she thinks of the doctor's wife and her high spirits drop. "Maybe she will stay on here," she says, somewhat crestfallen. "Don't worry," Feldhüter reassures her. "You can begin packing tomorrow [...] Dr. Bär and his wife shot themselves a couple of hours ago." "I always told you, Arthur," the Frau Doktor responds, "that the two of them were not quite in their right minds these last weeks." "And then," she adds in her testimony, "I was overcome by joy." Feldhüter warns her, however, that the whole town does not have to know about the suicides; the story is being put out, he says, that Bär accidentally shot himself while cleaning his gun and that when his wife saw what had happened she took her own life. "My good Arthur!" the Frau Doktor comments. "When I think of the harm the Jew did to him all those years and now he is concerned about saving his reputation. But Arthur was always like that — good-hearted and considerate." (p. 92) As if to confirm her judgment of him, Feldhüter announces that he is "glad the old man has croaked." "May that be the fate of all enemies of the fatherland," the Frau Doktor responds. "Who knows how many crimes Dr. Bär committed in his long life," she thinks. "Illegal operations and the like. I know that he was always against Paragraph 218 [the law prohibiting assisted abortions — L.G.]. Unlike my Arthur, who has always believed that the living embryo was especially sacred." (Lieselotte's "Malheur" is thus conveniently erased from the Frau Doktor's new consciousness as the wife of the town's prominent National Socialist doctor.)

The narrative continues in this vein. The Frau Doktor would have liked to refurnish the Bärs' villa with furniture bought from a fellow Party member, but "the good man was so expensive that one evening as it was getting dark I went to the store of the Jewish furniture dealer Kohn. To tell the truth, I went out of compassion, for old man Kohn is seventy-five now and what is the old man to do if no one buys from him any more? Naturally the Jew first tried to cheat me. He wanted to charge nearly as much as our good Party member. I gently pointed out to him that from a person of alien stock that is simply not acceptable. I was irritated that the man seemed not to have appreciated my kindness in coming to him. 'My prices have always been firm, Frau Doktor,' he said in his shameless Jewish way. 'Yes, before,' I answered quietly. 'I can't sell the furniture for less,' was the response. But anger now overwhelmed me. 'Don't you know that it's all over now with price-gouging.' I exclaimed.

'I am duty-bound to report you for trying to sell at higher than the set price.' […] The old man stood trembling in a corner, staring at me with his huge black eyes. Even if he is a sub-human," the Frau Doktor reflects, "the Bible tells us we must have compassion with animals. 'So, Herr Kohn,' I said encouragingly, 'we can surely come to an agreement. I will pay you half of what you are asking. And you will still be making a good deal.' […] At the time I still did not know that I would not have to pay the Jew anything at all. He delivered the furniture, but even before I got the bill he had been sent to a concentration camp for engaging in Communist plots." (pp. 100–101)

Two episodes recounted by the Frau Doktor anticipate the later narratives of the Countess and Kati. According to the Frau Doktor,

> despite the seriousness of the times, there are all kinds of things that make one laugh, as, for instance, when the Social Democratic Mayor of our town was made to march through the streets carrying a Swastika banner. […] If he slowed down he would get a good-humoured shove from one of our good SA men. He would then run for a bit, which sent the young people in the crowd into fits of laughter. The day after that the story went around that treasonous documents had been found in his home and that he was to be arrested. But suddenly our Mayor was nowhere to be found. […] Everyone in the town wondered where he could have gone, for the Swiss border was strictly guarded. I had my suspicions. There is only one person who can have hidden him. So I said to my future son-in-law, Baron Hellsdorf, "If I were you, I would do a house-search at Countess Agnes Saldern's place. I know for sure that that woman is a fierce enemy of our movement. So much so, that she no longer even greets me when we meet on the street. Besides, I suspect that there are Jews in her family line." (p. 96)

The story of the search is then told from the point of view of the Nazi investigators in anticipation of its subsequent retelling from the point of view of the anti-Nazi resistance, to which the reader has now been given good reason to suspect that the Countess has gone over. We learn that Countess Agnes adopted a haughtily correct, even provocative aristocratic tone with the men, that the Frau Doktor's future son-in-law, Baron Hellsdorf, was so incensed by it that he had to restrain himself from striking the old lady, and that Claudia was furious at the indignity done to her mother.¹⁸

A side-issue, satirizing the Nazi obsession with race, is introduced at this point when Feldhüter warns his wife against spreading a story about there being Jews among Countess Agnes's Saldern ancestors. He has already checked the matter out, he tells her and found — doubtless to his regret — that the family is 100% Aryan. "However, if this question interests you...," he adds maliciously, pulling out of his pocket a sheaf of papers containing the results of years of inquiry into the racial ancestry of prominent people. The Frau Doktor notices to her delight that the great grandmother of the Frau Major was a baptised Jewess. But to her consternation, Feldhüter's continued research into the racial ancestry of prominent local figures turns up evidence soon afterwards showing that the maternal great-grandfather of her future son-in-law Baron Hellsdorf, "that splendid, blond, typically Germanic young man," was a baptised Jew. Lieselotte is already thirty, the Frau Doktor reflects, and it will not be easy for her to find another man. Fortunately, the situation is saved when letters are discovered in the Hellsdorf family archives "demonstrating beyond doubt that his great-great-grandmother had had an affair with a Freiherr Elz von Rübernach and that her one child was the child of their love." Happily, therefore, there is not a drop of blood from an alien race in Hellsdorf's veins. The Frau Doktor allows herself to feel sympathy and admiration for the ancestor of her future son-in-law. Forced out of financial necessity to marry a man of alien race, she had had the courage to preserve the purity of her family's blood by engaging in an adulterous relationship. (pp. 104–05)

---

18   Zur Mühlen's choice of the name Hellsdorf was probably not arbitrary and was curiously prescient. The similarly named Wolf-Heinrich, Graf von Helldorff (1896–1944), was a relatively well-known figure of an "aristocrat" turned Nazi. He had taken part in the failed rightwing Kapp Putsch against the Weimar Republic and joined the SA in 1931. Zur Mühlen could not have known in 1934, when she wrote *Unsere Töchter die Nazinen*, that the National Socialist government would appoint him Chief of Police in Berlin in 1935 and that he would play an active role in the harassing and plundering of the Jewish population, or that, if Goebbels is to be believed, he proposed the construction of a ghetto in Berlin to be financed by the rich Jews themselves. He is also said to have been the brains behind "Kristallnacht" in November 1938. (All this did not prevent him from participating in the failed plot to assassinate Hitler — for which he was put to death in 1944).

A second episode anticipating the crucial, culminating event of the later narratives of Countess Agnes and Kati Gruber concerns the pursuit of a Communist by twenty young club-bearing Nazis. The Frau Doktor admits in her second testimony that some improper things have happened under the SA. The other day, for example, when about twenty club-bearing young men were running after a Communist, she relates, they paid no attention to the fact that she was also in the street. She had to dart quickly into a doorway to avoid getting hurt herself. "Cowardly, like all Marxists," as she puts it, unaware, as usual, of any irony in her words, "the Communist was running away as fast as he could. The whole lakeside square was full of running, shouting men." She admits that she was extremely frightened. But once she was out of danger, she relates, everything looked different.

> Goodness gracious! One has to have some understanding of the people's spirits and how fired-up they are. And in the end it really was a funny spectacle. Unfortunately, the Communist got away. But that was only because of that crazy Claudia, who stood in the way of the brave young lads, shreiking, and yelling out something about the dignity of the movement. For a moment, she made them hesitate. And that moment was enough to give the Marxist his chance. Claudia's lover was in command of the SA men. He laughed loudly at the frenzy of the old spinster and pushed her gently but vigorously aside, so that she collapsed against the wall of a house. I wondered about this event later. [...] Was it possible that this man-crazy woman was also involved with the Communist? The Salderns are Catholics and it is well known that the Jesuit poison has infected these people and made them thoroughly immoral. In a neighboring town, for instance, a priest, speaking from the pulpit, dared to slander our glorious Führer. The old man must have known he was not telling the truth. But naturally these international brothers, who let themselves be told what they are to do by a foreigner and who live in sin with their housekeepers are almost as un-German as the Jews. The old man is in a concentration camp now and it serves him right. Why doesn't he follow the example of our good Herr von Papen, who submits to the authority of the Führer in everything. (p. 103)

In gratitude for the many benefits that have now come her way — in her own words: "I am now much sought after and honoured" — the Frau Doktor ends her second testimony on words of praise for her fatherland — "the only land where true service is rewarded and where, as it is said in the Bible, 'He hath put down the mighty from their seats, and exalted them of low degree,'"[19] and on a prayer of thanks to God and to "the chosen instrument of His will, our Führer Adolf Hitler, the most German of Germans." (p. 108)

***

The broad satire, for which Zur Mühlen reveals a striking gift in the testimonies of the middle-class Frau Doktor, gives way in the concluding two testimonies by the aristocratic mother and the working-class mother to dramatic and pathetic narrative. Countess Agnes opens her testimony with an avowal and a commitment: "I am only a simple mortal, an old woman, who has perhaps sinned throughout a lifetime by withdrawing from everything. Now however, at seventy, despite my age, I would like to make up for all that I failed to do, I would like to help and to rescue people, and I would also like to witness the fall of those who currently wield power." The aristocrat has thus realized that it is time to leave the glasshouse in which in her 1929 autobiographical memoir Zur Mühlen had accused her class of having shut itself up, go beyond distaste and disdain, and join forces with the Social Democratic working class in active opposition to a regime that is the enemy of all humanity. Not surprisingly, therefore, it transpires that it was Countess Agnes who carried out the rescue of the town's Social Democratic mayor and ferried him in her motorboat to the safety of Switzerland on the other side of the lake, that — at great risk to herself, obviously — she has been providing temporary sanctuary in a well concealed room in her house for many other Communists and Social Democrats on the run from Nazi persecution, and that, affecting deep piety, she has been storing weapons for her new friends under piles of prayer books in an old prayer-stool that she brought out expressly for the purpose and ostentatiously placed in a prominent position in her living room. Despite searches of the house, the old lady's skilful planning, resourcefulness, sang-froid, and expert play-acting effectively thwart the Nazis' best efforts to locate an elusive loophole in their surveillance system. Her success is all the more remarkable as she does not conceal her contempt for them and their movement and appears to do nothing to allay their suspicion of

---

19 In the original: 'Er stößet die Gewaltigen vom Stuhl und erhebet die Elenden.' The passage, unattributed in the text, is from Luke, 1:52.

her. In fact, she uses her aristocratic hauteur as a useful disguise. Even Claudia's membership in the party becomes a situation to be exploited: it is invoked, for instance, to underline the unlikelihood that a resister is being concealed in a house inhabited by a Nazi.

What remains for a time unclear is whether Claudia knows more about her mother's activities than she lets on. Her disaffection from the party, or from its violent and "unchivalrous" tactics, already hinted at in her heated denial of Fritz's account of having being set upon by an entire gang of National Socialists in the Countess's first testimony, is hinted at again, twice, in the second testimony of the Frau Doktor. On the first occasion, Claudia wanted to jump in to stop the attacks on the delivery boy from the Jewish department store, and had to be held back by Toni; on the second, as we just saw, she tried to stop a crowd of club-bearing Nazi youths from beating up a lone fleeing Communist and was pushed aside contemptuously by her SA lover. The reason for Claudia's behaviour is made clear on that occasion by Claudia herself: the beatings of lone, defenceless victims by gangs of SA men, she shouts, are a discredit to the party and are inconsistent with what she takes to be its ideals.

That Claudia is deeply troubled by the actions she has witnessed emerges in Countess Agnes's second testimony from changes the Countess notices — and for which she has, as yet, no explanation — in the young woman's appearance and behaviour. Mother and daughter have by now been partly reconciled. They take their meals together and talk about indifferent matters, avoiding the topics that divide them. Countess Agnes notices, however, that Claudia has become thin and pale, has dark rings round her eyes as though she has difficulty sleeping, hardly eats, but smokes one cigarette after another. Sometimes, when she thinks she is unobserved, there is a look of despair on her face, and her hands shake. On one occasion when the Countess, thinking she has gone out, enters Claudia's room without knocking, she finds her daughter stretched out on the sofa, weeping profusely. A little later, Claudia comes home deathly pale, with a troubled expression that Countess Agnes recognizes from when she was little. Suddenly she falls to her knees and buries her face in the Countess's lap, saying only "Mother, mother." As the Countess strokes her hair, she notices that it has become quite grey. Claudia does not appear that evening for dinner.

5. Our Daughters the Nazi Girls. A Synopsis in English

When she goes in to say goodnight to her, Countess Agnes finds her lying in bed staring at the ceiling. There is a pool of water in front of the washbasin. "You certainly gave yourself a good wash this evening, Claudia," Countess Agnes says, partly to distract the young woman from her thoughts. "Not good enough, mother, not good enough," Claudia replies, looking with disgust at her hands and her thin body. "I shall never be clean again, never." Countess Agnes notices that she did not sleep that entire night for the light was burning in her room until dawn. (pp. 111, 113–14)

Claudia now begins to urge her mother to cross the border and settle in Switzerland, indicating on one occasion that she knows it was the Countess who made it possible for the town's mayor to escape over the lake into Switzerland. The Countess is puzzled. "Why do you want to get rid of me, Claudia?" she asks. The answer comes hesitantly, in a monotone, like something rehearsed: "Because a lot of shady elements have infiltrated the SA and it's not impossible now that, against the wishes of the leaders, those agents provocateurs…" Suddenly she breaks off and says in a whisper: "Go to Switzerland, mother, I beg you. Something could easily happen to you. Those people who claim to be National Socialists and in reality are something entirely different…" Countess Agnes looks at her and asks: "Since when have you started to lie, child. I always consoled myself with the thought that however you acted, you were always upright and honest at least. Have you now lost that one good quality too?" Claudia turns a deep red. Her hands shake and her lips tremble. She places a hand on the image of the Madonna on the prayer stool (in which the Countess stores the weapons of the resisters). "You have become religious again, mother. Pray, pray that everything doesn't…" Unable to complete her sentence, she simply stands still, looking lost and helpless. Countess Agnes feels a pain in her heart. "Come here, Claudia," she says softly."I want to tell you something." Claudia comes over and sits beside her. "We don't see eye to eye on anything, my dear," Countess Agnes continues. "We have almost become enemies in these last months. Perhaps I was too hard on you. I'll stop reproaching you. Just do one thing for me. Be true to yourself. Don't ever do anything that goes against your better judgment and your truest convictions." Claudia gives a bitter, desperate laugh: "My better judgment, good God, my better judgment." Suddenly she seizes her mother's hand: "Mother, how did you, you of all people, come by such a daughter. How is it possible that a child of yours is a coward, a pathetic coward?" "The bravest of us can feel fear," the Countess answers. "It's a question of overcoming it." Claudia gets up from the sofa and goes to the window. Yet Countess Agnes feels her daughter is closer to her than she ever was and in the midst of all the anguish and distress, she experiences a quiet happiness. (pp. 115–17)

Claudia soon has occasion to follow her mother's advice when her revulsion at her Nazi comrades' tactics provokes her to make the final — and fatal — intervention that becomes the tragic climax and conclusion of Countess Agnes's second testimony. The Countess is at home one day when she hears shots. She wonders who is being attacked this time and thinks of the old man who is in hiding from the Nazis and whom she is supposed to help escape to Switzerland that evening. As she is reflecting on a conversation she had had shortly before with Fritz, the gardener, and Toni's former friend Seppel — a conversation in which she had asked why Russia has not intervened, and been told in response by the two brave young Communists that she doesn't understand anything about politics — Toni bursts into the house, pale as death and eyes red from weeping. The Countess thinks something has happened to Kati. Toni, who, she notices, is no longer wearing her swastika badge, replies that she has not come to tell her about Kati, but about Claudia. "My God, what has she done?" the Countess asks. "Has she betrayed someone?" Claudia has betrayed no one," Toni answers. "You can be proud of her. Claudia is dead." She then relates how it happened. His would-be rescuers had waited too long with their escape plans for an old comrade (in which, as the reader already knows, the Countess was to have played a major role); he had been discovered and arrested that afternoon. The Nazis had tied a placard round his neck that read "I am Huber, the old big shot" and had driven him through the streets of the town, beating and shoving him as they went. Claudia had encountered the mob in the square by the lake. "I had already had to hold her back once before," Toni explains. "But today, she was alone. By the time I got there, it was too late." Claudia, it seems, stood watching the scene as though shell-shocked. "She saw how one young Nazi stuck out a leg in front of the old man, so that he tripped and fell, and how the lad then began to kick him as he lay on the ground. She saw how they raised the old fellow up and began beating him with their rubber truncheons. At that point she jumped forward and stood in front of the old man, shouting to the SA people: 'Leave the old man alone, you beasts, you murderers!'" Seemingly the old man told her she should go, for there was nothing she could do to help him. But Claudia stood her ground and shouted through the whole square: "Won't any of you step forward to help? Are you all cowards?" She then ripped the swastika from her breast and threw it in the leaders' faces, crying "The badge of murder, the badge of cowardice. Save the old man! Kill the beasts!" A big crowd had gathered, Toni went on. "One young man leaped from the crowd to stand beside Claudia and old Huber, pulling out a knife. A few voices struck up the International. The SA men were soon surrounded. But our people were unarmed. Then the shots rang out. I heard them myself. The young man was hit by the first, Claudia by the second. The Nazi procession moved on, leaving the two dead young people behind them. Our men picked them up and carried them away." (pp. 121–24)

Claudia's body is brought home that evening. The Countess has her child back. "In the midst of my pain, I also felt happiness," she writes in her diary. "Because now I could weep for my child... I held her cold hand in mine and I thought: 'How quickly she found her way back to me, my Claudia, much more quickly than I could have dared to hope... She is the last of our line and in her death she has brought honour to it. Poor confused heart, poor mixed up head, when the light finally dawned in you, you could only die, but in the service of a good cause. Others might have been smarter and not allowed themselves to be carried away, so that they could live to fight the enemy. You, my child, could fight only through your death. But that is something too, it is a lot. And I am proud of you." (p. 124)

Even as she expresses her pride in her child, the Countess thus hints at the limitations of aristocratic opposition to National Socialism. Claudia's objection is to the Party members' brutality and "unchivalrous" behaviour: the reader of Hermynia Zur Mühlen is inevitably reminded of little Erika's indignation at the fight of "four against one" in *Reise durch ein Leben*, Tante Aglae's reaction to a similar situation in *Ein Jahr im Schatten*, the distress and anger of the child in a *feuilleton* entitled "Man muß es ihnen sagen" when she comes upon a group of boys bullying a single one. There is no indication that Claudia has understood how the behaviour of the SA might be connected with a political program, the proclaimed ideals of which have a heroic and noble air. The goals Claudia took to be those of National Socialism — the transformation of a people, the building of a community united by the bond of brotherly love in which everyone has a part to play, escape from the lonely, alienated "ugly I" and rediscovery of the original "we" (in the words used by Erika in *Reise durch ein Leben*) — remain detached in her mind from any concrete analysis of social conditions, any consideration of the practical measures that might have to be taken in order truly to improve those conditions, any reflection on the measures proposed and carried out by the National Socialists. Claudia's politics were and remain a politics of pure will. The essentially aristocratic notion of fair play, valuable as it might be on occasion as an obstacle to certain kinds of inhuman behaviour, is not in itself, Zur Mühlen makes clear, a policy that can be the foundation of a new and better society. Aristocrats, as Countess Agnes points out several times, are literally a dying class: they are good at dying nobly for a cause; but "working people know how to live for one." It is they, not the aristocrats, who have the qualities needed to envision and to build a truly new and better world: patience, diligence, resilience, and the capacity to think things through.

The Countess's testimony does not therefore end with Claudia's courageous act of self-sacrifice. On the morning after the death of her child, the Countess calls on the family of the young man who was killed along with Claudia. "I did not know their name, they knew nothing of me, but we felt somehow that we belonged together. I think I shed more bitter tears in the little room of those working people than at the bedside of my dead Claudia. The young man was not yet twenty. [...] In the quiet hours, as I sat next to my dead Claudia, I had the feeling that something had come to its proper end, the feeling of a life fulfilled. But here, next to this dead half-child who had not yet reached maturity and whose life would bear no fruit, I was overcome by a different feeling [...] — hatred and a desire for revenge..." But then, "my gaze fell on the parents of the young victim and my rage and hatred gave way to a feeling of shame. Their features expressed infinite pain, but also something I had difficulty interpreting: a determination, a courageous, unyielding resoluteness that was stronger than death. I had the feeling that I was looking life itself in the face, unconquerable, indestructible life, the life that after the hardest winter frosts pushes forth buds that will become blossoms and fruit, the life not of individual humans but of an idea. What I found here was different from the unreflected outburst of my Claudia, who had thrown herself recklessly, following only her feelings of anger and disgust, into the arms of death. Nor was it the impotent rage of an old woman who, because she is descended from an ancient line that for centuries ruled over others, cannot believe that there is anything she cannot do. What I saw was the patient resilience of a class that is the bearer of the future and that for that reason, in spite of everything, cannot be vanquished. I spoke to these two people with the deepest respect. I felt that they stood higher than I, higher than the past." (pp. 125–26)

As the parents, fearing who might be laid next to him, do not wish their son to be buried in the local cemetery, the Countess suggests that the two children, "who had fought together and died together" — the aristocrat's daughter and the working-class couple's young son, *Ende* and *Anfang*, as the title of Zur Mühlen's autobiographical memoir runs — be buried alongside each other in her garden. At the burial ceremony, held in secret and under cover of darkness, an old man briefly placed a red flag on the graves. Being an aristocrat, in Zur Mühlen's view, had once meant being the beneficiary of the labour performed and the hardships endured by millions, in order that human culture might be developed in one privileged group of people. The new bearer of human culture, as she saw it, was now the working class. It was therefore appropriate that the old aristocracy make for the working class the sacrifices that working people had once made for the aristocracy. Though it is no longer the destiny of the aristocracy to be the carrier of human culture it can and indeed should — *noblesse oblige* — be ready to sacrifice itself for the sake of the class now destined to assume that role. It cannot live the new human culture that is dawning, but it can die for it.

***

Appropriately, therefore, the final testimony in Zur Mühlen's novel is not that of Countess Agnes but that of the working-class Kati Gruber. As usual, the new testimony advances the narrative itself beyond the point where it was left at the end of the preceding testimony. We learn that the Countess's motor boat has been seized, that Fritz has been arrested and taken away and that no one knows where he is or whether he is even alive, that the Countess herself is under so much suspicion that her villa can no longer be used as a hiding place for people, weapons, or documents, but that she still helps out in every way she can, often incautiously and at great risk to herself, that she was uncontrollably enraged when the workers' unions were banned — she who has probably lived a good part of her life, Kati muses, not knowing what a trades union is — and that she has become so unrelenting in her hatred of the Nazis that she is angry with Kati for having sheltered one of the leftwing SA men who had turned against his former comrades at the time of the murder of Ernst Röhm but managed to escape the fate intended for him. "She cannot or will not believe that beneath the brown uniform there can be a real human being who rues his error," Kati comments. "She, who used to be so much in favour of peace, has become unbelievably harsh and unforgiving in her hatred of the enemy. I think she would be capable of killing one of them with her own hands, quite calmly and in cold blood." (p. 153)

Toni, we learn, has now joined the resistance and is actively involved in dangerous activities such as the rescue of people who are under threat and the distribution of anti-Nazi leaflets. As more and more people, out of need or fear, come to support or join the Nazi Party (p. 136) — at one time, Kati reflects ruefully, you could count the small number of Nazis in the little town but now that could be said of the Social Democrats — those who are opposed to the Nazis increasingly sink their differences and make common cause. Outside Germany the Social Democratic and Communist parties continue their bitter feuding (pp. 136–37), but within Germany Social Democrats and Communists work together, alongside anybody else who opposes the regime. These may include a few upper class people, like the Frau General — the same independent-minded old lady who had refused to believe that the Communists set fire to the Reichstag, who also obstinately resisted her daughter's urgings that she recognize Frau Doktor Feldhüter, and who now goes out of her way to tip Kati off about an upcoming house-search (p. 136) — as well as some sincere Christians, chiefly Catholics, like the local priest, who ends up speaking out in his sermons against the National Socialists and is hauled off to a concentration camp. (pp. 137, 155) They may even include a few former National Socialists, who believed in a genuine German social revolution and have been disillusioned by the Party's denunciation of the "leftwing" faction within it and the murder of its leader. At one tense point in the narrative Kati is hiding in her apartment both one such disillusioned SA man and Toni's friend, the Communist Seppel. (pp. 143–46)

Ultimately, in light of the failure of other countries to come to the aid of Germany and, most notably, the failure of the Soviet Union to support the beleaguered German Left (Toni attempts to persuade her mother that there are strategic political reasons for the inaction of the Soviet Union but Kati remains unconvinced), the message of Zur Mühlen's book is that the Germans must unite to save themselves. In 1934, Zur Mühlen appears not yet to have given up hope that the regime might be overthrown by disaffected groups from within. In her second testimony Kati refers with what we now know was completely illusory optimism to growing discontent among the peasants (p. 150), workers, and small shopkeepers, and even among some Nazis who expected something different and now recognize that what they brought about was "no revolution for the people and the poor but a revolution for the rich and the 'leaders'." (pp. 155) "Our people were rounded up and murdered," Kati reflects, "but those [young Nazis] were deceived. What will happen when they grasp the extent of the deception. These men have been taught to kill defenceless people. What will happen when, having learned to despise human life, they turn against their leaders? Even the peasants, who were so strongly for Hitler, are beginning to have second thoughts…" (p. 150)

The last words of the novel express — once again with what can now be seen to have been misplaced optimism — the patient determination of the socialist working class to keep up the fight and retain confidence that in time they will triumph. On a fine summer's day Kati and Toni are watching construction workers putting up a house in the street opposite them. "When you look at those piles of bricks and stones, it's hard to believe that a house will ever be made out of them," Toni says. "But in a month's time, it will be there. And that's the way it is with us too. From the ruins we drag one stone after another. We stack them. We sort them carefully. And a new, free Germany will arise out of the stones. We are building it, mother, we are already building it." "Yes, Toni," Kati replies quietly. "You are right. We are rebuilding, we are rebuilding." (p. 157)

***

By making women — stereotypically impulsive and volatile but also focused on slow maturation and the long-term survival of the species — the central players in her political novel, Zur Mühlen may have intended to direct attention to one of the essential tensions of her narrative: the tension, within the opposition to National Socialism, between impassioned, almost instinctive revulsion and considered, clear-headed rejection, between impulsive, short-term protest and calculated, long-term resistance. By giving the last word to the patient, un-heroic, but resolute working class women, rather than the more reckless and heroic aristocrats, she gives precedence to the long, thought through view of historical action over the immediate, subjective personal reaction. Kati and Toni look toward the future, their eyes are trained on the objective of a far-off final victory, not on short-term actions that make a largely ineffectual moral statement or afford a sense of momentary, purely subjective moral satisfaction at having done the right thing and been "true to oneself." Consequently, they manage their resources carefully, avoid unnecessary risk, and refrain from actions that will not contribute to their long-term goals and might even detract from the realization of these goals. Toni, who is no less repelled by the behaviour of the SA than Claudia, does not sacrifice herself in noble protest, but withdraws in order to contribute to a larger, longer, planned struggle.[20] The two working class women thus become models of behaviour for all the other opponents of National Socialism. Seppel, for instance, goes wild when he learns that his mother has been placed

---

20   As Kati puts it, "I thought how full of despair we two old women were when our daughters became 'Nazinen' and how differently the two of them broke with the party. Claudia, like a madwoman, consumed by shame and disgust, Toni calmly and quietly, but surely, having thought it all over. I see the same difference between my dear Countess Agnes and me. Whenever others are in danger, she is sly and shrewd, but when it is a matter of herself alone, she cannot control herself… She refuses to see that her very life is valuable to us and must be protected." (p. 137)

under arrest and thinks of turning himself in to obtain her release. He has to be persuaded that that will do no good and that far more will be achieved by his continuing to work in the resistance. Countess Agnes who behaves recklessly wherever only her own life is at risk, fails to understand that, as Kati puts it, "We cannot afford to lose the services of a single one of us." (pp. 141, 154) The Countess and Claudia, as Zur Mühlen repeatedly points out, act according to the old, by no means unworthy, but in modern conditions unpractical and unproductive principles and values of a dying caste. In the Countess's own words, "I think that we — members of my old caste — can die for a cause, but we do not know how to live for one. We don't have the right strength for that. Dying is also easier." (p. 114)

Perhaps that was also how Hermynia Zur Mühlen — née Hermine Isabella Maria Victoria, Countess Folliot de Crenneville-Poutet — understood her own behaviour. Her heroines, usually aristocrats, are often portrayed as impulsive, moved by old aristocratic notions of chivalry and "fair play." To the degree that they identify with the workers' movement it is because that is the right thing for their dying caste to do. *Noblesse oblige*. Their historical role, in short, is to sacrifice themselves for the sake of the new rising class that is destined to be the living bearer of human values in the future. To this class they are joined by their shared rejection of the egoism, opportunism, and narrow utilitarianism that Zur Mühlen associates with the middle class and satirizes ferociously in the figures of the three Feldhüters.

6. Remembering Hermynia Zur Mühlen: A Tribute

Lionel Gossman

"Auch sie war unglücklich gewesen, kränklich und zart, aber welche Kraft sprach dennoch aus ihren Werken." [She too had been unhappy, sickly, and frail, but what strength came through in her writings.]

Hermynia Zur Mühlen on the poet
Annette von Droste-Hülshoff in *Unsere Töchter die Nazinen*[1]

Hermynia Zur Mühlen was a contemporary, give or take a few years, of many well-known writers and artists from the last decades of the Austro-Hungarian Empire: Hugo von Hofmannsthal, Oskar Kokoschka, Karl Kraus, Robert Musil, Joseph Roth, Egon Schiele, Stefan Zweig. While not in their league, she once enjoyed a modest but distinctive reputation both in Germany and in her native Austria as a translator from English, French, and Russian into German, as an author in her own right (an autobiographical memoir and six of her novels were published in English translation in the 1930s and 40s), and as a tireless fighter against National Socialism, anti-Semitism, and all forms of social injustice. "She was," it has been said, "one of the best known women writers of the Weimar Republic."[2] On her sixtieth birthday in 1943,

---
 1 Vienna: Gsur-Verlag, n.d. [1936], p. 40; Berlin: Aufbau Verlag, 1983, p. 37; first published 1934.
 2 Beate Frakele, "Reise durch ein Leben. Zum 40. Todestag Hermynia Zur Mühlens," in Siglinde Bolbecher, ed., *Literatur in der Peripherie* (Vienna: Verlag für

the BBC aired a tribute to her and the occasion was also celebrated at a party given in her honour by the Austrian and Czech PEN clubs in London. Since her death in 1951, however, she has been almost completely forgotten. Twelve years of exile in England and political views unpalatable to much of the Austrian public in the immediate aftermath of Germany's defeat in World War II did nothing to rescue her from the oblivion to which she had been deliberately consigned by the Nazis in her native land and in Germany, while in the country in which she had found refuge in 1939, she remained a marginal figure. Her books were allowed to go out of print, fell from public view, and were soon no longer read.³ Thanks to her strong left-wing credentials,

---

Gesellschaftskritik, 1992), p. 208. (All translations from German are by L.G. unless otherwise indicated). On German women writers in the Weimar republic, see Gisela Brinker-Gabler et al., *Lexikon deutschsprachiger Schriftstellerinnen 1800–1945* (Munich: DTV, 1986); Renate Wall, *Verbrannt, Verboten, Vergessen* (Cologne: Pahl-Rugenstein, 1988); Brian Keith-Smith, ed., *German Women Writers 1900–1933* (Lewiston: Edwin Mellen Press, 1993), especially the article by Edna Sagarra, "The German Woman Writer 1900–1933" (pp. 1–24); the opening section of Nicole Nottermann: *Strategien des Erfolgs. Narratalogische Analysen exemplarischer Romane Vicki Baums* (Würzburg: Königshauen und Neumann, 2002); Walter Fähnders and Helga Karrenbrock, eds., *Autorinnen der Weimarer Republik* (Bielefeld: Aisthesis, 2003).

3   "She was born to fabulous wealth, and died in bitter poverty. Her novels, short stories, novellas, and children's books went through many editions, and she was forgotten in her own lifetime. A great number of admirers showed respect for her literary achievement and testified to her stylistic sensitivity and personal courage. Greater still, however, has been the ignorance that caused the work of this important woman writer to be disregarded and the author herself abandoned to the oblivion into which she was cast by the cultural devastation of fascism." (Karl Markus Gauß, Introduction to a re-edition of Zur Muhlen's short story collection *Fahrt ins Licht* [Klagenfurt: Sisyphus Verlag, 1999], p. 7.) In the late 1940s and in the 1950s, however, short sketches ("*Humoresken*") — of varying quality — by Zur Mühlen did appear from time to time in the *feuilleton* pages of the newspaper *Frankfurter Rundschau*, the last of them on May 1, 1961, ten years after her death. For a list of Zur Mühlen's writings in Austrian newspapers and magazines, see Deborah J. Vietor-Engländer, Eckart Früh and Ursula Seeber, eds., *Nebenglück: Ausgewählte Erzählungen und Feuilletons aus dem Exil von Hermynia Zur Mühlen* (Bern: Peter Lang, 2002), pp. 259–73. Until the recently published monograph of Ailsa Wallace, the only studies of her work in English were the short but useful essay by Lynda J. King, "From the Crown to the Hammer and Sickle: the Life and Works of Austrian Interwar Writer Hermynia zur Mühlen," in Marianne Burkhard and Jeanette Clausen, eds., *Women in German Yearbook*, vol. 4 (Boston: University Press of America, 1988), pp. 125–54 and the even shorter essay by Deborah Vietor-Engländer, "Hermynia Zur Mühlen's Fight against the 'Enemy Within: Prejudice, Injustice, Cowardice and Intolerance,'" in *Keine Klage über England? Deutsche und österreichische Exilerfahrungen in Großbritannien 1933–1945*, ed. Charmian Brinson et al. (Munich: Iudicium, 1998), pp. 74–87.

a few were republished in the 1970s and 1980s by the Aufbau Verlag in the former German Democratic Republic. Some small presses in Austria also took her up again and a handful of dedicated scholars in the field of *Exil-Literatur* have done their best to revive interest in her. But these efforts have so far failed to produce sustained critical attention and have not resulted in the kind of revival recently enjoyed, for example, by the Russo-French writer Irene Nemirovsky. With the publication of Ailsa Wallace's *Hermynia Zur Mühlen: The Guises of Socialist Fiction* (Oxford University Press, 2009), adapted from the author's insightful and comprehensive Oxford D.Phil. dissertation, the time has come for some, at least, of Zur Mühlen's translated works to be made available again to English-speaking readers.[4]

***

Hermine Isabella Maria Victoria, Gräfin Folliot de Crenneville-Poutet, sometimes referred to as the "Red Countess," was born into a prominent Viennese aristocratic family on December 12, 1883. Her great-grandfather on her father's side had been a French *émigré* aristocrat who achieved distinction as a cavalry general in the service of the Austrian Emperor. At the Restoration, Louis XVIII several times pressed him to return to France, promising that he would be well compensated for properties confiscated during the Revolution, but Ludwig, Count Folliot de Crenneville (1765–1840), refused. "I will be poor," he declared, "but I will remain loyal to my ruler, from whom I have received many honours and marks of favour, and to his house. After the death of my king [i.e. Louis XVI], I became an Austrian and I shall remain one, as will my sons."[5] Her grandfather on her father's side, Franz, Count Folliot de Crenneville (1815–1888), had had a brilliant career as a high-ranking army officer and later as a prominent official at the court of Emperor Franz Joseph, who held him in high regard. Both ancestors appear to have had the conservative political views of most members of their

---

4   In addition, three novels in English translation were posted at the end of 2008 on a remarkable website devoted to women's literature: http://digital.library.upenn.edu/women/_generate/AUSTRIA.html, along with an earlier version of the present essay, 'Liebe Genossin: Hermynia Zur Mühlen: A Writer of Courage and Conviction', http://digital.library.upenn.edu/women/muhlen/gossman.html

5   Quoted by Oscar Criste in *Allgemeine deutsche Biographie* (1904), vol. 48, p. 617 (art. Ludwig Folliot de Crenneville).

caste. The Countess's grandfather on her mother's side, Ferdinand, Count von Wydenbruck (1816–1878), had had a diplomatic career and had seen service in London, where he met and married Zur Mühlen's grandmother, and in Washington, where he had been Franz Joseph's Envoy Extraordinary (1865–1867) at the time of the American Civil War.

As a child, the Countess herself relates, she received little care or affection from her socially prominent parents and was largely brought up by her widowed maternal grandmother, Isabella Luisa, Countess von Wydenbruck (1829–1900), whom she evokes lovingly not only in her lively autobiographical memoir of 1929 but in various guises in nearly all her fictional writings.[6] Countess von Wydenbruck was one of two daughters of St. John Blacker, a member of the Anglo-Irish gentry. Her mother was Welsh and her grandmother half Scottish. She and Ferdinand von Wydenbruck were married in London in 1854 and between 1856 and 1862 she bore him three children — two sons and a daughter.[7] As Austrian envoy, Wydenbruck had been charged with maintaining friendly relations between the democratic republic of the United States and the Habsburg Empire. For her part, Countess von Wydenbruck "had the liberal views of English women at that time," according to her granddaughter. She did not share the contempt for the bourgeois work ethic or for the classic political values of the bourgeoisie that was common among members of the Austrian aristocracy, even among those who, like not a few younger members of Countess Hermine's own immediate family, had apparently lost confidence in their caste and

---

6   The Countess's deep love and respect for her grandmother shines through the many pages devoted to the heroine's wise and humane grandmother in the novel *Reise durch ein Leben* (1933). Erika, the heroine of this novel, hardly ever sees her mother, who plays no role in her life and whose early death simply makes her absence irremediable — and causes the heroine confusion over her failure to react to it appropriately with tears. Even after her mother's death, she receives only rare visits from her father. To all intents and purposes, she is her grandmother's child. Countess von Wydenbruck is evoked again some years later in the powerful figure of Grandmaman Inez in *Ewiges Schattenspiel* (first published in book form in English translation as *We Poor Shadows* in 1943).

7   See Burke's *Genealogical Heraldic Dictionary of the Landed Gentry of Great Britain and Ireland*, 4th ed. (London: Harrison, 1862), vol. 1, p. 105; Constant von Wurzbach, *Biographisches Lexikon des Kaiserthums Österreich* (Vienna: K. Hof- und Staatsdruckerei, 1890), vol. 59, pp. 37–38; *Gothaisches Genealogisches Taschenbuch der Gräflichen Häuser* (Gotha: Justus Perthes, 1901), pp. 960, 1005; Latham C.M. Blacker, *A History of the Family of Blacker of Carrickblacker* (Dublin: Hodges, Figgis, 1901), p. 21.

taken to mocking its pretensions.[8] She subscribed to the liberal Viennese

---

8   See above, *The End and The Beginning*, p. 8. In the novel *Das Riesenrad* (*The Wheel of Life* [London: Barker, 1933], p. 104) Zur Mühlen invents the following conversation, in a train going to the Riviera, between the father of the heroine — a character who, according to the Countess's lifelong partner Stefan Isidor Klein, offers a faithful image of her historical father — and a fellow traveller, the dull and patriotic Prussian Count Luckner: "You are a fortunate man, Count Luckner." "Why?" "You still believe in yourself and your purpose in life." "Don't you, my dear Count?" "Good Lord, no. I know that we are done for as a caste and as human beings." A few pages earlier, the Count had poured cold water on his daughter's desire to be a writer: "That profession does not suit our class, Marieleine." "Why not?" "Because, as a rule, we are intellectual illiterates with a certain amount of culture. That is to say, we were formerly that type of person. Nowadays we have lost even our culture. [...] You see, Marieleine, we aristocrats always took everything and gave nothing. The little sums of money we gave artists and writers to keep them from starving did not really count for anything. We filled ourselves with beauty until there was no room left for anything else. And then, like people who have overeaten and who push aside the food they no longer enjoy, we said: 'Enough of that food.' Then we were interested only in sport. Perhaps this interest was one of the causes of our being done for" (pp. 93–94). In the strongly autobiographical novel *Reise durch ein Leben* several portraits of the heroine's male relatives offer a similar view of the Austrian aristocracy. One (based perhaps on what Zur Mühlen knew of her maternal grandfather, Ferdinand von Wydenbruck, as well as on his son, the writer's "Onkel Anton") has become utterly disabused and cynical and has withdrawn from society altogether; another, a former governor of Tuscany who signed hundreds of death sentences (probably based on her paternal grandfather, Franz Folliot de Crenneville, at one time Governor of Livorno or Leghorn), has dedicated his retirement to writing a learned book against the death penalty; the heroine's own father continues to "play the game" of the aristocracy without believing in it. (*Reise durch ein Leben* [Bern and Leipzig: Gotthelf-Verlag, 1933], pp. 99–100, 110–11, 127–28) An unflattering picture of the younger members of the aristocracy is provided by the heroine's cousin Nicki. Having twice failed his exams at the Gymnasium, the seventeen-year old has been sent by his parents to live with his great-aunt, the heroine's beloved grandmother, instead of accompanying them to the French Riviera where they regularly spend the winter. Interested only in clothing, looks, and horses, sporting a monocle (or making strenuous efforts to), puffing elegantly on cigarettes, full of contempt for the "provincial hole" he has been exiled to — the little lakeside town the heroine loves — and boasting of his "colossal success with women" (57), the immaculately groomed Nicki explains to his younger cousin that study is of no importance to an aristocrat: "What can that stuff matter to me? Am I a little Jew-boy that I have to get an education? Anyway, Papa wants me to take over Zahirsan [the family estate]. What do I need Greek and Latin for on the estate? Papa says I am dumb [...]. But Papa has such strange ideas. He keeps going on about a 'humanistic education.' Mama is more sensible. She says that if nothing works out, I can always become a diplomat." (56–57) Nicki, the cynical aristocrat, turns out, however, to have many saving graces — notably honesty and genuine feeling — compared with the heavy seriousness and hypocrisy of the good-looking German bourgeois the heroine marries, as no doubt the aristocracy she constantly criticized also did for Zur Mühlen, and it is with him that, some years later, after she has left her husband, she experiences the love of her life. In general, Zur Mühlen's

newspaper, the *Neue Freie Presse*, whose publisher and editor was Moritz Benedikt, a converted Jew, and whose Paris correspondent and regular *feuilleton*-writer in the 1890s was Theodor Herzl, and she was a Dreyfusarde at the time of the *affaire* — a consequence, perhaps, of her reading of Herzl's reports. She also supported voting rights for women, her granddaughter relates — albeit with the caveat that it might be wise not to move too fast in Austria, since most women there were likely to use their votes to support rightwing, anti-liberal parties.[9] When, at the age of thirteen, inspired by a budding concern with issues of social justice and equality, the little Countess founded a "Society for the Improvement of the World" (into which, as she herself recounts with characteristic irony, she dragooned a couple of her female cousins and a few local middle class girls eager to please the *Komtessrl*), her grandmother did not scold her, as her mother did, or make fun of her, as her father did. Instead, she accepted nomination as the first honorary member of the so-called Anchor Society and regularly allowed the *Anker-Zeitung*, the Society's monthly "publication" to be read aloud to her. Above all, she appears to have taken her moral obligations as a Christian seriously and instilled in her grandchild an unshakable conviction that all human beings are of equal worth in the eyes of God, together with a keen sense of personal responsibility for the welfare of others. The Imperial government's treatment of her husband can hardly have strengthened Countess von Wydenbruck's respect for the social and political establishment. Blamed for not having prevented the execution of Emperor Franz Joseph's brother Maximilian, the so-called "Emperor of Mexico," Wydenbruck was removed from his post in Washington and, according to another of his grandchildren, "retired from the diplomatic service in high dudgeon and spent the remainder of his life in his country home, a prey to deep despondency."[10]

---

portrait of her class resembles that presented by Joseph Roth in his celebrated novel *Radetzky March* and its short sequel *The Emperor's Tomb*. (See the essay by Patrik von zur Mühlen in the online supplement.)

9 See above, *The End and the Beginning*, p. 16.

10 Ferdinand von Wydenbruck's period of service as head of the legation in Washington coincided with the disastrous end of the brief and uncertain reign of Maximilian as Emperor of Mexico. Though he had consistently received instructions from Vienna to play down the Habsburgs' Mexican connection, which Washington opposed, and to give priority to maintaining good relations with the U.S. (Egon Caesar Count Corti, *Maximilian and Charlotte of Mexico* [New York and

The Countess's eldest son, Christoph Anton — the lively, cynical, much loved "*Onkel Anton*" of Zur Mühlen's memoir — was a more subversive influence on his young niece. A diplomat like his father and like Zur Mühlen's own father, Christoph Anton "first went to school in America," which resulted — in the view of his somewhat estranged daughter, the writer and translator Nora Wydenbruck — in "democratic predilections" and "violent disapproval of Austrian society and its Byzantine class distinctions." Those predilections and that disapproval were communicated to and shared with his niece.[11]

Questioning and rebellious from an early age, receptive to her grandmother's Christian ideals of social justice as well as to Romantic notions — no doubt partly derived from Tennyson's *Idylls of the King*, which she read in English with her grandmother — of the knights of old as brave and noble benefactors of humanity, the young Countess Folliot de Crenneville soon began to challenge the social conditions and conventions taken for granted in the world of her parents and strongly supported by her mother. (Her father was distinctly more ambivalent.) "At the age of eight or nine," she recounts later, with a nice sense of the irony in her words, "I considered the editorials of Herr Benedikt a New Testament, and an unshakable conviction crystallized within me: the government was always wrong."[12] As she grew up, the

---

London: Alfred A. Knopf, 1929], 2 vols., vol. 2, pp. 593–94, 756), Wydenbruck did in fact intervene vigorously with Secretary of State Seward in numerous letters and telegrams begging the U.S., which had never recognized Maximilian and had continued to support President Juarez of Mexico, to intercede with the latter and persuade him to spare Maximilian. (See the communications between Seward and Wydenbruck in *Message of the President of the United States, and Accompanying Documents, to the Two Houses of Congress at the Commencement of the Second Session of the Fortieth Congress* [Washington: Government Printing Office, 1868], "Papers relating to Foreign Affairs," Austria, pp. 558, 564–72.) Nevertheless, as Austria's envoy to Washington, Wydenbruck was judged responsible for failing to save the unfortunate Maximilian from the firing squad in June 1867 and was recalled soon afterwards. On his subsequent embitterment, see Nora Wydenbruck, *My Two Worlds: An Autobiography* (London: Longmans, Green, 1956), p. 3.

11   Nora Wydenbruck, *My Two Worlds: An Autobiography*, p. 3. On Zur Mühlen's close and warm relation to Onkel Anton, whose contempt for the way of life of the Austrian aristocracy she shared and with whom, she relates, she would have liked to go and live after her grandmother died, see *The End and the Beginning*, p. 49.

12   *The End and the Beginning*, p. 9. Countess von Wydenbruck seems to have exercised her influence on several members of her family. In addition to her granddaugher Hermynia and her son Christoph Anton, the latter's daughter Nora, the Countess's other granddaughter, was also something of a rebel (*My Two Worlds*, p. 53), had a

positive, constructive influence of her grandmother and the negative, corrosive influence of Onkel Anton and, to a lesser degree, of her own father, were supplemented, but never displaced, by the socialist ideas she began to pick up in books and through encounters with exiles from czarist Russia.[13] Drawn in early adolescence to idealistic,

---

literary career, like Hermynia, and married a commoner. Born in 1894 in London, while her father was in the Austrian embassy there, she later attended the same convent school in Dresden that Zur Mühlen had been sent to, disliked it as intensely, and ended up in London again in middle age. Like Zur Mühlen and Klein, she and her husband, a painter, lived for a time in cheap boarding houses (such as the one Zur Mühlen evokes in *Miss Brington*, reproduced in Chapter 4, '*Feuilletons* and Fairy Tales'), barely scraping by. The two cousins both spent the war years in England. The absence of Zur Mühlen from her cousin Nora Wydenbruck's autobiography (as of Nora from Zur Mühlen's autobiographical texts) is all the more striking in the light of these similarities as well as of Zur Mühlen's strong attachment to her "Onkel Anton." By leaving her husband, taking a young Jew as her lover, and joining the Communist Party, had Hermynia Zur Mühlen made herself literally unmentionable in all branches of her family? See below, note 21, on the character described as "Aunt Kitty" in Zur Mühlen's novel *Das Riesenrad*.

13   Zur Mühlen appears to have viewed Christianity as an anticipation of socialism, socialism as the appropriate present-day form of Christianity. The title-story of *Der rote Heiland* [The Red Redeemer] (1924), for instance, revives the Romantic conflation of Christianity and Revolution. This tendency became more pronounced in the author's later years. The titles of the three parts of *Came the Stranger* (1946), which is set in the period from just before the *Anschluß* until the German occupation of Bohemia and Moravia, are "Peace," "The Shadow of the Cross," and "The Passion" (the last being itself divided into "Gesthemane," "Ere the Cock Crows," and "There was Darkness over all the World"); the Biblical flight into Egypt becomes an allegory of the plight of refugees from Nazi Germany in the short story "Flüchtlinge" (*Zeitspiegel* [London], 23 December 1944); while in another short story about the setting up of a union of farm labourers in England in 1872, the working man who organizes the movement is presented as Moses leading his people out of slavery ("Die Vogelscheuche," in *Arbeiter Zeitung*, 11 June 1950). Zur Mühlen would have subscribed to the view expressed in 1937 by Rudolf Olden, a liberal journalist who emigrated from Germany in 1933: "Wer Christ ist, muß Sozialist sein" [Every Christian has to be a Socialist]. (Quoted by Hubertus, Prinz zu Löwenstein, *Abenteurer der Freiheit: Ein Lebensbericht* [Frankfurt/Berlin/Vienna: Ullstein Verlag, 1983], p. 178). As for the significance for her of her noble birth, it is hinted at in the words she attributes to Countess Agnes, one of the three heroines of the 1934 novel *Unsere Töchter die Nazinen*: "I have always been too proud to imagine I was anything because of my noble birth. For me, noble birth always meant responsibility. We had privileges, but precisely for that reason we were doubly responsible. Privately, I often felt that our time was over — as a class, but not as human beings." (Vienna: Gsur Verlag, 1936, p. 46) "Chivalrousness" — *Ritterlichkeit* — remains an important general human value for Zur Mühlen, whence the frequent expressions of moral outrage at uneven combat, at attacks by many against one, the strong against the weak, in both the *feuilletons* and the novels (e.g. the *feuilleton* "Man muß es ihnen sagen," the novels *Reise durch ein Leben* [Bern: Gotthelf, 1933, pp. 36–45], *Unsere*

humanitarian movements and causes, she was soon moving further and further in the direction of the radical political Left. A short and unhappy marriage to Viktor von zur Mühlen, a conservative German landowner from one of the Baltic provinces of the Czar — in itself an act of revolt, inasmuch as, in comparison with the urbane, aristocratic, and Catholic de Crennevilles, many of whom held positions at the court of Emperor Franz Joseph, von zur Mühlen occupied a distinctly lower rung on the social ladder and was a Protestant to boot — ended in separation and divorce. But not before outrage at the exploitation of their native Estonian workers by the ruling German landowners, which the headstrong, high-strung, and sharply critical young woman observed in the course of the five years (1908–1913) she spent on her husband's remote estate of Eigstfer in southern Estonia, had made a convinced socialist of her. Not coincidentally, these were years of rising tension, in the aftermath of Russia's defeat in the Russo-Japanese War and the 1905 Revolution, between the czarist authorities together with the German landowners, on the one hand, and local Estonian nationalist and revolutionary movements, on the other.

Severe respiratory problems, aggravated by the harsh Baltic climate, resulted in the young Countess's release from what she later portrayed in her autobiographical memoir as the oppressive environment of the German colony in Estonia. In 1913 she was sent for medical treatment to a sanatorium in Davos, Switzerland. Here, with a translation into German of an anti-war novel by the then well known and widely read Russian writer Leonid Andreyev — "the most popular, and next to Tolstoy, the most gifted writer in Russia today," according to his American translator[14] — she took the first significant step on the literary career she had until then been able to pursue only half-seriously.[15] The Andreyev translation was immediately followed by a translation — with an Introduction by the respected Danish critic Georg Brandes — of Upton

---

Töchter die Nazinen [Vienna: Gsur Verlag, 1936, pp. 56–58, 122–23], and *Ein Jahr im Schatten* [Zurich: Humanitas-Verlag and Büchergilde Gutenberg, 1935, p. 156]).

14 Leonid Andreyev, *The Seven Who Were Hanged*, translated by Hermann Bernstein (Garden City, N.Y.: Halcyon House, n.d. [c. 1941]), Foreword, p. 5. The work by Andreyev that Zur Mühlen translated was *Igo Voiny* [*The Burden of War*]. Her translation appeared in 1918 in Zurich, in a collection directed by the pacifist Alsatian writer René Schickele, as *Unter dem Joch des Krieges*.

15 See her own account of these early literary efforts in *The End and the Beginning*, p. 17.

Sinclair's *King Coal* (Zurich, 1918). Zur Mühlen went on to translate over seventy full-length books and innumerable shorter texts from English, French, and Russian. These included works by John Galsworthy (a bestselling author in Germany as in the English-speaking world), Harold Nicolson, Max Eastman, Edna Ferber, and the translator's "much adored" Jerome K. Jerome, for whom she also wrote the obituary in the *Frankfurter Zeitung*.[16] Zur Mühlen was particularly active in promoting the "muckraking" novels of Upton Sinclair, with whose leftwing views she strongly sympathized. She served effectively as Sinclair's literary agent in Germany and thanks largely to her translations of more than twenty of his novels and plays, succeeded in turning him into a bestseller in Germany in the 1920s. Her translation of *Oil!*, for instance, sold more copies in Germany in the first two years after its publication in 1927 than the original sold in the U.S. in the same period.[17] In addition, both her translations of Sinclair, several of which were illustrated by Georg Grosz, and the internationally popular children's fairy tales which she began to produce in the early 1920s, with the aim of spreading socialist ideas among the young and ill-educated, contributed to the success of the radical avant-garde Malik Press of Wieland Herzfelde and his better known brother, the Dada photomontage artist John Heartfield, with which she had become closely associated.[18]

---

16 No. 4370, 1927, reprinted in *Die Literatur. Monatsschrift für Literaturfreunde* (Stuttgart), Jg. 29, Heft 11, August 1927, p. 649.

17 Sales of *Petroleum* had reached 100,000 by 1929, whereas sales of *Oil!* in the same period were 75,000; see Dieter Herms, "Upton Sinclair: Forschungslage und deutsche Rezeption," in Dieter Herms, ed., *Vergessene Rebellen? Upton Sinclair Spanischer Bürgerkrieg* (Berlin: Argument Verlag, 1989), pp. 5–15, at p. 8. Kornelia Vogt-Praclik, *Bestseller in der Weimarer Republik 1925–1930* (Herzberg: Traugott Bautz, 1987) reports that *Petroleum* occupied one of the top places in the bestseller list of the *Literarische Welt* in both 1927 and 1928 (p. 116). Zur Mühlen's close decade-long association with Sinclair, whose work she not only translated but tirelessly promoted in Germany, came to a sad and rather ugly end when Sinclair, who did not know German, responded to a couple of reports that her translations were deficient by asking Herzfelde, without Zur Mühlen's knowledge, to find another translator. On Zur Mühlen's role as Sinclair's translator, see my essay "Zur Mühlen as Translator of Upton Sinclair," in the online supplement to this volume.

18 On the fairy tale in German-speaking countries and the political use to which it was put and on Zur Mühlen's activity as a writer of fairy tales, see my essay "Fairy Tales for Workers' Children: Zur Mühlen and the socialist fairy tale" in the online supplement to this volume.

At Davos Zur Mühlen also met her future life's partner, Stefan Isidore Klein, a Viennese Jew of modest background several years her junior, who had made a small reputation as a translator of literary works from Hungarian into German. In 1919 the couple moved to Frankfurt, then caught up in the revolutionary turmoil that had seized Germany after the defeat of 1918. On their arrival at the main railway station, Zur Mühlen recalled later, they found it bedecked with red flags. Soon the two of them with their dogs were a familiar sight on the streets of the old free Imperial city.[19] Zur Mühlen's career now took off.

---

19 The well known Hungarian writer Sándor Márai, who shared his living quarters with Zur Mühlen and Klein for a time in Frankfurt, writes that the couple "had two passions: literature and dogs." (See, in the online supplement to this volume, the extract from Márai's *Bekenntnisse eines Bürgers: Erinnerungen*, transl. from Hungarian by Hans Skirecki, ed. Siegfried Heinrichs [Munich/Zurich: Piper Verlag, 2000; orig. Hung, 1934], pp. 250–56.) Klein himself gives an example of this love of dogs in a letter to a friend. The only time in his life that he ever abandoned Hermynia, he relates, was one evening in Frankfurt, when the skies suddenly opened up and Hermynia, seeing a canine couple [*ein Hundeliebespaar*] standing miserably in the pouring rain, went over to the two dogs and held her umbrella over them. Instead of joining her, Klein confesses, he took shelter in a doorway. (Quoted by Manfred Altner, *Hermynia Zur Mühlen: Eine Biographie* [Bern: Peter Lang, 1997], p. 69) In addition to the heroine of *The End and the Beginning*, many of Zur Mühlen's fictional heroines, especially those closely resembling the author herself, are dog-lovers (e.g. Kitty in the novel *Das Riesenrad* (1932), Erika in *Reise durch ein Leben* (1933), Rita Ranke in the mystery story *Vierzehn Nothelfer* (1933). In the short story "Monsieur Bontemps und sein Freund" (in *Fahrt ins Licht* [Klagenfurt: Sisyphus, 1999; 1st ed. 1936], pp. 93–99), the hero's dog Argus is a prominent character and in "Äffchen" (*ibid.*, pp. 182–86) the loving and loyal dog Äffchen, betrayed by her selfish masters, is the heroine of the story. In *Reise durch ein Leben*, the death of the heroine's little dog Flocki marks the end of a paradisiac childhood in which there is no radical separation of humans, animals, and plants and all are experienced as parts of a single, unified, natural world. It is likely that for Zur Mühlen dogs always recalled this original fraternity of all living creatures. Interestingly, a similar view of the animal world was held by another German communist writer, Friedrich Wolf, best known for his socially engaged dramas *Cyankali* (1929; against the criminalization of abortion) and *Professor Mamlock* (1933; against the anti-Jewish laws being introduced by the Nazis), but also the author of "Kiki," a story about a heroic "black-haired English pointer with wonderful, intelligent, light brown eyes," of "Bummi, der Ausreisser," who is "a grey and white, wire-haired schnauzer," and of many other tales about animals for young and old. In every one of his animal stories, Wolf explained, the underlying idea is peace and brotherhood — "not that of nature red in tooth and claw, but the gentle melody of friendship and mutual aid between one animal and another and of friendship between man and beast." ("Antwort auf eine häufige Frage," serving as foreword to Wolf's *Märchen, Tiergeschichten und Fabeln*, vol. 14 of his *Gesammelte Werke*, ed. Else Wolf and Walther Pollatschek [Berlin: Aufbau Verlag, 1961], p. 6) The attachment of Zur Mühlen to her dogs was confirmed for me by a recollection of Wolf Thormann, the late head of the Modern

Despite the health problems that continued to plague her throughout her life, she was astonishingly productive — as she had to be. Having broken with both her husband and her family — though her divorce from Viktor von zur Mühlen was not finalized until March 1923,[20] she had already declared her independence by anticipating the post-War Austrian Republic's constitutional prohibition of titles of nobility and provocatively dropping the "von" in her husband's name — she could count on no income from either source, and, despite considerable activity as a translator, Klein appears not to have had much literary or financial success. Of the two, she, in all likelihood, was the breadwinner.[21]

Languages department at Goucher College, and an old personal friend from my years at Johns Hopkins. Thormann remembers Hermynia's coming with her dogs to his parents' apartment in Frankfurt around 1932 and his secretly feeding them chocolate. (Werner Thormann was a staunchly leftwing Catholic newspaper editor, journalist, and theatre critic who — like Zur Mühlen — advocated a popular front of Catholics and Communists against National Socialism. Like Zur Mühlen and Klein, he left Germany with his family in 1933).

20 Patrik von zur Mühlen, "Hermynia Zur Mühlens baltische Jahre" (unpublished essay), p. 6.

21 The couple of "Aunt Kitty" (the fourteen-year old narrator-heroine's much older cousin, described in the novel itself as an older version of the heroine) and her lover Robert in the autobiographically based novel *Das Riesenrad* (1932) may offer a clue to the relation of Zur Mühlen and Klein. Born into the aristocracy, Aunt Kitty has been excluded from good society because she abandoned her husband for her lover, Robert, who, to make matters worse, is a commoner, and worse still, a Jew. Robert is kind and loving, but somewhat passive, and he cannot make a living. Kitty, who has some talent as an artist, supports the couple financially by tirelessly painting the pleasant landscapes and portraits popular with the well-to-do winter residents of the Côte d'Azur. From time to time she rebels against the abuse of her talent, but to Robert such moments of revolt are a self-indulgent luxury that the couple cannot afford. Aunt Kitty's relation to Robert is complex: a mixture of tenderness, appreciation, companionship, protectiveness, resentment, and occasional feelings of great loneliness when the difference in their backgrounds and life experiences looms large and she is overwhelmed by the sense that they do not really understand one another. A somewhat similar relation of deep attachment and emotional dependency combined with resentment, even at times a degree of contempt, and a taste for freedom and independence — albeit without the class difference — characterizes the marriage of Martina and her long unsuccessful writer husband Clemmy (who, as Clemens, "Graf Follyot," bears Zur Mühlen's family name) in the later novel *Ein Jahr im Schatten* (1935), as well as that of Clarisse and Robert in the still later *Als der Fremde kam* (1946). In *Ein Jahr im Schatten*, as in *Das Riesenrad*, the woman is the more resourceful partner and with the arrival of hard times becomes the family breadwinner by sacrificing her talent and ambition as an artist. A sculptress, Martina spends her time producing kitschy clay dolls because they sell. Neither Stefan Klein's devotion to his wife nor Zur Mühlen's dedication of most of her novels to "St." or "My Husband" is evidence that their loyal and enduring partnership was not also fraught with difficulty — as almost all

In addition to innumerable translations in the 1920s and 30s and into the 1940s, Zur Mühlen turned out half a dozen detective novels with a socially critical slant under the American-sounding pseudonym of Lawrence H. Desberry, identifying herself as their "translator" — a plausible enough disguise in view of her reputation as the translator of Sinclair and other American writers. She also produced the children's fairy tales referred to earlier, in which the exploitation of the working class was exposed and interpreted for young readers from a socialist perspective. In the 1920s the fairy tale was viewed by the German Communist Party, which Zur Mühlen had joined some time between 1919 and 1921, as an effective means of promoting the political education of the masses. Illustrated by artists such as George Grosz, John Heartfield, and Heinrich Vogeler, Zur Mühlen's collections enjoyed considerable success not only in Germany but in Chinese, Czech, English, French, Japanese, Russian, Spanish, and Yiddish translations. There was even a translation into Esperanto. The fairy tales were thus a source of much needed income and a contribution to a cause to which their author was committed. Hundreds of anecdotes and sketches written for magazines and for the *feuilleton* pages of newspapers — chiefly leftwing — were another important source of income. Some of these generally well crafted pieces were satirical, some were humorous, most were marked by sharp and honest observation and all were critical of both social injustice and individual human cruelty. Zur Mühlen continued to publish short works of this kind, even during the years (1939–1951) she spent in exile in England, when they appeared in the German language newspapers that catered to the refugee community. Two book-length collections of short pieces — *Der rote Heiland* [The Red Redeemer] in 1924 and *Fahrt ins Licht. 66 Stationen. Erzählungen* [Journey into the Light. 66 Stations. Short Stories] in 1936 — also attest to a special talent for the short form, as does the largely paratactic structure of many of her longer narratives. On the whole these do not have a strong or intricate plot structure; the organizing pattern tends to be chronological, with interest focused on individual scenes in which the characters are portrayed in their shifting, sometimes perplexingly

---

the marriages in Zur Mühlen's writings are. It would be hard in fact to find another writer who presents as nuanced and honest a portrait of the complexities of the marriage relation.

contradictory relations to each other and to an evolving socio-political environment. The serialized form in which several of Zur Mühlen's novels first appeared — a common strategy for maximizing royalties at the time — may well have reinforced this tendency.[22]

In 1929 a charming, sharply observed, and often humorous autobiographical memoir of the years from childhood to the effective end of her marriage to von zur Mühlen was serialized in the respected, liberal *Frankfurter Zeitung*. By the end of the year it had been taken up and published in book form by S. Fischer Verlag (the publisher of Thomas Mann) under the title *Ende und Anfang, ein Lebensbuch*. Karl Kraus was one of this book's early admirers. An English translation, for which a foreword was solicited from Arthur Schnitzler, appeared in New York (Jonathan Cape and Harrison Smith) under the title *The Runaway Countess* a year later, a Polish and a Spanish translation a year after that.[23] The author used her own life experiences, presented in the form of more or less free-standing anecdotes chronologically arranged, to depict the inner moral and cultural decay (but also, to some extent, in the case of the pre-1914 Austrian aristocracy, the charm, wit, and refinement) of a world that she believed had come to a well-deserved end with the Russian Revolution of 1917 — the welcomed *Anfang* or New Beginning of the German title. The aristocratic Zur Mühlen clearly found no reason to regret the collapse of the bourgeois-capitalist society that had replaced the decadent *ancien régime* and that was characterized, in her eyes, having lost whatever emancipatory impulses might once have motivated it, by middle-class mediocrity, vulgar ostentation,

---

22 Likewise, the loose construction of her novels made it possible for her to publish brief sections from them in the *feuilleton* pages of popular newspapers and magazines — a valuable source of income for her. Parts of *Reise durch ein Leben* appeared in this way in *Der Wiener Tag, Neues Wiener Tagblatt, Das kleine Blatt, Bunte Woche,* and *Das kleine Frauenblatt* in 1933 and 1934.

23 On Karl Kraus's view of "the courageous Hermynia Zur Mühlen, who has lost her noble rank but not her nobility" and on the Polish and Spanish translations of *Ende und Anfang,* see the Preface by Manfred Altner to the 2001 Sisyphus Verlag (Klagenfurt) edition of Zur Mühlen's memoir, pp. 6, 9. On the proposed Schnitzler Foreword, see Athur Schnitzler, *Briefe 1913–1931*, ed. P.M. Braunwarth, R. Miklin, S. Pertlike and H. Schnitzler (Frankfurt a.M.: S. Fischer Verlag, 1984), 2 vols., vol. 2. p. 663 (letter to Prof. Otto Schinnerer, 6 February 1930). Schnitzler notes that he was reading *Ende und Anfang* along with Gide's *Les Faux Monnayeurs* on 7 July, 1929. (*Arthur Schnitzlers Tagebuch,* ed. P.M. Braunwarth et al. [Vienna: Verlag der Österreichsiche Akademie der Wissenschaften, 1997], vol. 9, p. 262). No foreword by Schnitzler was in fact printed.

moral hypocrisy, and the selfish pursuit of gain at the expense of others. At the same time, the author's literary talent is amply demonstrated by the skill with which she constructs her own persona and transforms the memories of a minor diplomat's daughter into lively images of a certain turn-of-the-century world.

Several works defined by the author herself as "novels" followed soon after. Two were highly fictionalized narratives of different phases of her own life: *Das Riesenrad* (Stuttgart: I. Engelhorns Nachfolger, 1932; English translation, *The Wheel of Life*, London: Barker, and New York: Frederick Stokes, 1933), told in the first person by its fourteen-year old heroine-narrator and concentrating on a short period of about six months, and the more expansive *Reise durch ein Leben* (Bern and Leipzig: Gotthelf,1933; English translation, *A Life's Journey*, London: Jonathan Cape, 1935), told in the third person and extending over a far longer period of time from childhood through adolescence and an unhappy marriage to the threshold of disillusioned middle age. Both novels skillfully exploit the author's own experiences in order to portray, through their heroines, the evolution of a young girl as she emerges from the sheltered, secure, and privileged space of her childhood, symbolized by the magical garden of her grandmother's (*A Life's Journey*) or her aunts' (*The Wheel of Life*) villa in the Alpine resort town of Gmunden, about 130 miles from Vienna, and discovers and engages with the larger social and political world beyond.

Both novels are about passing from a closed paradisiac world, cut off from the "real world" and seemingly innocent not only of class distinctions and social injustice but even of hard and fast boundaries between humans, animals, and plants — the prelapsarian world of the original "we" in the author's own terms — into a fallen, historical world of social divisions and injustice, egoism, competition, vanity, hypocrisy, and loneliness — the world of the "ugly 'I'" — and about the heroines' longing to return to the lost paradise or create a new one. In both novels leaving the garden and discovering the world beyond it are presented as at once painful and essential to the fulfillment of the heroines' humanity. The basic structure of both novels, in short, is that of the Judeo-Christian story of the Fall and the pursuit of redemption. At the same time, their realism allows both novels to be viewed as belonging to the traditional German genre of the *Bildungsroman* — except that the leading figure is a woman instead of a man and the focus is on the social world, which the heroine discovers and unmasks, as much as on the heroine herself. Above all, both novels offered a critical response to the conventional literature of the time for girls and young women, the so-called *Backfischroman*, which presented its readers with an idealized view of the social world and in particular of sex and marriage, and which Zur Mühlen had already subjected to stinging criticism in an article of 1919.[24] In her two girls' "growing-up" novels, Zur Mühlen did not shy away from topics sedulously avoided in the conventional literature: menstruation, childbirth, miscarriage, abortion, and above all, the stresses and strains of living with another person, whether in a legally and religiously sanctioned marriage relationship or in a "free" relationship outside of marriage. All Zur Mühlen's heroines are naturally independent and seek to make their own way in the world; all reject the *Backfischroman* ideal of submission to convention and the established order; but the independent life is never presented as painless or trouble free.

1933 also saw the serial publication in the Vienna *Arbeiter-Zeitung* of *Vierzehn Nothelfer*, a clever detective novel with striking expressionist touches that was also a trenchant and witty social satire, and the appearance of a comic novel, *Nora hat eine famose Idee* (Bern and Leipzig: Gotthelf; English translation, *Guests in the House* [London: Frederick Muller, 1947]), which contained many references to the current political situation and which received favorable reviews in newspapers in Berlin, Vienna, Prague, and Basel.[25]

During the Frankfurt years, Zur Mühlen and Klein had come under intermittent police surveillance because of their Communist affiliations.

---

24 "Junge-Mädchen-Literatur," in *Die Erde*, 1919, no. 14/15, pp. 473–74. See also Altner, p. 94. This literature is also severely criticized by Zur Mühlen's contemporary and compatriot Stefan Zweig in the chapter entitled "Eros Matutinus" of his autobiography, *The World of Yesterday* (New York: Viking Press, 1943).

25 The endpapers of *Reise durch ein Leben*, also published in 1933, contain clips from favorable reviews of *Nora hat eine famose Idee* in the liberal *Berliner Tageblatt* (3 September 1933), the *Wiener Tag* (6 June 1933), the *Prager Presse* (21 March 1933, and the Basel *Nationalzeitung* (26 March, 1933). According to the reviewer in the *Tageblatt*, Zur Mühlen's novel offers "something truly valuable," an "accurate and unsentimentalized [*unverkitschte*]" account of society in a "witty presentation [...] Behind the farcical plot, the intelligent reader will find the spirit of a sharp observer and, even more than that, a language and tone of truly creative, poetic quality."

After the publication of one novella — *Schupomann Karl Müller* (1924), in which the policeman hero breaks ranks and sides with the revolutionaries his job requires him to oppose — Zur Mühlen was even taken to court on a charge (later dropped for lack of convincing evidence) of high treason. In fact, though Zur Mühlen did give readings to workers in factories around Frankfurt, the gatherings at the couple's apartment, which the authorities considered highly suspicious, may well have been more leftwing-Bohemian than conspiratorial.[26] In any case, around 1931 or 1932, Zur Mühlen left the Communist Party. She appears to have been discouraged by the oppressiveness of the Stalinist regime in the Soviet Union (one of the writers whose work she had translated and who was also a personal friend and admirer — the French socialist, literary critic, and journalist Henri Guilbeaux — was a fervent supporter of Trotsky) and by the authoritarian dogmatism of the German Party itself, which found it more important to combat the Social Democrats than to join with the latter in combatting National Socialism. In her novels of the late 1930s and the 1940s her characters begin to express doubts about the wisdom and goodness of "the masses" and even about the point of political action. However contradictory and imperfect, the individual emerges more and more clearly from these later works as the highest value, and the the emphasis falls increasingly on basic conditions of human existence — the fleetingness of happiness, the difficulty of relationships with others, even those we love, the persistence of malice, the sadness of ageing, and the finality of death. Still, though she later described herself to Hubertus Prince zu Loewenstein as having joined the ranks of the "Left Catholics,"[27] Zur Mühlen did not trumpet her withdrawal from the Communist Party. Even the change she made to her 1929 memoir when it was republished in the socialist women's magazine *Die Frau* in 1949–1950 — she dropped the original final chapter hailing the Russian Revolution of 1917 and substituted a brief narrative

---

26 See the extract from Sándor Márai's *Bekenntnisse eines Bürgers: Erinnerungen*, reproduced in the online supplement to this volume. There may well be a recollection of them in an unflattering description of a gathering of artists and intellectuals at Aunt Kitty's in *Das Riesenrad* (*The Wheel of Life*, pp. 201–09). Klein later claimed that the account of the life of Kitty and Robert in that novel offered a true picture of "our life in Frankfurt a. M." ("Zur Wahrheit über Hermynia Zur Mühlen," *Österreichisches Tagebuch*, 2 June 1956; quoted in Altner, *Hermynia Zur Mühlen*, p. 24).

27 See Manfred Altner, *Hermynia Zur Mühlen*, p. 153.

of her life from 1917 to 1949 — stops well short of a repudiation of her lifelong commitment to socialism. Overcoming the pessimism, despair, and sense of isolation that she projected convincingly on to several of her women characters, identifying with the oppressed, and taking an active stand against injustice remained the primary imperative of the lapsed Catholic as well as the former Communist. Not surprisingly, individual Communists remain, along with truly devout Christians, among the most decent and admirable characters in her fiction. In fact, the two — sincere Christians and Communists — make common cause, along with sincere Social Democrats, in *Unsere Töchter die Nazinen* (1934, 1936) and *Als der Fremde kam* (1946), against the worst of enemies, the cruelty and inhumanity represented for Zur Mühlen, in her own time, above all by National Socialism. In light of their political orientation and reputation, therefore, as well as Klein's situation as a Jew, the couple made the decision to leave Germany in 1933, immediately after Hitler's *Machtergreifung*, for their native Austria. Short of money, as always, they settled in an extremely modest *pension* — "a flea-ridden boarding-house," according to Zur Mühlen[28] — in the Alserstrasse in Vienna's Ninth District.

Outraged by what she saw as the blindness or indifference of her countrymen and women to developments in Germany, Zur Mühlen was especially provoked when a well-meaning local newspaper editor advised her to stay away from politics and provide him instead with entertaining stories and sketches. She responded by turning out one of her most politically engaged novels, *Unsere Töchter die Nazinen,* in the record time of three weeks. The contemporary situation is illuminated in this polemical and vigorously satirical work by the interlocking first-person narratives of three women from different social classes in a small town in Southern Germany, three mothers whose daughters join the Nazi Party — a working class Social Democrat, a lonely aristocrat who, buffeted by life, has withdrawn into a world of her own, and the resentful, frustrated, and ambitious middle-class wife of a scheming

---

28 See p. 167, above. Another residence was apparently found later, for Klaus and Erika Mann report in 1939 that when they saw Zur Mühlen "for the last time, she was living in an old house in the middle of a garden which looked haunted, in a suburb of Vienna. She is not likely to be found there now," they add, alluding to the *Anschluß* of 1938. (Erika and Klaus Mann, *Escape to Life* [Boston: Houghton Mifflin Company, 1939], p. 60).

doctor whose practice has lagged far behind that of the popular and respected local Jewish doctor. The appeal of National Socialism — to young women in particular — is explained in psychological, as well as economic and social terms, and the ultimate message of the novel is that all decent people, be they Christians or Communists, working people or aristocrats, conservatives or Social Democrats, must unite in organized resistance, a truly popular front, to a fundamentally evil and inhuman regime.[29]

Serialized in a leftwing Saarbrücken newspaper in the summer of 1934, a year before the Saar voted to rejoin the new German Reich,[30] this novel could not find a publisher in Austria willing to take it on, Zur Mühlen's outspoken denunciations of National Socialism having made her *persona non grata* in the Third Reich. One episode in particular had branded her as an enemy of the Reich. In 1933 the highly respected S. Fischer Verlag, under extreme pressure because of its Jewish ownership, asked three of its most prominent authors, Alfred Döblin, René Schickele, and Thomas Mann — all of whom were generally known to be opposed to National Socialism and all of whom had been approached by Thomas Mann's son Klaus about contributing to his newly-founded, Amsterdam-based, anti-fascist review *Die Sammlung* — to make an unequivocal statement of their intention to refrain from publishing in émigré magazines. For various reasons, including concern for Samuel Fischer, who was ailing, and for the future of his firm, which at the time was still pursuing an accommodation with the Nazis, all three

---

29   This work has not been translated. For a full account of it in English, with many quotations from the text, see Ch. 5 in the present volume.

30   On the failure of the campaign to persuade the Saarlanders to vote in favor of the status quo (in which the Saar was under the jurisdiction of the League of Nations), see the personal testimony of Gustav Regler, a native Saarlander, in *The Owl of Minerva*, transl. Norman Denny (London: Rupert Hart Davies, 1959), pp. 221–29. See also the third volume of the autobiography of Regler's friend, the Austrian Manès Sperber, *Until my Eyes are Closed with Shards*, transl. Harry Zohn (New York and London: Holmes & Meier 1994), pp. 61–65. Both Sperber and Regler suggest that the Communist attempt to turn opposition to Fascism into support for a "Red Saar" did enormous damage to the anti-Nazi campaign. By the time the Communists came around to supporting the broad-based popular front of Socialists, liberals, and Catholics that Zur Mühlen's novel had advocated, it was too late. The disabling effect of competition and distrust between Communists and Social Democrats in the struggle against National Socialism is narrated with uncommon vividness by the Austrian Communist Ernst Fischer in his remarkable *Erinnerungen und Reflexionen* (Reinek bei Hamburg: Rohwolt, 1969).

complied with their publisher's request and sent telegrams explaining that they had mistakenly understood Klaus Mann's review to be purely literary and non-political. Stefan Zweig responded in the same way to an identical request from the Insel-Verlag. The Engelhorn Verlag, the Stuttgart publisher of *Das Riesenrad*, wrote to Zur Mühlen in similar vein, assuring her that, if she complied with the firm's request, she would find herself "in the best of company." Zur Mühlen's cutting reply of 25 October 1933, a scathing rejoinder to the statements of Döblin, Schickele, Mann, and Zweig, was immediately made public both in Wieland Herzfelde's Prague-based *Neue Deutsche Blätter* (no. 3, 1933), and in the leftwing Vienna *Arbeiter-Zeitung* (26 October 1933). "As I do not share your view that the Third Reich is identical with Germany and that the 'leaders' [*Führer*] of the Third Reich are identical with the German people," Zur Mühlen declared,

> it would be incompatible both with my convictions and with my sense of personal integrity for me to follow the unworthy example of the four gentlemen you refer to. Apparently it is more important to them that their work be printed in the newspapers and their books sold in the bookshops of the Third Reich than that they remain true to their past and to their convictions. To this "best of company" I prefer solidarity with those who, in the Third Reich, are persecuted because of their convictions, shut up in concentration camps, or "shot while attempting to escape." One cannot serve Germany and the German people better than by joining in the struggle against the horror tale become reality that is the Third Reich. That struggle cannot therefore logically be described as hostile to Germany by anyone truly connected with the German people and German culture. As for the accusation of betrayal of the homeland, I should point out, if that emotion-laden term must be used, that in view of the way the Third Reich has treated Austria, I, as an Austrian, would be guilty of betraying my homeland if I did not oppose the Third Reich with all the modest means at my disposal.[31]

---

31 Quoted in Manfred Altner, *Hermynia Zur Mühlen*, pp. 139–40. For a summary account of this extremely interesting episode, see Jean-Michel Palmier, *Weimar in Exile: The Antifascist Emigration in Europe and America*, transl. David Fernbach (London and New York: Verso, 2006; orig. French 1987), pp. 369–71, 382–92. For a more detailed study and a judicious, nuanced view of the particular position of each of the writers involved, see Hans-Albert Walter, "Der Streit um die 'Sammlung': Porträt einer Literaturschrift im Exil," *Frankfurter Hefte*, 1966, 21: 850–860 and 1967, 22: 49–58. For the letters exchanged between Klaus Mann and Thomas Mann and between Klaus Mann and Stefan Zweig in this affair, see Klaus Mann, *Briefe und Antworten*, ed. Martin Gregor-Dellin (Munich: Verlag Heinrich Ellermann, Edition

With such public attacks on National Socialism Zur Mühlen had burned her boats as far as publishing or even selling any of her work in Germany was concerned. In addition, as most publishers in the smaller German-speaking lands were dependent on the German market, they were loth to alienate the German authorities by bringing out overtly anti-Nazi books. This was especially the case in Austria, where National Socialism already cast a long shadow. The most prominent publishing houses in Vienna, even when owned by Jews, Zur Mühlen told the Jewish-American novelist Nathan Asch, four of whose books she had translated into German, were unwilling to publish Jewish writers or, for that matter "gojim," as she put it, who, like herself, were on the Nazis' black list, for fear of being excluded from the German market.[32]

Unsere Töchter die Nazinen was finally brought out in 1936 by the Gsur Verlag, the director of which was the strongly anti-Nazi Catholic Vice-Mayor of Vienna, and which had an explicit policy of publishing

---

Spangenberg, 1975), 2 vols., vol. 1, pp. 121–22, 131–32 (K. Mann and Zweig) and 122–24, 132–35 (K. Mann and T. Mann). Zur Mühlen couched her reply in terms that would not have been in the least surprising to conservative Austrian opponents of National Socialism (such as Ernst Karl Winter), who regularly emphasised both Austria's distinctiveness and independence in relation to the German Reich and the country's mission, in the current situation, to stand up for "the true values of German culture, which have been suppressed in today's Germany," as the author of an article entitled "Wir brauchen einen österreichischen Verlag" in the weekly paper *Sturm über Österreich* (25 August, 1935) put it. (See Murray G. Hall, *Österrechische Verlagsgeschichte 1918–1938* [Vienna/Cologne: Böhlau Verlag, 1985], vol. 2, pp. 188–91).

32   Letter dated Vienna, October 1, 1935. Louise Pettus Archives & Special Collections, Winthrop University. For a richly informative study of the process by which Paul Zsolnay, the owner-director (allegedly of Jewish extraction) of a major *"Judenverlag"* ["Jewish Publishing House"] which had become the foremost Viennese publisher of modern Austrian and German literature and counted Franz Werfel, Heinrich Mann, and Emil Ludwig among its authors, was pressured into ditching all his Jewish and leftwing writers, in some cases even before they were officially banned in Germany, and promoting instead writers acceptable to the policymakers of the Third Reich (i.e. in sympathy with National Socialism and the doctrine of "Blubo" ["Blut und Boden," "Blood and Soil"]), see Murray G. Hall, *Österrechische Verlagsgeschichte 1918–1938*, pp. 482–521. The Zsolnay case provoked a sustained and angry public controversy in the Viennese press in the years 1933–1935, of which Zur Mühlen was obviously fully apprised. In 1937, the Austrian Jewish writer Joseph Roth, well known in the English-speaking world as the author of *Radetzky March* and other novels, made a similar comment: "Many *bien-pensant*, worthy and thoroughly Austrian 'Anti-semites' will be painfully surprised to learn that the *Jewish* publishers in Austria are the very ones who are eagerly seeking to meet the demands of Goebbels and Rosenberg." (Quoted in Hall, p. 509).

anti-Nazi works,[33] only to be immediately banned by the authorities under pressure from the German Ambassador to Austria, Franz von Papen, on the grounds that it was offensive to a neighboring power, insulting to its leaders, and filled with "Communist propaganda."[34] It

---

33 Ernst Karl Winter, editor of the *Wiener Politische Blätter* — the first number of which (April 16, 1933) was immediately banned in Germany — was appointed vice-mayor of Vienna by Dolfuss after the February 1934 government attacks on and arrests of leading Social Democrats. His motto was "rechts stehen, links denken" ["stand on the Right, think on the Left"] and his political vision seems to have been of a corporatist "Volksmonarchie." G.E.R. Gedye, "the greatest British correspondent of the interwar years," who was based in Vienna fom 1925 until 1939 and was fired by his paper, *The Daily Telegraph*, for his strongly interventionist anti-Nazi views, wrote of him: "Winter was a curious character, a religious, non-Marxist Socialist, a Monarchist, a liberal and a man who really meant well by the workers. He did no good of course, and in October 1936 he was dismissed for advocating to Schuschnigg [Dolfuss's successor as Chancellor] the obvious remedy for his dilemma — the formation of a Popular Front to fight the Nazis." (*Betrayal in Central Europe. Austria and Czechoslovakia: The Fallen Bastions* [New York: Harper & Brothers, 1939], p. 196) Rightly or wrongly, the extreme left remnants of Austria's socialists were suspicious of Winter's efforts to make peace between the workers and the Dolfuss and Schuschnigg regimes and distrusted him. "Links reden, rechts handeln" ["talk Left, act Right"] was their parody of his motto. In their view, he was an "Arbeiterbändiger und Oberdemagoge" [worker-tamer and super-demagogue], an "Agent des Faschismus," a "mit Würden, Geld und Einfluß gekaufte Kreatur des Dolfuß" [creature of Dolfuss, bought with honours, money, and influence] — at best "der Hofnarr des Faschismus" [the court clown of fascism]. On the other hand, the Communist writer Ernst Fischer describes him in his memoirs as "an upright Christian socialist, a man who deeply respected Otto Bauer [the leader of the Austrian Social Democratic Party] and strove to reconcile socialism with the corporate state." (*Erinnerungen und Reflexionen*, p. 303). Winter was undoubtedly a sincere Austrian patriot, consistently and courageously opposed to National Socialism. He was certainly a loyal supporter of Zur Mühlen: he personally reviewed her 1935 novel *Ein Jahr im Schatten* in the *Wiener politische Blätter* very favorably and expressed dismay that it had had to be published in Switzerland because Austrian publishers, caving in to pressure from Germany, had become unwilling to publish any author banned by the Nazis. In 1936, following his dismissal, the *Politische Blätter* were banned — on the same grounds that Zur Mühlen's novel was banned, namely that the latest issues "expressed socialist ideas and served the propaganda of the Marxist Popular Front." In 1938, just before the *Anschluß*, Winter left Austria, by way of Switzerland, for the U.S. where he had a career as a professor of sociology and social philosophy at the New School in New York. He returned to Austria in 1955. (See *Widerstand und Verfolgung in Wien 1934–1945. Eine Dokumentation*, 4 vols. [Vienna: Österreichischer Bundesverlag für Unterricht, Wissenschaft und Kunst, 1975], vol. 1, pp. 554–74; Murray G. Hall, *Österrechische Verlagsgeschichte 1918–1938*, vol. 2, pp. 178–92; and Karl Hans Heinz, *Ernst Karl Winter: Ein Katholik zwischen Österreichs Fronten 1933–1938* [Vienna: Böhlau Verlag, 1984]. See also the entry under "Gsur Verlag" in the "Notes on Persons and Events" above.)

34 For facsimile reproductions of the text of the German Embassy protest (dated 15 December 1935, transmitted orally) and of the report of section 13 of the Austrian

was not published again until the Aufbau Verlag brought it out in 1983 in the former German Democratic Republic.

Even in a less overtly polemical work from this period, the novel *Ein Jahr im Schatten*, which appeared in 1935 in Zurich with the émigré Büchergilde Gutenberg (a book club founded in 1924 with the aim of publishing culturally edifying books at prices the proletariat could afford) and in English translation soon after (*A Year under a Cloud* [London: Selwyn and Blount, 1937]), the personal dramas of the heroine and other members of her aristocratic but in the post-War Austrian Republic no longer wealthy or influential family are increasingly overshadowed by events "up there," i.e. in Germany. Still, with the couple's finances as fragile as ever and the German market closed to her, Zur Mühlen had to find alternate sources of income. Resourceful and hardworking as always, she appears to have won a contract to supply Belgian radio with documentaries on prominent historical figures. No fewer than eleven such documentaries by her were broadcast in Flemish in 1937 and 1938 — on Queen Isabella of Spain, Christopher Columbus, Louis XIV, Cardinal Richelieu, Frederick the Great, Joseph Fouché, Metternich, Florence Nightingale, Woodrow Wilson, Bethmann-Hollweg, and Lord Edward Grey.

The *Anschluß* in 1938 obliged Zur Mühlen and Klein to uproot once more. This time they headed for nearby Bratislava, in Slovakia, where they decided to get married. Just before they left Vienna, Hermynia came into some money from her mother's estate. To collect it in post-*Anschluß* Austria, however, she was required to sign an affidavit affirming that she was of pure Aryan descent. Though the couple needed the money badly, Zur Mühlen refused. With the German occupation of Bohemia and the establishment of an independent Slovak puppet state under Father Tiso in 1939, she and Klein fled to England, where they lived

---

Federal Chancellery recommending that the book be banned and all extant copies confiscated — not so much because of the alleged insults leveled in it at the leaders of a neighboring country, it was stated in an apparent effort to assert that the Austrian government was acting independently and not under pressure, as because of its "almost undisguised Marxist-communist propaganda" — see http://www.literaturepochen.at/exil/multimedia/image under "hzm1" through "hzm5". See also Murray G. Hall, *Österreichische Verlagsgeschichte 1918–1938*, vol. 2, pp. 186–87. For a rough translation of the German Embassy protest and of the Austrian government official's recommendation regarding it, see the prefatory remarks to the synopsis of *Unsere Töchter die Nazinen* in Ch. 5 in the present volume, note 3.

a penurious existence until their deaths a few years after the end of the Second World War. The small income Hermynia derived from the short pieces she wrote for the exile press, from some radio broadcasts for the BBC,[35] and from a couple of longer works published in wartime England had to be supplemented by intermittent financial assistance from refugee agencies in Britain and the U.S. In addition, she suffered greatly from poor health and a lack of regular medical attention. The English climate aggravated her respiratory problems; and in the last months of her life, she rarely left the modest dwelling she occupied with Klein in the small suburban town of Radlett, Hertfordshire, some twenty miles north of London. Zur Mühlen died there, seemingly of a heart attack, in 1951, without ever having returned to Austria. Klein died nine years later in nearby St. Albans. In the local church records the woman who had once been the spoiled "Komtesserl" of a high-ranking Austrian aristocratic family and who had achieved some celebrity as the writer Hermynia Zur Mühlen is identified, no doubt in accordance with her Slovak marriage certificate, simply as "Hermyna Kleinova."

The two longer works that date from this last and most difficult stage in Zur Mühlen's career are in some ways her most ambitious. They appear to have been intended as parts of a planned trilogy in which the social, political, and cultural history of Europe, and in particular of Austria and Central Europe, would be analyzed and represented by following the fortunes of the Herdegens, an old Austrian aristocratic family, through many generations and many individual fates, from the Congress of Vienna and the final defeat of Napoleon to the rise of Hitler and the end of Austrian independence. Zur Mühlen may have been inspired by the success of "family novels" such as Mann's *Buddenbrooks* (1901) or Galsworthy's *Forsyte Saga* (1906–1921), but these last works, while they may be "cast in what is perhaps an unoriginal mould" (in the words of an otherwise very favorable contemporary review in the *TLS*[36]), are more richly informed historically than Galsworthy's, and Zur Mühlen's canvas is wider and more complex. Though the central

---

35 On Zur Mühlen's work for the BBC and on her interest in radio in general, see Deborah Vietor-Engländer, "Hermynia zur Mühlen and the BBC," in *'Stimme der Wahrheit' — German Language Broadcasting by the BBC*, ed. Charmian Brinson and Richard Dove (Amsterdam: Rodopi, 2003), pp. 27–42. (Yearbook of the Research Centre for German and Austrian Exile Studies, University of London, 5).

36 *Times Literary Supplement*, March 11, 1944, p. 125.

scenes of the action are the ancestral Herdegen estate not far from Vienna ("Wohan" in Moravia in the first novel, "Korompa" in Slovakia in the second)[37] and the family palaces in Vienna, some of the principal characters are foreigners (French, Polish, Prussian, Spanish, Swiss) who either married into the family or found refuge and employment in it. On their side, some Herdegens marry foreigners and go off to live in the land of their spouse; others marry out of their social class. The "exile" who has attachments to two or more countries — or social classes — but no longer feels completely at home in any one thus plays a pivotal role in the family saga, as well as among the secondary characters, reflecting no doubt the experience of the author herself, but at the same time multiplying the historical perspectives of the novels and presenting a paradigm of humanity as inescapably hybrid. It is "Because we are patchwork" — seemingly the title of a presumed missing component of the planned trilogy[38] — that we are all both disconnected from an imagined "home" and potentially connected with each other, sharing the same destiny as parts of a single patchwork humanity. A cosmopolitanism rooted in the condition of the aristocracy of the Habsburg Empire opens here on to a global humanism that is no less relevant today than in the dark decade of the mid-30s to mid-40s when Zur Mühlen conceived, wrote, and published her family saga.

The first work in the trilogy — *Ewiges Schattenspiel* — which covers the period from the Congress of Vienna to the 1848 Revolutions, was probably written shortly before Zur Mühlen and Klein left Vienna for Bratislava, for, though it was not published in German as a book until

---

37 The real Korompa (in Hungarian; Krompachy in Slovak) is actually quite far from Vienna. It lies in Eastern Slovakia, near Kosice. Beethoven's student Teréz Brunszvik, Gräfin von Korompa (1775–1861), was a relative of Zur Mühlen's Aunt Maria.

38 "Patchwork" [*Flickwerk*] — perhaps a reminiscence of a famous phrase in Montaigne's *Essays* (II, 1): "nous sommes tous de lopins" — is already the title of one of the closing chapters of *A Life's Journey*. It refers there to a patchwork quilt on which the last remaining servant at the dilapidated and, in the aftermath of the Great War, probably no longer affordable villa of the heroine's beloved grandmother has been working all her life. To the heroine who has returned saddened, bereft, and bewildered to the scene of her innocent and protected childhood, it is both the symbol of her disintegrated world and fragmented personal life and, at the same time perhaps, the model of a new, looser kind of personal identity and social community — one made up of many individual parts, each of which retains its autonomy.

1996, it appeared in serialized form in the Bern newspaper *Der Bund* between November 1938 and March 1939. An English version, entitled *We Poor Shadows*, was published by Free Austrian Books in London in 1943 and again that same year by the London publisher Frederick Muller, with a second printing the following year. As the title page of this English version gives the name of the author as "Countess Hermynia Zur Mühlen" and as there is no indication anywhere that it is a translation, it has sometimes been assumed that Zur Mühlen wrote the novel in English. This is manifestly not the case. It is very likely, however, that she took an active part in translating it into English and in adapting it to the taste and interests of the English reading public. (The English version is shorter than the German one and some of the detail that gives the rich and wide-ranging original, with its vast cast of characters, its historical vividness and density has been cut.)

The second major part of the presumed trilogy to be published after the departure from Vienna — *Als der Fremde kam* — is an insightful portrait of the period from 1937 (i.e. just before the *Anschluß*) to the end of Austrian independence, the secession of Slovakia from the Republic of Czechoslovakia and its establishment as a fascist puppet state, and the occupation of Bohemia and Moravia by German troops in March 1939. Even if earlier parts of it were written in Bratislava, therefore, it seems virtually certain that most of it was written after Zur Mühlen and Klein arrived in England. Notwithstanding that in this case the English version — *Came the Stranger* (London: Frederick Muller, 1946) — preceded the German version (Vienna: Globus Verlag, 1947[39]) and again bore no indication that it was a translation (the author is identified here too simply as "Countess Hermynia Zur Mühlen"), it is most likely that it too was originally written in German and translated — perhaps by Zur Mühlen herself — from German into English, rather than the other way round, as was at one time believed. At least one further novel, it is assumed, was intended to fill in the story of the Herdegens between 1814 and 1939. In her correspondence Zur Mühlen mentions a work to which she refers by an English title, "Because we are Patchwork" — but that, once again, in no way implies that the text itself was written in

---

39 The work was republished in the German Democratic Republic in 1979 (Berlin and Weimar: Aufbau Verlag) and again in Austria in 1994 (Vienna: Promedia Verlag).

English. How far along she got with this novel is not known, and no trace of it has been found.[40]

***

It is my hope that the present republication by Open Book Publishers of Zur Mühlen's autobiographical memoir will encourage readers to explore this courageous and talented author's other writings. Equally, it is hoped that other publishers will be encouraged to follow the lead of openbookpublishers.com by reissuing the now virtually inaccessible English translations of her novels of the 1930s and 1940s. Though fairly traditional in technique — she was no Virginia Woolf or Gertrude Stein or even Marieluise Fleisser — Zur Mühlen was an accomplished writer who succeeded in combining passionate political commitment with a strikingly broad and rich historical sweep, sharp Marxist-influenced insight into the dynamics of social and political change, a keen eye and ear for individual and class characteristics and speech, humor, ironical self-awareness, and an undogmatic (perhaps especially feminine) sensitivity to the complexity of individual character and human relations and to the irremediable sadness of loss and death. Among many women writers of novels and short stories of her time in German — Anna Seghers, Princess Mechthilde Lichnowsky, Gina Kaus, to say nothing of the stupendously successful Vicki Baum — hers is a distinctive voice. Above all, she stands out as an insightful witness and portraitist of a crucially important period in modern history, as the creator of convincing and emancipating narratives of girls growing up, and as a fearlessly outspoken champion of human rights at a time when there were not a great many of these. I close this brief tribute to her by citing an earlier tribute that appeared shortly, after the publication of *Ende und Anfang*, in *Die Weltbühne*, a leftist weekly featuring work by many well-known figures in German letters in the Weimar period — among them Erich Kästner, Else

---

40 It would be imprudent, in the absence of documentary evidence, to rule out completely the possibility that Zur Mühlen wrote *Came the Stranger* and the presumed missing part of the trilogy, *Because we are Patchwork*, directly in English. Other Austrian writers, notably Robert Neumann, did make the switch from German to English with some success; see Richard Dove, "Almost an English Author: Robert Neumann's English novels." *German Life and Letters*, 51 (1998), 93–105; the same author's *Journey of No Return* (London: Libris, 2000); and Sylvia Patsch, *Österreichische Schriftsteller im Exil in Großbritannien* (Vienna and Munich: Brandstätter, 1985), pp. 33–72.

Lasker-Schüler, Arnold Zweig, and Erich Mühsam — until it was shut down by the Nazis in March, 1933. Though the author of the tribute, the French communist Henri Guilbeaux, a friend of Lenin and Trotsky, was less consistent in his politics than Zur Mühlen (he defected from the Party and subsequently became an admirer of Mussolini), his words convey something of the appeal of Zur Mühlen's writing and personality:

> Klugheit, lebhafter Geist, Empfindsamkeit, Geschmack und Charme machen sie in der Tat zu einer guten Fee. Ohne Unterschied nimmt sie sich eines verlassenen Hundes, eines armen Teufels ohne Dach und Geld, eines Verirrten an. Sie hat nichts gemein mit kommunistischen Funktionären, die mechanisch und bureaukratisch ihr tägliche — achtstündige — Pflicht erfüllen. Obwohl sie noch ihre Illusionen, was die Parteiführer betrifft, hat, so ist sie doch von einer grossen geistigen Unabhängigkeit, und ihr Horizont ist nicht begrenzt. [...] Alle die wissen, dass revolutionäre Kunst nicht Phraseologie... ist, alle die auf der Suche nach einem fruchtbaren, frohen Talent sind, haben die herzlichsten Gefühle für die grossen schriftstellerischen Gaben und den frischen Geist der Hermynia zur Mühlen.[41]

---

41 *Die Weltbühne*, 8 July 1930, p. 68: "Intelligence, liveliness of mind, sensibility, taste, and charm make her truly a good fairy. A stray dog, abandoned by its master, a poor devil without a penny to his name or a roof over his head, a lost soul — she takes them all equally under her wing. She has nothing in common with communist officials mechanically and bureaucratically working their eight-hour-day shifts. Although she has not yet lost her illusions about the Party leadership, she retains great independence of mind and her horizons are in no way limited. [...] Everyone who understands that revolutionary art is not just phraseology, everyone who is on the look-out for a creative and joyful talent responds to the great literary gifts and the free spirit of Hermynia zur Mühlen."

7. Works by Hermynia Zur Mühlen in English Translation

The Runaway Countess. Transl. Frank Barnes (New York: Jonathan Cape and Harrison Smith, 1930).

The Wheel of Life. Transl. Margaret Goldsmith (London: Barker, 1933).

A Life's Journey. Transl. Phyllis and Trevor Blewitt (London: Jonathan Cape, 1935).

A Year Under a Cloud. Transl. Ethel K. Houghton and H.E. Cornides (London: Selwyn and Blount, 1937).

We Poor Shadows (London: Frederick Muller, 1943), no translator named, http://digital.library.upenn.edu/women/

Came the Stranger (London: Frederick Muller, 1946), no translator named, http://digital.library.upenn.edu/women/

Guests in the House (London: Frederick Muller, 1947), no translator named, http://digital.library.upenn.edu/women/

8. Image Portfolio

Fig. 1: George Grosz, illustrations for Hermynia Zur Mühlen, *Was Peterchens Freunde erzählen* (Berlin: Malik-Verlag, 1924). Clockwise: front cover, p. 4, p. 25, and facing p. 17.

https://doi.org/10.11647/OBP.0140.08

Fig. 2: Heinrich Vogeler, illustrations for Hermynia Zur Mühlen, *Es War Einmal und Es Wird Sein* (Berlin: Verlag der Jugendinternationale, 1930). Clockwise: cover design, p. 4 (from "Warum?"), p. 16 (from "Der Knecht"), and p. 28 (from "Die Brillen").

... ein Schlag, der ihn aufhob, als sei er eine Feder (S.13)

Mc. Givney nahm das Geld vom Tisch (S.79)

Besser von der Polizei verprügelt werden, als sich von der deutschen Artillerie in Stücke zerreißen zu lassen. (S.111)

Fig. 3: Upton Sinclair, *100% : Roman eines Patrioten. Autorisierte Übersetzung aus dem Amerikanischen von Hermynia Zur Mühlen; mit 10 Lithographien von George Grosz* (Berlin: Der Malik-Verlag, c. 1921). Clockwise: cover design by John Heartfield, illustrations by George Grosz facing pp. 32, 128, and 64.

Bei jedem Schlag brüllte Glikan einen neuen Fluch (S. 209)

Häßlicher Hohn verzerrte die Züge des Detektivs; mit bösem Spott grinste er Peter an. (S. 235)

„Mit Blut ist die Geschichte der Industriearbeiter der Welt geschrieben" (S. 331)

Fig. 4: Upton Sinclair, *100% : Autorisierte Übersetzung aus dem Amerikanischen von Hermynia Zur Mühlen; mit 10 Lithographien von George Grosz* (Berlin: Der Malik-Verlag, c. 1921). Clockwise: illustrations by Grosz facing pp. 224, 256, 332.

List of Illustrations

Frontispiece:	Hermynia Zur Mühlen, photograph taken in the garden of her husband's estate at Eigstfer, Estonia, c. 1910. Courtesy of Patrik von zur Mühlen.	ii
	Advertisement by Samuel Fischer Verlag, Berlin, for the newly published *Ende und Anfang*.	6
1a.	George Grosz, front cover design for Hermynia Zur Mühlen, *Was Peterchens Freunde erzählen: Sechs Märchen*, 2nd edition (Berlin: Der Malik Verlag, 1924 [1st ed. 1921]). Courtesy of Princeton University Library, Department of Rare Books and Special Collections, Cotsen Children's Library.	437
1b.	George Grosz, illustration in Hermynia Zur Mühlen, *Was Peterchens Freunde Erzählen*, 2nd edition (Berlin: Der Malik Verlag, 1924 [1st ed. 1921]), p. 4. Courtesy of Princeton University Library, Department of Rare Books and Special Collections, Cotsen Children's Library.	437
1c.	George Grosz, illustration in Hermynia Zur Mühlen, *Was Peterchens Freunde Erzählen*, 2nd edition (Berlin: Der Malik Verlag, 1924 [1st ed. 1921]), p. 25. Courtesy of Princeton University Library, Department of Rare Books and Special Collections, Cotsen Children's Library.	437
1d.	George Grosz, illustration in Hermynia Zur Mühlen, *Was Peterchens Freunde Erzählen*, 2nd edition (Berlin: Der Malik Verlag, 1924 [1st ed. 1921]), facing p. 17. Courtesy of Princeton University Library, Department of Rare Books and Special Collections, Cotsen Children's Library.	437

2a. Heinrich Vogeler, front cover design for Hermynia Zur Mühlen, *Es War Einmal und Es Wird Sein* (Berlin: Verlag der Jugendinternationale, 1930). Courtesy of Princeton University Library, Department of Rare Books and Special Collections, Cotsen Children's Library.   438

2b. Heinrich Vogeler, illustration for Hermynia Zur Mühlen, *Es War Einmal und Es Wird Sein* (Berlin: Verlag der Jugendinternationale, 1930), p. 4. Courtesy of Princeton University Library, Department of Rare Books and Special Collections, Cotsen Children's Library.   438

2c. Heinrich Vogeler, illustration for Hermynia Zur Mühlen, *Es War Einmal und Es Wird Sein* (Berlin: Verlag der Jugendinternationale, 1930), p. 16. Courtesy of Princeton University Library, Department of Rare Books and Special Collections, Cotsen Children's Library.   438

2d. Heinrich Vogeler, illustration for Hermynia Zur Mühlen, *Es War Einmal und Es Wird Sein* (Berlin: Verlag der Jugendinternationale, 1930), p. 28. Courtesy of Princeton University Library, Department of Rare Books and Special Collections, Cotsen Children's Library.   438

3a. John Heartfield, cover design for Upton Sinclair, *100% : Roman eines Patrioten. Autorisierte Übersetzung von Hermynia Zur Mühlen. 10 Lithographien von George Grosz* (Berlin: Der Malik-Verlag, 1921. Die Rote Romane-Serie, 2). Courtesy of Princeton University Library, Department of Rare Books and Special Collections.   439

3b. George Grosz, reproduction of a lithograph in Upton Sinclair, *100% : Roman eines Patrioten. Autorisierte Übersetzung von Hermynia Zur Mühlen. 10 Lithographien von George Grosz* (Berlin: Der Malik-Verlag, 1921. Die Rote Romane-Serie, 2), facing p. 32. Courtesy of Princeton University Library, Department of Rare Books and Special Collections.   439

3c. George Grosz, reproduction of a lithograph in Upton Sinclair, *100% : Roman eines Patrioten. Autorisierte Übersetzung von Hermynia Zur Mühlen. 10 Lithographien von George Grosz* (Berlin: Der Malik-Verlag, 1921. Die Rote Romane-Serie, 2), facing p. 128. Courtesy of Princeton University Library, Department of Rare Books and Special Collections.   439

3d. George Grosz, reproduction of a lithograph in Upton Sinclair, *100% : Roman eines Patrioten. Autorisierte Übersetzung von Hermynia Zur Mühlen. 10 Lithographien von George Grosz* (Berlin: Der Malik-Verlag, 1921. Die Rote Romane-Serie, 2), facing p. 64. Courtesy of Princeton University Library, Department of Rare Books and Special Collections. 439

4a. George Grosz, reproduction of a lithograph in Upton Sinclair, *100% : Roman eines Patrioten. Autorisierte Übersetzung von Hermynia Zur Mühlen. 10 Lithographien von George Grosz* (Berlin: Der Malik-Verlag, 1921. Die Rote Romane-Serie, 2), facing p. 224. Courtesy of Princeton University Library, Department of Rare Books and Special Collections. 440

4b. George Grosz, reproduction of a lithograph in Upton Sinclair, *100% : Roman eines Patrioten. Autorisierte Übersetzung von Hermynia Zur Mühlen. 10 Lithographien von George Grosz* (Berlin: Der Malik-Verlag, 1921. Die Rote Romane-Serie, 2), facing p. 256. Courtesy of Princeton University Library, Department of Rare Books and Special Collections. 440

4c. George Grosz, reproduction of a lithograph in Upton Sinclair, *100%. Autorisierte Übersetzung von Hermynia Zur Mühlen. 10 Lithographien von George Grosz* (Berlin: Der Malik-Verlag, 1921. Die Rote Romane-Serie, 2), facing p. 332. Courtesy of Princeton University Library, Department of Rare Books and Special Collections. 440

This book need not end here…

At Open Book Publishers, we are changing the nature of the traditional academic book. The title you have just read will not be left on a library shelf, but will be accessed online by hundreds of readers each month across the globe. OBP publishes only the best academic work: each title passes through a rigorous peer-review process. We make all our books free to read online so that students, researchers and members of the public who can't afford a printed edition will have access to the same ideas. This book and additional content is available at: https://www.openbookpublishers.com/product/746

Customise

Personalise your copy of this book or design new books using OBP and third-party material. Take chapters or whole books from our published list and make a special edition, a new anthology or an illuminating coursepack. Each customised edition will be produced as a paperback and a downloadable PDF. Find out more at: https://www.openbookpublishers.com/section/59/1

Like Open Book Publishers

Follow @OpenBookPublish

Read more at the Open Book Publishers BLOG

You may also be interested in:

Fiesco's Conspiracy at Genoa
Friedrich Schiller. Translated by Flora Kimmich, with an Introduction by John Guthrie

https://www.openbookpublishers.com/product/261

The Life of August Wilhelm Schlegel
Cosmopolitan of Art and Poetry
Roger Paulin

https://www.openbookpublishers.com/product/25

Telling Tales
The Impact of Germany on English Children's Books 1780-1918
David Blamires

https://www.openbookpublishers.com/product/23

Brownshirt Princess
A Study of the 'Nazi Conscience'
Lionel Gossman

https://www.openbookpublishers.com/product/18